RIFLE GUIDE

SAM FADALA

STOEGER PUBLISHING COMPANY

Editor: Mike Toth
Production Editor: Charlene Cruson Step
Book Design: Cat Alfano
Cover Design and Photography: Ray Wells

On the Cover: Ruger No. 1 standard rifle (top) in 7mm Rem. Mag. with 26-inch barrel; Sako Deluxe Rifle (center) in Medium Action, 243 Win., with European walnut stock featuring basket-weave hand-checkering and high-gloss finish; Winchester Model 94 Side Eject Rifle (bottom) in 30-30 Win. with 20-inch barrel and checkered forearm and stock.

Published by Stoeger Publishing Company
5 Mansard Court
Wayne, New Jersey 07470

ISBN: 0-88317-171-6
Library of Congress Catalog Card No.: 92-85565
Manufactured in the United States of America

In the United States:
Distributed to the book trade and to the sporting goods trade by Stoeger Industries, 5 Mansard Court
Wayne, New Jersey 07470

In Canada:
Distributed to the book trade and to the sporting goods trade by Stoeger Canada, Ltd., 1801 Wentworth Street, Unit 16, Whitby, Ontario L1N 8R6, Canada

PREFACE

My heroes were gunwriters. As a lad I was laid up much of the time with chronic asthma, which gave me a lot of reading time. By age 11, I'd whipped the wheeze-and-cough game and was spending hours—even days—in the desert around Tucson. I began, in a most modest way, to shoot as many different firearms as I could get my hands on. Every one of them taught me something, not only about the gun in question, but about its ammo as well. I found out about the good, the bad, the great, the terrible.

My shooter's evolution was not so different from that of any dedicated rifle lover. Curiosity has to be satisfied. You can't shoot all the rifles out there, so you study the subject through literature, counting on the expertise of others for sound information.

And, of course, you shoot as many longarms as you can buy or borrow to verify or refute what you read. Shooters seek rifles to hunt with, but Dave Andrews, formerly of CCI-Speer, knew the answer when he was asked where all those bullets his company sold went to. "Into dirt banks," Andrews said. He was right. By far, the vast majority of bullets end up in dirt banks, the butts behind the targets or tin cans. But it's hardly a matter of frivolous shooting. Riflemen shoot to improve their marksmanship, to sight in, to test handloads and factory ammo for accuracy, to enjoy a great sport and to learn all they can.

Dedicated riflemen are never happy with mediocrity. They want their shooting machines to perform at cloud level for a specific intended task, from harvesting small game or big game to clustering bullet holes close on the target. These things don't happen well without a full understanding of and appreciation for the instrument that guides the projectile downrange, as well as the missile itself.

This book deals with both firearm and cartridge, including the peripheral gear and gadgetry that attend the sport of rifle-shooting. Burying bullets in dirt banks for its own sake is never enough. That's why shooters talk about internal and external ballistics, tenets of accuracy, downrange energy, bullet drift caused by rotation and wind, trajectory, brush-bucking, wound channel and the many other aspects of shooting dealt with in this book. Having chronographed, hunted with, and otherwise tested rifles and cartridges for over three decades, I hope that these experiences are sufficient to form the foundation of this text.

The more a shooter learns, the more he or she wants to know. And for every question answered, two more questions pop up. Nobody ever learns all there is to know about this sport. The quest goes on forever. That's what makes rifle shooting the fascinating endeavor that it always was and always will be.

AUTHOR

A technical editor with *Rifle Magazine,* Sam Fadala is also blackpowder/knife editor for *Gun Magazine,* a regular contributor to *Gun World,* feature writer for *Muzzleloader Magazine,* and a contributor to Harris Publications of New York. Sam has freelanced for various hunting and shooting publications over the years and somehow has found the time to author 15 books as well. Among them are: *The Book of the Twenty-Two, Great Shooters of the World,* and *Legendary Sporting Rifles*—all recently published by Stoeger.

Sam was born in Albany, New York, in 1939, but from age five, was raised in Arizona. He has lived in Canada, and today calls Wyoming his home, where he has resided for the past 15 years. Hunting is one of Sam's passions. He has hunted in many states in the U.S., including Alaska; also Canada and Africa. He has fired every kind of rifle—from the 22 rimfires to muzzleloaders to high-power, long-range big bores and elephant rifles. He brings to this book many years of shooting and testing experience.

CONTENTS

THE DIVERSE AMERICAN RIFLE

1 The American rifle is as diverse as the American public—long, short, light, heavy, strong, mild, accurate, not so accurate, well made and otherwise. Our rifle's ancestors were born in Europe, where most shooting innovations originated, including jacketed bullets, telescopic rifle sights, smokeless powder and rifling. The word "rifle" denotes the lands and grooves that are spiral-cut into the bore, causing a projectile to spin on its axis.

The Jaeger—German for "hunter"—is a good starting place for telling the American rifle story. This stout big-bored (some were as large as 70 caliber) hunting rifle was well thought of in the Old Country, in spite of its powder consumption, high trajectory and medium authority at medium range. People seeking a new life in the New World brought the Jaeger with them in one form or another. Although a good rifle, it was not quite right for conditions on our side of the ocean.

German, Dutch and other European craftsmen set to work, and a new style of rifle metamorphosed. If you think of the Jaeger as being of the male gender, the resulting Pennsylvania longrifle (also referred to as a "Kentucky" rifle) would be a female. Here was a slimmer firearm, not necessarily lighter in weight, but with a much longer barrel and a far smaller bore. Pennsyl-vania longrifles generally averaged between 38 and 45 caliber, with thousands made in the latter size. Shooters usually loaded it with a patched round ball. The well-constructed, finely rifled "Kentucky" was quite accurate. Even in the comparatively small 45 caliber size, good bullet placement made this rifle deadly.

A pouch that could hold only a few 60 or 70 caliber lead spheres could carry many more round balls of 45 caliber. The long barrel gave the Pennsylvania rifle a long sight radius—the distance from rear sight to front sight—for a clear sight picture. The long barrel also provided good balance. Coupled with a lot of drop at the comb of the stock, the up-front weight of the long barrel promoted excellent offhand shooting.

The Pennsylvania rifle was a flintlock—matchlock and wheellock ignition styles of the past were not employed. The flintlocks were (are) not foolproof, but they were far more reliable than some modern gunwriters believe. If the flintlock were as hit-and-miss as I've read in some contemporary literature, the settlers would have been driven back into the sea by hostiles on both two and four legs.

So the Pennsylvania rifle had everything: accuracy, beauty, reliability. It was at home at the turkey shoot as well as on the hunt or war trail. But something called Westward Expansion al-

The Thompson/Center Pennsylvania rifle (top) is long barreled and adheres to the original concept in early caplock rifles that followed the "Kentucky." By comparison, the T/C Scout below is a short-barreled modern muzzleloader.

tered the usefulness of this handsome rifle. President Jefferson believed, correctly, that the western half of America was worth acquiring. He wanted an American presence west of the Mississippi River to thwart inroads made by French and English explorers. The adventurers who entered what was known in the 19th century as the Far West of course took with them whatever rifles they owned—including their "Kentuckies." But the slim smallish-bore longrifle was not right for the Far West. It didn't fit well on a horse, and horse travel was the main mode of transportation over such vast expanses. The rifle broke easily, especially at the wrist area of the stock. And there were huge animals in that wild region, such as grizzly bears and Rocky Mountain elk.

A new rifle was born. Called the Plains Rifle, it was epitomized by examples crafted by the brothers Hawken, Sam and Jake, who eventually settled in Denver, Colorado. The Hawken, to use that name generically, carried a shorter barrel than the Pennsylvania rifle but had a bigger bore, usually 50 caliber or more. It was a halfstock rifle instead of a fullstock, which improved its strength. And it was altogether more rugged if not nearly as eye-pleasing as its Pennsylvania/ Kentucky predecessor.

Compressing a good deal of history into a small space, we see the plains rifle in turn supplanted by the repeater. These early repeaters were absolute pipsqueaks. The Volcanic, for example, shot a "Rocket Ball," which was a hollowed-based bullet with a wee supply of black powder in the base.

The Volcanic shot many times in succession, but no single hit was worth much on a big-game animal. Nonetheless, it led the way to better (and bigger) inventions. Caseless ammo left a lot to be desired. It was not nearly as powerful as the paper cartridge, which was not much more than a tube containing bullet and powder. In its more sophisticated form, the paper cartridge was used

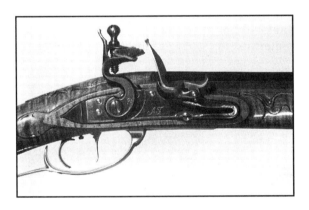

The custom work of Andy Fautheree proves that the modern rifleman can have it all, including hand-made replicas of the Kentucky/Pennsylvania longrifle. Above is Andy's hand-made flintlock; below is his carved patchbox, replicating that of an original longrifle.

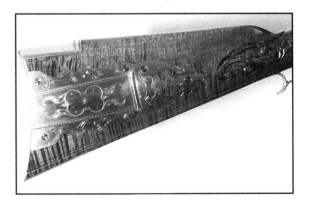

in the Sharps breechloader. The paper round was shoved into its open breech; when the falling block action was returned to battery (shooting position), its sharp edge sliced off the back of the paper cartridge, exposing the powder charge to a channel. Fire emanating from a percussion cap dashed through the channel to ignite the powder charge.

SMOKELESS POWDER REVOLUTIONIZES SHOOTING

The fuel at this time was of course black powder—in everything from muzzleloader to paper cartridge breechloader. Smokeless powder formulas were on the scene very early, but they weren't workable in the open system of the muzzleloader. Nor was smokeless powder acceptable for the early breechloader and its paper cartridge. A stronger package was needed to help contain the pressures developed by this newer grind. What evolved was the metallic cartridge. This type of cartridge acted as a seal at the back of the breech. For quite some time, black powder was housed in the new cartridge case, but as stronger steels were invented and used in barrelmaking, smokeless powder became workable in the metallic case as well. The world of shooting was changed forever.

Before 1886 the 8mm Lebel, a French Army cartridge, was loaded with smokeless powder. This round, technically the 8×50R Lebel (8mm bullet, 50mm case, "R" for rimmed), was chambered in a bolt-action rifle. The combination of a good 8mm bullet, smokeless powder and a bolt-action rifle could have proved ideal for sporting purposes, but the Lebel was never popular in the hunting field. The round and rifle were apparently considered too military for sporting use. American sportsmen had taken to the lever-action rifle, and a bolt-action hunting arm was not to their liking at this time.

The 30 US Army, which is known today as the 30-40 Krag, was an American smokeless powder military cartridge chambered in a bolt-action rifle. While some hunters saw its field application, the lever guns continued to serve the American hunter. Then came the first *sporting* smokeless cartridge, the 30 WCF (30 caliber

This original can (note small size) of "Kentucky Sporting" grade black powder symbolizes the beginning of shooting.

tridges, such as the 38-55 Winchester and 45-70 Government, gave way to the smaller, faster smokeless powder rounds that shot a lot flatter and actually dropped deer-size game faster than the big slow bullet—although large-bore blackpowder rounds were better than the smokeless smaller-bores on larger-than-deer game at close range.

Today we have it all. The modern rifleman has access to the finest 22 rimfires ever made, a multitude of middle-sized centerfires, and some big bores built to handle anything in the world, including pachyderms. The modern shooter is spoiled. Even in the days of the blackpowder cartridge, there were at least 100 different rounds to choose from. We have the same situation now, but there are fewer gaps in the lineup. Everything—from 4000 foot-per-second 17-caliber centerfires to cartridges pushing huge bullets at

Originals of timeworn favorites abound, many in safe working order. This Winchester Model 1876 rifle is a perfect example that remains in use today.

Winchester Center, or Central, Fire). Its little sister, the 25 WCF, is not generally recognized as a smokeless powder sporting "first." However, this metallic was introduced concurrently with the 30 WCF, and both were chambered for the one-year-old Model 1894 lever-action Winchester rifle that used a nickel-steel barrel. These rounds were popularized as the 30-30 Winchester and the 25-35 Winchester; the former went on to become the favorite sporting cartridge around the world, while the latter faded into obsolescence.

Our current sporting rifles developed from these origins. Smokeless powder and the metallic cartridge case paved the way for hundreds of different rifle styles. Popular blackpowder cartridges ended up as smokeless powder rounds. For example, the little 22 rimfire, born as a blackpowder load, became a perfect smokeless number. The older big-bore blackpowder car-

medium speed—is available, as well as the most accurate and useful rimfires ever known. We're blessed also with air-powered rifles of fantastic close-range accuracy and good small-game performance. Furthermore, blackpowder arms are still in heavy use, by at least five million shooters in this country. If anything, interest in muzzleloaders is growing.

The realm of rimfires is dominated by 22 calibers: the 22 Long Rifle, the lesser-used 22 Short and 22 Long, and the only cartridge of its kind in the world—the 22 Winchester Magnum Rimfire (WMR). An improvement of the earlier rare military air rifles of old that were capable of dropping a soldier at long distance. The Lewis & Clark Expedition of the 1800s, spearheaded by President Jefferson's Far West campaign, was noted for carrying a powerful air rifle. But the average sporting air rifle of the past was no match for the high-speed model of today.

The 22-caliber rimfire rifle is also at a zenith, in spite of a decline in pump-action models. And of course we have today the finest collection of centerfire rounds known in the history of shooting. The following is a brief overview of the action styles offered the modern marksman.

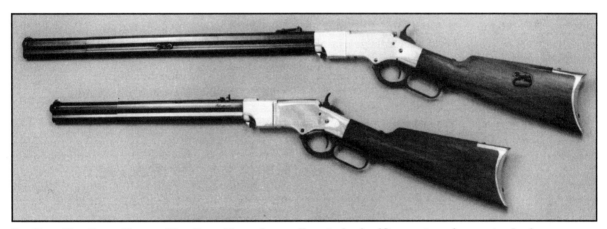

Replicas like these Henry rifles from Navy Arms allow today's riflemen to enjoy yesterday's guns without risking collector value.

22 Winchester Rim Fire (WRF), the 22 WMR shoots a jacketed bullet. The styles of modern rifles discussed in this book include early designs as well as recent designs because the old ones never died. Muzzleloaders are still with us, and lever-action designs that originated in the 19th century are also in use today. Dozens of old rifle styles have been kept alive through replication. Therefore, in order to speak of the modern rifle, we have to include muzzleloaders (of old and new design) as well as replica cartridge arms.

The modern air rifle is the most accurate of its kind ever made. It is also more powerful than most previous air rifles, with the exception of the

SINGLE-SHOT RIFLES

Action styles of yesteryear remain with us, beginning with the single-shot. Who would have thought that a single-shot rifle would survive in the space age? There are many single-shots of various designs. Thompson/Center offers a break-open single-shot Contender Carbine, for example, currently chambered for 22 LR, 22 Hornet, 223 Remington, 30-30, 35 Remington and others. The same company has a break-open Single Shot also in numerous calibers, including the 223, 22-250, 7mm-08, 308 Winchester, 30-06 and other popular rounds. This rifle is also chambered for the 32-40 Winchester—almost

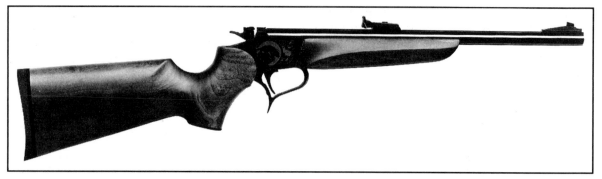

This Thompson/Center Carbine is a good example of a modern single-shot. Scaled down for the smaller marksman, this rifle is chambered for a number of excellent cartridges.

shocking—because the 32-40 came out in the early 1840s and was washed up 100 years later with no rifle chambered for it. But the 32-40 Winchester was always heralded for its potential accuracy, and T/C brought the cartridge back.

Other single-shots include the replica Sharps falling block. The Sharps rifle is popular in 45-70 Government, but can also be purchased in smaller and larger chamberings, right up to the 50-140-700 Sharps round, which arrived too late in time for the buffalo runner to use, but makes an interesting big bore for today's rifleman. The Remington Rolling Block, almost as popular as the Sharps rifle in buffalo days, is also replicated today in 45-70 Government, and is chambered for 22 LR, 22 WMR, 22 Hornet and 357 Magnum. The rolling block is a strong, unique design, with the nose of the hammer locking the action. Browning's Model 1885 with

28-inch barrel is a high-wall falling-block rifle chambered for various excellent rounds, including the 7mm Remington Magnum. And the Ruger No. 1, another single-shot on the falling block principle, is currently available in numerous configurations with a host of chamberings, including the 270 Weatherby Magnum.

LEVER-ACTION RIFLES

The lever-action rifle remains viable in spite of its age. Browning's Model 81 is offered in two action lengths, one for cartridges like the 308 Winchester and another for rounds like the 30-06 Springfield. Here is a lever-action model for all major calibers. The fan of big bullets can choose the 81 in the excellent 358 Winchester cartridge, which handles 200- and 250-grain projectiles. Magnum devotees can select the 7mm Remington Magnum for long-range au-

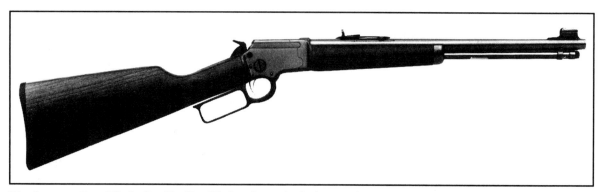

The lever-action 22-rimfire Marlin rifle has been built in one form or another since the 19th century. This is a recent version, the Model 39TDS.

thority. Browning has built several replica lever-action rifles in recent times, including the Winchester Models 1886 and 1895, plus a Model 71 in its original 348 Winchester chambering, as well as a Model 53 in 32-20 Winchester. There are plenty of Winchester Model 1873 copies sold by various companies, as well as Winchester's

One advantage offered by the lever-action repeater is good round capacity, because its tubular magazine can run the full length of the barrel. Here rounds are introduced into a Winchester Model 94.

Model 66, made with many variations.

Marlin's lever-actions are still highly regarded. They're easy to find in just about any sporting goods store. The 22 rimfire is represented in the famous 39A, with the 336 action housing the 30-30, 35 Remington and other rounds. A 336-type action noted as the Model

1895 in honor of that great old Marlin can be purchased in 45-70 Government chambering for up-close, heavy-duty work. Marlin's lever-actions also chamber the 22 WMR as well as the 25-20 Winchester and 32-20 Winchester.

The great Savage Model 99 lever-action is still available in calibers 243 Winchester and 308 Winchester, and in its various chamberings will remain a lever-action favorite for a long time. Used-gun racks all over the country carry Model 99 Savage rifles in an assortment of chamberings. These used rifles are also available through arms newspapers such as the *Shotgun News* and *The Gun List*.

Of course the famous Winchester Model 94 remains on line. Today, it's a stronger-action rifle than ever before and is available in 307 Winchester and 356 Winchester chamberings, two powerful rounds. It is also sold in 7×30 Waters and 30-30 Winchester. Empty brass ejects out to the side in this modern version of the 94, making central scope mounting over the bore feasible.

SLIDE-ACTIONS

Although offered by few companies in limited configurations, the slide-action rifle continues to appeal to some rifleman. A little Timber Wolf Pump is available in 357 Magnum (which will also shoot the 38 Special cartridge) and also in 44 Remington Magnum. The strong Remington 7600 Slide Action rifle remains with us too. Better than ever, it is chambered not only for the ever-popular 30-06 Springfield cartridge, but also for the 243 Winchester, 270 Winchester, 280 Remington, 308 Winchester and the powerful 35 Whelen—not long ago a wildcat cartridge. Built on necked-up 30-06 brass, the 35 Whelen is today a Remington factory round.

THE BOLT-ACTION

All in all, the bolt-action is king today. There are so many different models in so many different chamberings that attempting to list them all would be difficult, if not impossible. Cartridges from 22 Short through 460 Weatherby Magnum, not to mention hundreds of wildcats (the 17-caliber centerfire wildcats are particularly interest-

The pump-action rifle in 22 rimfire, an example of which is this Winchester Model 62 "trombone" action, was once highly popular. Today the bolt-action and semiauto rimfire rifles have taken over.

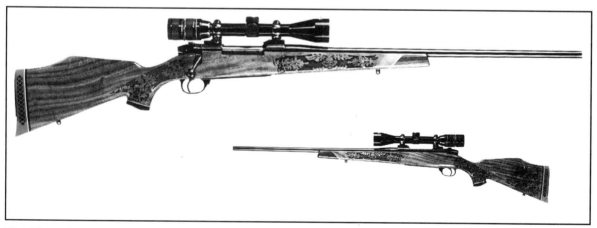

The king of rifles today is the bolt-action. This luxurious bolt-action is Weatherby's Mark V with special laser carving on the stock.

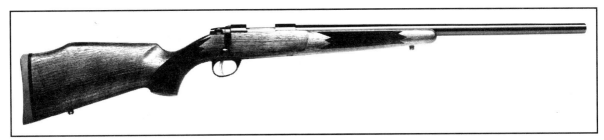

Sako's heavy-barreled Varmint rifle in 22 PPC USA and 6mm PPC USA is a super-accurate single-shot bolt-action.

ing) plus the 17 Remington factory round, are all chambered in bolt-action models.

THE BOLT-ACTION SINGLE-SHOT

Deserving special mention is the single-shot rifle that is also a bolt-action rifle. A shooter immediately thinks of the 22 rimfire single-shot in this instance, because here was a sturdy little "boy's rifle" that could be purchased with the contents of one modest-sized piggy bank. However, the single-shot, bolt-action rifle is far more than a 22 rimfire today. It represents accuracy that can be safely described as incredible. For example, at the moment the most accurate factory rifle (out of the box without further tuning) is the Sako heavy barrel model chambered for the 22 PPC USA and 6mm PPC USA cartridges. This single-shot, bolt-action rifle is capable of grouping five bullets into a 1/3-inch cluster as measured from the centers of the two most distant bullet holes in the group at 100 yards from the bench. Groups of 1/4 inch center to center are not uncommon with the Sako bolt-action, single-shot rifle.

Savage brought back its single-shot Model 112FVS based on the Model 110 bolt action. In calibers 223 Remington and 22-250 Remington, this rifle wears a free-floated heavy barrel 26 inches long, tapered with recessed muzzle. In keeping with the concept of the single-shot, bolt-action rifle, the 112 has a rigid solid bottom receiver. And in accord with the trend of the times, the 112 wears a fiberglass polymer stock. The single-shot, bolt-action rifle gained fame in winning national benchrest competitions, thereby promoting the introduction of the Sako and Sav-

age single-shots listed here. These commercial bolt-action single-shots are not as heavy as benchrest rifles; however, they do fall in the nine-pound class. There are also target-type 22-rimfire bolt-action, single-shot rifles, as mentioned below in brief.

THE SEMIAUTOMATICS

These are self-loading actions in which the rifles do not continue to fire with a single pulling of the trigger. Rather the trigger must be pulled and then released each time the rifle is to be fired. That's where the semiautomatic name comes in, although "self-loading" probably describes this action style more aptly. Self-loading rifles were designed a long time ago, with actions on the drawing board in the 19th century.

Dozens of rimfire semiauto rifles are in the marketplace, from the AMT Lightning with its military look and 30-shot magazine, to the Ruger 10/22 Autoloading Carbine and its unique detachable rotary magazine. Brownings little auto remains in the lineup, along with Remington's well-known 552 and a host of Marlin 22 rimfires.

Marlin's Papoose is a smartly designed 22-rimfire autoloading takedown that fits into a handy case. On the other end of the semiauto continuum is the full-scale BAR—Browning Automatic Rifle. No rimfire, this semiautomatic big-game rifle is available in 243, 270, 280 and 30-06. But the story does not end there; a special Magnum BAR is chambered for the 7mm Remington Magnum, 300 Winchester Magnum and 338 Winchester Magnum cartridges for big power with rapid fire. Remington's Model 7400 continues the long history of that company's

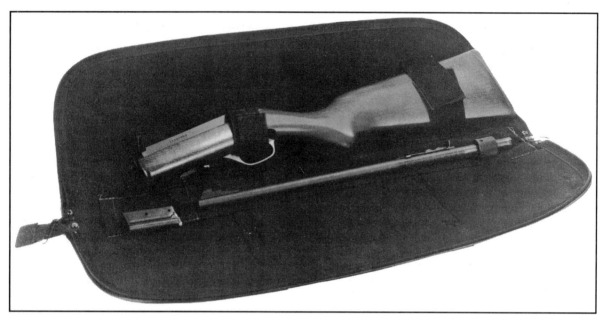

Indicative of the numerous rifle styles offered the modern rifleman is Marlin's Model 70P Papoose: a 22-rimfire semiautomatic takedown, sized for the younger shooter.

semiauto big-game rifles. The fine-looking current model has a Monte Carlo stock and is chambered for the 243, 270, 280, 308 and 30-06. A carbine version of the 7400 comes with an 18.5-inch barrel in caliber 30-06 only. The handsome Model 7400 Remington uses a detachable four-shot box magazine.

Somewhat in a world all its own is the Marlin Camp Gun. The Model 9 is chambered for the 9mm Parabellum cartridge; the Model 45, for the 45 ACP cartridge. This is a slick-working, accurate semiauto. My tests of this firearm included the consumption of 10 boxes of ammo—500 rounds—without cleaning. Not one single round misfired in the test. Shooting 500 times without cleaning is, of course, not recommended practice and must be considered abusive, but the Marlin took it in stride. The 16.5-inch barrel of the Camp Gun has Micro-Groove® rifling, a Marlin specialty. Overall length is under 36 inches.

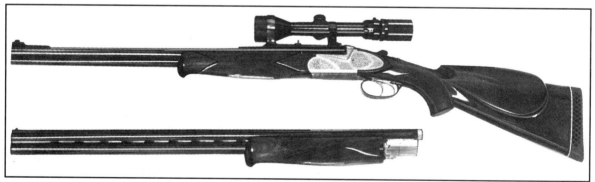

An example of a multi-barreled rifle is this Armsport Model 4000 over/under, shown here with scope in place and additional shotgun barrels.

MULTIPLE BARREL RIFLES

Savage Arms continues to offer its Model 24 in a variety of styles. The Model 24F-12T Turkey Gun is an over/under rifle/shotgun with synthetic camouflaged stock. Its upper barrel is available in a choice of 22 Hornet or 223 Remington, while the lower barrel handles 12-gauge, three-inch magnum shotgun shells. The standard 24 is available in various combinations, including a 30-30 Winchester/12-gauge model.

A number of multiple-barrel rifles are strictly rifles. Beretta's Model 455, for example, is a side-by-side that can be ordered in 375 H&H Magnum, 458 Winchester Magnum, 470 Nitro Express, 500 Nitro Express, 416 Rigby and 9.3×74R. In keeping with double rifles, the Ber-

16-inch barrel, 22-rimfire semiauto can take a 50-shot magazine. Mitchell offers several 22-rimfire military-like rifles, including an AK-22 self-loader in either 22 LR or 22 WMR. Centerfire autoloaders of military style include numerous models, far too many to list here. Auto-Ordnance's Thompson 27 A-1 is a 30-shot unit in 45 ACP (Automatic Colt Pistol) chambering. But hold onto your hat—you'll need to if you shoot the Barnett Light-Fifty Model 82 A-1 Auto rifle with 29-inch barrel and 10-shot detachable magazine. Its big 50 BMG cartridge shoots bullets in the 700-grain and heavier class. The 223 Remington round is well represented in the world of military-like sporters, as are the 9mm Parabellum and the 308 Winchester.

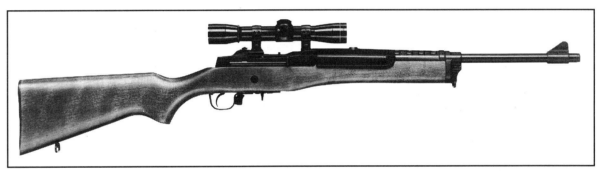

Military influence on sporting rifles is clearly evident in this Ruger Mini-Thirty. Not only is its configuration military, this model is also chambered for an army round, the 7.62mm Russian.

etta is not available at a bargain-basement price. You can buy one for about $20,000, or if you prefer the fancier model, $44,000. Not all doubles are so costly, however. The Bernardelli in 9.3×74R is under $8,000. The Tikka Model 412S over/under double rifle in caliber 9.3×74R is imported from Italy by Valmet; it's a good buy at under $1500.

THE MILITARY INFLUENCE

There has been a tremendous military influence on sporting firearms over the past decade. Rimfire and centerfire rifles have taken the look of soldiers' issue arms. For example, the Auto-Ordnance 1927-A is a visual replica of the Thompson submachine gun Model of 1927. This

RECENT RIFLE TRENDS

The military sporting rifle is part of a trend. When Springfield Armory brought out its M-1A rifle in 7.62mm NATO (that's the 308 Winchester), with 5-, 10- or 20-shot magazine, it was clear that the military trend was on a serious track. The M-1A, also available in 243 Winchester, was offered to the shooting public not only in a standard version, but also in a National Match model and a Super Match model. This replica rifle, in other words, was meant for serious shooting. Trends are dangerous. They can be difficult to identify and they may disappear right before your eyes. However, unlike clothing fashions, the current trends in rifles seems stable and long-lasting.

Shooters have zeroed in on high-precision accuracy, for example. This trend has been well satisfied by many target rifles, one fine representative being Remington's 40-XR KS in 22 rimfire. This single-shot, bolt-action competition-grade rifle with synthetic stock weighs 10 pounds with its heavy 24-inch target barrel. It is built to ISU specs so that it can be used within the framework of serious target shooting. Remington's 11.25-pound 40-XB, with synthetic or wood stock, is chambered in a variety of centerfire calibers, including the 222 Remington, 222 Remington Magnum, 223, 220 Swift, 22-250 Remington, 6mm Remington, 243, 25-06, 7mm Remington Magnum, and some esoteric num-

manufactured today are not offered with optional fiberglass stocks, or stocks of other synthetic materials. The so-called "mountain rifle" trend has slowed a bit, but this style of rifle remains in demand. The simple classic American-style stock is more appreciated now than it has been for years and many synthetic stocks carry this design.

The flyweight rifle persists, but the glitter has worn off that creation. Some hunters who just couldn't wait to get their hands on a five-pound 300 Magnum couldn't wait to turn loose the same rifle after owning one. I am one of those hunters. I don't mean the sensible lightweight rifle, but rather the "trifle," as I call it. For example, my

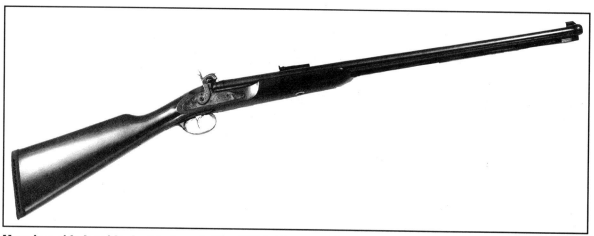

Here is a side-by-side double barrel rifle, CVA's Express 50-caliber muzzleloader.

bers, such as the 7mm BR (Benchrest) and 30-338 wildcat. The Parker-Hale M-8 Sniper Rifle is a 10-shot 308 Winchester that weighs 12.5 pounds with scope and McMillan fiberglass stock. It is designed to group bullets at long range, including 1,000 yards. The M-87 Target Rifle also by Parker-Hale is similar, but comes in a variety of calibers, including 243, 6.5×55, 308, 30-06 and 300 Winchester Magnum. These are only some of the accuracy-oriented repeaters and single-shots now on the market.

Lightweight synthetic stocks are a relatively new invention that are here to stay. At this point, however, the synthetic stock has not replaced wood altogether, since a few major hunting rifles

Ruger International 308 Model 77 weighs only 7½—not 5½—pounds with scope sight. It is a rifle, not a trifle. I found that a super lightweight rifle was a joy to carry, but not to my liking when absolute field stability was demanded. Give me some weight, please, not only to control and steady the rifle for a good shot, but also to dampen recoil. The notion that these flyweights don't "kick" because they wear synthetic stocks is applesauce. One of the more important factors involving recoil is the weight of the firearm. If the rifle and the bullet weighed the same, the rifle and bullet would take off at the same speed. For me, lightweights yes, flyweights no. I'm happy to see what was a strong trend toward flyweights dying out.

As far as cartridges go, during the past decade wildcats have been added to the ranks of factory rounds with uncommon regularity. This movement has seen the 22-250 graduate from wildcat to factory round as the 22-250 Remington. The 25-06 has experienced a similar history. The 308 Winchester necked down to handle 7mm bullets used to be a wildcat as well. Today the 7mm-08 Remington is a factory reality. The 7mm Remington Magnum has been so successful and popular that we tend to forget it also was a wildcat at one time. The 35 Whelen is another. This former wildcat, the 30-06 necked up to handle 35 caliber bullets, now bears the Rem-

modified to use a small rifle primer. The case is 1.520 inches in length, compared with the 2.015 inches for the regular 308 Winchester case. Mention of these rounds doesn't scratch the surface of cartridge development today. Consider also the number of handgun cartridges that are currently chambered in rifles.

Part of modern cartridge trends is bringing back the "oldies." Out of circulation at one time were the 25-20 and 32-20 Winchesters. Not that they were no longer manufactured as factory ammo. It's just that no new rifles were chambered for either cartridge. Not true today. Although the 32-40 Winchester has been offered in the Sharps single-shot for quite some time, I

Marlin's Model 9 is one example of a rifle chambered for a handgun round, the 9mm Luger.

ington name. Remington, obviously, has taken notice of good wildcats and tamed them for factory use. So has Sako, which brought the 22 PPC and 6mm PPC out as factory rounds: the 22 PPC USA and 6mm PPC USA. Winchester's 7-30 Waters is the factory version of Ken Water's wildcat based on necking the 30-30 case down to hold 7mm bullets.

Other interesting cartridge developments include the evolution of the 6mm BR (Bench Rest). This round is based on a Remington creation, a modified 308 Winchester case designed to use a small rifle primer. The round went factory in 1989. Remington is also responsible for a 7mm BR, which is also a shortened 308 case

was surprised that it was back in a modern rifle. Other cartridges that remained in production, but with few to no factory rifles chambered for them, include the 220 Swift, 250 Savage, 257 Roberts, and 300 Savage. All of these have seen recent chamberings.

CHOOSING THE RIGHT RIFLE FOR YOU

How would a shooter go about picking the right rifle? It's not an easy matter nowadays. The following list is barely a starting point, but it will put the shooter on the right trail.

1. The Cartridge. The cartridge is the first consideration in picking a rifle. It does the work. Obviously, you pick a target round for target shooting, a long-range number for long-range duty, a varmint cartridge for varmints and so forth.

2. Application. Both cartridge and rifle are chosen on the basis of application. Nobody needs a heavy magnum rifle for whitetail hunting in the thickets. On the other hand, a short-barreled 35-caliber rifle is not really the ticket for hunting the western plains.

3. Terrain. The preceding consideration leads to this factor: "lay of the land." A rifle is chosen on the basis of where it will be used.

4. Style and Action. These related factors are somewhat personal. Today all action styles are offered in a range of cartridges. For example, even the semiauto is chambered for rounds up to mid-magnum size, such as 338 Winchester.

5. Portability and Handling. Rifles must be stored, carried and handled. The shooter should consider these points before buying a rifle. Size and weight make a big difference in storage, carrying and handling.

6. Stability and Accuracy. These two are lumped together. The most stable rifles are generally of heavier-than-average barrel weight. Stocks are usually substantial rather than sliver-like. On the other hand, how much accuracy and shot-to-shot stability is required of a brush rifle?

While a benchrest shooter may fire dozens of shots in a short time, a whitetail hunter is unlikely to get more than a couple of bullets out of the muzzle in a whole day of hunting. My Ruger Model 77 International is not as stable as my Ruger No. 1, nor does it have to be. The little 77 is ideal for big-game hunting in close cover, and has been known to do well in the open, too. But for many successive shots, my No. 1 is more stable, although not more accurate, than my 77. On the plains, give me the No. 1 in 270 Weatherby Magnum chambering. Along the creek bottoms where whitetails roam, I'll take the Model 77 with its 18.5-inch barrel in caliber 308 Winchester.

7. Price. Buying twice is poor economy. If a shooter knows what he wants and the price tag is not beyond his pocketbook, he should part with the money and buy the rifle. He shouldn't try a rifle he does not truly want, only to trade it in later at a loss so he can purchase the shooting machine he should have bought in the first place.

This is a look at the American rifle today. The American rifle is a single-shot, a repeater, a big bore, a small bore. It's a muzzleloader. It's an air rifle. It is mild mannered. It is powerful. It works wonders at the target range. It is perfect for big game. No wonder the modern shooter is considered the most fortunate marksman ever.

THE CARTRIDGE: THE RIFLE'S "ENGINE"

2 If not for the cartridge, the world of rifle shooting today would not be as advanced as it is. The first "guns" were little more than a sometimes-cylindrical fixture with two holes in it. The larger hole formed a bore into which black powder was loaded; on top of that a projectile was rammed home. The smaller hole provided a channel for a spark or flame to reach the powder charge. When the powder went off, it created a great volume of expanding gas that forced the bullet from the muzzle of the bore. As long as this open system prevailed, no true high-pressure situation could exist. And without sufficient pressure behind it, the missile could never achieve a very high velocity. Muzzle velocities with patched round balls eventually reached around 2000 feet per second (fps). But speeds in the 3000 and even 4000 fps domain were a long way off.

Shooters soon invented a *paper "cartridge"* only because carrying powder and ball separately was not convenient or efficient. Born in 16th-century Europe, the paper cartridge in its original form of fixed ammunition thrived into the 19th century (and even beyond) all over the world. The term "cartridge" meant then what it means today: a container. The original paper cartridge was simply a tube that held the bullet and the powder as a unit. The paper tube was tied off with string or the powder end was glued shut. Grease could be applied to the paper to protect the powder from moisture, and grease also helped seat a stubborn projectile downbore.

This precursor to the metallic round was not made only by hand. Paper cartridges were in fact manufactured, with thousands of rounds made for wartime use, in the American Revolutionary War as well as the Civil War. The United States Cartridge Company catalogue of 1904 carried a list of "Cartridges for Small Arms, 1839." The list included prepared paper-cartridge loads, such as the 64-caliber Musket paper cartridge, which contained one round ball and 130 grains of black powder (noted as "Musket powder"). Also listed was a standardized Musketoon load: a paper cartridge with one round ball and only 85 grains of black powder. A U.S. 69-caliber standardized paper cartridge, manufactured from 1794 to 1842 carried one full-size round lead ball topped by two large buckshot pellets— the "buck 'n' ball" load. Conical projectiles were also loaded into paper cartridges. These elongated bullets took on a multitude of forms.

The paper cartridge initially was used only as a container. The shooter ripped away the end of the paper tube, poured the powder downbore and seated the bullet. However, when the breechloader came along—especially the Sharps model—the paper cartridge rose in stature. The falling-block Sharps breechloader could accept the paper cartridge into its waiting chamber. When the action of the rifle was closed, the upward movement of the falling block brought a razor-sharp edge of steel against the paper cartridge, slicing the rear portion away and exposing the powder charge. A spark generated by a percussion cap could then reach and detonate the waiting powder. This was a major step towards a "real" cartridge. The problem, still, was lack of a gas seal. Paper cartridges did nothing to keep the gas from escaping into the mechanism of the rifle and sometimes right at the shooter as well.

Smokeless powder of course achieved its potential because of the gas seal provided by the metallic cartridge case. Some caseless ammo had been tried successfully. The Rocket Ball, for example, which was used in the Volcanic and sim-

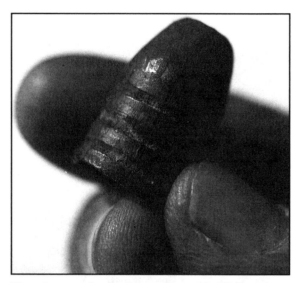

The elongated missile, such as this Minie, allowed more mass per caliber.

ilar early repeating arms, was essentially a bullet with a hollow base that held the powder charge—but it made a pitiful load. Caseless ammo is under study to this day because elimination of the case would allow soldiers to carry a larger supply of ammo into the field. But so far, the metallic case is king. It alone allows the fantastic accuracy, power and reliability exhibited by the modern rifle. Furthermore, the metal case can be reloaded, an art that began soon after the first metallic cartridges became available.

The *rimfire* was the first successful metallic cartridge. In it a priming mixture was distributed along the rim of the cartridge case. When this outer portion of the case head was struck by the firing pin, the concussion detonated the priming mixture, which in turn sparked the powder charge to life. Rimfires could not be reloaded, however. But the rimfire concept continues to thrive—witness the millions of 22-rimfire rounds that flow from ammo plants daily in this country and abroad.

Rimfire cartridges were originally offered in a huge variety of calibers. The 22 Short, introduced by Smith & Wesson, was on the scene by November of 1857. This little rimfire became the point of a spearhead that drove onward into the 19th century with hundreds of rimfire variations.

Before the cartridge was the patched round ball, loaded downbore as shown here, usually with a short starter.

The box on the left contains Garrett's special 45-70 Government ammo—a 19th-century cartridge that remains chambered in many rifles today. Below the box is an original Civil War paper cartridge, along with a number of old-time rounds, including the 50-140 Sharps. On the far right are bullets for the rifled musket, along with black powder and a few percussion caps.

There was also a 30 Short, a 30 Warner and a 30 Long as well as a host of 32 rimfires, some of them excellent for small game and turkey hunting. The 32 Long rimfire could probably be used today for these purposes with total success.

At the other end of the spectrum were bigbore rimfires that shot heavy bullets. The 58 Storm, for example, was a 58-caliber rimfire that propelled bullets weighing from 480 grains to 611 grains with a blackpowder charge averaging around 60 grains. But this was not the big boy on the rimfire block. Larger rounds included a 69 Roberts rimfire, a 69-caliber Musket rimfire and, incredibly, a one-inch caliber known as the "1-inch Gatling." The latter burned 330 to 360 grains of black powder behind a bullet that

weighed 3,840 grains.

On the smaller side, there were at least a few 14-caliber rimfires, among them the 14 Alton Jones and 14 Garrison, as well as a host of 17s. These were smokeless-powder loadings, as was the ill-fated 20th-century 5mm Remington Magnum rimfire, a 20-caliber cartridge that offered the rimfire fan well over 2000 fps mv. Rimfires were offered in the straight-case wall style as well as the bottleneck design.

As interesting and useful as the rimfires were (are), right up to military rifle application (as with the 41 Swiss rimfire round), the design eventually gave way to a better idea: the *centerfire (or "central fire")* cartridge. The big difference, of course, was the replacement of the

The priming mixture of a rimfire cartridge lies in the rim—hence, the name of the round.

priming mixture around the rim of the casehead with a centrally located primer. This made reloading possible, for when the spent primer was expelled, a new one could be installed in its place.

The balloonhead copper centerfire case, also called a folded head case, soon was improved by a solid head design that could withstand high pressure. That upgrading of the case is vital to understanding where we are today, for without cartridge case strength, our present high-velocity/high-pressure loads would be impossible.

CARTRIDGE COMPONENTS

The idea of a centrally located detonator, or primer, required an avenue for the spark to travel

from the primer to the powder. This channel was provided by a flashhole, or passageway, through the head of the cartridge and into the body, which contains the powder supply.

Imagine a cartridge case resting on the table in front of you. It is a metal tube, usually brass, with one closed end and one open end. When the bullet is pointing upward, the case is resting on its *head,* that is, the back portion of the case that is away from the bullet. The body of the case consists of the *walls.* On a straight-wall case, the walls run from the head to the bullet end. The end of the case that holds the bullet is called the *mouth.* A straight case can be tapered so that the mouth end is smaller than the head end.

However, in order to achieve a larger body size coupled with a smaller mouth size, the *bot-*

The priming mixture of the centerfire cartridge is centered in the head of the round, as shown here in this old 33 Winchester load (note "W" for Winchester in center of primer).

tleneck case was born. This type of case tapers rather radically at the *shoulder,* then straightens out toward the mouth of the case to form a *neck,* which holds the bullet in place. The basic statistics of a bottleneck cartridge case include: the *head size,* which is the diameter of the head; the *overall length* of the cartridge case, measured from the head to the mouth; the length from the head to the beginning of the neck; the length from the front of the extractor groove to the beginning of the shoulder; the diameter of the front of the extractor groove; and the diameter of the neck.

Also of interest is the *shoulder angle* of the case. This is the measurement in degrees of a line drawn along the taper that forms the shoulder. In the 30-06 Springfield, for example, the shoulder angle is a bit over 17 degrees. Other measurements can be taken, of course, but these give a good general idea of case size, shape, internal capacity and shoulder design.

A shooter interested in comparing cartridge cases needs only to check a few measurements. For example, there are numerous cartridge cases with the same head size as the 30-06, which has a head diameter of .473 inch. The 22-250 Rem-

ington and the little 6mm BR Remington both have a head size of .473 inch. So does the 243 Winchester, 250 Savage, 270 Winchester, 300 Savage and 308 Winchester. The indication is clear: these rounds are related to the 30-06. Indeed, they were designed by altering either the 30-06 case or a case derived from the '06. A single case can be used to build many different types of cartridges. The mere necking down or necking up of the case drastically modifies the finished product.

The head of the case contains vital information. The *headstamp*—the lettering impressed into the bottom of the head—usually tells you the manufacturer and the type of ammunition. An example of a commercial headstamp would be: "norma .308." This means the cartridge is made by the Norma ammunition company of Sweden and the round is the 308 Winchester. Military ammo is a mild exception to the rule, for the information on its headstamp differs from commercial data. An early cartridge headstamp might read "U.M.C. 40-3¼." Quite different from modern nomenclature, this old reference is to the Union Metallic Cartridge Company (UMC) and a 40-caliber cartridge with a case 3¼ inches long.

There are hundreds of variations, and all re-

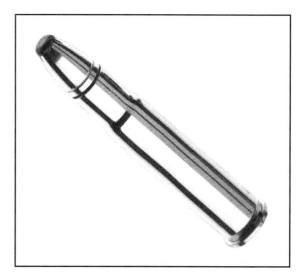

The rimmed centerfire cartridge is not outdated. The relatively new 356 Winchester cartridge shown here is of the rimmed type.

These two bottleneck cases are interesting in that the 8mm Lebel (left), probably the first smokeless cartridge, is rimmed, whereas the 30-06 (right) is rimless.

fer to cartridge identification. Consider these two: "W.R.A. CO .32 W.S." and "Super Speed .303 British." The first represents Winchester Repeating Arms Company and its 32 Winchester Special cartridge. The second is also a Winchester factory load, for Super Speed is a Winchester logo; the round is apparently a sporting version of the 303 British military cartridge.

The *style of cartridge head* used is an important part of the cartridge's design. The *rimmed cartridge* is a rather basic head style, in which the head of the case is wider than its body; the ever-popular 30-30, for example, has a rimmed case. When fired, the rifle's extractor "grabs" the rim and pulls the spent cartridge out of the chamber.

The *rimless case* has a head diameter close to, but not exactly the same as, the diameter of the case body. Because no rim protrudes for an extractor to grab, the rimless case has an extractor groove cut into it. The 30-06 is an example of a rimless design cartridge case.

While rimmed and rimless represent the most popular cartridge head styles, there is also a *semi-rimmed* variation. The head of this case is larger than the case body, but it also has an extractor groove cut into it. (A few semi-rimmed

cartridge cases have a rim diameter a trace smaller than the body diameter.) The 220 Swift with its semi-rimmed cartridge case was built from the semi-rimmed 6mm Lee Navy cartridge case necked down from 24 to 22 caliber. The diameter of the Swift rim is .473 inch, but the diameter of the body in front of the extractor groove is .445 inch.

Another design is the *rebated rimless case.* The 284 Winchester is one of few examples of this style. The idea of the rebated rimless case is to "fatten" the body of the cartridge without going to an overly large head size. The 284 Winchester dimensions shows a 30-06 head diameter of .473 inch. However, on the 30-06 case, the diameter in front of the extractor groove is .470 inch, whereas on the 284 Winchester case this measurement is .500 inch—a full half-inch across. Obviously, the 284 case is fatter than the '06 case at this point.

The *belted* or *belted magnum case* is yet another cartridge case head style that dominates today. The fine Weatherby cartridges exemplify this case design. Roy Weatherby began his experiments in high velocity using 30-06 brass, but soon moved to the basic 300 H&H Magnum case because of its improved capacity as well as its belt. The belt is not a necessity for strength as many believe. Charles Newton, the arms and ammo designer, proved that with his powerful

This "antique" balloon-head cartridge is an example of a straight-wall case. Note its size in relation to the dime.

The headstamp of the cartridge lists the precise nomenclature of the round. Note the different head sizes (diameters).

30 Newton, a big case with no belt whatsoever. But the band of metal—think of it as a girdle or a ring—rests in front of the extractor groove. It is an excellent case design and has given us a number of powerhouse rounds, including the 458 Winchester, the 300 Weatherby Magnum and the 460 Weatherby Magnum.

Headspace is the distance from the face of the breech to that point in the chamber where the cartridge is held in place when it is locked in the breech. Headspacing holds the round in place when the rifle is fired so that the cartridge case does not fly forward. This is not a complete description of headspace, but it serves our purpose, which is to note that the various head designs described above will headspace differently.

The rimmed case headspaces on the rim itself. The headspace measurement is taken from the face of the bolt to the forward portion of the rim. In other words, the headspace dimension on the rimmed case is about the thickness of the rim itself. The rimless cartridge case design headspaces from the head of the cartridge case (the most rearward portion) forward to that point where the beginning of the shoulder makes contact with the chamber. The belted case headspaces on the belt. This is measured from the rearward portion of the head to the forward portion of the belt.

CARTRIDGE NAMES

Maybe the world would be a less interesting place for it, but I believe in basic standardization. I appreciate right-hand screw threads and shirt sizes that mean something. Unfortunately, those responsible for naming cartridges over the years felt differently. The result is a hodgepodge of names, many of which make very little sense.

Some attempts were made to standardize cartridge-naming. For example, the old 45-70-500 Government is easy to decipher. The case contains a bullet of 45 caliber, a load of 70 grains of black powder and a bullet weight of 500 grains. Another sensible approach can be credited to the Sharps line of rounds. For example, the 45-120-550 3 1/4-inch Sharps is a 45-caliber cartridge that holds 120 grains of black powder and a 550-grain bullet in a case 3 1/4 inches long.

Early attempts at naming smokeless powder loads include the 30-40 Krag and the 30-30 Winchester. But neither of them were so-named by their inventors. The 30-40 Krag was really the 30 USA or 30 Army, and the 30-30 Winchester was really the 30 WCF (Winchester Center Fire). After the fact, these rounds got their popular titles, the 30-40 Krag suggesting a 30-caliber bullet and 40 grains of smokeless powder; the 30-30, a 30-caliber bullet with 30 grains of smokeless powder. Neither of these rounds were blackpowder numbers; they were smokeless designs from the start. As it turns out, the latter number wasn't ideal anyway, because smokeless powder changed. Today, neither the 30-40 Krag nor the 30-30 Win. necessarily digests the powder charge weights these numbers once signified.

Common-sense cartridge names didn't last long. Take the 270 Winchester. It was developed by Winchester. That, along with the fact that the groove diameter of the rifle is .270 inch, is all you know for certain. Bullets for the 270 Winchester measure .277 inch so that they can en-

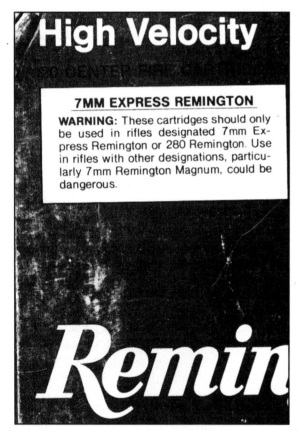

High Velocity

7MM EXPRESS REMINGTON

WARNING: These cartridges should only be used in rifles designated 7mm Express Remington or 280 Remington. Use in rifles with other designations, particularly 7mm Remington Magnum, could be dangerous.

Remin

Proof positive that cartridge names are extremely important. A new loading of the 280 Remington introduced a new cartridge name as well, the 7mm Express Remington. However, buyers were sometimes confused and ended up purchasing 7mm Express Remington ammo for their 7mm Remington Magnum rifles. Remington was obliged to print an explanation on the box, as shown here.

grave in the rifling. In that regard the 270 part make sense. But you have to read the information provided on the box of ammo to find out what the bullet weighs. You don't know the powder type or the weight of the charge. To add to the confusion, the 270 is really a 7mm/30-06 with a case slightly longer than the '06, because the 270 Winchester shoots 7mm bullets.

Although the cartridge names don't always relay a lot of pertinent data, they do say something of their nature. The 5.6×50mm Magnum, for example, is a 5.6mm (22 caliber) bullet with a case 50 millimeters long. The 7×57 Mauser is a 7mm (specifically 7.2mm) bullet with a 57mm case. The 219 Donaldson Wasp, developed by Harvey Donaldson, does not, on the other hand, shoot .219-inch bullets at all, rather 22-caliber (.224-inch) bullets.

Remington's fine 280 Remington round, essentially a 7mm/30-06 with a case length a bit longer than either the '06 or 270 case, came along in 1957 in Remington's Model 740 autoloader. The case was made longer than the 270 Winchester to prevent any chance of someone forcing a 280 Remington round into a rifle chambered for the 270. When Remington decided to offer some upgraded loads for its 280, the company also decided to change the name of the round to the 7mm Express Remington. That caused confusion. Remington was prompted to print a warning on the box to the effect that the 7mm Express Remington was never to be loaded into a rifle chambered for the 7mm Remington Magnum. Some shooters apparently confused the 7mm Express with the 7mm Rem. Mag.

THE MAGNUM CARTRIDGE

Although the magnum title has been abused, it's wrong to think of the magnum cartridge as a salesmanship gimmick. Most rounds so-named deserve it, for magnum means "bigger than average." The little 22 Winchester Magnum Rimfire (WMR) is a good example. The average 22 rimfires out there are the 22 Long Rifle and its smaller sisters the 22 Long and 22 Short. The 22 WMR shoots a jacketed 40-grain bullet much faster than the 22 LR shoots a lead 40-grain bullet. Any 22 LR ammo that attains 1300 fps muzzle

These are both 270-caliber cartridges. On the left is the 270 Weatherby Magnum, on the right, the 270 Winchester. Note the larger case capacity of the magnum, and the belt.

velocity is pretty fast. But 1900 fps with the 22 WMR is common. In fact, RWS 22 WMR ammo has been chronographed at 2150 fps at the muzzle.

In spite of all efforts to blow standard centerfire brass out to outlandish proportions, such as the 25-06 Improved, magnums generally give the shooter what he wanted in the first place: more velocity without on-the-edge pressures or case-forming problems. My own 25-06 wildcat had to huff and puff and almost blow a gasket in order to push a 120-grain bullet at 3300 fps muzzle velocity. My 257 Weatherby Magnum drives the 120-grain bullet at 3400 fps mv—only 100 fps faster, but without concern for popped primers and undue case loss.

An even better example of the magnum is the 270 Weatherby Magnum. I've loaded the 270 Winchester for well over three decades. A 140-grain bullet at a flat 3000 fps mv is an accom-

plishment with this round. My own 270 Weatherby Magnum chambered in a Ruger No. 1 rifle gets 3400 fps with the same 140-grain bullet. That's not an apple-to-apple comparison, because my chronographed data out of the 270 Winchester is derived from a 24-inch barrel, while the barrel of my Ruger is 26 inches long. However, I've also tested 26-inch barrel 270 Winchesters and in no way does the standard 270 achieve the bullet speed achieved by the magnum 270.

But are magnums necessary? The answer depends on what is required of the rifle. I use a 7mm Remington Magnum for long-range big game hunting in the West. But I don't care for this magnum in the whitetail thicket. I have a 308 Winchester and a 9mm Mannlicher that work just fine in that habitat. So bigger is not always better, and magnums aren't always worth bothering with. But when the ultimate in bullet speed is desired or required, the magnum round is the ticket. The 270 Winchester gets 2799 foot-pounds of muzzle energy with its 140-grain bullet starting at 3000 fps. My load in the 270 Weatherby Magnum for the same bullet develops 3595 foot-pounds at the muzzle. What's more, the 270 Weatherby bullet retains more energy at 100 yards from the muzzle than the standard 270 develops at the muzzle. But, again, if you don't need the extra zoom, don't bother. Magnums cost more to shoot, make more noise and "kick" harder than the standards.

HANDGUN CARTRIDGES IN RIFLES

This trend is nothing new. Convenience may have originally prompted the development of AC/DC ammo. How nice to buy one box of ammo and feed both your rifle and sidearm with it. Original oldies include the 32-20 Winchester, which was at home in a Colt sixgun as well as in a rifle. The 38-40 Winchester was another example that was a pretty fair close-range deer round out of a rifle. So was the 44-40 Winchester.

Today, you don't know what will happen in handgun/rifle cartridge development. A cartridge we think of so decidedly as an auto-pistol number—the 9mm Parabellum (9mm Luger)—has found a home in a rifle. My own Marlin Camp

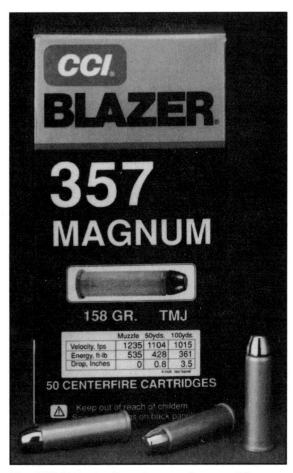

The 357 Magnum is only one of many different handgun rounds that are chambered in rifles. The practice is nothing new, for in the 19th century the 44-40 Winchester round, among others, was also chambered in rifles and revolvers.

Gun in this caliber fires rapidly and true. The 45 ACP (Automatic Colt Pistol) cartridge was intended for the handgun. But it, too, has found its way into the ranks of rifle fodder. The 357 Magnum, 357 Maximum, 41 Remington Magnum and 44 Remington Magnum handgun cartridges are all good close-range deer rounds when shot from a rifle. And the 22 rimfire in all its forms has been at home in both rifle and handgun for ages.

The advent of pistols designed to handle high-intensity cartridges is the reverse of the handgun-ammo-to-rifle-chambering phenomenon, but it has been successful. The Thompson/Center pistol is ready to go in 30-30 Winchester, for example, along with a number of even more powerful rounds. Remington's handsome XP-100 pistol is chambered for the 35 Remington and can accommodate other rifle rounds of similar power and then some. Therefore, thinking of a cartridge strictly as either a rifle round or a handgun round is never a certainty. When the 45-70 can find a home in a handgun, which it has, and a 9mm Parabellum sees a chambering in a rifle, it's difficult to draw the line so readily.

CARTRIDGE DESIGN

The theory that a cartridge can have built-in accuracy within the dictates of its design has bothered many shooters over the years. If a specific cartridge design is inherently accurate, why are so many mundane-looking rounds so accurate? The puzzle is pieced together by looking not at the big picture, but at only a part of it—not accuracy, but ultimate accuracy. For example, the 32-40 Winchester has always been regarded as an accurate round. But would it win a modern benchrest match against cartridges truly designed with ultimate accuracy in mind? Perhaps not. Put just about any cartridge in a well-executed rifle with a solid action of close tolerances and an accurate, correctly bedded barrel, and if the bullets are concentric and correct, accuracy will result—but not necessarily ultimate accuracy. In short, good bullets out of good barrels generally mean accuracy, but cartridge case design is a factor in top accuracy.

Several key elements of cartridge design promote accuracy. The sum of these elements can be summarized in one sentence: ''The most inherently accurate cartridges are short and fat as opposed to long and skinny.'' That's no more scientific than casting monkey bones on the ground to reveal your future, but it holds up fairly well all the same. In spite of the fact that visually long and narrow rounds, such as the 300 H&H Magnum, have won shooting matches for a very long time, no such cartridge will be found at today's benchrest events. This is not only because of obviously excessive recoil, but also because short fat rounds would whip its tail in delivering bullets into tight clusters. The 300 H&H has won long-range matches, but shooters agree that the most accurate 30-caliber round is the 308 Winchester—a short, squat round in comparison.

The most accurate cartridge in the world today, based on the fact that it has set hundreds of new benchrest records, is the 6mm PPC USA round. When shot out of the Sako single-shot bolt-action rifle, the 6mm PPC proves to be the

222 Remington with a fine custom barrel. Although a custom-barreled rifle is usually more accurate than one with a factory barrel, the results proved otherwise. The 6mm PPC won every contest between the two rifles, with the same bullets and in spite of the fact that the 222 cases were hand-selected and matched.

How powder burns in a short rotund case probably has a lot to do with accuracy. There is also the factor of "100 percent load density," which means that a cartridge, when properly and

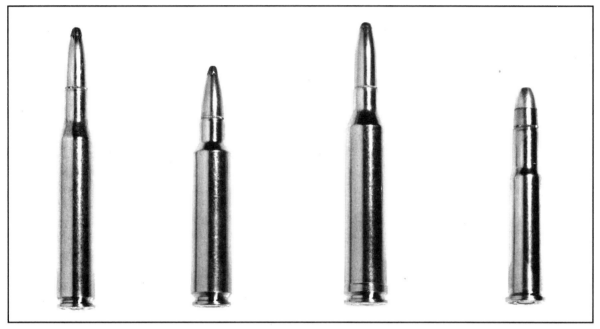

A variety of case designs: (from left) the 270 Winchester, a rimless/bottleneck; the 284 Winchester with a rebated rim (note that the body is larger than the casehead); the 7mm Remington Magnum with belted case; and the 30-30 Winchester with a rimmed case.

most accurate chambering a shooter can buy from the local gunshop. While this cartridge has many special features—including uniformity of case-wall thickness, a drilled flashhole (instead of punched), and the benchrest (BR) primers— a main factor in its accuracy is its short and wide overall profile.

In an attempt to satisfy my disbelief about cartridge design and accuracy, I worked with two single-shot Sako rifles: a 6mm PPC USA and a

prudently loaded, has a full case of powder, with no air space. Too much can be made of this, of course, and shooters get the idea that an efficient cartridge is perfect for everything. Not so. For example, on elk in cross-canyon situations, I'd prefer a well-loaded 300 H&H Magnum to a 308 Winchester, even though the latter is a far more efficient cartridge. Efficiency here equates to how much a cartridge produces versus how much is put into it. The little 308 Winchester can develop well over 3000 fps with a 130-grain bullet and about 50 grains of powder. The 300 H&H Magnum can push that same bullet to 3500 fps, but it might use almost 80 grains of powder to get the job done. That's about a 15-percent increase in bullet speed for an almost 40-percent increase in fuel. Not efficient. But 500 fps is a big gain in velocity, all thoughts of efficiency aside.

One other factor is shoulder angle. Sloping shoulders, as found on the 300 H&H Magnum, are supposedly less conducive to efficient powder consumption than sharper shoulders. Ideally, accuracy experts say, the shoulder should be sharp, but not too sharp. The shoulder angle of the prize-winning 6mm PPC USA cartridge is 30 degrees. That is not terribly sharp, nor is it sloping. A lot of trial and error went into the devel-

opment of the 6mm PPC; and its co-inventor, Dr. Lou Palmisano, decided on a 30-degree shoulder for a reason. After much study, this astute shooter concluded that a 30-degree shoulder for the 6mm shorty was just right.

The cartridge is the engine of the rifle—it makes the whole thing go. The sweetest, best-looking, finest-working rifle in the world is no better than its cartridge. Furthermore, cartridge selection is paramount to duty. You don't pick a rifle and then expect it to do a specific job in a specific way without regard for the cartridge. You wouldn't take a 375 H&H to a benchrest match or a 6mm PPC on a Cape buffalo hunt. Understanding the cartridge, its caliber and the bullets the cartridge shoots are vital to a marksman's overall success.

ALL ABOUT CALIBER (POWER)

3 Technically, the word "caliber" refers to the diameter of the bore of a rifle barrel, which is measured in decimals of an inch or in millimeters. In a practical sense, "caliber" can also mean "cartridge." "What caliber is your rifle?" someone asks. You respond that it's a 30-06, referring to the cartridge—technically incorrect, but entirely proper. In this book, "caliber" is used both ways, the technical and the conversational. The U.S. and England measure caliber in hundredths of an inch. Most other countries measure caliber in millimeters. Somewhere, far too long ago to remember, a decimal point was placed in front of the caliber—incorrectly. But it stuck.

Today most ammo texts continue the practice. We see in print: .30 caliber, which is $^{30}/_{100}$ *of one caliber,* not 30 caliber. Each single caliber means in fact $^{1}/_{100}$ of one inch. So properly stated, it should be 30 caliber, or $^{30}/_{100}$ of one inch, not $^{30}/_{100}$ of one caliber.

As for metric designations, caliber can be ascertained through multiplying by four. This is not exact, but it's close enough for our purposes. A 7mm is 28 caliber ($4 \times 7 = 28$). A 6mm is 24 caliber. The European 7.62mm is 30 caliber—four times 7.62 equals 30.48, which rounds off to 30 caliber—not exact, but close.

The diameter of the bullet must be larger than the diameter of the bore. If a rifle bore is measured from land to land at exactly $^{30}/_{100}$ of one inch (30 caliber), the measurement from groove to groove would be more like .308 inch, indicating that the depth of each groove is .004 inch. The 30-caliber bullet would not engrave (take on the impressions of the rifling) if it were not larger than 30 caliber. Therefore, our 30-caliber bullets have a diameter of .308 inch (sometimes a little smaller, sometimes a little larger). When the .308-inch bullet is shot down a .30-inch bore, it will be engraved by the lands of the rifling.

BIG BORES AND SMALL BORES

Quite a range of calibers exists, both big bores and small bores. American shooters consider the 22 caliber a small bore, with everything else in the big-bore class. Of course, there are other interpretations, but if you attend an American shooting match and enter the small-bore competition, 22-caliber rifles will probably be used. But if you are in Africa and someone tells you to grab your small bore for an afternoon hunt, don't be surprised if he means a 30-caliber rifle. The 375 H&H Magnum, which we consider large, would be classified there as a medium bore. Only those rifles of 40 caliber and larger would be considered "big bore," and even that's not always the case. The 416 Rigby, for example, is thought of as a big bore by some hunters on the Dark Continent, but as a medium by others. There would be no question, however, about a 45 caliber like the 458 Winchester—that's a big bore anywhere.

In the days before smokeless powder, caliber equated to power. High velocity as we know it today was out of the question with black powder, even though medium bullet speed was achieved. A round ball could be driven at around 2000 feet per second (fps), but certainly not 3000 or 4000 fps. Conicals usually departed the muzzle at more like 1500 fps.

The round ball depended on caliber for power, more so than the conical. For example, a .310-inch round ball for a 32-caliber squirrel rifle weighs only 45 grains—five grains heavier than our standard 22 Long Rifle bullet. Even a round ball of .445-inch diameter weighs just 133 grains. A .490-inch ball for a 50-caliber muzzle-loader brought the heft up to 177 grains, and in a 54-caliber, the .535-inch ball weighed 230 grains. The weight of the round ball grew way

Caliber was paramount in gaining power in the old-time round-ball rifle. The round ball shown here is a 12 bore of 494 grains weight, compared to the 180-grain, 30-caliber modern bullet on the right.

out of proportion with the diameter, so bore size was vital to projectile mass.

Somebody figured out that if you wanted to get more weight in a given bore size, the round ball should be abandoned in favor of an elongated ball. ("Ball" simply referred to the projectile.) Caliber was not quite so important once the conical bullet took over, because a 500-grain elongated bullet could be moulded for a 45-caliber bore—plenty of weight without going to a bore size noble enough to hide a donkey. But caliber never lost its importance, regardless of the bullet style used. To this day, the caliber of the rifle dictates power.

Suppose you're minding your own business on a quiet afternoon in Africa. You walk around a thorn tree and there standing in your path is a Cape buffalo about as big as a barn door. You know right away that he doesn't like you. Let's pretend you have an immediate mythical choice of cartridges. Make a wish and one of the following will be at your command to dispatch this four-legged tank: 6mm-06 wildcat, 25-06 Remington, 6.5-06 wildcat, 270 Winchester (which is essentially a 27-06), the 7mm-06 (ballistically the 280

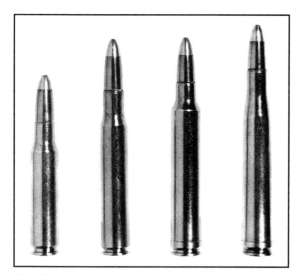

The 30-06 Springfield cartridge (second from right) is shown with three 30-caliber sisters: the 308 (left); 300 Winchester Magnum (immediate right); and 300 H&H Magnum (far right). Because of case capacity and design, these three rounds offer different ballistics, even when shooting the same bullet.

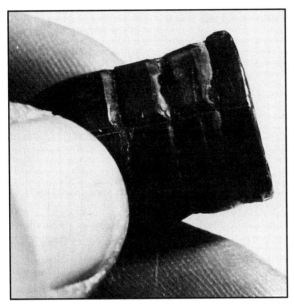

The vintage Minie ball, like the 525-grain 58-caliber one shown here, provided more weight per caliber than did the round ball.

proximations based on existing chronographed data. While near maximum loads, they are not necessarily pet loads. Certain rifles may surpass these ballistics; others may not achieve them, depending upon exact chamber/bore dimensions of the individual rifle. See the top chart on the next page.

More information on muzzle energy (in ft.-lbs.) and 100-yard striking energy data look like that (rounded for convenience) in the second chart. The figures are close enough for our purposes, although a particular rifle might gain a little more punch from its specific cartridge over another rifle chambered for the same round. Apples are compared to apples because the parent cartridge for each caliber is the same: the 30-06. The 30-06 is shown with its progeny to illustrate what transpires ballistically when a cartridge is necked up or down. Here is a perfect illustration of caliber significance when a modern cartridge case of one specific capacity is used, but with different bullet diameters.

On the basis of delivered energy and no other

Remington), the 30-06 Springfield, the 8mm-06 wildcat, 338-06 wildcat (same as the 333 OKH), 35 Whelen (which is a 35-06), and the 375-06 wildcat (375 Whelen). Which one of these cartridges would you want to tackle the buff?

A lover of fast bullets might insist that one well-placed high-speed pill from the 25-06 would be enough. A big-bore fan would insist on the 375 caliber round, but only because a 45 caliber or larger bore cartridge isn't listed.

Before you make your selection, perhaps you should be privileged to a little ballistic data. The 6mm-06 drives a 100-grain bullet at 3300 fps muzzle velocity (mv). The 25-06 puts a 120-grain bullet out at 3200 fps mv. The 6.5-06 sends a 140-grain bullet away at 3000 fps mv. The 270 also drives a 140-grain bullet at 3000 fps mv. The 7mm-06 pushes a 160-grain bullet at 2900 fps mv. The 30-06 propels a 180-grain bullet at 2800 fps mv. The 8mm-06 throws a 220-grain missile at 2500 fps mv. The 338-06 expels its 250-grain bullet at 2500 fps mv. The 35 Whelen shoots a 250-grain bullet at 2500 fps mv and the 375 Whelen scoots a 300-grain bullet downrange at 2500 fps mv. These velocities are close ap-

The little 25-grain, 17-caliber bullet is proof that high velocity deals out great energy. This bullet is deadly on the largest varmints when fired with a muzzle velocity in the 4000 foot-per-second realm.

Caliber	Bullet Size	FPS Muzzle Velocity
6mm-06	100 gr.	3300
25-06	120 gr.	3200
6.5-06	140 gr.	3000
270 Win.	140 gr.	3000
7mm-06	160 gr.	2900
30-06	180 gr.	2800
8mm-06	220 gr.	2500
338-06	250 gr.	2500
35 Whelen	250 gr.	2500
375 Whelen	300 gr.	2500

factor, the winner of this showdown is the 375 Whelen, largest of the calibers. It leads the energy contest all the way out to 300 yards. Remaining energy at 300 yards is 2860 fp for the 375 Whelen and only 1610 fp for the speedy 25-06, the former with a 300-grain spitzer bullet, the latter with a 120-grain spitzer bullet. The 30-06, firing a 180-grain spitzer, shows a 300-yard energy of 1905 fp—more than the 25-06, but significantly less than the 375. If no other attributes are assigned to this family of 30-06-based cartridges, the 375 Whelen is clearly the best of the lot. Of course, there's more to a big-game cartridge than energy. If there weren't, we'd all be shooting some form of shoulder-mounted big-bore cannon.

TRAJECTORY

Trajectory is another caliber attribute. As the accompanying trajectory table shows, small bores shoot flatter than big bores (case capacity being equal). For our purposes, each cartridge was judged with a 200-yard sight-in to promote uniformity of comparison. The 6mm-06, shooting the smallest diameter bullet of the group, is the flattest shooting cartridge of the family. Sighted in for 200 yards, the 100-grain spitzer "rises" (meaning above the line of sight) 1.25 inches at 100 yards, dropping 5.5 inches at 300 yards. By comparison, the 375 Whelen 300-grain spitzer rises 2.5 inches at 100 yards when zeroed in for 200 yards, but drops 9.5 inches at 300 yards.

Elmer Keith's belief that big bores were viable for long-range shooting is supported by the rather flat trajectory of the 375 caliber on the '06 case. A properly sighted 375 Whelen—zeroed at 225 yards, not 200 yards—has a bullet drop of about eight inches at 300 yards. Holding the crosswires on the chest of an elk or even a mule deer at 300 yards would result in a hit. A high-shoulder hold on the smaller pronghorn antelope would bring a strike at 300 yards, which is very

Caliber	Foot-pounds Muzzle Energy (fpme)	Ft.-lbs. at 100 Yards
6mm-06	2420	2020
25-06	2730	2300
6.5-06	2780	2400
270 Winchester	2780	2445
7mm-06	2990	2645
30-06	3135	2670
8mm-06	3055	2700
338-06	3470	3080
35 Whelen	3470	2715
375 Whelen	4165	3690

ENERGY/TRAJECTORY FIGURES FOR TEST CARTRIDGES

The following are energy figures and average trajectory patterns for test cartridges that were built on the 30-06 Springfield case, either necked up or down. All rifles were sighted in for 200 yards for comparison purposes, although 200 yards is not a suggested sight-in distance. All figures are rounded off.

Caliber	Distance	Energy (Foot-pounds)	Trajectory (Inches)
6mm-06	Muzzle	2420	
(w/100-grain	100 Yards	2020	+1.25
Spitzer bullet at	200 Yards	1670	0
3300 fps mv)	300 Yards	1370	−5.5
	Muzzle	2730	
25-06	100 Yards	2300	+1.5
(w/120-grain	200 Yards	1995	0
Spitzer at 3200 fps mv)	300 Yards	1510	−6.0
	Muzzle	2780	
6.5-06	100 Yards	2400	+1.5
(w/140-grain	200 Yards	2050	0
Spitzer at 3000 fps mv)	300 Yards	1740	−7.0
	Muzzle	2780	
270 Winchester	100 Yards	2445	+1.5
(w/140-grain	200 Yards	2125	0
Spitzer at 3000 fps mv)	300 Yards	1840	−7.0
	Muzzle	2990	
7mm-06	100 Yards	2645	+1.5
(w/160-grain	200 Yards	2325	0
Spitzer at 2900 fps mv)	300 Yards	2030	−7.0
	Muzzle	3135	
30-06 Springfield	100 Yards	2670	+2.0
(w/180-grain	200 Yards	2260	0
Spitzer at 2800 fps mv)	300 Yards	1905	−9.5
	Muzzle	3055	
8mm-06	100 Yards	2700	+2.5
(w/220-grain	200 Yards	2380	0
Spitzer at 2500 fps mv)	300 Yards	2090	−9.5
	Muzzle	3470	
338-06	100 Yards	3080	+2.5
(w/250-grain	200 Yards	2730	0
Spitzer at 2500 fps mv)	300 Yards	2410	−9.5
	Muzzle	3470	
35 Whelen	100 Yards	2715	+2.5
(w/250-grain	200 Yards	2335	0
Spitzer at 2500 fps mv)	300 Yards	2105	−10.0
	Muzzle	4165	
375 Whelen	100 Yards	3690	+2.5
(w/300-grain	200 Yards	3255	0
Spitzer at 2500 fps mv)	300 Yards	2860	−9.5

far in spite of "campfire" and "typewriter" shots of twice that distance. Nonetheless, the smallest bore of this test group did shoot the flattest.

Anyone who has picked up a shooting magazine during the past few decades has seen the 270-versus-30-06 argument in print. It's a natural. I ran a comparison of these two famous rounds for my own edification. I've always liked the 270. However, as far as sheer energy delivery is concerned, the 270 loses to the 30-06. The 270 Winchester shoots *slightly* flatter than the 30-06 Springfield, but the latter has more energy at all ranges when properly loaded. Even a 140-grain bullet at 3000 fps mv (instead of a 130-grain bullet at 3150 fps mv) in the 270 fails to beat the energy of the older cartridge. Squeezing the neck of the 30-06 down to 27 caliber produces a slightly flatter-shooting cartridge that "kicks" the shooter a little less, but that's it. A bit flatter trajectory with a little less recoil is a good bargain, but in the cold light of ballistic reality, the 30-06 is "more cartridge" than the

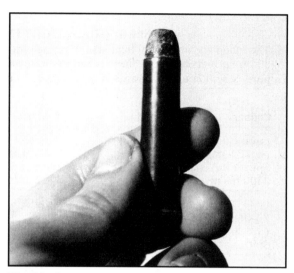

The blackpowder cartridge, exemplified by the 45-60 round above, followed the same tradition as the muzzleloader: the larger the caliber, the more power.

270—with all apologies to 270 fans, including me.

RECOIL

Recoil is an important criterion of caliber comparison. Recoil tables show that small bores jolt the shooter less than big bores. I always wanted a Mannlicher carbine. As my longing grew closer to reality, I began to look at the old-time carbine with an eye to ballistics as well as aesthetics. If I were to own a Mannlicher, I would hunt with it. Antelope? Sometimes. Mule deer? Yes, though not in the high mountains for cross-canyon shots. White-tailed deer? Certainly. The carbine is a natural on the creek bottoms north and west of my home where I pursue the flagtail. Elk? Why not? Black timber and elk were made for each other. A quick-action carbine with iron sights is fine for woodland elk.

I had to decide. Which of the original Mannlicher cartridges to pick? The 6.5mm was the darling of the rich and famous hunters of the early 1900s who carried the Mannlicher carbine all over the world. A few hunted elephants with the little gun. Even Elmer Keith, the big-bore guru, stated in *American Rifleman* magazine that the 6.5mm was deadlier than its bore size. But an

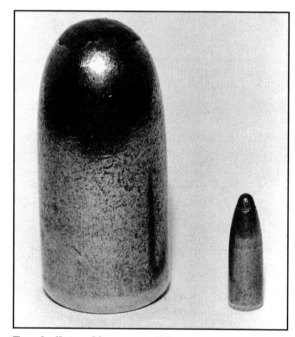

Two bullets of immense difference: the 900-grain projectile on the left is for the 600 Nitro Express, while the bullet on the right is a 17 caliber of only 25 grains weight.

unfired Model 1905 Mannlicher in 9 × 56mm came my way. Luckily, its groove-to-groove diameter happened to be .358 inch. Bullets would not have to be swaged to .354, .356 or whatever other hole-in-the-barrel size Mannlicher chose to use at the time of manufacture. So I bought the 9mm.

Having shot both the 9mm and the 6.5mm, I can attest to the fact that the 6.5mm in a seven-pound carbine is pleasant to shoot. The 9mm in the same lightweight rifle is manageable, but it delivers noticeably more push at the shoulder than its little brother. The moral of the story: Considering recoil only, smaller holes in the barrel are better than bigger ones when similar-sized cartridge cases are used, because smaller bores "kick" less than bigger ones.

CALIBER AND PENETRATION

Bullet diameter, bullet weight, sectional density and ballistic coefficient all affect projectile penetration. These factors determine how far a bullet will travel, not only in the atmosphere, but in a solid medium as well (see Chapter 4).

Devotees of the aforementioned 6.5mm Mannlicher cartridge pronounced that good penetration was due to a long 160-grain bullet with a .328 sectional density. By comparison, the 9mm's .358-inch, 250-grain bullet has a sectional density of .279. The 6.5mm can do about 2300 fps from an 18-inch barrel with its 160-grain steeple-like bullet. My 9mm carbine handloads register just shy of 2300 fps from a 20-inch barrel with its fat 250-grain missile, for an almost identical muzzle velocity. In my bullet testing box (described in the next chapter), penetration was in favor of the 9mm Mannlicher in spite of a sectional density advantage for the 6.5mm Mannlicher.

What about downrange energy for these two cartridges of similar case capacity? Remember that the 35-caliber, 250-grain bullet from the 9mm Mannlicher cartridge weighs roughly 35% more than the 26-caliber, 160-grain bullet. Although muzzle velocities are almost identical, muzzle energies are not. The 6.5 has a muzzle energy of 1880 foot-pounds, while the 9mm carries a muzzle energy of over 2900 fp. The 250-

grain, 35-caliber round-nose bullet retains almost a long ton of energy at 100 yards. The 160-grain round-nose bullet falls to about 1400 fp of energy. Of these two rounds of similar powder capacity, the 9mm Mannlicher delivers more pasta than the 6.5mm Mannlicher.

It does not matter how many elephants D.W.M. Bell shot with the 6.5—it does not whip its larger-caliber brother. The bullet-box tests showed that not only do big-bore missiles have greater penetration potential than small-bore projectiles, they also have more "force." While a 180-grain, 30-caliber bullet at high velocity penetrated well and pushed test media aside, a 58-caliber, 600-grain lead projectile at much slower striking velocity passed entirely through the box, blowing apart its wooden sides.

Another factor linked to bullet size is "brush busting." That term applies to bullets smashing through foliage like little charging rhinos. Most of us have long believed that big fat bullets were better than little skinny bullets for pushing through nature's garden on the way to the target. There may be something to the idea that a bullet of high momentum (momentum = mass × velocity) shoves more brush out of the way than a bullet of lesser momentum. But simple demonstrations do not show this to be true. The shooter can test for himself by arranging a target behind a screen of brush and shooting at it five times with Bullet A and five times with Bullet B. Don't

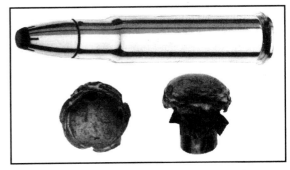

No cartridge is ideal in brush, not even the larger calibers. However, modern cartridges continue to use caliber for power. The 356 Winchester is a strong round because of its 35-caliber bullet. Shown here are two views of the 356's recovered 250-grain bullet.

Nancy Fadala took this mule deer with her bolt-action Sako chambered for the 7mm-08 cartridge: a perfect example of a load that reduces the caliber of a cartridge to change its characteristics. The 7mm-08, based on a necked-down 308, is a fine all-around cartridge.

be surprised when a .277-inch diameter, 130-grain spitzer finds the bull's-eye as often as a .277-inch diameter, 170-grain round nose, or when a 30-caliber bullet does as well as a 35-caliber pill.

The bottom line is that even large-caliber, heavyweight bullets fare poorly in penetrating a screen of brush or twigs. On the other hand, the worst bullets for getting through brush are high-speed varmint pills, due in part, no doubt, to the fact that they are designed to blow up. They explode and come apart on brush instead of breaking through as a solid unit. Thin-shelled bullets designed to fragment are not built to penetrate anything, including brush. But the low momentum of such bullets may also play a role in their inability to drive through brush.

So far, it may seem that choosing the larger caliber is best. However, that is not always true. Appropriateness plays a role in selecting a caliber. A 35-caliber bullet is not necessary to harvest a deer, although it's certainly excellent for such game. Furthermore, a 7mm Remington Magnum is not needed to drop a deer at 150 yards. In spite of this, I carry a Big 7 for high country mule-deer hunting because in the mountains, it's possible, prudent and ethical to shoot across a canyon at a buck with an accurate rifle—one that is fitted with a powerful, high-resolution telescopic sight, and that is chambered for a cartridge which generates more punch at 300 yards with handloads than many popular factory cartridges have at the muzzle.

So the Big 7 has a place in the deer field for those who feel comfortable with that much cartridge. But a 7mm Magnum isn't best for everyone. When my wife and eldest daughter wanted to hunt deer and elk, I chose rifles chambered for a smaller-cased 7mm, because Nancy and Stephanie had no intention of shooting at long range. Both women ended up with 7mm-08s—Nancy's a Sako, Stephanie's a Remington. The first season, Nancy's dropped a hefty mule-deer buck with one shot. She also got an elk with one shot. Daughter Stephanie's 7mm-08 gave equal results. Bottom line: hunt elephants with a big bore, varmints with a small bore and the rest of your game with something in between.

Ballistically speaking, larger bullets cause good things to happen, provided the fatter bullet retains decent ballistic properties—especially sectional density and ballistic coefficient. With all regard for the fine 35 Whelen, it appears from the data presented in this chapter that the 338-06 (333 OKH) provides more downrange ruckus. Each cartridge is capable of driving bullets of similar weight at similar velocities, but 33-caliber bullets have more going for them ballistically than 35-caliber bullets of the same weight. For example, a 200-grain, .338-inch Hornady bullet has a sectional density of .250 with a ballistic coefficient of .403, while a 200-grain, .358-inch Hornady bullet has a sectional density of .223 and a ballistic coefficient of only .295. These are bullets of about the same profile from the same company, yet the 33-caliber bullet is ballistically superior. So in this comparison, the smaller caliber bullet wins over the larger caliber one, because their weights are equal, making the smaller caliber bullet "longer for its diameter."

Two bullets that demonstrate power through caliber: on the left is a 500-grain 45-caliber bullet; on the right, a 51-caliber, 600-grain bullet. Fired from the 500 Van Horn Express cartridge, the latter bullet produces terrific energy levels.

PRESSURE

As calibers grow, pressure relationships change. As bullet size increases, surface area of the base grows out of proportion. A 35-caliber bullet has far more surface than a 30-caliber bullet for gas to push on. The bigger bore also offers more volume for gases to react in.

Compare a 270 Winchester and 30-06, disregarding sectional density or ballistic coefficient

CUP stands for Copper Units of Pressure, just as LUP represents Lead Units of Pressure (used for lower pressures, such as those in blackpowder firearms). The term derives from the crusher method of determining pressure, whereby a pellet of known dimension is placed in the path of a rod activated by a piston. The piston derives its force from a bleed-out hole in a pressure gun. The more the copper pellet is crushed, the higher the pressure. A micrometer is used to determine just how much deformation the pellet suffers and the figure is translated into a pressure term. Therefore, when we have 50,000 CUP, it means 50,000 Copper Units of Pressure. The value is comparative, in that ascending numbers equate to higher pressures.

for a moment. Based on data from the Lyman loading manual, 46th edition, a 130-grain bullet leaves the muzzle of the 270 at 3125 fps with a CUP (Copper Units of Pressure, see box) rating of 53,600 when burning 60.0 grains of H-4831. A 130-grain bullet from the 30-06 takes off at 2923 fps mv with a pressure rating of 41,600 CUP when burning 61.5 grains of H-4831. (The 30-06 H-4831 load is at 61.5 grains with the 130-grain bullet because of case space, not maximum pressure.)

A 150-grain bullet from the 270 departs the muzzle at 2824 fps mv with 47.0 grains of IMR-4064 powder and a pressure rating of 52,800 CUP, while a 150-grain bullet leaves the muzzle of the 30-06 at 3012 fps with 53.0 grains of IMR-

4064 and a pressure rating of 49,600 CUP. Remember, we're not concerned with best loads for either cartridge. We're only interested in bullet weight for a pressure comparison with the same powders.

One more comparison is in order, this time using the 264 Winchester Magnum and 7mm Remington Magnum. The only difference between these two cartridges is the size of the bullets they shoot; but in using Reloader 22, the 264 maximum charge is considerably below the 7mm's maximum charge, both firing a 140-grain bullet. There's something to this pressure/caliber business, as the laws of physics support. Bigger holes in the barrel allow a greater volume for expansion of gases, while at the same time, larger bullets have more base surface for those gases to push on.

RIFLE WEIGHT

Caliber can help determine rifle configuration. While it's possible to build a lightweight rifle chambered for a large-capacity big-bore round, it's not practical. I shot a seven-pound 458 Winchester in Africa. Not fun. Powder capacity of the cartridge is important to weight of the rifle because the amount of powder burned is one factor in assessing actual recoil energy. My Wells custom pre-64 Model 70 in 7mm Magnum weighs 9½ pounds. I like it that way. My wife's Sako 7mm-08 weighs about two pounds less. That's as it should be. The 7mm Magnum produces more recoil, which the heavier rifle helps dampen. The smaller cartridge creates less recoil, so a lighter rifle is OK. Small-bore cartridges of modest case capacity naturally work well in lighter rifles. Case capacity also suggests different barrel lengths. The 7mm Magnum does well with a 24-inch barrel, while the 7mm-08 realizes sufficient potential from a 22-inch barrel.

I've heard the notion that a 338 Winchester featherweight rifle can be designed to recoil like a 22 rimfire. However, while there may be a Santa Claus, no flyweight big-cartridge rifle kicks like a cap pistol. Wristwatch-weight rifles in big calibers buck plenty. One way to reduce recoil in a particular rifle weight is to reduce bullet size, even in small-capacity rounds, because lighter

Available in chamberings from 22 Hornet to 7mm Remington Magnum, the Thompson/Center single-shot rifle offers a large continuum of power per caliber. A 12-gauge slug is yet another bullet option for this firearm.

bullets from a given cartridge can offer less recoil. A perfect example of this is a comparison of the 308 Winchester and 7mm-08 Remington. The latter is the former necked down from 30 caliber to 28 caliber. The 7mm-08 renders less recoil than the 308, while retaining good down-range authority due to the excellent ballistic properties of 7mm bullets. Of course the 308 is more potent than the 7mm-08, but when you don't need the extra thump, the 7mm-08 is a good choice.

What about accuracy and caliber? Forget it. I have seen too many big bores drill ragged one-hole groups in the target to get dewy-eyed about small bullets dominating accuracy. Benchrest rifles shoot small projectiles because big bullets are not necessary for shooting at paper, and because the little bullet achieves good velocity without undue recoil. However, a rifle chambered for the 308 Winchester won an interna-

tional benchrest match in 1968. Furthermore, in bench-testing a 416 Weatherby Magnum, I found that the Mark V rifle was capable of producing excellent three-shot groups at 100 yards—the smallest a shade over a half-inch center to center, the largest three-fourths of an inch. I wasn't surprised. A friend has a custom 375 H&H Magnum that performs at the same high level of accuracy.

When it comes to caliber, I'm a moderate, not a radical. A smaller bore allows a pleasant-shooting lightweight rifle. All things being equal, the smaller bore cartridge shoots flatter than the big bore. For these reasons, small bores are easier to hit with than big-bore rifles, except when the latter are in the hands of highly experienced shooters.

Conversely, the big bore enjoys a greater potential for translating the powder charge into delivered bullet energy. The large bullet offers high energy, a large wound channel, good penetration and that elusive commodity known as "stopping power." When facing a dangerous beast like the Cape buffalo, big bores are best. Finally, a big-bore bullet of good ballistic property delivers more downrange energy than a lighter bullet, even though the latter may have higher velocity.

The range of calibers is great: 17 through 45 in modern over-the-counter cartridges; from 14s to you-name-it on a custom basis. Each caliber has its merits. The little 17 Remington is a joy in the varmint field. On the other hand, a 460 Weatherby Magnum, which is capable of shooting a 500-grain bullet at over 2600 fps, is life insurance in dangerous game country. In black-powder days, big bullets were necessary for power. There was no way to achieve high velocity before smokeless powder came along. Today, thanks to smokeless powder efficiency, medium-sized game can be hunted with medium-sized bullets fired from mid-sized cases.

QUICK CALIBER COMPARISON

14 Caliber. Caliber 14 is a custom proposition only, not a practical bullet diameter for the "average" shooter.

17 Caliber. The only 17-caliber factory cartridge is the 17 Remington. An amazing round, it is capable of driving a tiny 25-grain bullet at over 4000 fps, resulting in total bullet destruction. Recoil is extremely light. This bore size demands careful reloading, as pressures can rise significantly with small variations of powder charge. Bore cleaning can be a problem as well, but it's all worth it to the 17 fan. Caliber 17 is extremely popular in air rifles. It offers good velocity, fine accuracy and worthy effectiveness on small game at practical air-rifle distances.

20 Caliber. A rare caliber, there are 20-caliber custom-made bullets. A 20-222 wildcat round shoots 20-caliber bullets weighing 45 to 48 grains. The 20 caliber is also excellent in an air rifle and is referred to as a 5mm. The Sheridan air rifle has been offered in 20 caliber for years.

22 Caliber. King of the rimfires and most popular of the centerfire varmint cartridges, the 22 is truly America's darling. The 22 Long Rifle (LR) is the No. 1 rimfire in the world and the 22 Winchester Magnum Rimfire (WMR) occupies

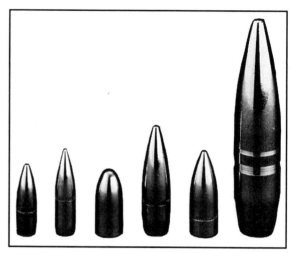

Caliber size dictates the final bullet to a great degree. These Speer bullets (left to right) are: 55-grain 22 caliber, 62-grain 22 caliber, 110-grain 30 caliber, 150-grain 30 caliber, 123-grain 31 caliber, and 647-grain 50 caliber.

a specific ballistic niche all by itself.

Dozens of superb bullets are available to the handloader of 22 centerfire rounds. There are .222-inch and .223-inch diameter 22-caliber bullets, but most 22s shoot bullets of .224-inch diameter. Some 22 centerfires shoot .226-inch and .228-inch diameter bullets. The 226 Barnes wildcat cartridge, for example, shoots a long .226-inch bullet that weighs 125 grains. The old 22 Savage Hi-Power cartridge used bullets of .227- to .228-inch diameter.

23 Caliber. No commercial cartridge is made in this size, although custom 23-caliber bullets are available. Some shooters have designed 23-caliber rounds for use in areas where 22 centerfires are not allowed for big-game hunting.

24 Caliber. Also known as the 6mm, this caliber is currently popular in a number of rounds. The 243 Winchester, for example, is a favorite round west of the Mississippi River. This caliber is noted for modest recoil with reasonable downrange performance on deer-sized game. It's also a good varmint caliber. The 6mm PPC USA is renowned as the most accurate cartridge in the world.

25 Caliber. Years ago, the 25 was a rimfire round, considered good for small game and wild turkey. The 25-20 Winchester has once again found a home in a factory rifle and Remington has made the former 25-06 wildcat a legitimate factory cartridge. The 25-06, originally built by necking down the 30-06 to shoot 25-caliber bullets, is highly regarded by deer and antelope hunters out West. The super 257 Weatherby Magnum is the power king of the 25s, shooting a 100-grain bullet at 3600 fps and a 117-grain bullet at 3400 fps from the muzzle.

26 Caliber. Few 6.5s have been made in America. The 6.5mm shoots a bullet of .264-inch diameter. The 264 Winchester is a 6.5mm Magnum capable of propelling a 140-grain bullet at 3200 fps muzzle velocity. This powerful cartridge was supposed to put the 270 Winchester on relief, but it never did. The only other American 6.5 of note is the 6.5mm Remington Magnum, a short belted number that drives a 140-grain bullet at 3000 fps.

27 Caliber. The 270 Winchester and 270 Weatherby Magnum are the only commercial 27s available as this is written. In spite of that, the 270 Winchester is second only to the 30-06 for hunting in the West, and the 270 Weatherby Magnum is second only to the 300 Weatherby Magnum in that lineup. The 270 Winchester shoots a 130-grain bullet at 3100 fps mv, while the 270 Weatherby Mag. scoots the same bullet away at 3400 fps mv. Top handloads find the 140-grain bullet doing 3300 fps mv using IMR-7828 powder. (See *Hornady Handbook of Cartridge Reloading.*) In my own Ruger No. 1 rifle chambered for the 270 Weatherby Magnum, the 140-grain bullet achieved a muzzle velocity of 3400 fps with a Hornady load listed as one grain *under* maximum.

28 Caliber. The 7mm Remington Magnum is third in western hunting popularity behind the 30-06 and 270. This bullet size, .284-inch diameter, was always well regarded by European shooters. It failed to make a big splash in this country, though, until Remington's magnum came out in 1962. The 280 Remington is essentially a 7mm-06, although the case is longer than that of the 30-06. The 7-30 Waters is essentially a necked down 30-30, with case dimensions also varying from the original wildcat. The 7mm-08, a necked-down 308 Winchester, is gaining ground. This is a good bullet size, with high ballistic-coefficient possibilities.

30 Caliber. This is still the most popular "big-bore" caliber in America. One reason may be that two early smokeless-powder rounds—the 30-40 Krag and 30-30 Winchester—caught on. It's also because of the 30-06 Springfield, which took over both as an army round and a sporting round in this century. There are many good 30s, but the 308 Winchester is probably the most inherently accurate 30-caliber round in America.

32 Caliber. The vintage 32-20 Winchester has made a modest comeback. But depending on the rifle, it may shoot bullets of .308-inch diameter, making it a 30 caliber instead of a 32. The 32 Winchester Special once had a great many fans, but not today. It was a true 32 caliber, shooting bullets of .321-inch diameter. The 32-40 Winchester, thought long defunct, has also made a quiet showing lately in new chamberings.

The family of 8mms can be considered 32s, for they shoot bullets of .323-inch diameter. The 8mm Mauser was popular in the U.S. after World War II, because so many 8mm German Mauser rifles were brought into the country. But today, the only American 8mm of importance is the 8mm Remington Magnum, using a long belted magnum case and driving a 220-grain bullet at 2900 fps mv.

33 Caliber. The 33 Winchester was a pretty hot round in its day. It shot a .338-inch bullet of 200 grains at around 2200 fps mv and was chambered in the famous Model 1886 Winchester lever-action rifle. But caliber 33 was not well-known in recent times until the 338 Winchester Magnum was born; it shoots a 225-grain bullet at 2800 fps mv. Weatherby's 340 is another 33; this big boy shoots a 225-grain bullet at 3100 fps mv and will take down just about anything with one shot. The 33-06 is a wildcat, but may not remain so for long.

34 Caliber. Only one 34-caliber American cartridge made a splash in America's pool of rounds: Winchester's 348. Chambered exclusively in the Model 71 lever-action Winchester rifle (an improvement on the Model 1886), this cartridge fired a 200-grain bullet at 2500 fps mv and was well thought of by elk and moose hunters in timber.

35 Caliber. Many fine 35s have proved themselves in this country—the 35 Winchester, the 35 Remington (highly regarded for deer at modest range) and the 358 Winchester. But 35s have never been terribly popular in the U.S. The 35 Whelen, a recent factory loading of the former wildcat, has not set the shooting world on its ear, for example, and the 350 Remington Magnum is scarce as money in the street. The big 358 Norma, which shoots a 250-grain .358-inch bullet at 2800 fps mv, has never been widely used in this country either.

38 Caliber. Jumping from 35 to 38 caliber, we find an updating of the well-liked blackpowder 38-55 Winchester in a newly designed 375 Winchester (the two rounds are not interchangeable). This is a true 38-caliber round, shooting a bullet of .375-inch diameter. The 375 H&H Magnum, which shoots a 300-grain .375-inch bullet at 2550 fps mv, has never found a lot of use in America, but it's well known everywhere. The 378 Weatherby Magnum is a bigger 375, as it were, capable of driving that same 300-grain bullet at 2900 fps mv. It's a powerhouse cartridge.

40 Caliber. This size was once loaded in the U.S. Lists of old cartridges include 40s like the 40-60 Winchester and 40-60 Marlin, which both shoot 40-caliber bullets. Today, the size is not popular in rifles, but new 40-caliber handgun ammo is gaining a foothold.

41 Caliber. In the early 1990s, the 41-caliber rifle cartridge refused to sit down any longer. Ruger chambered an extremely nice dangerous-game rifle in 416 Rigby, a 1911 British cartridge. Remington brought out its own 41 caliber: the 416 Remington, shooting a .416-inch bullet. And Weatherby necked down its 460 to shoot the 41-caliber bullet. A 400-grain bullet leaves the Rigby and Remington rounds at 2400 fps mv; the Weatherby 41-caliber round exits at 2700 fps mv. The 41 Remington Magnum handgun round, which shoots .410-inch bullets, continues to be chambered in some rifles.

44 Caliber. The 44 Remington Magnum handgun cartridge has been chambered in rifles for a long time. Its 240-grain bullet can be pushed out at around 1900 fps mv from a rifle barrel. The 444 Marlin is a rifle round that shoots a 44-caliber, 240-grain bullet at 2300 fps mv. Bullets for both of these 44s are actually 43 caliber, being .430 inch in diameter.

45 Caliber. This is the practical limit in North America. The age-old 45-70 Government round is still chambered in a number of rifles. Of course, America's own elephant cartridge, the 458 Winchester, has gained wide popularity both here and in Africa. The 458 shoots a 500-grain bullet at 2150 fps, making it too much cartridge for most American hunting, but a few Alaskan guides prefer a 458 in the brush when hunting the big coastal grizzly, better known as the brown or Kodiak bear. Weatherby's version of a 45-caliber rifle round is in keeping with the company's motto that faster is better. The 460 Weatherby Magnum can drive a .458-inch bullet at more than 2600 fps mv.

BULLETS FOR BIG GAME

4 The rifle is designed, engineered and constructed for one purpose: to deliver a projectile to a target. If that fails, then the match is lost, or there is no game for the larder. The projectile is everything to success.

This chapter deals primarily with bullets for big game because missiles for target shooting, plinking, simple paper-punching and all other non-hunting aspects are required to do one thing only: deliver accuracy. Those bullets come from custom bullet makers and bullet manufacturing companies all over the world. They are uniform of jacket, concentric, homogeneous of construction and, in short, they are accurate. It is the big-game bullet that "gives us fits" because it must do so many important things after reaching its destination.

Projectiles for dependable performance on big game were on the drawing board and in the test field early in the shooting game. The lead round ball was no marvel of aerodynamics, but it seated properly in the bore so that it or the patch around the ball was engaged by the rifling. Rotation of the ball compensated for spherical imperfections, averaging any lopsidedness on a common axis. The lead globe was capable of good accuracy, even when cast slightly imperfectly.

The all-lead conical that followed was also accurate and dependable. But it required more careful production because the conoidal shape had to affect an almost perfect gyroscope for accuracy, the center of gravity coinciding with the center of form. In the bore, the bullet was forced to rotate around its center of form. It could do nothing else. But after exiting the muzzle, it had to rotate around its center of gravity, so conicals had to be concentric, i.e., have a common center. Conical accuracy hinged on both static and dynamic stability. Imbalance in the conical—due to cavities, eccentric points, oblique bases, or any other defect displacing the mass from the axis point—destroyed accuracy.

The "round ball" was so-named because it was a sphere, and all projectiles were referred to as balls. That's why we also have the "conical ball," even though the latter is not round in shape. The round ball did not fall into immediate disuse when the elongated missile was invented. A number of seasoned and respected hunters maintained a preference for the lead sphere. As Fremantle quoted in *The Book of the Rifle*, "Mr. Greener says in his book, 'Gunnery in 1858,' that . . . small-bore elongated bullets were very rapidly adopted for sporting purposes, and as rapidly abandoned, because they did not 'kill dead.' " In the same time frame, S.W. Baker, famous elephant hunter and explorer, concurred

These all-lead bullets are examples of 19th-century styles. Note the fins, which probably were introduced into the rifling groove.

fully, preferring the spherical ball over the conical ball because he said the conical made "too neat a wound," and it did not dispatch game, such as elephants, with complete authority. Captain Forsyth and Major Shakespear, noted sportsmen of the same era, also gave the nod to the round ball over the conical.

Not all round balls were simple lead spheres. A great deal of imagination and intellectual effort were lavished on this most basic lead projectile. A Spanish officer in about 1725 developed a belted lead ball to enhance accuracy in the muzzleloader. The belted round ball was wrapped in a greased patch. The projectile itself received little, if any, engraving. The patch and the belt translated the rotational value of the rifling to the mass of the missile without the rifling touching the projectile.

An expanding bullet with a hole in its base, the cavity filled with a wooden plug, constituted another step toward an accurate lead round-ball projectile that could be loaded without undue effort. It was called the Greener Expanding bullet. The wooden plug was driven forward by the gas from the powder charge and the plug expanded the walls of the under-bore-sized bullet for engagement with the rifling.

If Greener's Expanding bullet sounds like a Minie ball, it should. Captain Minie of the French Army had been paid 20,000 English pounds by the British government in 1852 for an open-based projectile. To this day, Minie's name remains attached to the hollow-base conical black-powder bullet. Greener protested, saying that he was the originator of the idea. After much litigation, the courts finally capitulated, granting Greener 1,000 pounds compensation for "the first public suggestion of the principle of expansion, commonly called the Minie principle, in 1836."

General Jacobs, in 1846, developed his important bullet design, which overcame a bad trait associated with the belted ball—tipping after exiting the muzzle. Jacobs' bullet was significant because it was one of the first conicals to gain recognition as accurate and dependable. It could be counted on at up to 600, even 800 yards for military purposes.

Many conicals followed, their aerodynamic

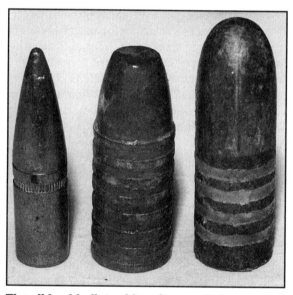

The all-lead bullet seldom fragments because of high molecular cohesiveness. The two lead bullets on the right were cast for use in a 45-caliber rifled musket. The center bullet weighs 480 grains, while the projectile far right, weighs 550 grains. Compare these to the 180-grain 30-caliber bullet on the left.

improvement over the sphere recognized by all students of ballistics. There were literally hundreds of designs: some had iron points; some were grooved; some looked just like our heavy round-nose lead projectiles of today; others had super-sharp spire points; and some exploded when they hit, and were tried on dangerous game in Africa and Asia.

The cross-cut bullet, associated with Lord Keane, was a standard lead conical; however, a "core peg" was forced into the nose of the bullet during manufacture so that the front of the projectile split into segments like a banana peel. Then the bullet was swaged and, in the swaging

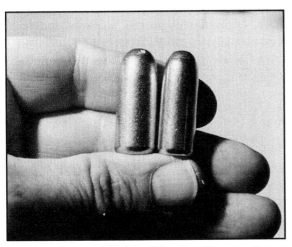

Two examples of jacketed lead bullets are these 51-caliber heavyweights.

process, the nose sections were again united to form a normal bullet point. When this bullet struck its target, the divided sections of the nose separated again, causing a significant change in the shock wave and greater delivery of projectile energy.

One of the most remarkable bullet designs was the Hebler-Krnka Tubular Bullet. Both ends had an ogive and through its center was an "air passage" or hole all the way through the bullet. A sabot (cup) formed a gas seal at the otherwise open base of the bullet. The bullet was composed of lead, or sometimes a non-lead noted only as a "soft metal" in the literature. This particular style was supposed to thwart the ravages of the

atmosphere. Of course, a missile with a hole completely through it will work as a rocket on the Venturi principle, i.e., more gas is forced out of the larger open end of the rocket than the smaller open end. But the Hebler-Krnka was a bullet, albeit an odd one, not a ramjet missile, and it did not gain prominence with shooters.

Pure lead was a good material for making the old-style cast round ball or cast conical. Lead was plentiful, cheap and dense—heavy for its volume—and melted at only 621 degrees F., making it possible to "run ball," as casting was sometimes called, at the campfire site. Lead had high molecular cohesion, promoting good penetration without fragmentation.

JACKETS AND ALLOYS STRENGTHEN THE LEAD BULLET

Soon, however, the lead bullet would wear a jacket or "envelope." Many think of the jacketed bullet as developing concurrently with smokeless powder and high velocity, but that's not the case. Jacketed bullets preceded high velocity. A "mantel" bullet was available in Europe in the 1850s, developed, it's believed, to thwart barrel leading and to inflict a less ghastly wound on the battlefield. However, it is undeniable that high velocity did attack the all-lead projectile. Early supersonic velocities, usually in the 1200 to 1500 fps range, were no threat; however, at twice the speed of sound, lead molecules began to separate and bullets often failed to perform correctly, sometimes breaking up before reaching the target or when hitting it.

Alloys helped to make lead bullets stronger. Tin and antimony in various small amounts produced a harder lead bullet. Mercury was also used for a while, and shooters found that heat-treating their finished cast missiles hardened them. But no alloy rendered the lead bullet tough enough to withstand the ravages of hot smokeless-powder gases, the high forward velocity and increased revolutions per second (RPS) of the missile. Since the base of an elongated projectile does most of the "steering," as noted by Dr. F.W. Mann, bullet bases damaged by smokeless-powder pressure caused bullets to go astray. A metal cap on the base of the bullet would have helped.

Modern bullet casters know that "gas checks" allow higher velocity and accuracy, but even with gas checks, the lead or lead alloy bullet was not strong enough.

In 1895 the 25-35 Winchester and 30-30 Winchester were offered to American sportsmen with smokeless powder. These cartridges, as well as previous smokeless rounds, such as the 30-40 Krag and 8mm Lebel, furthered the development of the jacketed bullet—the logical choice for higher smokeless powder velocity.

Since RPS is a function of exit velocity and rate of twist, as velocity went up, so did revolutions per second. Smokeless powder rifles had a much faster twist than blackpowder rifles. The 25-35 Winchester in the Model 1894 rifle, for example, demanded a 1:8 rate of twist, while rifles chambered for the 6mm Lee Navy had an even faster 1:7.5 twist. By 1895 the jacketed bullet, or "envelope," was well established and fast becoming a reality on the ammo shelf. External as well as internal ballistics required the new projectile, because a high-speed bullet could penetrate very well on big game *if* correctly constructed.

Although the jacketed or "envelope" bullet was not developed because of smokeless powder and higher velocities, it did provide a metal casing around a lead core that helped to prevent bullet skid on the rifling in the bore. It also helped to prevent damaged bullet bases and shanks, which lead projectiles suffered at high velocity. Soft steel was tried for jacket material. It actually worked without causing undue bore wear; however, cupro-nickel proved less susceptible to corrosion. Cupro-nickel constitutes an amalgam

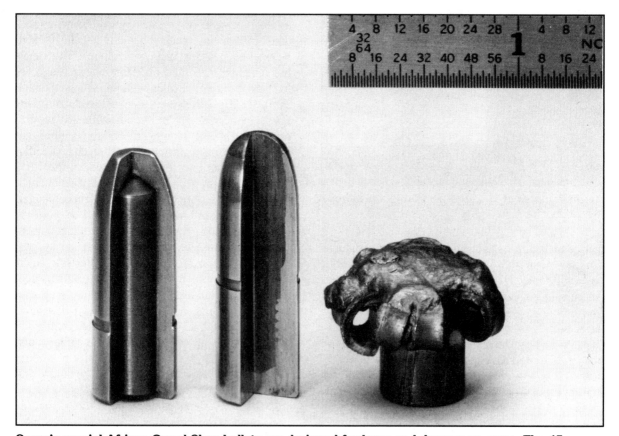

Speer's special African Grand Slam bullets are designed for large and dangerous game. The 45-caliber, 500-grain bullet on the left is a "solid," designed for maximum penetration. The bullet next to it is a 500-grain, 45-caliber soft-point, shown expanded on the right.

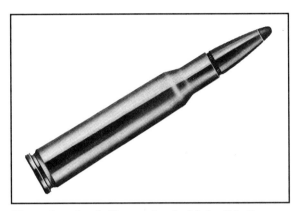

The soft-point bullet, as loaded into this 7mm Mauser round, is the most popular design for big game.

of 60 percent copper and 40 percent nickel. This metal was, in fact, the old German silver (sometimes called electrum) that was used for years by blackpowder shooters. Gilding metal, an alloy of copper and about 5 to 10 percent of zinc, was also employed.

Initially, the jacket was a big horsefly in the oatmeal. To promote the all-important gyroscopic effect, the jacket had to be uniform and concentric. A lopsided jacket would upset balance. The jacket also had to withstand high velocity and RPS without disengaging from the core. And the core of the jacketed bullet had to be homogeneous to promote precision. A lead core with voids, heavy spots or light spots, hurt accuracy. Further experimentation with lead continued. Winchester's famous Lubaloy, for example, was an alloy of lead with a small percent of tin. England had a similar product, which British gunners called Nobaloy.

A misconception about jacketed-bullet accuracy eventually arose. Some shooters felt the jacket should come all the way to the nose to affect best accuracy because, they said, a flattened bullet nose caused trouble. Even into the 1950s, gunwriters proposed that the most accurate projectile had to have a full metal jacket (FMJ) because "points will not deform or upset when heavy breech pressures are introduced behind them" (so said Dr. Hagie, a respected arms author of the era).

The concept that flattened lead points on sharp-profiled, soft-point projectiles destroyed accuracy survived for a long time, even though it wasn't true. But hunters of soft-skinned game were aware of their needs: not an FMJ bullet, but rather a good soft-point projectile. The first widely used soft-point, big-game bullets in America were offered in the 30-30 and 30-40 Krag, along with the 25-35. An exposed lead tip allowed bullet "mushrooming," the term that caught on for external bullet upset on the target. These bullets were excellent for deer, but on larger game the jacket sometimes shed away on impact.

Expansion was desired, but bullet blow-up was not. For example, the original dum-dum bullet, a jacketed projectile with lead exposed at nose and base, was designed for expansion. According to Townsend Whelen, the dum dum's problem was loss of the jacket on impact. When the bullet blew its jacket, it also blew all chances for good penetration. Experienced hunters wanted penetration *and* expansion, just as seasoned hunters today want the same in a big-game bullet for consistently reliable results under varying hunting conditions. The quest was for *controlled* expansion in a big-game bullet, not simply random mushrooming.

EARLY DESIGNS

Many experiments in big-game bullet design ensued. Early round-nose soft-points with a lot of exposed lead were reliable. Designs with a small lead tip were tried for greater penetration. Western Cartridge Company came out with a good jacketed hollow-point bullet for big game. But hunters were calling for a sharp-pointed, lead-tipped expanding missile. In 1924, Townsend Whelen reported a desire for such a bullet, but even 20 years later he felt that the "perfect" pointed expanding bullet had still not been developed.

Improvements were recorded, however. Winchester Repeating Arms Company introduced a Pointed Expanding Bullet with a sharp nose clothed in an extremely thin jacket of gilding metal. The mini-jacket over the nose of the bullet progressed downward between the main bullet covering and the bullet core.

Remington designed its Bronze Point early on, with a little metal wedge splitting the bullet apart after entry into game. It was and still is a very interesting projectile and quite effective with "boiler room" hits. Western's 220-grain, soft-point, boat-tail bullet was highly touted by Stewart Edward White, who used it on lions in Africa. But the factory load, at an advertised 2300 fps mv, was not reliable on deer; the bullet was so strongly constructed that it just whistled through a buck like a sharp needle through paper. Winchester's 130-grain Protected Point for the 270 also carried a thick jacket, and was noted for good penetration with reliable expansion.

The 1933 Peters Belted bullet had a thick band of gilding metal surrounding the outside of the jacket. About a half-inch wide and situated about one-fifth of an inch below the point on a 220-grain 30-caliber bullet, it looked "like a ring on a finger," in Whelen's words. Although the Belted bullet offered excellent penetration with reliable expansion, it was abandoned. Just before World War II, the Peters Inner Belted and Remington Core-Lokt—bullets of excellent jacket/core integrity—replaced it. They were less costly to make, using a thickened gilding metal jacket to correspond with the band of the Peters Belted bullet. The "belt" here was more a fatter portion of the jacket, and of course was of internal rather than external design.

The Winchester Silvertip appeared with a silver-colored, cupro-nickel cover over its soft point. This thin jacket was drawn down well along the core of the bullet. The protected point of the Silvertip ensured good penetration. Trophy hunter Grancel Fitz often relied on the Silvertip bullet in his 30-06 rifle for game from deer to moose.

European bullet makers had been working on a reliable hunting bullet for years. D.W.M. (Deutsche Waffen und Munitionsfabrikin) developed the Strong Jacket and R.W.S. (Rheinische-Westfaelische Sprengstoff) offered its H-Mantel (we spell it Mantle) bullets—just two of the many special premium big-game projectiles offered by overseas manufacturers. The Strong

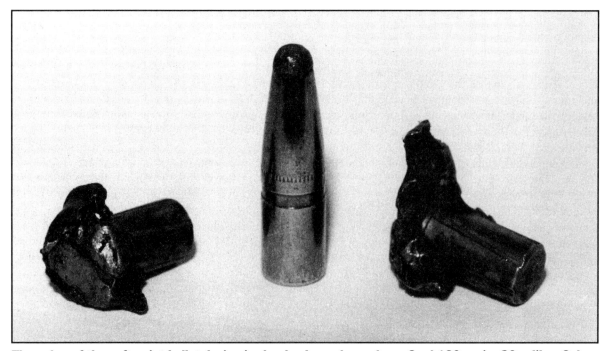

The value of the soft-point bullet design is clearly shown here. An unfired 180-grain, 30-caliber Sako Hammerhead bullet (center) is flanked by two of the same brand recovered from moose. Note the perfect "mushrooming" effect, which imparts energy.

Jacket had a fragile forward portion, with a very tough base. The front was supposed to expand readily, while the base of the bullet remained intact for better penetration; unfortunately, it did not work well.

In the early 1950s, John A. Nosler was forced to expand his operation to meet the heavy demand for his Partition Bullet. After much field use, no rupture had occurred at the partition with the Nosler bullet, and its fine reputation was sealed. The modern Nosler bullet is more accurate than its predecessor; but from the start, Noslers were sufficiently accurate for hunting purposes. In the early 1960s, I hunted caribou off the Denali Highway in Alaska, using a 270. I noted a significant improvement in dispatch when I switched from a mushy 130-grain pill to a Nosler.

Erroneous bullet concepts were dissipating. The idea that deformed points destroyed accuracy had been squelched. (That notion had brought forth a little gadget which fitted into the forward portion of the magazine, its function to protect the soft lead point from being smashed, thereby "guaranteeing accuracy"). Some of us experimented by shooting five-shot groups with three normal bullet tips and two noses deliberately smacked flat—the latter staying right in the group. Later high-speed photos illustrated that

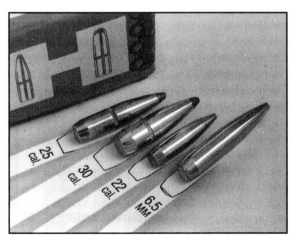

The boat-tail design, shown by these Hornady bullets in calibers 25, 30, 22 and 6.5mm (26 caliber), flattens trajectory and increases energy at long range.

Examples of the hollow-point design are these 100-grain Hornady 7mm bullets, which are meant to fragment on the target.

the forward section of the bullet was severely flattened by the atmosphere (although the photograph itself distorted the truth by greatly exaggerating it). Nonetheless, there was a small degree of truth in the bullet-flattening statement. The atmosphere was blunting the nose of the projectile, but not to the extent suggested by some of the photographs.

Bullet makers continued to strive for a perfect big-game hunting projectile. Serious hunters defined and redefined their desires, asking for the seemingly impossible—mushrooming at all terminal velocities with good bullet weight retention, but without "bust-up," in order to ensure penetration, which creates the wound channel.

Hunters of limited experience were thrilled with explosive bullets. Stripped core/jacket "blow-up" gave dynamite-charged performance. Lung area strikes, with total disruption of the high-velocity projectile, destroyed no edible meat. Total penetration was unnecessary. Kills were astonishing. But these same bullets were not too shiny when the animal didn't cooperate for perfect boiler-room placement. A shoulder shot with the soft-shelled missile often failed miserably. In Africa, I had a chance to conduct autopsies on about 45 game animals, ranging from the Stembok to Cape buffalo, and the high correlation between bullets that stayed together and clean harvests was startling. So was the reverse. One of our hunters used an older-style bullet that blew apart every time on larger game, and every time we were on the spoor after the shot.

The same soft bullet, however, killed like lightning on chest-struck little stuff. Many consecutive examples of harvests are instructional, and if sectional density and penetration are not married, they are at least going steady, for good bullets of high sectional density created longer wound channels than the same caliber bullets of lesser sectional density.

Over the years, I've also looked at the relationship between bullet energy and penetration. My experiences suggest, and the laws of physics support, that high terminal energy and penetra-

teresting H-Mantle (still with semi-partition), the TUG, TIG, Cone Point and other styles designed for expansion without separation of jacket and core.

Incidentally, the R.W.S. solid proved itself on safari. While another brand of FMJ style blew to confetti on a Cape buffalo, the R.W.S. penetrated and remained intact, fulfilling the requirements of a full-jacket big-game stopper: bone breaking ability with deepest possible penetration. Hornady, Remington and Winchester solids all behaved the same—after deep penetration in large game, each recovered bullet looked like new.

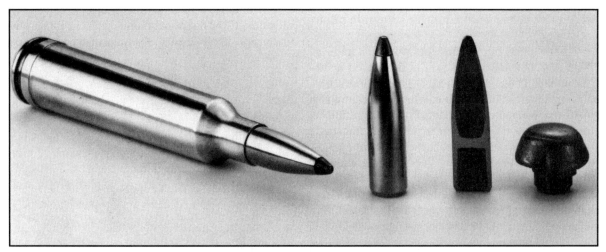

Nosler's Partition bullet (for the 7mm Rem. Mag. at left) guarantees that the front portion of the projectile will not expand past the belt. This ensures mushrooming without jacket/core separation.

tion go hand in hand; but, again, without sound bullet construction, forget it. The bullet still has to stay together to deliver a long wound channel and leave an exit hole, which many of us credit for additional harvesting effect through loss of body fluids.

American bullet crafters studied projectile effectiveness on big game, responding with bonded cores and controlled expansion on bullets especially for game larger than deer. Not one current premium big-game bullet manufacturer advertises explosiveness as a selling point. Neither do European big-game bullet makers. RWS, for example, offers its in-

NO SINGLE BIG-GAME BULLET SATISFIES ALL SITUATIONS

Hunters learned that no single big-game bullet would be perfect for all situations. Fortunately, more high-performance big-game bullets are offered today than ever before, and in a variety of styles to match the game that is hunted. It is up to the shooter to pick the right bullet for the job.

Quite by accident I recently rediscovered the 308 Winchester as a hunting cartridge. A Ruger Model 77 International with its Mannlicher-style full-length stock interested me for brush and timber hunting. I got one in caliber 308 Win-

Northern Precision bullet company offers many different styles. These 416-caliber bullets, for example, range in weight from 200 grains to 450 grains, with obvious shape differences.

chester and found accuracy excellent. But I had a bullet lesson to learn. On a hunt to fill an additional antlerless deer license, I tried the 308 with the beautiful Vulkan bullet from Norma. I shot a mature mule deer doe chest-center with this 180-grain, strongly constructed bullet. The deer simply walked away. Tracking proved that the deer walked 300 yards and fell over. Had I not followed the animal, I would have lost it.

From that lesson, I switched to a bullet better matched for the game: a 150-grain Sierra boattail. Using the Sierra bullet in the 308, I've taken several deer with ideal results. So match the bullet design to the game.

Dozens of fine bullets are available to choose from. Hornady's Interlock design is one. A particularly accurate Frank Wells 7mm Magnum produced several witnessed 200-yard groups

Although these are all .277-inch diameter bullets, they vary in both style and weight. Pairs from left: 130-grain Sierra BT, 140-grain Sierra BT, 140-grain Hornady BT, 140-grain Armfield and 160-grain Nosler (single bullet) on far right. Note the rounded BT design of the Armfield projectile.

These Speer 22-caliber bullets exhibit great variation. From the left: 46-grain flat-point with cannelure, 50-grain TNT for extra explosiveness (light jacket hollow-point), 52-grain Match bullet, 62-grain hollow-point with cannelure for heavier varmints, and 68-grain Match hollow-point with boat-tail design.

under an inch, center to center, with Interlock bullets. Speer's excellent Grand Slam bullet offers proper mushrooming without bullet "bust-up." The Nosler Partition remains as viable as ever as a premium big-game projectile. A-Square offers a bonded bullet with a very strong jacket. Swift has a fine bullet of partition design. Barnes bullets are noted for strong jackets; their 195-grain 7mm bullet is proof. Bitterroot's Bonded Core bullets use thick copper tubing for jacket material and pure lead for cores. Winchester offers a new boat-tail Silvertip. Remington has its time-tested Core-Lokt. There are many excellent premium bullets made by small manufacturers, such as Allred Bullets, which are double-jacketed projectiles, and the phenomenal Jensen J26 bullet—it has just about everything and is essentially "made by hand."

Blackpowder shooters can take advantage of many newly designed bullets too. The Buffalo Bullet Company offers a long line of conicals, for example. Furthermore, bullets can be made at home. The art of casting lead projectiles survives and thrives today, with many good books on the subject. Making excellent jacketed bullets at home has gained wide acceptance, partly because of the availability of good equipment offered by such companies as Corbin Manufacturing.

Chapter 6 deals with the sectional density and ballistic coefficient of bullets, as well as tests and test media used to determine bullet performance. But before that, what keeps a bullet on track during its flight?

THE STABLE RIFLE BULLET

5 No matter how superbly designed or well constructed, the bullet must remain stable from muzzle to target if accuracy is to be achieved. In theory, a perfect round ball (lead sphere) will shoot straight at modest range from a smoothbore. In practice, this is not the case, which is why rifling was invented.

Rifling forces the projectile (whether it is a round ball or a jacketed bullet) to rotate on its axis, giving it a gyroscopic effect. The effect remains in force as long as the projectile maintains adequate spin. When rotation falls below that ideal level, the elongated projectile yaws or otherwise tips off its axis. It may "keyhole," causing the projectile to reach the target in a haphazard way. This is often illustrated by an imprint of the bullet's profile on the paper, rather than a round hole in the target.

There is no one perfect rate of rifling twist. RPS (revolutions per second) must vary in accord to the nature of the bullet in question. It is difficult to prove that a bullet can be overstabilized, although it's easy to show that rifling can provide a rate of twist that is too rapid. In such a case, the bullet "rides" over the rifling instead of being guided by it. This condition is known as "stripping the bore," and it was noted very early in the study of firearms. When a bullet strips the bore, it cannot be stabilized. It may

yaw, tip, go end over end, or otherwise take an erratic flight pattern.

THE IMPORTANCE OF BALANCE

Ideally, a bullet should exhibit both static and dynamic balance. *Static balance, or stability,* is the inherent uniformity of the projectile at rest. Static balance manifests itself in *dynamic balance,* the bullet's posture in flight. As alluded to in Chapter 4, an unbalanced missile behaves in the bore because it is forced to rotate on its axis, but after exiting the bore, that "bad" bullet must rotate on its center of mass.

A bullet may be unbalanced for various reasons: voids or cavities in the core, eccentric points, oblique bases, asymmetrical jackets, or any other defect that displaces the mass center from the axis point. Damage may also affect a bullet's flight, depending upon the location of the damage. My own attempts to test damaged bullets confirmed that spitzer soft-nosed bullets with flattened noses usually will group consistently. Shank damage, however, may lure the bullet off the path, and base damage can misguide it even more.

Some missiles with minor damage did not go off course regardless of the damage location, possibly because their imbalance was controlled by the spinning of the bullet. Also, the effect of base damage varied for different bullets. An untrue bullet may wobble in flight, yet still hit the bull's-eye point-forward! Conversely, overspinning of a damaged bullet can magnify discrepancies. Overspinning may manifest itself in a wobbling bullet that does not find its way into the group, because increased spin causes bullet imperfections to reveal their aerodynamic problems. The bullet wobble will increase beyond the ability of the bullet to maintain point-on flight.

is a 90-degree change in attitude, whereby the projectile may strike the target sideways.

Mann states his concept of overspinning bad bullets in his classic book, *The Bullet's Flight*. Dr. Mann says, "If the twist is increased above its normal [level] to keep an unbalanced bullet from tipping, it fails to do so, as our experiments indicate, since the increased twist magnifies the angle of tangent to bore spiral, thus throwing axis of the unbalanced bullet out of line with in-

If perfectly formed, the round ball (far right) would in theory fly correctly. However, groups from rifled arms surpass groups from smoothbores because, in part, the spinning of the ball equalized imperfections on a common axis. Note other bullet forms shown here. The patch imparts the value of the rifling to the round ball.

Is there any such thing as overspinning a bullet? A physicist might answer by saying, "stability varies directly as the square of the axial movement and invariably as the first power of the transverse movement." Yaw, or tipping in flight (when the nose of the bullet no longer points forward) is one stability problem, as noted above. Dr. F.W. Mann, student of ballistics, stated that a six-degree yaw would tumble a projectile. The bullet may keyhole. A true keyhole

creased force when set free from the muzzle." Mann goes on to say that "increasing the twist also shortens up time of oscillation of an unbalanced bullet and lengthens its gyration, and a slow-gyrating bullet makes an air spiral with a long pitch, thus giving the air a longer time to act in any given direction before its axis is altered to allow air to deflect it in another direction." In short, problems are magnified, and the result of overstabilization is reduced accuracy.

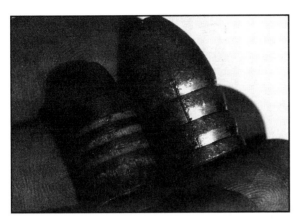

Although these large-caliber Minie-type blackpowder bullets are heavy, they do not possess great ballistic coefficient and will stabilize from a relatively slow-twist bore.

Much of Dr. Mann's efforts in *The Bullet's Flight* speak obliquely, if not directly, about bullet stabilization. Mann's borrowed 32-40 Winchester smoothbore rifle proved that even elongated (conical) missiles can achieve some form of stability without spinning. Examples of non-spinning, but stable, projectiles abound, from rockets and rifled shotgun slugs to socks with sand in the toe. The trouble is *how* they stabilize, which may or may not be point-forward. Mann learned that some bullets at some juncture in their flight turned end over end, losing their stability. He computed a 3300 RPM (revolutions per minute) for one tumbling bullet.

Shape is important to stability, especially of non-spinning missiles. Dr. Mann puzzled over *how* unstable bullets flew through the atmosphere. Of course he worked only with linear or Newtonian physics, as we still do. It is my guess that linear physics could not then and cannot now answer all the questions of unstable, yet repeatable flight characteristics.

A missile might tumble through the air, but not randomly. It may tumble with a pattern. The science of chaos, or non-linear physics, may determine when such patterns emerge, just as this branch of science deals with thousands of randomly placed dots on a piece of paper that eventually form a pattern. When non-linear physics is applied to ballistics, we should learn more about the oddities of bullet flight. For now, the exploration follows a traditional trail. Remember that in the bore, the bullet is forced to rotate on its center of form, but in flight the bullet rotates around its center of gravity in a gyroscopic manner. The bullet is ruled by the rifling until it departs the muzzle, then its flight is guided by the "instructions" of RPS.

BULLET SPIN AND RATE OF TWIST

RPS is a function of rate of twist and exit velocity. A 1:10 rate of twist means that the bullet will rotate one complete revolution within 10 inches of bore. Even if the barrel is only two inches long, the 1:10 rate of twist still prevails. The key is *rate,* not barrel length. A bullet from a 20-inch barrel with a 1:10 rate of twist turns twice before it exits the muzzle. Cut the barrel down to 10 inches and the bullet still turns twice in 20 inches. Of course, the missile will be 10 inches in front of the muzzle when it makes its second complete revolution.

RPS does not fall off nearly as rapidly as forward velocity because of the Law of Conservation of Angular Momentum. Consider a toy top. Bal-

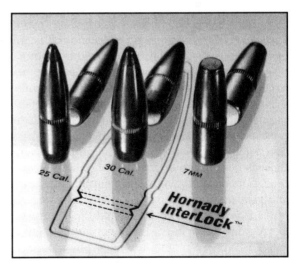

Bullet shape has much to do with stabilization. Note the differences in these Hornady InterLock bullets—high ballistic coefficient on the left, a little less C in the middle and less yet with the flat-point design on the far right.

These four handgun cartridges are all employed in rifles. Note the shape of their bullets (left to right): 9mm Parabellum with round nose, 45 Auto with flat nose, wadcutter style of the 44 Magnum and blunt profile of the 45 Colt bullet. While aerodynamics may not seem to be a consideration, all of the bullets are ballistically correct for their intended use, and accurate.

anced on its point, a top falls over every time. But spin the top on its point and it stabilizes. When the top slows too much, its axis of rotation changes dramatically, and it falls over again. Angular momentum becomes a vector (directional impetus) when the top tumbles.

Instability can also bring directional change in a bullet. The angular momentum of an object, such as a bullet or a gyroscope, remains constant unless external torques act to alter this momentum. Angular momentum changes slowly because these external forces must be comparatively strong to affect change. Otherwise, angular momentum (assume RPS in this case) tends to remain fairly constant. Couple this with the short time of flight associated with a projectile and these two forces act simultaneously in bullet stabilization: conservation of momentum along with short time of flight. Because of these factors, RPS holds up extremely well from muzzle to target.

Velocity of spin contributes to bullet stability. To improve bullet stability from a bore, it would seem correct simply to raise the muzzle velocity. Since RPS results from rate of twist and exit velocity, it follows that more velocity produces more spin. But how much extra rotational velocity is required? If the bullet is almost sta-

bilized anyway, a bit more velocity may do the trick. But if the bullet is far from stabilized, it would be impossible to get it going fast enough to stabilize, considering maximum working pressures.

Mann had a test rifle with a 1:21 rate of twist from which the bullet was not stabilized with a powder charge of 18 grains. When he increased the powder charge to 23 grains weight, the same bullet suddenly stabilized. "To the surprise of some riflemen acquaintances, increasing the velocity at the muzzle, in the 21-inch twist, caused the bullet to make perfect prints," Mann says in *The Bullet's Flight*. At 18 grains of powder, bullets "tipped badly and would not reach the tar-

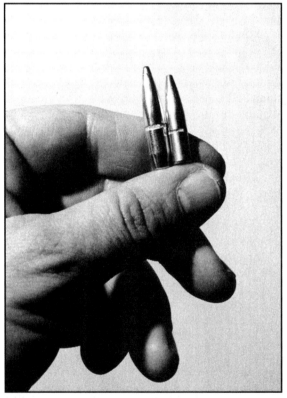

Two spitzer bullets: a boat-tail design on the left, a flat base on the right. Although the 162-grain 7mm bullet (left) can be expected to "carry up" better than the 30-caliber, 180-grain bullet on the right, the flat-base bullet remains an excellent design, especially for medium-range shooting.

Each bullet in this lineup presents a different configuration and each will stabilize somewhat uniquely, although the first four will achieve a proper flight attitude with a 1:12 rate of twist. The four bullets starting from the left are all .375-inch diameter, while the bullet on the right is a 180-grain 30 caliber for comparison.

get," but at 23 grains of powder, the same bullets flew point-on.

This is conjecture, but I suspect that the missiles in Mann's test rifle above were almost stabilized with the 18-grain charge. Had the twist of his rifle been slower than 1:21, the increased powder charge and higher exit velocity would not have been sufficient to stabilize the bullet. Increasing twist has more practical effect on RPS than increasing muzzle velocity. Slow twist yields slow spin. For example, an Enfield (Snider) rifle with 1:78 twist produces only 200 RPS when the bullet leaves the muzzle at 1300 fps. The Martini-Henry rifle with 1:22 rate of twist *and the same* 1300 fps mv produces 714 RPS for the same bullet. But the 256 Mannlicher's 160-grain bullet at 2400 fps mv develops 3657 RPS because of its 1:8 twist (actually 1:7.87). When RPS reaches ridiculous levels, energy is robbed from the powder charge. Instead of expanding gases working to propel the bullet forward, some gas energy is diverted to create RPS.

Fremantle, in *The Book of the Rifle* (1901) noted that "the stability of a bullet in flight, if it starts with an ample spin, is very remarkable." Fortunately, each bullet diameter and weight does not demand one and only one rate of twist to stabilize it. There is an allowable *range* of RPS/ stabilization for a given projectile in accord with caliber, weight and shape.

BULLET SHAPE AND MASS

Shape plays a role in bullet stabilization. Mann discovered that flat-based bullets stabilized well in a given test rifle, while bullets with oval bases tipped after they had traveled only 50 yards. Certainly it was not slow-down in RPS that caused the oval-based bullet to forsake its axis in only 50 yards. Boat-tail bullets stabilize beautifully and fly like a dream. But when RPS is marginal for stabilization, a boat-tail bullet may wobble, while a flat-based bullet of the same weight stabilizes from the same bore.

Weight for weight, the boat-tail bullet is longer than its flat-based counterpart. I asked Steve Hornady of Hornady Manufacturing Company why he did not offer a 175-grain 7mm boat-tail bullet. "Adding a boat-tail to the 7mm 175

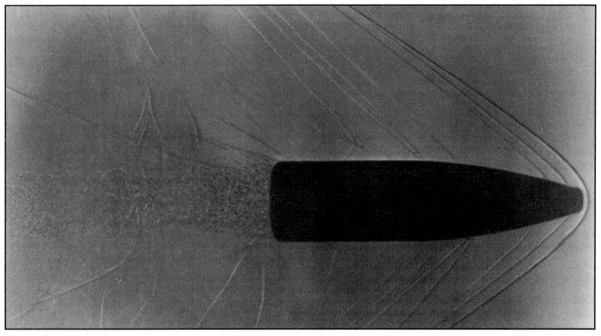

This Sierra 180-grain, 30-caliber soft-point bullet has been captured in flight through spark photography. Note the many waves that attend the bullet's flight. Different projectile designs will impart different waves.

lengthens the bullet," he said, "to the point where stability is marginal even in some of the faster 7mms around." In order to add the boat-tail, the sharp profile of the 175-grain Hornady 7mm bullet would have to be altered—made more blunt—not a trade-off that Steve wanted. He preferred to maintain a sharp profile rather than trading that rocket-like nose shape for a boat-tail base.

Obturation is the enlarging of the bullet while it is still in the bore. The bullet is slightly fore-shortened and made a bit larger by its own inertia trying to hold itself in place, while high-pressure expanding gas is working on the bullet's base. Obturation plays a small indirect role in bullet stabilization. As Mann discovered, a bullet tends to conform to the bore because of obturation. Mann recovered tapered lead bullets and found they were no longer tapered. "These bullets when recovered from the snow, however, were found to be cylindrical, made so by the rifle's bore. . . ." I've noticed a slight shank section on round balls I've recovered after firing with heavy powder

charges and Minie skirts may flare out from high pressure.

Obturation enhances bullet stability through improved engagement of the missile to the rifling that guides it in the bore. Depth of groove and consequent height of land also apply, as they aid in getting the bullet off to a good start. The effect of the these rifling characteristics is engraved upon the surface of the bullet, except with paper-patched conicals and cloth-patched round balls, where twist is translated to the projectile via intermediate mediums (paper and cloth).

Also important to bullet stability is *mass of projectile*. The round ball shows this very well. A small-caliber round ball needs far more RPS than a large-caliber one to stabilize it. This is why the catch-all 1:48 rate of twist that so many muzzleloading rifle manufacturers insist upon for all calibers does not compute. Some historians believe that the 1:48 rate of twist entrenched itself because it was used by the famous Hawken Brothers. Sam and Jake had one rifling machine. It carried a 1:48 twist. They used 1:48

because they had it. Others believe that a turn in four feet is magical, stabilizing round balls and conicals equally well regardless of the rifle's caliber. "The reason you see so many rifles with a 1:48 rate of twist," one writer told me, "is that it was proved long ago that 1:48 is perfect."

Not so. For example, a 32-caliber round ball demands a faster RPS (by comparison) than a 64-caliber round ball. A 1:30 twist may be fine for a 32-caliber round ball, but I'll take a 1:70 or slower for a 64-caliber round ball. Again, there is a range of acceptable twist per caliber. A 1:48 rate of twist will stabilize a 32-caliber round ball and a 1:90 will stabilize a 64-caliber round ball. Velocity plays a role, of course: a 64-caliber ball-shooting rifle with a 1:48 rate of twist loaded down to subsonic velocities may group its projectiles fairly well due to the low velocity, hence reduced RPS.

C.E. Harris explained in the August 1983 issue of *American Rifleman* that "For a given rate of twist the ratio of spin to forward velocity is a constant, and the only improvement in gryoscopic stability due to loading hotter results from the slight decrease in overturning moment coefficient with increasing velocity." Spinning the bullet faster keeps it flying point-on because of greater gyroscopic impetus due to higher RPS. In these terms, a stability factor of more than 1.0 is necessary for any hope of stabilization, with 1.5 to 2.0 falling into the realm of the ideal range. Generally, less than 1.5 suggests an unstable bullet. Over 4.0 is unnecessary, and when 5.0 is reached, things begin to reverse themselves. Too much RPS brings destabilization. Example: take a 30-06, 152-grain FMJ flat-base bullet at 2750

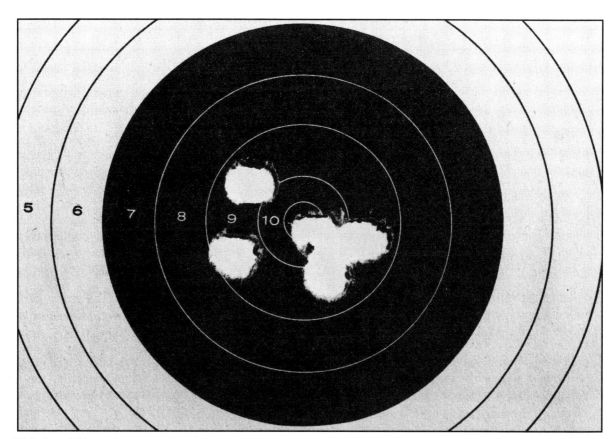

This is a 100-yard group, shot with round balls. When properly stabilized and fired from a good bore, the round lead ball is capable of high-grade accuracy.

fps mv. The gyroscopic stability factor rate (S) from a 1:16 twist is 1.3. With the same bullet/velocity from 1:13 twist, S equals 2.0. With the same bullet/velocity from a 1:12 twist, S equals 2.3; from a 1:10 twist, S equals 3.3. It's easy to see how important rate of twist is by these figures.

STABILIZATION AT THE TARGET

Another important aspect of bullet stabilization is in performance on game. Bullet stabilization in flight is a common concern. However, when the bullet is called upon to create a proper wound channel to harvest big game cleanly, it must also maintain a sense of stabilization. This statement will fall on deaf ears for those who believe that good bullet performance is total disintegration of the projectile upon striking game. Those who want a long wound channel and an

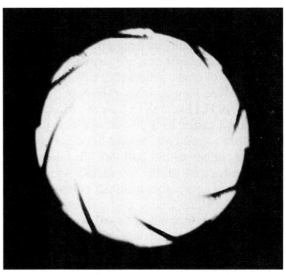

This is what the bullet "sees" as it rests downbore. The rifling that will guide its flight in the bore will also cause the bullet to fly point-forward out of the bore due to spin.

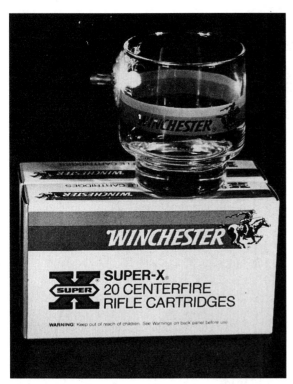

When this Winchester bullet hit its target (a water glass), the energy was imparted to the glass; however, the projectile maintained its proper attitude in flight and did not tip.

exit hole feel differently, as do those who shoot solid projectiles on dangerous game.

"I want to collect a springhare for the museum back home," said a hunter on one safari I attended. He grabbed a 223 with full-patch ammo and began to stroll away from camp in search of this African mammal that looks like a cross between a rabbit and a kangaroo. The camp was divided. Half of us felt the 223 solid would ruin the hide. The other half said it would not. The hunter returned later with his quarry. The hide was ruined in spite of an FMJ bullet that should have, in theory, punched a narrow hole. Yes, the full metal jacketed bullet was stable in flight, but it was not stable in the game.

Tipping, or the buzz-saw effect, is a matter of interior stabilization: how the bullet reacts when driving through game. Round-nose bullets are supposed to make neat, straight wound channels. Spitzers should veer off course. After studying many wound channels, I still don't know if there is any practical truth to the round-nose versus spitzer argument. I've seen crooked wound channels and straight wound channels with both. I have also seen FMJ pointed bullets that should have zipped through with a pencil-

A lineup of bullets visually depicts why different calibers, shapes and ballistic values demand different rates of twist for stabilization. The following Speer projectiles are (from left): 243 (6mm, 100 grain), 257 (100 grain), 7mm (145 grain), 30 caliber (150 grain), and a 35-caliber (250 grain) bullet.

like wound channel that instead created a large exit hole. Exit holes in game are a matter of shock wave in front of the bullet. If the bullet tips and tumbles, those shock waves are altered.

Sometimes when you think you have a shooting problem solved, an individual rifle steps

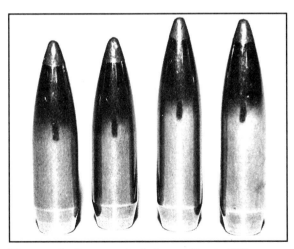

The two bullets on the left are Sierra 270 (.277-inch) caliber 130-grain boat-tails. The twin bullets on the right are Sierras of the same diameter, but 150-grain weight. All of these projectiles will fly correctly from a 1:10 rate of twist.

in to muddy otherwise clear waters. I have a 7mm Magnum that clouds the water badly. Twist is 1:9. Riflemaker Dale Storey found it hard to believe when I told him that bullets over 150 grains weight were never accurate in that rifle. He rebedded it free of charge after learning that what I said was true. It didn't help. Free-floated, pressure-pointed—nothing mattered. Bullets of 160 grains and 175 grains weight stabilized to 300 meters in our tests, but they did not shoot accurately—even though they were definitely striking the target point-on. Downgraded accuracy with bullets over 150 grains weight from a twist that is supposed to be right for heavier bullets is a puzzle. I'm sorry to say we never found the right pieces to give us a picture of what was, and still is, going on in that rifle.

OTHER FACTORS

Many external factors affect bullet stabilization, including obstacles in the path of the bullet, such as brush. In theory, the more stabilized missile should get through more brush. In practice, all bullets are sent off course by twigs and such. Muzzle damage may also affect bullet stability. We know less of this factor than we would like to. All of us have seen rifles with badly worn and even damaged muzzle crowns put their bullets right on target, while modest damage to other muzzle crowns sent bullets off on wild paths. Unfortunately, and all too often, we have to weave in and out of stabilization questions with conditionals and surmises.

Drift, however, is a certainty we have to live with. *Drift* is the horizontal departure of the bullet from its intended line of flight due to the direction of rifling twist and the RPS of the bullet. A right-hand twist, with consequent right-handed RPS, sends the bullet to the right, with a left-hand twist doing the opposite.

Wind drift is another matter. It's the horizontal departure of the bullet from its intended flight path due to the force of air movement. Drift, for all practical shooting, is not a big problem. Wind drift can be a severe one. For example, a bullet can be deflected by the wind so badly that it will strike far from its intended bull's-eye. A 30-06 shooting a factory load with a 180-grain bullet a 2700 fps mv can drift off course by about two feet at 300 yards in a 30 mile-per-hour crosswind—a wind velocity not unknown on the western plains. Therefore, hunters must understand wind drift if they are to place bullets correctly under windy conditions.

There are other stability factors. Mann found that "oblique base bullets make about the same size groups as normal bullets, only in different places." This statement refers to bullet integrity, something modern shooters don't have to worry about very much in practical terms, although benchrest shooters trying to set world records certainly study the concentricity of their projectiles before an important match. All factory bullets are amazingly uniform these days. Bullets from Sierra, Hornady, Speer, Nosler and others are superb. And custom bullets are also available for the shooter whose goal is that elusive "one-hole group."

THE BULLET IN MOTION

6 Ballistics is the science of a bullet in motion. Interior ballistics deals with the bullet before it leaves the muzzle of the rifle. This chapter is concerned with only external ballistics—what happens to the bullet after it leaves the rifle muzzle. A great many things happen to a bullet in its journey from muzzle to target, as well as after the bullet strikes the target.

POTENTIAL ENERGY

Place a bullet in the palm of your hand. As it rests there motionless, it transfers no power. However, it does have the *potential* to deliver power, as does any object, from a rock to a rocket. The ability of the bullet to turn into a power-delivering entity depends on its weight, and also on its caliber and shape. A 30-caliber 200-grain spitzer and an old lead round ball of the same weight, if both driven at the same speed, deliver exactly the same energy at the muzzle, because they weigh the same and are traveling at the same velocity. But it's no secret that down-range the 30-caliber spitzer will have far more retained energy than the round ball.

EVALUATING THE BULLET

Sectional density is one means of evaluating the potential energy capability of a bullet. It re-

lates to how the bullet reacts not only in the atmosphere between muzzle and target, but also after the bullet hits the target. A basic explanation of sectional density is "weight of the bullet per caliber." A 200-grain 30-caliber bullet has a much better sectional density than a 200-grain 45-caliber bullet because the 30-caliber bullet is "longer for its weight" than the 45-caliber bullet.

More precisely, sectional density is: *the ratio of a bullet's weight to its diameter.* The weight of the bullet is expressed in pounds and the diameter in inches. In the formula, the square of the bullet's diameter is used. The ratio emerges as a number, and the larger the number, the greater the sectional density.

The weight of the bullet must be converted from grains to pounds, one pound equaling 7000 grains. This figure is divided by the cross-sectional area of the bullet in inches squared. The mathematics are not of concern here because every bullet manufacturer offers sectional density figures for its bullets.

Going back to the comparison of the 200-grain 30-caliber bullet with the 200-grain 45-caliber bullet, we find that the former has a sectional density of .301, according to the *Sierra Rifle Reloading Manual, 3rd Edition.* The same manual shows the sectional density of a 45-caliber bullet as .140. It's easy to see why the 30-

Bullets at rest represent latent, or potential, energy. When put into motion, that energy is then spoken of as kinetic.

caliber bullet has a higher sectional density: it is long for its caliber, while the 45-caliber bullet is short for its caliber.

Sectional density is helpful in evaluating the potential of a bullet's downrange performance. It's not enough, though, because sectional density does not deal with the style of bullet. For example, the ever-popular 180-grain bullet so often fired out of the 30-06 Springfield and 308 Winchester—as well as a host of 300 magnums and other 30-caliber cartridges—has a sectional density of .271 regardless of its shape. A streamlined 180-grain 30-caliber spitzer bullet has a sectional density of .271. A round-nose, 180-grain 30-caliber bullet is also worth .271 sectional density. Obviously, this won't do in dealing with downrange bullet performance, because in no way do these bullets behave the same way downrange. The round-nose loses far more of its energy over 200 yards compared with the spitzer

equivalent, because the spitzer fires through the atmosphere better. The atmosphere—not gravity—is the bullet's biggest enemy.

Ballistic coefficient defines the aerodynamics of the bullet. Ballistic coefficient is noted as C. The C of a bullet is also expressed by a number starting with a decimal point. However, C is more valuable than sectional density, because C is the ratio of the bullet's sectional density to its coefficient of form.

Think of it this way: Imagine a "perfect bullet" in terms of shape, then think of another bullet from the real world. Let's say the closer the real bullet comes to matching the mythical perfect bullet, the higher the score, with the maximum being 1.00. Of course, 1.00 won't be reached, because the perfect bullet doesn't exist. Realistically, a bullet with a C of .500 will hold onto more of its original velocity and energy than will a bullet with a C of .250.

Returning to the 180-grain 30-caliber bullet, we find that the round-nose has a C of .267, while the spitzer, a C of .435. These figures are correct only for a specific range of velocity, because a bullet's behavior in the atmosphere depends on its speed. But the only true value of the C figures dealt with here is in comparison. We use C figures to compare bullets. The C number says that a bullet is better than, or not as good as, another bullet in terms of retaining its velocity/energy. But C isn't everything. If a particular round-nose bullet load works beautifully in a specific rifle on deer in the brush, don't trade that bullet for one with a higher C.

The modern rifleman must understand that by comparing the various C factors of different bullets, he can determine which bullet has the best potential for retaining its original energy. Again, compare the 30-caliber 180-grain round-nose and spitzer bullets. With 30-06 handloads, muzzle velocity for each is exactly 2800 fps. At the muzzle, each earns an energy rating of 3133 foot-pounds. But at 200 yards from the muzzle, the 180-grain spitzer still carries 2300 foot-pounds of energy, while the 180-grain round-nose is left with 1953 foot-pounds. The spitzer has even slightly more energy at *300 yards* (1956 foot-pounds) than the round-nose at 200 yards.

POWER

The bullet is now in motion. How much force does it have? Here we are dealing with another kind of force: *kinetic energy.* Shooters have always wished for a formula that could define the potency of a particular cartridge in terms of "killing power." A cartridge that earned, say, 100 would be twice as good on moose as a cartridge that earned a score of 50. No such formula exists. Momentum theories abound, but in determining bullet power, only one formula is accepted by science—Newton's model.

Newton's laws include one for energy. The formula refers to the amount of force required to lift one pound of weight one foot high. Thus, the resulting figure is expressed in foot-pounds. Bullet foot-pounds of energy is calculated by first squaring the velocity of the projectile. A fast round with a modest-weight bullet might fare better than a slow round with a big bullet. The 220 Swift with a 48-grain bullet at 4000 fps mv is worth 1706 foot-pounds. The 45-70 with a 500-grain bullet at 1200 fps is credited with not quite 1600 foot-pounds of energy. But which one would perform better in stopping a charging grizzly bear? I'll leave that question open.

Newton's formula is the only one accepted worldwide by all ammo and bullet manufacturers. A shooter will never see the power of a cartridge expressed in any other form. Foot-pounds of energy prevails. The reason? All in all, it's the best formula we have. And it keeps bullet weight in the picture. To compute with Newton's kinetic energy formula, the velocity of the bullet is squared. That figure is then divided by 7000, to convert from grains to pounds. That number is then divided by 64.32 (the Galileo constant of gravity); the result is then multiplied by the weight of the bullet to derive foot-pounds.

Let's compare two handloads: a top load for the 257 Weatherby Magnum and a top load for the 30-06 Springfield. These are real chronographed loads—not fabricated models. The 257 Weatherby Magnum load drives a 120-grain

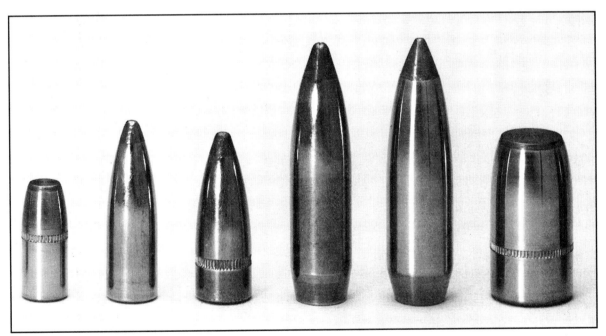

Sectional density is thought of as the relationship between a bullet's diameter and length. That is only a visual expression—not an accurate assessment of sectional density itself. However, it's no trick to pick out bullets of high or low sectional density among this collection of Speer missiles (from left): 75-grain 25 caliber, 120-grain 7mm, 125-grain 31 caliber, 225-grain 338 caliber, 270-grain 375 caliber, and 350-grain 45 caliber.

bullet at a flat 3400 fps mv. The 30-06 load pushes a 180-grain bullet at a flat 2800 fps mv. The ballistic results are as follows:

257 Weatherby Magnum
$3400 \times 3400 = 11,560,000 \div 7000 =$
1,651.4285
1,651.4285 is divided by 64.32
(the Galileo constant of gravity)
with the end result: 25.675194

This is the energy for only *one* grain of bullet weight. That is, each grain weight of the bullet is worth about 26 foot-pounds of energy. But our bullet weighs 120 grains; so 25.675194 is multiplied by 120 for: 3081.0232 foot-pounds (rounded off to 3081) of muzzle energy.

The 30-06 load computes to 3134 foot-pounds. Interestingly, because of the lower velocity of the 30-06, each grain weight of bullet is worth only about 17 foot-pounds, compared to about 26 foot-pounds for each grain weight of the 257 Weatherby Magnum bullet. So this is where bullet weight enters the picture. Because of its heavier bullet, the 30-06 still wins the contest, but not by much. In fact, for all practical purposes, the two loads are in about the same ballistic ballpark. This may make fans of either round see red, but according to Newton's formula, that's the way the bullet bounces.

Bullet energy is of concern because hunters want to harvest big game quickly and efficiently. I've taken game with the two loads described above. Both deliver good results, but with different wound channels. A buck deer standing 200 yards out sideways and struck directly in the chest cavity would probably expire quicker with the 120-grain bullet from the 257 Weatherby. The 180-grain bullet from the '06 would probably be the better bullet if the projectile landed directly at the point of the shoulder and bone had to be penetrated. So killing power is no easy subject to conquer and no formula in the world could define the big-game killing power of a cartridge. Too many factors are at work, including the construction of the bullet and the location of the bullet hit.

Colonel Townsend Whelen, famous hunter,

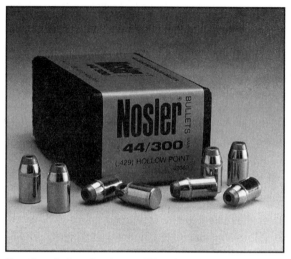

Sectional density is readily visualized here with these 44-caliber 300-grain bullets. While not high, the sectional density of these projectiles is considerably greater than that of the usual 240-grain 44-caliber bullet. In terms of ballistics, the relationship of caliber and bullet weight are extremely important, because it means that this bullet, fired from a rifle at close range, offers formidable authority.

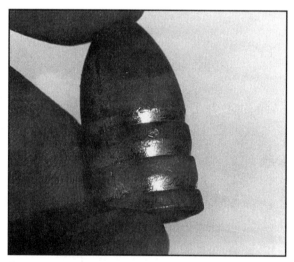

One of the biggest ballistics questions regards bullet weight/velocity, i.e., a heavy bullet at modest speed or a lighter one at high speed. Obviously, the greatest energy is associated with a heavy bullet at high speed; however, this big Minie 58 caliber slug weighing over 500 grains becomes a force at modest velocity.

The obvious "bottom line" is field performance. Both of these mature trophy bucks dropped instantly, the one on the left to a bullet from a 7mm-08, the other on the right to a bullet from a 7mm Remington Magnum.

soldier, ballistician and shooter, derived a theory about killing power after many years of experience and a great deal of thought on the subject. Whelen says in his book, *The Hunting Rifle* (1940), "The killing power of a bullet in flight depends entirely upon the average size of the wound it makes in the animal, and upon nothing else. The size of the wound in turn depends upon the size, weight, construction, and shape of the bullet, and the velocity with which it strikes, and upon no other details." In the past half century or so, a truly better explanation of bullet efficiency on big game has not shown up.

BULLET CONSTRUCTION

Whelen's remark about bullet construction is so vital to the entire subject of practical ballistics that it deserves expansion. Bullets are constructed in dozens of different ways. There are the full-metal-jacket (FMJ) models and hollow-points, heavy jackets over lead cores, light jackets over lead cores and these days bullets of homogeneous construction with no lead core whatever. I have samples of German hunting bullets that are a couple decades old, and they are made of solid copper. There is no single ideal bullet construction, because no single demand is made of a hunting bullet. The little 25-grain bullet from a 17 Remington, for example, is designed to explode into oblivion, which is just what it does after modest penetration.

On small animals, such as prairie dogs, the 25-grain bullet kills instantly with extreme destruction of tissue. On larger rodents, like woodchucks, tissue destruction is more an internal affair. On varmints of coyote size, the result of a strike with the 17 Remington within a reasonable range where bullet speed remains high—such as 200 yards—is a tiny entrance hole, no exit hole at all and generally a complete halt of locomotion, similar to a movie film suddenly put on stopframe. It's quite normal for bullets from much larger cartridges to work far less swiftly on these smaller targets than the 17 Remington with its minuscule 25-grain bullet at high speed. Meanwhile, no one in possession of his faculties would

The author's bullet box shown here was used to determine the effect of a bullet on various test media, such as water, clay, wet newspapers and even old phone books.

think of trying to stop the charge of a Cape buffalo with a 25-grain bullet at any speed.

TESTING A BULLET

It is up to the shooter to select the bullet that will serve best for the specific task at hand, be it varmint control in a ranch pasture or harvesting a bull elk for the freezer. Over the years, I have used a device I call a "bullet box" for testing projectiles.

A bullet box can be constructed in many ways. Mine is a wooden structure with compartments. The first compartment gets a water balloon; the second, a clay block; the third, wet newspapers; and the fourth, a backup of old phone books. Bullets that "come apart" in the test box come apart on game. Bullets that hold together in the box hold together on game. Although a multiple-medium bullet box probably gives the best results, bullet construction can also be tested against an ordinary clay bank or with a box of damp newspapers.

WOUND CHANNELS

Dedicated hunters make autopsies on big game. They also study small-game carcasses. The reason for these inquiries is to determine the wound channel produced by a particular bullet. Of course, striking velocity alters wound channels. A bullet hitting from 50 yards will deliver different results from the same type of bullet shot at 200 yards. Nonetheless, wound channel information is important to the shooter so that he can determine how his load performs in the field. A wound channel—the path created by the bullet within the carcass—includes the exit hole, although it is clear that much of the channel, including the hole itself, is made *indirectly* by the bullet.

Experienced hunters will recall numerous exit holes in big and small game that were far larger than the expansion possibilities of the bullet they used. A few years ago, I examined the carcass of a deer harvested with a 300 Winchester Magnum rifle. The exit hole in the rib cage was about two inches across. The 30-caliber bullet of the 300 Magnum, about a third of an inch across, did not flatten out to two full inches. It did not, therefore, directly make the exit hole in the rib cage of the deer. What did? The best answer we have is shock wave, for lack of a more descriptive term. High-speed photography has provided us with photographs of bullets striking objects, as well as pictures of bullets in flight. There is no doubt that attending the bullet are various shock waves, which in front of the bullet, punch the hole. Of course, the shock wave was created by the bullet, so the bullet's particular function was responsible for the wound channel.

That is why bullet construction as well as shape are important to exterior ballistics. Early in this chapter, it was noted that ballistic coefficient is more important than sectional density in terms of a bullet's ability to retain velocity and energy. But there is no doubt that the sectional density of a projectile has much to do with the shape of the resulting wound channel. Bullets of high sectional density seem to penetrate better than bullets of low sectional density, which immediately reflects on wound channel.

The 226 Barnes QT is a wildcat cartridge of small caliber that is known for its deep penetration. It is built on a necked down and fire-formed 257 Roberts case or 7mm Mauser case. With a .226-inch diameter, it can be considered 22 caliber, although it can be argued that it is 23 caliber since it goes over .225-inches; mathematical rounding off could bring it into the next link on the caliber chain. The bullet's virtue, however, lies in its length, not its velocity, which is generally around 2600 to about 2700 fps mv. Its 125-grain bullet is about 1 1/4 inches long, and has been witnessed to pass totally through the chest cavity of a caribou. One shooter reported that the bullet traveled completely through a bull moose. High sectional density would have to be credited with such penetration powers for this small bullet.

Different bullets create entirely different wound channels. Always a surprise to me is the much-maligned round ball. A large-caliber round ball makes a long wound channel, much longer than a shooter might guess. I have seen a .530-inch round ball out of a 54-caliber muzzleloader shoot from one side of the chest cavity to the other on a bull elk at close range. One factor at

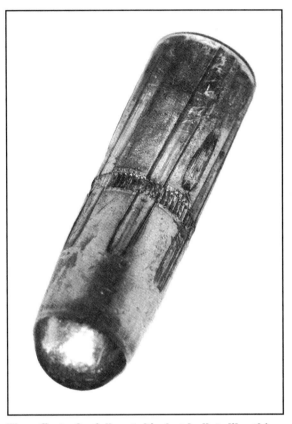

The effect of a full-metal-jacket bullet, like this 300-grain RWS 375 caliber taken from a Cape Buffalo, lies in penetration and bone breakage—more than instant delivery of energy to one specific body location.

work here is bullet integrity. The pure lead round ball, because of its high molecular cohesion, tends to stick together as a unit rather than fragmenting. Fragmentation causes bullets to produce short wound channels.

A bullet should do the best possible job on the type of game being hunted. That means matching construction of the projectile to the medium in which it must travel. A super tough bullet that does not open up is all wrong for deer-sized game, because this bullet fails to impart its energy in the target. It tends to punch through the game, leaving a narrow wound channel. Much of the bullet's energy is transferred to the landscape behind the animal.

On the other hand, an extremely tough bullet,

even an FMJ, may be necessary to reach the vitals on truly large or thick-skinned quarry, such as Cape buffalo or rhino. Most of us won't be going after either of these, but we still have to be cautious with bullet selection. A varmint bullet for any big-game cartridge, such as the 30-06, is wrong for big game because it is too fragile. It is meant to "blow up," not stay together.

An acquaintance of mine liked to use 110-grain varmint bullets in his 30-06 for antelope. Pronghorns are neither large nor thick-skinned, and since my friend is a good shot, he had no problem when the 110-grain lightly constructed bullets hit home—until one day when he hit the front shoulder instead of the chest region. Fortunately, he was successful putting two more bullets into the buck. The first bullet had come apart with little penetration and minor effect on the quarry.

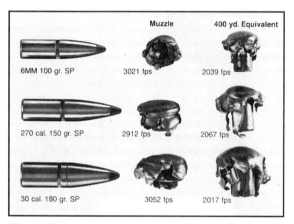

The delivery of ballistic energy is not merely a matter of potency at the muzzle—downrange delivery is another factor. These bullets show the effect of striking velocity on the shape of the projectile at the muzzle and all the way out to 400 yards.

As Colonel Whelen pointed out, the weight, shape and velocity of the bullet dictate the size and shape of the wound channel. There is no such thing as a perfect wound channel. A long, straight wound channel of modest width may be perfect for harvesting a medium-sized game animal, while a far shorter, wider wound channel may be better for quickly dispatching a smaller animal. A very narrow, but extremely long wound channel, as made by a tough-jacketed or FMJ bullet, may be necessary to reach the vitals of dangerous game, as well as break the bones to deter locomotion of that animal—especially locomotion straight at the hunter.

TRAJECTORY

An obvious factor in external ballistics is the path that the bullet follows from the muzzle to its final destination. The curve that a bullet takes is called a *parabola*. If the muzzle of the rifle is held horizontal to the earth, the bullet, even a high-speed missile, will strike the ground after a relatively short distance. That's why the muzzle is elevated somewhat when a rifle is sighted in. The idea is to take advantage of the parabola, whatever it may be.

It's a shame when hunters of open places, i.e., plains or mountains, sight a long-range rifle in dead-on for 100 yards. They destroy the ability of that rifle to function over a greater distance with no hold-over necessary for a perfect hit. The opposite sight-in—patterning bullets at very long range—is equally unfortunate, because the projectile must travel quite high above the line-of-sight in order to strike a distant bull's-eye. This means that an animal may be hit too high, or the bullet may sail over its back.

Furthermore, high-shooting occurs at both uphill and downhill angles. It may seem illogical, but it's true. And it's a matter of trigonometry, not gravity. No one is good enough to judge precisely how high a bullet will strike above the norm when a downhill or uphill angle is encountered. The smart rifleman simply knows this for a fact and guards against it by holding a little lower on these angled shots.

One deer season a few years ago, I had not filled my tag and there were only a couple days left to do that. I got up early in the morning and headed for a mountainous area that I knew held good numbers of mule deer. I found myself in the upper reaches of the range when my 10X50 B&L binoculars picked out a 4×4 mule deer buck. The buck knew I was there, too, and he climbed up, up out of the canyon. I could not get a clear shot because of the pine trees between us. I waited. The deer continued to climb upward and soon was well above me, standing in front of a huge dirt backdrop. I took a prone position over a fallen log, rested the forearm of the rifle on the log, moved the scope to 10X and took aim. Although the deer was now at long range, I held the crosswire low on the chest area and fired. The bullet struck only a few inches below the spine. Although I had accounted for angle, the effect was greater than I had anticipated. Had I not considered angle at all, the bullet would have zoomed over the deer.

SIGHTING IN

Each given bullet at its particular velocity requires its own sight-in. Fortunately, however, there is an acceptable range of forgiveness. The accompanying sight-in chart, simplified for easy use, takes this latitude into account. Changing bullets can of course alter trajectory. A 30-06 shooting a 150-grain boat-tail bullet shoots dead-on at about 270 yards by sighting in to hit three inches high at 100 yards. This bullet, at 3000 fps mv with handloads, travels flat enough to allow hold-on sighting for deer or antelope out to 300 yards. If, in the same rifle, a 220-grain round-nose bullet loaded at 2500 fps mv is sighted in three inches high at 100 yards, the bullet will fall into the line-of-sight path at closer to 200 yards, not 300, and that's quite a difference. Don't short-change your rifle by sighting in below its ballistic capability. Don't short-change yourself,

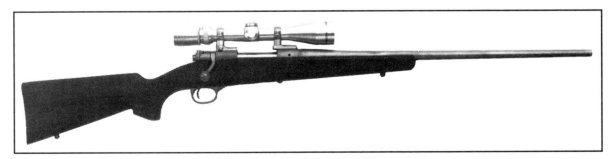

This is what long-range ballistics is all about—an accurate scope-sighted rifle like this Model 70 Winchester.

either, by sighting your rifle beyond its ballistic capability.

There are many ways to achieve a flatter trajectory. The most obvious is velocity increase. Smokeless powder cartridges, such as the 30-30, were considered a marvel for their flat-shooting nature when compared with the blackpowder pumpkin-throwers of the late 19th century. Today, the 30-30 is considered a middle-of-the-road cartridge, if that, regarding trajectory. A flat shooter like the 270 Weatherby Magnum can be sighted dead-on at a full 300 yards and the bullet won't even strike three inches high at 100 yards. But the old 45-70 was fortunate to enjoy a 100 yard sight-in with its original load.

High velocity aids flatness of trajectory, but bullet shape is also helpful in getting a projectile to hug the line-of-sight a bit closer. The most streamlined bullets nowadays are of the VLD (Very Low Drag) design. These shapely missiles are so long for their caliber that they can't be

Drag is an important aspect of bullet ballistics. This is a VLD bullet, which stands for "very low drag." This 105-grain 6mm bullet even looks "racy." A high rate of twist is necessary for stabilization, something like 1:8.

shot in ordinary rifles. I tested a special 6mm rifle using a VLD 105-grain bullet; a 1:8 rate of twist was required for stabilization. The VLD bullet is, at the moment, a long-range target proposition. Its mission is to punch holes in paper with minimal drift and hold-over. But its target construction and tiny hollow-point opening are not ideal for big-game hunting because reliable expansion cannot be guaranteed.

The boat-tail design also promotes a flatter-shooting attitude. In the past, shooters believed that the boat-tail bullet had no trajectory advantage until it reached a very long range of several hundred yards. This is not true. With the boat-tail design, modest improvements in trajectory are seen at only 200 yards, depending on the bullet used, its muzzle velocity, etc. Any shooter can prove that the boat-tail bullet picks up a little trajectory. All he needs to do is sight-in with a flat-base bullet for 200 or 300 yards, then shoot again at the same target with a boat-tail bullet of the same weight and velocity.

This is not to suggest that boat-tails are the only way to go. There are too many fine flat-base bullets to say that. Besides, we're often speaking in terms of an inch or two trajectory advantage with the boat-tail (along with higher arrival velocity and energy). Shoot the bullet that is most accurate in your rifle. It may prove to be a flat-base projectile. Also, it's obvious that the overall shape of the bullet promotes flatness of trajectory. That is why we have spitzer and spire-point configurations as well. Furthermore, bullets of blunt-nose design are necessary in big-bore rifles with tubular magazines.

Ammunition manufacturers have recently become more sensitive about trajectory, which has led to the introduction of some factory loads designed to extend range. Examples of these include the handsome Winchester Silvertip bullet with its boat-tail design, as well as Extended Range ammo from Remington.

BLACKPOWDER BALLISTICS

Blackpowder power for big-game hunting hinges on a large-caliber projectile of good weight at medium velocity. Factors of sectional density and ballistic coefficient put the standard muz-

STARTER SIGHT-IN CHART

The following figures represent good starting points for a few popular cartridges. The shooter might wish to sight his rifles with these recommendations, later refining sight-in at a preferred distance.

22 Long Rifle

(40-grain bullet, 1250 fps mv)
1. Sight in at 20 yards.
2. Move out to 85 yards. Zero group at this range.
3. At 100 yards, bullets will fall about 2 inches low.

22 Win. Mag. Rimfire (WMR)

(40-grain bullet at 1900 fps mv)
1. Sight in at 25 yards.
2. Move target to 150 yards for final sighting.
3. Bullet will strike about 2.5–3.0 inches high at 100 yards with this sight-in and of course will be dead-on at 150 yards, which is a good maximum distance for this cartridge.

22-250 Remington

(50-grain bullet at 3900 fps mv)
1. Sight in initially at 25 yards.
2. Move target to 100 yards and sight so group lands about 2.5 inches high at this distance.
3. Rifle will now zero at 300 yards and bullets will hit about 8 inches low at 400 yards.

243 Winchester

(100-grain bullet at 3000 fps mv)
1. Sight in 1 inch high at 50 yards.
2. Move target to 100 yards, print groups 3 inches high at this distance.
3. Bullet will now zero at 275 yards and hit about 3 inches low at 300 yards.

270 Winchester

(130-grain bullet at 3100 fps mv)
1. Sight to group bullets 1 inch high at 50 yards.
2. Move target to 100 yards, sight to hit 3 inches high.
3. Bullets will group on target at about 275 yards, around 3 inches low at 300 yards.

7mm Remington Magnum*

(162-grain bullet, 3165 fps mv)
1. Sight to strike 1 inch high at 50 yards.
2. Move target to 100 yards and sight so bullets hit 3 inches high at this distance.
3. Bullets will group dead on at 300 yards and 8.5 inches low at 400 yards.

30-06 Springfield

(handloaded 180-grain bullet at 2800 fps mv)
1. Zero initially at 50 yards.
2. Move target out to 100 yards and print group 3 inches high at this range.
3. Rifle will be sighted in for 250 yards with bullets falling about 6 inches low at 300 yards.

The above recommendations realize the potential trajectory inherent in the popular cartridges listed. Other cartridges with similar ballistics can be sighted in similarly. The closer-range starting point is ideal for getting the rifle on paper with a minimum expense of ammunition. However, it is also ideal because in each case the rifle will print its groups relatively close to the second phase sight-in distance. As always, rifles vary. The averages shown here may not pertain to your individual rifle.

*The 7mm Remington Magnum load above is exactly as chronographed with a 162-grain RWS factory load. My own handloads have matched this velocity in my 7mm Rem. Mag. rifles.

zleloader projectile in the shade when compared with modern streamlined, jacketed missiles. Compare the ballistic coefficient of the popular 150-grain 30-caliber spitzer with that of a 54-caliber round ball. The 150-grain 30-caliber Sierra boat-tail has a coefficient of .394, while the .535-inch 225- grain round ball carries a coefficient of only .075. Blackpowder conicals are ballistically stronger, but a coefficient of .150 is considered good for these. Bullets for the rifled musket are more aerodynamic, especially for the heavyweight 45 caliber, but the initial statement stands: Blackpowder power comes from comparatively heavy projectiles that often start out larger in diameter than some modern bullets end up after expansion.

EXAMPLES OF MUZZLELOADER BALLISTICS

54-caliber round ball (.530 diameter, 225 grains)
1970 fps mv = 1939 foot-pounds of muzzle energy
1162 fps velocity at 100 yards = 675 foot-pounds of energy

58-caliber Thompson/Center Maxi-Ball (555 grains)
1351 fps mv = 2250 foot-pounds of muzzle energy
1100 fps velocity at 100 yards = 1492 foot-pounds of energy

BARREL LENGTH AND VELOCITY

One important factor of velocity is barrel length. Since velocity dictates both energy and trajectory, bullet speed is an important commodity. Knowingly reducing bullet speed is fine, provided there is a reason.

Long barrels can be bothersome, but the barrel of a rifle should be long enough to realize most of the ballistic potential of the cartridge. Over the years, it's been fashionable to provide a velocity loss figure for big-bore rifles. It usually goes like this: "For every inch of barrel cut off,

25 fps muzzle velocity will be lost." That's absolute fantasy. In the first place, individual rifles vary in the velocity they obtain from identical ammunition. Therefore, it is impossible to say how many fps will be lost when a rifle barrel is lopped off.

Furthermore, what about the cartridge? A magnum round burning more than 80 grains of powder is one thing. A smaller cartridge holding 50 grains of powder is quite another. Then there's cartridge design (again). If some rounds burn powder more efficiently than others, does it not follow that there will be a variation in velocity loss per barrel length among these various rounds?

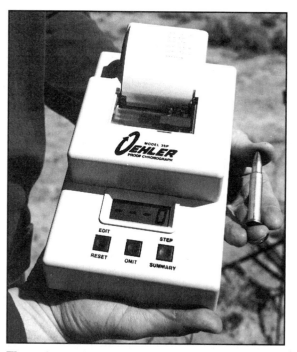

The only way to record exact velocities is with a chronograph, such as this high-tech Oehler 35P Proof model with instant readout.

Having chronographed rifles for over three decades, I've found that velocity loss per barrel length varies with all of the above factors. Here are some actual figures that were derived from chronographed data.

257 Weatherby Magnum (120-grain bullet handload w/IMR-4831 powder)

26-inch barrel	3415 fps mv
24-inch barrel	3226 fps mv

308 Winchester (180-grain bullet, factory load)

22-inch barrel	2533 fps mv
18.5-inch barrel	2529 fps mv

30-06 Springfield (150-grain bullet, handload w/W760 powder)

22-inch barrel	2900 fps mv
18.5-inch barrel	2608 fps mv

the 22-inch barrel got 2910 fps mv, while the 18.5 barrel dropped to 2703 fps with the identical load. Using IMR-4350 powder, the 22-inch barrel drove the 150-grain bullet at 2940 fps mv, while the 18.5-inch barrel got 2690 fps mv with the identical load.

The 257 Weatherby Magnum obviously suffered a significant velocity loss with the shorter barrel in this particular test. Both rifles, incidentally, were Mark V Weatherby models. The 30-06 also suffered high velocity loss when the barrel was pruned from 22 inches to 18.5

Each of these projectiles deals out its energy in a slightly different fashion. The all-lead round ball (far left) can penetrate surprisingly well in its 230-grain 54-caliber form, while the big 625-grain round-nose Minie next to it carries a great punch to the target. A similar Minie (far right) in 525-grain weight deals out less disruption per striking velocity than the flat-nosed 625-grain Minie to its left. The 150-grain 30-caliber bullet (center) is designed to deliver its punch through more bullet disruption than any of the lead projectiles.

The loads tested above were identical—out of the same box. The rifles, of course, were not. However, I have chronographed a single rifle while cutting the barrel off an inch at a time, and many variables still pertain. The exact powder used is one of those factors. The two 30-06 rifles tested above did not show the same degree of velocity loss with other powders. For example, using H-414 powder with the 150-grain bullet,

inches. But the 308 Winchester cartridge was not hurt so much when its barrel was truncated from 22 inches to 18.5 inches. Finally, observe that the 25 foot-per-second figure sometimes quoted didn't show up with any of the test rifles. The 257 Weatherby lost 94.5 fps per inch of barrel cut off. The 308 Winchester lost only four feet per second with the particular factory ammo tested.

KEY FACTORS OF RIFLE ACCURACY

7 What is accuracy? It all depends. A rifle for the brush that never sees duty past 50 yards is plenty accurate if it places four-inch groups at 100 yards. The serious plains hunter, on the other hand, who may earn one opportunity at a long-distance pronghorn in a week of hunting may as well have a South American bolo if his rifle won't produce better groups than that. And the benchrest shooter—if he doesn't want to be laughed off the range—has to consider only rifles that do quarter-inch 100-yard groups or better.

Demands for close-grouping of missiles has changed over the years. Accuracy of long ago was more in the realm of wishful thinking than reality. Consider this quote from an ancient battlefield record: "There dieth not so much as one man, for the harquebussiers content themselves with making a noyse." This was after a volley of 10,000 shots was fired! With some of the early British Army muskets, you couldn't count on hitting a cathedral dead center at 600 yards. If you aimed at the steeple, you might hit the door.

Things of course have improved. Between 1793 and 1805, the Reverend Alexander Forsyth worked on his percussion cap, which promoted the invention of a fairly accurate percussion musket. By the mid-1800s, accuracy much as we know it now was established. We consider one-inch groups at 100 yards satisfactory for a well-made, bolt-action hunting rifle; half-inch groups become the mark of super accuracy from a firearm (except for precision benchrest competition). In the 19th century, 10-shot groups of only one inch center to center at 220 yards were shot with scoped target rifles, especially the "40 rod gun," a rifle that could weigh 30 or more pounds. It was the forerunner of our benchrest rifle.

The myriad criteria pertaining to firearm accuracy were seriously studied in the 19th century, as they are today. That search for greater accuracy is perhaps the most interesting aspect of firearm advancement.

An expert of many years proclaimed not long ago that a free-floated barrel provided the best possible accuracy. Another expert promised that only pressure-pointed barrels shot their best. And a third shooting expert guaranteed that barrel bedding had little to do with accuracy. A local gunsmith who gave lectures on rifle accuracy declared adamantly: There is only one way to gain full accuracy potential from a good barrel— pressure point it, using an integral raised fiberglass pad near the forend of the barrel channel. Such juxtaposed viewpoints are commonplace.

Forget such opinions. Rifles are individual in nature because they are fraught with variables,

What causes accuracy? Certainly a precise bullet—round or otherwise—is necessary.

from exact bore dimension to barrel flex. When you hear or read of a single device or method that guarantees accuracy across the board, shun such mental mayonnaise. It will only smear the truth.

Dr. Mann, famous student of shooting, concluded that accuracy was a product of good bullets from precise barrels. That's true as far as it goes, but it doesn't go far enough. Earlier chapters have spoken of cartridge design and accuracy, for example. What about barrel bedding, triggers, the stiffness of the action, and other factors?

The idea of the Western film hero trimming

the moustache off the bad guy with a well-placed revolver bullet from 100 yards is no more true than some stories I've heard. One fellow proclaimed through the campfire smoke that his 30-06 was so accurate he could consistently hit antelope at 700 yards, even in the wind.

On the other hand, consider how much flak the benchrest boys and other accuracy aficionados catch from shooters who consider good accuracy the ability of rifle and rifleman to put ten shots in a washtub at 100 yards. These fellows just laugh when they hear of under-an-inch clusters at 100 yards. When a magazine article printed that I owned a custom hunting rifle capable of delivering three-shot one-inch groups at 200 yards, I was greeted with a few "doubt letters" as well as a local challenge from a fellow shooting club member. The local challenger and I met at the range. The rifle in question was feeling its oats that day—the three-shot group at 200 yards measured .75 inch.

On "average," a well-tuned, bolt-action hunting rifle firing proper ammunition should manage about a minute-of-angle accuracy. A minute of angle is 1.047 inches at 100 yards; but for our purposes, it means one-inch center-to-center groups at 100 yards, two-inch groups at 200, three-inch groups at 300 yards, and so forth. Dale Storey, a gunmaker who is devoted to building accurate rifles, has produced many rifles that slice that level of accuracy in half.

The most accurate factory rifle I know of is the Sako Varminter in caliber 22 PPC USA or 6 PPC USA. One-third-inch groups at 100 yards are commonplace. One-fourth-inch 100-yard groups with this rifle aren't uncommon either. Using a benchrest rifle in 6 PPC USA, Dr. Lou Palmisano shot an unofficial (but club-verified) group of one-third inch at 300 yards. He used a custom 70-grain bullet backed by 28.5 grains of H-322 powder. The smallest group of my lifetime was a five-shot, half-inch cluster made at 300 meters using a 300-meter competition rifle with 6mm 105-grain VLD (Very Low Drag) bullets.

THE ACCURATE BARREL

A good threading job with tight fit, minimal headspace so a "go" gauge can just be felt as the action is closed, a chamber cut with a match-grade reamer, lapped lugs for precise bearing surface, and a clean meeting of bolt face and breech are basics of rifle accuracy. Furthermore, the throat or leade of the chamber must be cut correctly. This aspect of barreling requires gunsmith knowledge and care. The bullet should be presented to the chamber in a concentric fashion and held in that attitude awaiting its ride downbore. Naturally, the rifling must be precise. A barrel may shoot better if the rifling is lapped, which smooths overly sharp lands. Sometimes a bore requires "shooting in," whereby the lapping is accomplished with bullets.

A specific number of lands and grooves is not essential to accuracy. Some multi-grooved barrels are accurate, but not all. A 100-yard 10-shot group of only .138 inch center to center was fired by Ferris Pindell. The rifle, a custom 222 Remington Magnum, had three-groove rifling.

The muzzle crown is important. It protects the rifling from damage and helps to achieve a uniform effect on the base of the missile as it departs the bore. The crown of the muzzle must be clean. After all, this portion of the bore is the last contact the bullet makes with the rifling before it heads downrange. Crown damage can impair accuracy. Sometimes the recrowning of a muzzle restores lost accuracy.

Rifling twist must be correct for bullet stability. Twist has parameters, however, as established in Chapter 5 on bullet stabilization. It is not a matter of a bore stabilizing only one bullet, but rather a modest range of bullets. As long as

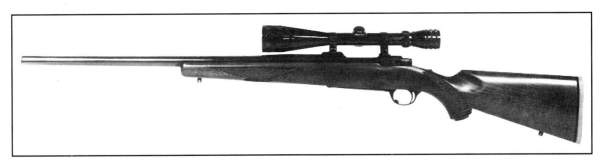

Accuracy is also within the system that finally sends the bullet downrange, i.e., the rifle. Precision within that system promotes tight bullet grouping. This Ruger Model 77 (M-77V) rifle is built for accuracy, then chambered for an accurate cartridge: the 308 Winchester.

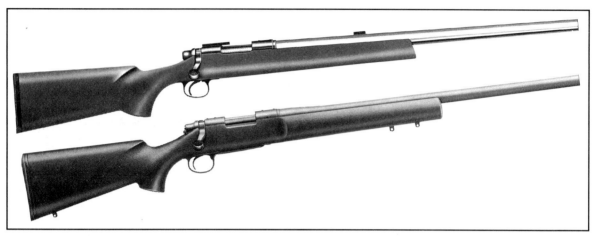

Two accurate Remington rifles are: the Model 40-XBBR KS Bench Rest (above)—a bolt-action, single-shot with Kevlar synthetic stock; and the Model 700 Police (223 Remington or 308 Winchester), with heavy barrel and stiff action, two ingredients that lead to tight bullet grouping. Stability is gained through weight.

the bullet has proper gyroscopic effect, it will fly point-on when less than perfect, and even damaged bullets maintain acceptable accuracy. The good barrel is precisely rifled and carries the correct twist for bullet stabilization. The bore should be straight, although exceptions have occurred when slightly crooked barrels produced acceptable groups. But straight barrels are best.

Barrel Bedding. Free-floating a barrel is a good way to begin the quest for rifle accuracy. A pressure point can be tried later on a free-floated barrel. But if the barrel is fully bedded in the channel, or even pressure-pointed, later free-floating requires additional gunsmithing. Dale Storey's modern plains rifle, which is made with a rigid stock/action and heavy Douglas match-grade barrel, is initially free-floated and then tested for accuracy. My particular model required later pressure-pointing for best accuracy. After placing a thin leather pad between barrel and forend, accuracy improved markedly.

Free-floating supports uniformity because there is no barrel contact over most of the channel. The barrel is liberated to vibrate at will. Expansion from heat does not alter the relationship of the barrel to its channel because the free-floated barrel does not touch the channel. Floating can work with all barrel weights. Also, at-

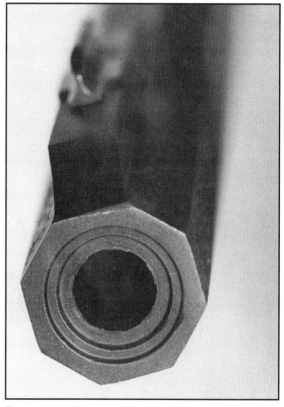

Damage at the muzzle can often cause accuracy deterioration. This muzzle is recessed to prevent damage at the crown area.

mospheric changes, such as humidity and consequent stock expansion, have less effect on a floated barrel.

Barrel Weight. Lightweight barrels can be accurate. While some flyweight rifles have proven accurate at the bench, generally these rifles give fair accuracy results in the field because they do not "settle down." Benchrested, a couple thin-barreled rifles I shot resulted in half-inch 100-yard groups.

Despite this, heavy barrels are used for *consistent* accuracy. In the first place, heavy barrels lend stability because of their mass. They are said to be less sensitive to bedding (they certainly heat up less rapidly than thin-walled barrels). And heavy barrels are generally more rigid than thin ones. However, all barrels, light or heavy, do sag. This is called "barrel flex." In measuring the "droop" of one 22-rimfire target barrel at rest in a vise, the barrel sagged by about .010 inch at the muzzle.

Exterior Barrel Pressure. To maintain accurate sight-in and tight groupings, don't rest the barrel on a hard surface when shooting. In a test using three rifles (one a 22 rimfire), the bullet group climbed higher as exterior pressure was applied on the barrel. The 22 Long Rifle bullet climbed almost one foot higher than its original sight-in at 100 yards when the forepart of the barrel rested firmly on a hard surface under considerable pressure. Furthermore, groups opened up when the barrel, rather than the forestock, was rested.

Barrel Life. "Truths" concerning barrel wear are still under scrutiny. A long-standing belief that gas cutting destroys the groove of the rifling is especially under attack. Inspections of halved barrels show very little wear in the groove. At this point, we don't know all of the factors present in barrel wear. Heat is certainly a culprit, and rapid fire can reduce barrel life. However, as noted previously, extension of the leade due to throat erosion may not ruin a barrel nearly as quickly as once thought. In many instances, seating the bullet very slightly outward in the case has restored lost accuracy in a deteriorating

Triggers also help a rifle gain in potential accuracy: the double-set triggers of this Zollinger custom rifle can be set for an extremely light let-off.

rifle barrel. While bore wear does eventually destroy accuracy, more study is necessary to determine precisely which factors are at work and how to thwart them.

Bore Condition. Benchrest shooters clean the dickens out of their barrels. They use bore guides to prevent damage to the chamber area. They use solvents and bore brushes to remove metal as well as powder fouling. The use of Flitz™—a mild abrasive compound that removes copper fouling—is condoned by some precision

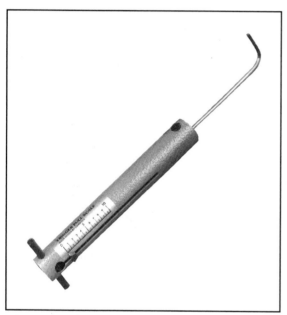

Concerned riflemen can check their own trigger pull weights with a trigger pull scale, such as this one from RCBS.

shooters. I use Flitz™ in all of my rifles, and haven't noticed any bore deterioration. However, after using Flitz™, I remove it from the bore with solvent before firing the rifle.

Lightly oiling the bore is wise for storage, but for shooting, a dry bore is best. Some tests conclude there is no effect from oil in the bore of a rifle; other tests disagree. My experience revealed accuracy deterioration with some rifles when shooting them with oily bores.

THE ACCURATE ACTION

Very accurate 22-rimfire rifles (and pistols) have been built with semiautomatic actions. However, the bolt action is king among accurate rifles because of its rigidity and its ability to "lock up" a cartridge in the breech.

Lock Time. Lock time—the interval between the disengagement of the sear and the detonation of the primer—is essential to accuracy. The shorter that time is, the less possibility of error from rifle motion. In an attempt to increase this lock-up characteristic, a new bolt-action design has been patented. It is the Poff/Palmisano action, and has a 45-degree locking lug aspect. In one stringent test run by H.B. White labs, additional projectiles were installed in the bore to be fired out by the bullet in the cartridge. Even though the barrel actually blew downrange, the action was not "set back." This is the sort of action strength and rigidity now being studied for use in super-accurate rifles of the future.

Action Bedding. The action should be bedded tightly in the stock mortise. But even this is not an absolute. Rifles with tightly bedded barrels but free-floated actions have demonstrated accuracy. However, benchrest rifles demand a unified action/stock relationship. To guarantee rigidity throughout the action area, the benchrest rifle is usually a single-shot bolt-action. There is no magazine interruption. A steel plate beneath the bolt promotes action rigidness. The action can be carefully bedded into a wooden stock or fitted in fiberglass. Accuracy is achieved either way, but "glassing" the action, or even gluing it in place, promises a precise fit.

STOCK MATERIAL

Wood has always been an excellent stock material. The super-accurate Sako Varminter has a wooden stock. Wood does flex, of course, just as barrels flex. Synthetic stocks can have less flex, depending upon their design and composition. Some synthetic stocks are extremely stable, however, more stable than wood, and laminated stocks in my tests were found to be so.

Not all synthetic stocks are moisture-resistant, however. Some are quite the opposite and can change constitution with the weather.

Dale Storey checks the target with a spotting scope mounted on a rifle stock. Good benchrest form and a solid benchrest promote accuracy.

Laminated stocks must be properly finished for a correct seal against the elements. An unfinished laminated stock may eventually have problems with separations and may even warp.

SIGHTS

The telescopic rifle sight is first rate for realizing accuracy potential. My hunting rifles wear variable scopes that take advantage of both lower and higher power bands. When hunting, I keep a scope on low power for field-of-view advantage, but zip it to maximum magnification whenever opportunity allows.

The exactness of bullet placement increases with magnification of the target. Anyone who doesn't believe this fact need only attend a benchrest match. Scopes of 20X and even 36X dominate when precision of bullet placement is at stake.

Pick the right reticle. If you hunt brush or timber exclusively, choose a large dot or heavy crosswire. I prefer a very small dot or duplex reticle with fine center wires. Potential rifle accuracy is realized when the target can be seen clearly, which means that the reticle must not obliterate the aimpoint. If your reticle subtends two inches at 100 yards, defining a one-inch bull's-eye is difficult, if not impossible. See Chapter 8 for more on sights.

LAPPING SCOPE RINGS

The mount is also important to accuracy. While most modern mounts hold the scope in a precise fashion, it is difficult to guarantee perfect alignment of the rings. Shooters who strive for accuracy may lap the scope rings (or have the job done by a gunsmith). It's a simple process: A round metal bar of one-inch diameter is placed in the one-inch scope rings. The bar, laced with polishing compound, is rotated in the rings. From time to time, the rings are tightened on the bar. The insides of the rings are thereby trued up, with discrepancies polished away. Now the scope will be more precisely supported in the rings, with even pressure applied all around. Lapping in scope rings is a good idea for the benchrest rifle shooter who is willing to try everything for ultimate accuracy. But for hunting rifles, I've

lapped my last scope in.

THE TARGET

At the shooting range one day, I looked at a 200-yard group that was not at all exceptional. But the rifle had been built for accuracy, embodying many of the features discussed here. Plus, it was fitted with a high-power scope. "What would you do?" the shooter asked me, "to improve the accuracy of this rifle?" I suggested that he start with a better target. The black six-inch bull's-eye would not allow for precision aiming. My own sight-in and accuracy-check targets are the same big black bull's-eye, but with one difference—there is a narrow white cross in the center of the black bull, formed with two stick-on labels. This narrow cross gives a precise aimpoint, which helps the shooter hold his sights on the same spot shot after shot.

AMBIENT LIGHT

Light diminishes steadily in proportion to the square of the distance from the target. Light rays

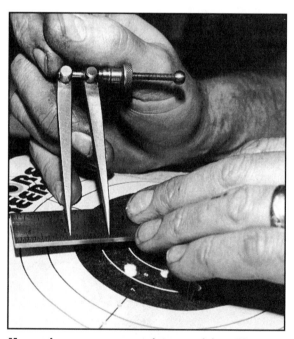

Measuring accuracy requires precision. Here calipers are used to determine the distance between the centers of the two holes that are farthest apart in the group.

also scatter. A candle flame one foot away from an object equals one foot-candle of light. Move the candle two feet from the object and the light has been reduced to one-fourth foot candle. Move the object 10 feet away and the resulting light to the object is only 1/100 of one foot-candle.

Image sizes perceived by the human eye diminish greatly with distance too. We can assume that at 50 yards, the size of the target diminishes to 1/50 optical dimension. The size of the image is to the size of the object as the distance of the image is to the distance of the object. The shooter in pursuit of top-grade accuracy from his rifle recognizes these two interlocking factors—that light diminishes rapidly with distance to the target, and that perception of the image grows small with distance. A scope thwarts the latter problem. As for lighting, if you want to test a rifle for its potential, shoot on a bright day and try to orient your target to receive the most available light.

FACTORS THAT AFFECT AMMUNITION

Cartridge Design. As discussed in Chapter 3, I used to place little credence in the "accurate cartridge" theory. The reason was that I had owned and tested too many accurate rifles chambered for cartridges of mundane design. However, while it's true that cartridges of ordinary design prove accurate in good rifles, these rounds never win serious benchrest matches today.

As previously discussed, the 22 PPC USA and the 6 PPC USA embody the major tenets for premium accuracy: a short, squat case of medium powder capacity; a short, but adequate neck; very little body taper; a 30-degree shoulder; the use of a small rifle primer, undersized concentric flash holes, and a strong case.

If you had to single out one cartridge as the most accurate in the world, it would be the 6 PPC USA. The short, fat 6mm PPC is a model for the meaning of accuracy, because the longer the case, the more difficult to draw it with uniformity of body wall thickness, and the greater the case stretch. Also, the shape of the powder charge is important to accuracy. A short, fat powder column is known to be best.

Cartridge Case Uniformity. Case-wall uni-

Two cartridges built with accuracy in mind are the 22 PPC USA (left) and the Remington 7mm Bench Rest with 140-grain factory load. Both enjoy the small-capacity short case associated with accurate cartridges.

formity, case-neck thickness, squareness of the cartridge head and other criteria attend the accurate case. The recoil axis of the cartridge head is coincidental with the recoil axis of the barrel. Case polishing is a good idea, but buildup of media alters powder capacity.

In small-calibered, high-intensity cartridges, media residue can cause blown primers through overly high pressures. Residue buildup reduces powder space within the case, raising pressures. Following tumbling, wash cartridge cases with a household cleaner and water. Then dry them thoroughly. After air-drying, use a cotton swab to capture leftover moisture.

For top-flight accuracy, it is wise to make certain that primer pockets are uniform—use a Sinclair Primer Pocket Uniformer. Square-up and clean the interior portion of the flash hole with a Sinclair flash hole deburring instrument. For hunting accuracy, flash hole uniformity is no problem. However, little time and energy are required to make and keep a cartridge case uniform.

Standard Deviation. Both factory loads and handloads must be made carefully in order for accuracy to be achieved. A modern chronograph allows a shooter to find out more about his ammo than just its raw velocity. Some chronographs offer an automatic readout of standard deviation. This factor can also be figured mathematically.

Standard deviation will not prove accuracy. After all, a poor bore, a badly bedded rifle, an unstable or imprecise bullet, or one of many other factors may ruin accuracy. But standard deviation will show how reliable ammo is via a simple number. The number gives a good idea of how much variation exists in the ammo. The lower the number, the better. For example, ammo with a standard deviation of only 10 or 20 fps supports the fact that this ammo is consistent from one shot to the next. Ammo with a high standard deviation figure suggests unreliability from shot to shot.

It is fashionable at present to downplay standard deviation. However, any shooter will agree that if the velocity of individual rounds in a batch of ammo varies widely, good groups are just about impossible attain. Suppose you own a 30-06, and suppose the velocity in a given batch of rifle ammo varies by a couple hundred feet per second, would you expect bullets to cluster closely from this sort of velocity spread? Hardly.

Base damage to a conical projectile tends to throw it off course. This Minie ball was purposely damaged and tested, the result of which was its landing out of the normal group.

Bullet Seating Depth. The manner in which the bullet greets the leade of the chamber can affect accuracy. Freebore (a long-throated chamber) supposedly reduces accuracy potential. Perhaps. However, I had two rifles built to test this theory. Both were very accurate. After establishing their accuracy, I had the barrels pulled and put the reamer back to work, creating a long throat. Both rifles shot as well with freebore as they had without.

However, for grain-of-sand accuracy, be aware of bullet seating depth. My mentor of benchrest shooting, Dr. Palmisano, starts with a seating depth of .015 inch from bullet tip to rifling land. As the rifle throat erodes, bullets may have to be seated outward to make up for the change in distance from the bullet tip to the rifling land.

Some rifles seem very sensitive to bullet seating depth. A friend unsuccessfully tried just about every trick to make his 6.5/06 shoot accurately. Once he altered the bullet seating depth, groups immediately improved from 1.25 inches at 100 yards to .65 inch.

Chamber Pressure. Shooters are sometimes surprised to find that the most accurate load in a pet rifle is not one with a reduced powder charge, but rather a full-scale (but safe) load. My own top accuracy loads in both 22 PPC and 6mm PPC are with full, safe powder charges. Powders seem to establish a "balance point" with the case and the bullet. Once the balance is exceeded, accuracy is impaired. This happened with my 17 Remington. By cutting back a half grain with one particular powder, accuracy decidedly improved.

Individual rifles are unique in performance in spite of identical cartridges and loads. Many factors pertain to muzzle velocity and pressure variation in a given rifle, including the throat of the chamber, actual bore diameter and consequent bore drag, true bullet diameter, rate of twist (bore friction), height of land (bore friction), smoothness of the bore (friction again) and cartridge neck thickness and length. Thick or overly long necks can raise pressures to the danger level. *Therefore, always trim cases to proper length.* Also pertinent are the bearing surface of the bullet due to its design (especially the shank

HOW TO RESTORE ACCURACY

A rifle that has been your best friend, shooting fantastic groups, may suddenly go sour. Nobody knows all of the answers to this problem, but here are a few hints for restoring accuracy in that favorite rifle which has fallen from grace.

1. Check for throat wear. If the leade of the rifle has advanced, loading projectiles minutely farther forward in the neck may prove beneficial.

2. Clean the bore. Be sure that metal and powder fouling are removed.

3. Check for a warped stock. If the stock has warped, the barrel channel may be introducing varying pressures to the barrel. A rebedding job may be in order. Ask your gunsmith to try free-floating first, but be willing to have him install a pressure point if floating does not restore accuracy.

4. Have a gunsmith check for a change in headspace. If a headspacing problem exists, have it corrected.

5. Check for loose bolts and screws. An accurate rifle can start to fail when the relationship between action/barrel and stock alters due to loose screws or bolts.

6. Check scope mounts. Loose scope mounts will destroy bullet grouping.

7. Check the scope for damage. Before having extensive work done on your rifle, remove the scope and install another in its place for group testing. If the new scope brings the rifle back to its former grouping ability, the original scope was the problem.

8. Check your ammo. If your new handloads don't shoot as well as previous ones, a change in component characteristics could be the culprit. Generally, slight alterations in powder lots or primers will not affect accuracy appreciably, but some rifles are finicky. Try different ammo before working on your rifle.

9. Check for damage from cleaning. Bore and action cleaning are essential to continued rifle accuracy and longevity, but damage can be inflicted inadvertently. Have a gunsmith check the lands for cleaning rod damage.

10. Inspect the muzzle crown if your rifle has gone awry suddenly. If the muzzle of the rifle seems worn, or in any way damaged, a recrowning job could improve accuracy.

---

of the projectile), the hardness of the bullet jacket, and the actual dimensions of the chamber. The modern shooter should keep all these factors in mind.

Concentric, Balanced Bullets. A book the size of an unabridged dictionary could be written on the design, construction and physics of the bullet. An accurate bullet is many things at once. It is concentric, and will prove itself so on a spinner. Although it is true that a stabilized bullet, with proper gyroscopic motion, will fly to the bull's-eye in spite of non-uniformity, the very best bullets—those that win benchrest matches—are concentric and balanced, with uniform jacket thickness all around and homogeneous lead cores. The bullet base, especially, is undamaged and clean, because the base seems to affect "steering" more so than the nose.

Hollow-pointed jacketed bullets are highly accurate, the most accurate having very small (but not closed) nose cavities. Reduced accuracy results when hollow points have large nose openings.

Monolithic bullets like the Barnes X-Bullet have no core/jacket problems because there is no lead core. The Barnes is made entirely of copper (see Chapter 4). Initial accuracy and bullet-integrity tests for monolithic bullets are encouraging. The jacket/core problem experienced with some hunting projectiles cannot occur with the X-Bullet, since of course there is no core to divorce itself from a jacket. Weight retention of 95 to 98 percent prevailed in tests. Field autopsies revealed long wound channels. On the other hand, the finest groups in the world have been achieved by bullets with lead cores and metal jackets. Sierra, Hornady, Speer, Nosler and other bulletmakers all produce jacketed projectiles that achieve excellent accuracy.

Powder Measure Technique. The best groups in the world have been made with powder measured charges, not scale-weighed charges. The precision shooter, however, knows how to use a measure—no haphazard affair. Methods differ widely among benchresters, but uniformity prevails. A routine is established, followed.

One of my measures seems to work best when I raise the handle slowly but fully, keeping a hand on the side of the unit to prevent any sideways slippage of the rotor. Then the handle is brought back, with the powder charge falling through the drop tube and into the mouth of the cartridge case.

Accurate loads can be produced with a powder measure because powder is not 100 percent efficient. A minute difference in a powder charge cannot be ballistically detected, not even with the finest chronograph.

Primers. In testing the PPCs for accuracy, the primers made a significant difference. That led to a study of primer accuracy in my 17 Remington. In the 17, switching from a standard small-rifle primer to a benchrest small-rifle primer definitely upgraded accuracy. Accuracy also improved in two 7mm Magnum test rifles—both of them liked magnum primers.

Primer selection is another of the do-it-by-shooting choices a shooter needs to make. By keeping all loading components constant and switching only primers, records of groups may reveal that your rifle prefers a given primer.

Factory Ammo. Not long ago, factory ammo was not as accurate as handloaded ammo. Manufacturers studied the problem, and today we have the most accurate factory ammo the world has ever known. A few examples of super-accurate factory ammo include: Federal Match, RWS Match, Winchester Supreme and Remington Extended Range.

TRIGGERS

Getting the greatest accuracy from a rifle involves a good trigger, with crisp letoff (break) and light pull. A trigger that requires too much pressure to break sear engagement disturbs the tranquility of the rifle. The shooter must be able to control the shot by squeezing a trigger that "lets go" without undue force. Of course, the trigger must be safe as well as light and crisp.

RECOIL

There is little direct correlation between accuracy and recoil. However, the best benchrest groups are fired from rifles having mild recoil. Recoil bothers the shooter a lot more than it disturbs the solidity of the rifle. High-speed bullets are in the barrel for just milliseconds; the barrel can rise before the bullet exits. But for all practical purposes, heavy-recoil rifles cannot be considered inaccurate directly because of the recoil.

OTHER FACTORS THAT AFFECT ACCURACY

This chapter did not include a discussion of 22-rimfire accuracy because it is a study all its own, involving nose slump, priming material distribution, region of disturbance (how the 22 bullet reacts to velocities above the speed of sound), bullet configuration, proper lead alloy, and many other criteria.

Other factors encompass the reaction of the bullet to the atmosphere, range altitude, temperature and wind. There are benchrest techniques to consider—feet flat on the ground, for example, rifle under control and returned to the same position shot after shot. Even shooting methods are meaningful to accuracy. Allow a cartridge to "cook" for a few minutes in a hot chamber and the bullet may detour from the group.

The shooter is also a focal point in the accuracy picture. Being in good physical condition is important for body control. A shooter's visual acuity is critical in discerning and maintaining the aimpoint over and over again. While recoil can have a physical effect on accuracy in barrel whip and rise, recoil can affect the shooter personally in that it disturbs the senses. Even though no true physical harm may befall the shooter, he may react to recoil by flinching, which ruins aim.

THE BEST RIFLE SIGHTS

8 Rifle accuracy is useless without some sort of aiming device to help direct the bullet to the target. Early firearms had no such implements. Battles in which thousands of rounds were fired without telling effect were fought with firearms that had the most rudimentary aiming instruments, if any at all.

Eventually, rifle sights became as much a part of the firearm as the stock. But it took a while to progress from the crude lump of metal on the front of the barrel to the best variable-powered riflescopes made today.

THE OPEN IRON SIGHT

The open iron sight may seem crude compared to the scope or the adjustable-aperture sight, but it was, and still is, a highly workable model. In theory, groups no better than four inches center to center are possible with open irons from a distance of 100 yards. Often, groups are bigger. Fortunately, however, this bit of "fact" from the shooting world is a shade off the mark. The human eye, we're told, isn't good enough to focus simultaneously on rear sight, front sight and target, visually holding the three points in relation to each other to produce better than that four-inch group. It is true that open iron sights make heavy demands on the eye, and those three focal points become more difficult to

master as eyes age. But the major problem with open sights—even when young eyes and steady hands are at work—is the design of the sights themselves. On many open sights the bead is so large it covers an elephant's behind at a hundred paces, while the rear sight notch is not always a perfect optical fit for the front sight.

Open sights would be obsolete today if it weren't for a few factors. First, some hunters still like the challenge of the open sight. Second, some rifles don't wear a scope all that well. The famous old-style Model 94 Winchester rifle is one. The new Model 94 ejects empty brass out to the side, but the old one shoots spent cases straight up in the air. Owners of the older 94s often stick with open sights. Additionally, open sights are extremely fast-aiming if the rifle fits the shooter. Finally, in many states with blackpowder hunting seasons, only iron sights (no scopes) are allowed by law.

Even crude open sights serve the brush hunter whose shots are always close. But for longer shots, especially at smaller targets, open irons require some refinement. Admittedly, my advice on open irons comes from personal preference as well as research and study. I like open irons, not only on muzzleloaders, but on a few other rifles I own as well. I enjoy shooting rifles with open sights. The challenge is interesting.

Most of my open sights undergo a little surgery, however, generally by replacing the blob of a front sight with a gold or white bead about 1/16-inch or 3/32-inch, usually available at the local gunshop. The front sight on my last iron-sighted rifle was refitted with a 1/16-inch gold sheared bead. The sheared bead is effective because it is flattened on the shooter's side so that it does not reflect light.

My best shooting with an iron-sighted muzzleloader produced frequent two-inch groups at

bashed on one of my journeys, I want to be back in business as fast as possible, if only with open iron sights. My backpack contains the necessary tool kit (Lyman's handy compact set) to remove the scope in minutes.

One important point to keep in mind is sight picture. You don't want a fat front sight with a mismatched rear notch, because the result is a poor sight picture. What you want instead is a small front bead matched with a notch large enough to admit light on both sides of the bead.

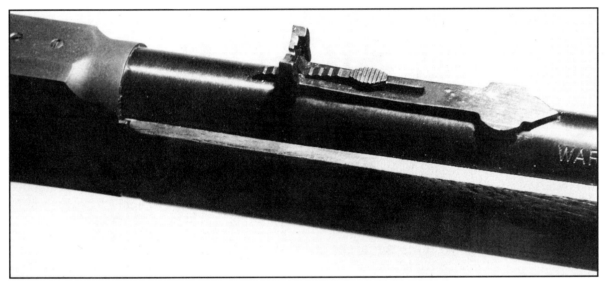

Open iron rear sights can be quite effective, especially when used by practiced marksmen. Note the ladder or elevator bar used to raise and lower the rear sight to change point of impact.

100 yards, with a few clusters going smaller. My best open-iron-sight shooting with a modern rifle came recently with three 3-shot groups fired during the sighting of a Model 77 Ruger International 308. At 100 yards, all three groups were about an inch center to center. I wouldn't bet a deflated dollar against a new truck that I could do it again. But a deer at 100 yards would be in the freezer with that iron-sighted rifle. This particular Model 77 carries open irons even though the little 18.5-inch barrel fullstock rifle is scoped. In this instance, the open irons perform an important function: backup duty. The 308 Model 77 has done serious backcountry and creekbottom whitetail work for me. Should the scope get

The reason for this is frame of reference. If the front bead or blade fits fully (optically speaking) into the rear sight notch, there can be no frame of reference. It is impossible to tell if the bead or blade is truly centered in the rear sight notch. But if there is a little light on either side of the bead as it rests in the open rear sight, that makes for frame of reference. The shooter knows when the sights are aligned and when they're not.

Hundreds of open-sight designs have been developed over the years, including, for example, the buckhorn rear sight. Although not appreciated by modern gunwriters, the buckhorn is one sight I've had good success with. A shooter interested in open-sight styles should consult any

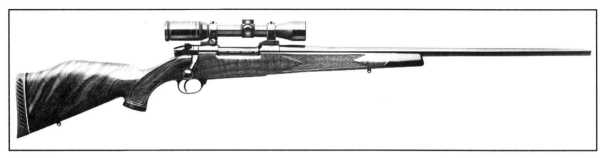

The Western big-game rifle looks like this: a bolt-action model with a scope sight. This Weatherby Mark V carries no iron sights, indicating the trust modern shooters have in glass sights.

book that pertains to a specific rifle company history (such as *The Winchester Book* by George Madis). Books like these usually include sight styles that were offered for the guns under study.

THE APERTURE SIGHT

There are dozens of different aperture or peep sight styles. Some of the more interesting models have been installed on the cocking piece of the rifle. The Model 71 Winchester lever-action rifle, for example, was offered with this sight as an option. Mannlicher's carbine had an optional peep sight that was somewhat unique. It was spring-loaded, allowing it to fold out of the way when the bolt was drawn rearward after firing the rifle. In this manner, the peep sight could be mounted low on the receiver so the eye would pick it up quickly, yet it would not impede the rearward progress of the bolt.

The micrometer aperture sight, with its extremely fine adjustment capability, provided a far better iron sight than the open sight. The major reason for peep sight superiority is its function. Remember that open iron sights require the eye to focus on three objects simultaneously: rear sight, front sight and target. The peep sight, however, demands that the eye focus on only two visual planes at once: the front sight and the target. Visual accommodation—the ability of the eye to function in a focus/refocus situation—is not so taxed by the peep sight. The eye will naturally focus on the point of greatest light, which just happens to be the dead center of the peep. Naturally, for the most precise point of aim, a tiny hole is best.

For hunting, a large aperture is better than a small one. While a large disc with a small hole is good for targets, a small disc with a larger

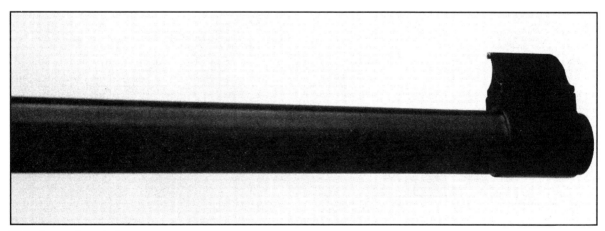

This front sight is integral to a ramp and includes a tiny bead.

"peep" makes more sense for hunting. The hunter looks through the peep aperture—not at it. He doesn't have to center the front sight in the peep, because his eye does that automatically. All he needs to do is to place the front sight on the target, hold it there and squeeze the trigger. Shooters who say the peep sight is no good probably use it incorrectly, consciously trying to center the front sight in the "hole." That's working too hard.

SIGHTING IN WITH IRONS

Rifles with open iron or peep sights are sighted in by moving the rear sight in the direction required of the next bullet. If the shooter wants the bullet to hit to the right, the rear sight is moved to the right. The rear sight is moved left for a desired left-hand strike of the next bullet on the target. Moving the sight up puts the next bullet higher. Moving the rear sight downward means the next bullet will strike lower on the target.

If the rifle is printing its group low and to the right, then the rear sight must be moved up to make the pattern hit higher, and to the left to make the pattern go left. A quality micrometer-adjustable aperture sight moves in precise increments, often quarter-minutes. This translates to $1/4$ inch at 100 yards for each click. The usual open rear sight is generally drifted in a dovetail notch for left/right adjustment and raised or lowered on an elevator bar (ladder) or in a sliding fashion, as with Lyman's folding rear sight.

A few rear sights are "fixed," as on some muzzleloaders. That means they are not designed to move up or down; they can usually be moved right or left in their dovetail notch. In such a case, the front sight can be used to aid in sighting the

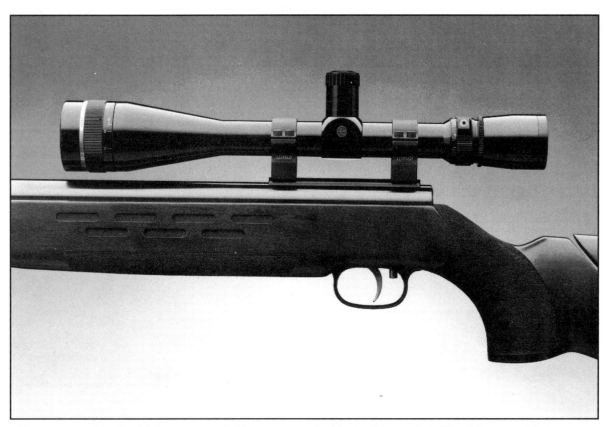

Riflemen can elect for high-power variable scopes today, including models like this Leupold that ranges from 6.5X to 20X.

This excellent Lyman micrometer peep sight is attached to a Storey Conversion custom Model 94 Winchester rifle. Note the elevation marks.

rifle in, but the reverse procedure is used: the next bullet will strike opposite on the target in reference to the direction that the front sight is moved. In other words, if the front sight is filed down to make it shorter, the next bullet will hit higher on the target; if the front sight is replaced with a taller sight, the next bullet will hit lower on the target. The front sight is drifted to the right if the shooter wants the next bullet to hit to the left on the target and so on.

THE ONE V BY INTERAIMS

The One V is a special sighting device that deserves mention. Made in Japan and distributed in the U.S. by Stoeger Industries, Inc., of South Hackensack, N.J., the One V lies somewhere between irons and scopes. It is compact, weighing only 3.9 ounces and measuring 5¼ inches long. The illuminated red dot within the tube is parallax-free, making for a fast-action sight that offers a clear aiming point. The bright red dot changes size via a turning knob, and appears as an unattached sighting point with no crosswires. Eye relief is unlimited. The One V is fast especially in dim light, because the shooter has only to place the red dot on the target—no further effort is required. The sight and target are on one plane, not three as with the open iron sight, or two as with the peep.

Interaims has manufactured the One V with a standard one-inch tube that fits the popular one-inch scope ring, or a 30mm tube for the 30mm scope ring. The One V will work on a rifle, sidearm or shotgun.

This tang peep sight is fitted on a Model 1894 takedown rifle in 30-30 caliber.

THE SCOPE SIGHT

The most-used sight in the North American hunting field today is the scope. The reason for its success is of course magnification. Magnification is not always necessary when shooting, but often it's a great boon. While close-range shots in the brush can be made with the most simple open iron sights, shooters encounter plenty of other situations.

Not long ago, I decided to set up a rifle for brush-hunting on whitetails, and chose my 308 Model 77 International. For prior test purposes, I had affixed a 2.5X-8X scope to this short carbine. After the tests, I removed the scope, for most of the rifle's work would transpire at close range, I felt.

It didn't take long for me to realize that the rifle deserved a scope. Nor did it take long to find out that even from an 18.5-inch barrel a 150-grain bullet could achieve a muzzle velocity of over 2900 fps with the right handload. So I set up the rifle with a 4X scope. It worked, but it wasn't exactly right for super-close shots because the 4X didn't have a particularly wide field of view. Worse yet, the 4X didn't allow me to pick a precise aimpoint on a deer in the brush. I passed up several opportunities of this nature, especially when hunting from the elevated sidebanks of creekbottoms, searching for deer below in the tangle. Deer I found, but never a "whole one." It was always a piece of deer showing through a screen of brush. I put a Bushnell 2.5X-8X on the 308 and there it rests to this hour. Close-range aiming speed was then possible, coupled with long-range target definition.

Scopes are not perfect sights, but they are

very, very good. The advantages of the scope sight are a single focal plane, a precise aimpoint coupled with a magnified target, target recognition in low light, and simple sight-in.

The first advantage is a big one. The target and the reticle of the scope appear on the same plane, so the eye does not have to focus back and forth between sights and target. The second is a double value. The reticle of the modern scope offers great precision because it can be aimed at a small spot on the target. And if you want to see exactly where to place the crosswires of your scope, magnify the target. Plus, the glass hunting sight is ideal in low light, because magnification helps a shooter discern the target.

The scope is easy to sight in—just follow the

This front sight is known as a "globe." The rifle is a Whitworth rifled musket noted for its long-range accuracy and winning of 1000-yard shooting matches.

arrows, as it were. Most scopes have arrows showing which way to adjust to move the bullet hole on the target—right or left, up or down. There are either clicks or some sort of reference mark to guide the degree of change, i.e., so many clicks per inch or so many marks per inch. It's really pretty simple to sight a scoped rifle, especially if the shooter starts up close to his target to get the rifle on the paper, moving out to longer range only after the rifle is zeroed for close range first.

A SHORT HISTORY OF SCOPES

Scope sights are hardly new. Research shows the famous scientist Sir Isaac Newton, who lived from 1642–1727, mounting a telescope on a firearm. Proving that Newton was way ahead of his time, riflescopes didn't "take off" for a couple more centuries. During the U.S. Civil War, scopes were mounted on a few rifles, and given to so-called "sharpshooters." These long telescopic sights had small fields of view and their optics were not on a par with modern lenses, but they couldn't have been too bad because they made a big difference in hitting a distant target. Many "buffalo runners" of the late 19th century used scoped rifles, too. Sometimes these scopes were 20X and had stadia wires for judging range. Many bison were shot from long-range with Sharps and Remington single-shot breechloading rifles wearing scope sights.

It would seem that by the 20th century just about every shooter would have a scoped rifle. Not so. As late as the 1950s, and even into the 1960s, many veteran hunters declared the scope sight a nuisance. They said it could fog up, might fail to remain sighted in and could self-destruct from the slightest bump. Remarkably, it took strong advice from prominent 20th-century gunwriters, such as Jack O'Connor, Elmer Keith and Townsend Whelen, to convince modern shooters to try a glass sight. Gunwriter Dr. C.E. Hagie said in his 1946 book, *The American Rifle*, "At the very outset I am going to hazard the opinion that toters of telescope-sight-mounted big-game rifles would kill 25 per cent more game if they left the telescopes at home and equipped their rifles with iron sights adapted to their individual needs."

Hagie was no beginner when he penned these words. He was a noted Montana rifleman of vast experience. Hagie believed the glass sight was delicate, not adapted to rough handling, unsuited to scabbard-carrying, likely to fog, might frost over or become lens-blocked by debris on the trail. It was no good for running game, and it magnified unsteadiness, making sighting of even a standing target slow and cumbersome. He felt the scope was only good for those "who like to put on their favorite hunting rifles all the fancy gadgets that can be procured." And he added, "It provides that much more to talk about and brag about and coddle along on a hunting trip." His remarks were not unique, for in the late 1940s through the early 1960s, many other celebrated hunters felt the same way about the glass hunting sight.

Otherwise intelligent shooters dove off the "deep end" when it came to scopes. One rifleman-writer said he disliked scopes because rifles so outfitted could not be held as steadily as iron-sighted pieces! Another writer admitted that scopes did not bring on a palsy, but he said he didn't like the *apparent* added rifle motion magnified by the scope. Glass sights broke, fogged, fell off, and pinched the view so drastically you couldn't get on target. They unsighted themselves magically, getting knocked out of whack if you ran over a candy bar wrapper on the road to the shooting range, said some detractors. A few early scopes deserved negative criticism. Shooter trust was a long time in coming. But the scope would rise above its bad press and take its place in the evolution of hunting sights.

The tube sight was presumably the forerunner of the scope. It was a long metal cylinder, often of barrel length, that looked very much like the later scope sight, although it had no glass in it. The tube sight, often $3/8$ to $5/8$ of an inch in diameter, clamped to a sliding base at each end, which allowed for horizontal adjustment. Vertical movement was via a movable pin. It wore an eye cup with a centered peep hole. At the opposite end was a pin head for a front sight. The object of the tube sight was *concentration* on the target.

It seems a natural transition from tube sight

This particular aperture sight is adjusted via dials for both windage and elevation.

to scope sight. Regular telescopes had been around for a very long time—Newton had, after all, mounted a telescope on a rifle centuries before. We also know that terrestrial telescopes were in use by outdoorsmen in the 16th and 17th centuries and that Old Gabe (Jim Bridger) carried a telescope with him on his forays into the unmapped regions of the Far West in the middle 1800s. "Feby. 22d Mr Bridger according to his usual custom took his telescope & mounted a high bluff near encampment to look out for 'squalls' as he termed it. . . ." (*Journal of a Trapper*, Osborne Russell 1834–1843).

As far back as the Continental Congress of 1776 is a notation authorizing the purchase of telescopic rifle sights. Historians feel these were actually tube sights. Or were they? Why did our founding fathers call them telescopic? Could it be that some Yankee Trader had a scope on the drawing board that our forebears found interesting? We don't know. Snipers of the Civil War era used scoped rifles. According to A.G. Gould in *The Modern American Rifle*, records show that Whitworth rifles fitted with scope sights were delivered to the Confederate Army Sharpshooters. Also, General Berdan's Union Sharpshooters employed scoped rifles.

Although it is impossible to credit one inventor, the *modern* scope was certainly advanced by William Ellis Metford, born in 1824 at Flook House, Tanton, Somerset. His father, a medical doctor, promoted rifle-shooting. Young Metford's interest in long-range marksmanship—out to 2,000 yards—prompted him to develop a workable scope sight.

His design probably constituted the first truly practical telescopic rifle sight. Attributes of a Metford 8X scope sight included high precision of manufacture, good optics and fine, accurate adjustments, with the scope sturdily mounted on the rifle. The Metford scope of 1854 was considered by some the best of its time. Others felt that John W. Sidel made the best scope. A later model Sidel scope was favored by Dr. F.W. Mann, the well-known shooter-researcher. Ned Roberts, of 257 Roberts fame, said his Sidel was the best of the early scopes, too.

Another good scope came from Syracuse (N.Y.) designer, William Malcolm. He built a quality instrument of the period and had a good following. In a December 1934 *American Rifleman*, Ned Roberts said of the Malcolm sight: "I have owned and used Malcolm telescopes for over 30 years, and still use a fine 8-power scope of that make." From the late 1800s beyond the middle of the 20th century, the Malcolm Rifle Telescope Company of Auburn, N.Y., manufactured the product.

Although sparsely used, scopes gained ground in American sport hunting during the early 20th century. By 1901, rifles with telescopic sights were seen at Bisley. The same year,

For night shooting and for use with heavy and large bore rifles we particularly recommend the following scopes:

AJACK 7.5 x 50

$84.00

Magnification, 7.5 X
Field of view, 6 yd. at 100 yd.
Luminosity—50

Length—14"
Tube Diameter, 26½ mm.
Eye Relief—3"
Weight, 500 Grams (18 oz.)

AJACK 10 x 50

$120.00

Magnification, 10 X
Field of view, 4.5 yd. at 100 yd.
Luminosity—50

Length—15¾"
Tube Diameter, 30 mm.
Eye Relief—3"
Weight, 880 Grams (31 oz.)

Early telescopic riflesights were good, but not nearly as excellent as the modern glass sight. These are examples of early high-class scopes.

The variable power scope sight is king today. Previous faults have been erased.

the J. Stevens Arms & Tool Company acquired the Cataract Tool & Optical Company. The latter had made a glass sight, which the new owners were committed to improving. The company's optician, F.L. Smith, was given one full year to upgrade the product. The result was the Pistol Telescope, Model No. 115, used on takedown rifles as well as pistols. The Stevens Multiscope No. 575 was a variable with 3/4-inch tube. The 1907 Stevens catalogue was careful to label the No. 575 a new model, not a new invention, for variables had been in use for a long time. Stevens called its $40 variable the first *practical* model. It was 6X-12X, with a sliding erecting lens. The Stevens scope was ahead of its time in another

way—it was *sealed* against the elements, with eyepiece, lenses and crosswires encompassed in a solid brass tube—no screws.

By 1916, Winchester offered a practical hunting scope "made in two styles and three powers." Style A, the superior model, was 5X. Style B offered powers 5X, 4X and 3X. Both ocular and objective lenses were adjustable for focusing. The company was proud of its riflescope, stating that "the Winchester Telescope Sight eliminates entirely the element of chance in its use." Interchangeable reticles included single and double crosshairs, triangle, aperture and pinhead. The Winchester scope was adjusted for sight-in through its mount system, and the

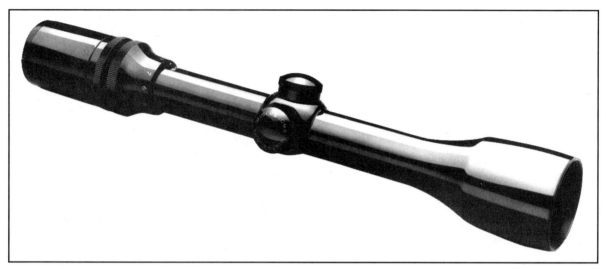

The 3X-9X, like this Bausch & Lomb model, is one of the most popular variables due to good high-end magnification coupled with reasonable low-end field of view.

manufacturer encouraged the shooter to dismantle his scope for cleaning.

Despite the existence of a few sporting scopes, when World War I broke out, there wasn't a single practical American sniper scope. The German army, however, had good sniper scopes built by manufacturers such as Zeiss and Hensoldt. The first widely accepted hunting scopes in America after WW I were also of Zeiss and Hensoldt manufacture, especially the Zeiss Zielklein 2½X and the Hensoldt Zielklein 2¾X, both with ⅞-inch tubes.

By World War II, American soldiers did have a sniper's rifle with scope sight. Wollensak of New York made the Model 82 scope for allied snipers. Telescope No. M73B2, made in Paris, France, was fitted to the Springfield 1903A4 rifle. The Weaver 330, notation "M73B1," was also fitted to the 1903A4 Springfield. In 1944, an army correspondent following the German campaign noted that one James McGill of Pennsylvania used his sniper rifle to drop the enemy from a distance of an estimated 600 yards, registering several hits on a machine gun nest. Without a doubt, knowledge of sniper scopes in WW II had an effect on sporting scopes to follow.

During this time period, the sporting scope continued to evolve. Captain Paul A. Curtis, a well-known shooter of his day (see *Great Shoot-*ers of the World, Stoeger Publishing, 1990), credited himself as father of the American sporting riflescope. "Between 1920 and 1925," he said in his 1943 book, *Guns & Gunning*, "I experimented with several foreign rifles fitted with scopes." Curtis ended up with a Zeiss Zielklein mounted on a Springfield sporting rifle. "I experimented with it for several months and then launched my sporting scope campaign." After a successful hunt in Alberta, Curtis wrote of his adventures with the scoped rifle. Zeiss sales jumped immediately. "In consequence, I feel justified in considering myself the father of the modern sporting telescope sight in America," Curtis concluded.

Between the world wars, there was a great rush to provide good scope sights for American sportsmen and many companies competed in the race. By 1933, Bill Weaver, then in Kentucky, had his Model 3-30 in production. It was to become the famous Model 330, 2¾X scope, the model perhaps most responsible for ushering American riflemen into the world of glass sights. The 330 was followed by the 440—basically the same scope, but with higher magnification. There was a discrepancy between advertised magnification and real magnification, however. The 330 was actually about 2X and the 440 about 3X. Eye relief was long and non-critical. Optics were good. Weaver's K-series—the K1, K1.5, K2.5, K3, and especially the K4—eventually eclipsed the early strain of Weaver models. The K3, incidentally, was suggested by arms author Jack O'Connor.

Lyman's famous scopes—the 5A, for example—were prominent in the 1930s, too. The 5A sold for $46.50. It boasted quarter-minute click adjustments. The Targetspot, 8X or 10X, sold for $60. There was also a 3X Stag at $55. Unertl had its acclaimed 1¼-inch target scope on the 1930 market, too. The Wollensak 4X was also a noted scope of the hour. Scopes were also made by Marlin, Mossberg, Fecker, Souther, Belding & Mull, Pechar, Noske, and others. Malcolm scopes were still around, too.

Despite continued resistance from American shooters, gunwriters praised the scope. In a December 1944 issue of *American Rifleman* magazine, Elmer Keith spoke highly of the glass sight. Ned Roberts advised glass sights for Schuetzen target matches as well.

As scopes developed, they became streamlined. The established firm of Leupold & Stevens (dating back to 1907) offered superior quality with aesthetic lines. The Leupold 4X of the 1950s proved exemplary of a vogue continuing to this hour: sleek, low-mounted scopes. The 4X Pioneer boasted a 35-foot field of view at 100 yards. It weighed only 8 ounces, and had a fixed reticle with adjustments in the mounts.

Redfield was making a name for itself in the realm of handsome glass riflesights as well. In the same time frame, an excellent Bausch & Lomb series of fixed reticle was introduced. It included the Baltur 2½X and Balfor 4X models, both at $65, and a Balvar 2.5X-4X variable at $80. The adjustable mount was another $25.

Reticles, also called reticules or graticules, were improving. Graticule No. 7 for the Zeiss scope was a post/crosshair arrangement, and there were many other styles as well. Crosshairs were made of all manner of materials. Phil Sharpe recounted the story of a fellow on the range who found that one of his crosswires had come off its station. The man wanted to finish shooting, so he fashioned another set of crosswires with human hairs. Scopes were not sealed anyway, and

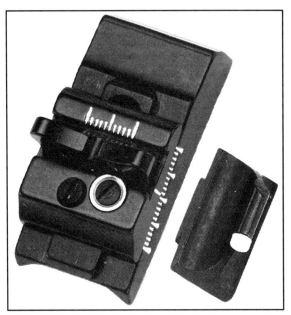

This CVA Micro Adjustable Sight Set is of the open variety. Note the windage adjustment calibration (white markings), and the white bead front sight at right.

takedown was common.

"This human hair has done excellent service," reported Sharpe in *The Rifle in America*. "It has been used for target and test shooting under the recoil of various Springfield loads." The web of the yellow field spider was found to be even better than human hair. Terrible reticles—pickets, heavy crosswires, thin crosswires, multiple crosswires, big dots, little dots, lots of dots, apertures, and sometimes a clutter of various combinations of the above (such as the Winchester triangle, which was an X with a horizontal wire, leaving a triangle to aim through in the center) were on the decline. The finest reticles ever presented in telescopic sights, such as the excellent standard Duplex crosswire, were gaining ground.

Mounts came a long way, too. The original German mounts were huge, clumsy and not necessarily strong. After a few shooting sessions with one of the early German models, Jack O'Connor reported that it allowed the scope to wiggle back and forth, not conducive to your best accuracy. The Stith scope mount of the 1930s was better

Today's mounts are generally rugged, but handsome. This Tikka bolt-action big-game rifle is fitted with Sako mounts and integral dovetail.

than most overseas counterparts. So was the Tilden mount of the same era, a bridge-type unit. Another good bridge mount of the 1930s was the Redfield. But there was still an inherent distrust of the scope sight. High mounts with see-through passages to the iron sights were prominent; however, the scope was often positioned too high with this arrangement, which made for uncomfortable shooting. The rifleman had to adjust his face on the cheekpiece in order to see through the center of the scope. Griffin & Howe's double-lever bracket mount, however, with permanent base on receiver and micrometer control for windage, offered quick scope removal with precision replacement and retained zero.

WHERE ARE SCOPES TODAY?

Today, the initial principles of the scope sight have been realized. Scopes are reliable. They are truly sealed instruments now. They sight in easily and remain sighted in. Eye relief (distance from eye to ocular lens) is good. Objective lenses are larger, offering a wider field of view.

Optics are much improved. The target is not merely magnified, it is also better defined—the sight picture is bright and clear. There are compact units of comparatively high magnification, such as the B&L Balvar Compact 2X-8X model. Field of view per magnification is good. Scopes focus easily to suit the individual eye, and crosswires are constantly centered (not long ago, crosswires were cock-eyed after sight-in). The variety of scopes is broad, with models to meet the needs of every shooter, including scopes for handguns and shotguns.

The variable scope is king, its previous faults overcome. Reticle size used to expand with magnification. As the shooter increased magnification for a far-away shot at a small target, the crosswire grew fatter, obliterating part of the target. Today, the opposite effect occurs. The reticle retains its optical size as the target magnifies, allowing more precision of aim.

The old variable had modest power adjustment, often 2.5X to 4X. Today, the range is tremendous, as in B&L's 2.5X-10X and 6X-24X, and Leupold's 4X-12X models. One new Bausch & Lomb variable even ranges from 12X to 32X!

The variable affords a wide field for quick shots, while offering power increase for improved long-range precision of aim. Some shooters feel that isn't necessary for big-game hunting; after all, an elk is much bigger than a woodchuck. However, the added precision of aim proves highly valuable, especially on longer shots.

"But I always set my variable for one power and leave it there," I hear. That's a matter of retraining. The shooter has to learn to use his variable as a variable. It makes no more sense to buy a 2.5X-8X scope, leaving it on 4X all the time, than to drive a 4-speed auto constantly in second gear. I carry my variables on a low setting for close shots, winding the power up for long shots. High magnification pays off in good bullet placement.

In early morning or late afternoon, when most big-game species are feeding, the variable

Quick-detachable scope mounts allow the shooter to remove the scope sight for iron sight use.

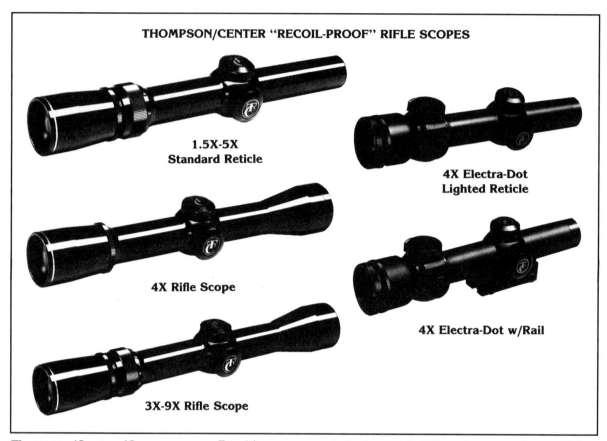

THOMPSON/CENTER "RECOIL-PROOF" RIFLE SCOPES

1.5X-5X Standard Reticle

4X Rifle Scope

3X-9X Rifle Scope

4X Electra-Dot Lighted Reticle

4X Electra-Dot w/Rail

Thompson/Center rifle scopes are offered in numerous styles to match different arms and uses. This is typical of today's scope makers.

scope can be increased in power to compensate for the lower light level. This is a matter of twilight factor, and is the opposite of what many shooters believe to be true. They want to use the lowest setting to gather more light. Optics don't work that way. All things being equal, the higher power will reveal the target better under low light conditions. One morning, I spotted a trophy antelope buck on the plains. Only the clear definition afforded by the variable scope's higher setting allowed a shot. I wouldn't have harvested that buck without the added magnification.

Modern variables are becoming more compact. My Frank Wells custom rifle wears a 3.5X-10X Leupold variable. While not a compact scope, this variable is sized very much like the older 3X-9X, and offers a specific aimpoint at a distant target, especially in the high Rocky Mountains where I frequently hunt. A recent test of a 3X-9X compact against its standard-size 3X-9X counterpart revealed no appreciable loss in optical excellence for the smaller scope. Combine a variable and a compact and you have tomorrow's scope sight.

Once upon a time, even in the middle of this century, the scope-sighted rifle was in the minority. Today, west of the Mississippi River, I doubt that you'd find more than one or two out of a hundred deer rifles lacking a glass sight. Distrust has been replaced by faith. Shooters understand the value of the glass sight and they know that modern scopes are the best ever, offering something for every gunning circumstance in every hunting locale.

THE SMALL GAME RIFLE

9 The cottontail rabbit is the most popular small-game animal in North America. The several species of tree squirrels are second on the list. Although these two small-game animals have short life spans (especially the rabbit), controlled hunting has no significant effect on their populations. Both game animals offer great hunting opportunities and are good sources of high-protein food.

Shotguns are often used for rabbit hunting, although Western hunters prefer a rifle. The favorite firearm for squirrel hunters, both Eastern and Western, is a rifle, typically a 22 rimfire. Today's small-game rifle is more than just a rifle for small game, however. It's also a plinking and practice gun, and can take game larger than rabbits or squirrels. Calibers for today's small-game rifles include the 22 WMR (Winchester Magnum Rimfire), the 25-20 Winchester, and the 32-20 Winchester, plus special handloads in big-game rifles and sub-loads for the interesting 17 Remington round.

RIMFIRE ROUNDS

The 22 Rimfire. The 22 rimfire began life in the 19th century as a blackpowder cartridge. Over the years, there have been hundreds of variations on the basic theme—far too many to discuss in one chapter. Except where noted otherwise, the 22-rimfire rounds covered here are those currently offered to the shooting public. Most of these rounds, it's safe to say, will remain in use for years to come.

BB Cap. The BB (bulleted breech) Cap is no more than a rimfire cartridge case with a round ball for a bullet. The story of this interesting little round is discussed more fully in *The Book of the Twenty-Two*, a Stoeger title recommended for anyone interested in 22-caliber rimfires and centerfires.

The BB Cap has limited use. It carries very little powder or none at all. Velocity and energy are low. Yet this none-too-popular 22-rimfire round has some applications. It can be used (with a safe backstop) wherever shooting is allowed by law, indoors or out. It isn't highly accurate, but it shoots well enough to pop a small pest—up to sewer-rat size at least—and can be used on cottontail rabbits and even squirrels at extremely close range, if only head shots are taken. The BB Cap is not sufficiently powerful to penetrate deeply on even small game.

The RWS ammunition company of Germany continues to offer the 22 BB Cap because its report is extremely quiet. The round ball of the RWS cap weighs 15.5 grains. This cap has a tiny powder charge underneath a cardboard wad. From a 22-inch barrel, muzzle velocity is 812

The cottontail rabbit is the most popular small-game animal in America. The only proper shot for a rifleman is the head region, offering a target of about two inches wide on most cottontails.

fps for a muzzle energy of 22.7 foot-pounds. This is deadly force, and must be respected—always shoot this load with a proper backstop.

CB Cap. In contrast to the BB Cap, the CB (conical bullet) Cap shoots a conical bullet, or an elongated projectile. The RWS CB Cap is loaded with a pointed 16-grain bullet and a light powder charge for a mv of 950 fps with a muzzle energy of 32 foot-pounds. Uses of the CB Cap are generally the same as those ascribed to the BB Cap: close-range targeting, pest disposal, and small-game hunting for the expert shot, taking head shots only.

22 CB Short. This cartridge uses a standard 29-grain bullet—typically associated with the 22 Short—as well as a 22 Short case. Its muzzle velocity is only 750 fps, however, with 36 foot-pounds of muzzle energy. This is a useful load for small game and pests at close range.

22 CB Long. This is a fine little cartridge, perhaps the best of the CB line, because it uses the standard 22 Long Rifle cartridge case with a 22 Short bullet. The 29-grain bullet takes off at

essentially the same velocity as the 22 CB Short, but the longer case makes this round operable in most 22 rifles. For example, my Kimber 22-rimfire rifle can handle the 22 CB Long in the clip, just as it feeds the 22 Long Rifle. Its uses are exactly the same as those of the 22 CB Short.

22 Short. The 22 Short comes in a variety of loads, including match grade, standard velocity, high velocity, and hollow point. The Short remains a good little plinking round and is very useful for cottontail rabbit and squirrel hunting (head shots only, hollow points preferred) at close range. The usual velocity/energy rating of the 22 Short is about 850 fps mv for a 29-grain bullet in the standard-velocity loading and about 1050 fps mv for the same bullet in the high-velocity loading.

22 Long. Most literature I've read about the 22 Long suggests that this cartridge has no reason for being and shouldn't exist. But I'm one shooter who disagrees. The 22 Long's ballistics are approximately those of the 22 Short, but with a Long Rifle cartridge case, which feeds better than the Short in many 22-rimfire rifles. For those concerned with throat erosion caused by using the 22 Short in the 22 Long Rifle chamber, the Long is the answer when 22 Short ballistics are desired. Furthermore, there remain a few old 22-rimfire rifles that handle the Long better than the

The 22 Long Rifle (center) is the most popular rimfire round of all time. Here it is flanked by two BB Caps that shoot round balls.

Long Rifle; a good example is the Model 12 Remington 22 pump. The standard-velocity Long propels its 29-grain bullet at about 910 to 915 fps mv. The high-velocity Long shoots the same bullet at about 1135 fps mv.

22 Long Rifle. Far and away the king of 22 rimfires, the 22 Long Rifle was born about 1887.

John Fadala poses with two cottontail rabbits harvested with a fine original Winchester bolt-action, chambered for the 22 Long Rifle.

Gun history is seldom entirely clear, but this date is close enough. Generally, the Long Rifle is the most accurate 22-rimfire round for most 22 rifles. It's more powerful than all the 22 rimfires mentioned thus far, although it falls behind the older 22 WRF (Winchester Rim Fire) and well back of the 22 WMR. The 22 Long Rifle is offered in many different loadings to fit different shooting circumstances. These run the gamut from serious match competition to hyper-velocity hollow points meant for varminting. Bullet styles also vary, but the standard round nose is most prevalent. Other designs include blunt-nosed bullets for small-game hunting, cone points and, of course, hollow points. There are even subsonic 22 Long Rifle loads with standard 40-grain bullets to satisfy shooters who want to keep their bullets below the speed of sound, theoretically reducing noise levels.

The 22 Long Rifle standard-velocity round shoots a 40-grain bullet at around 1100 fps mv. The 22 LR high-velocity load fires this same bullet at about 1200 to 1300 fps mv, depending upon the individual load tested. Hyper-velocity 22 Long Rifle rounds aren't magical. Higher speed is achieved by using a lighter bullet out of the 22 LR case, along with a charge of powder intended to gain good speed from that bullet. The Italian company Fiocchi makes hyper-velocity 22 Long Rifle ammo—Wasp is its trademark—chronographed at 1450 fps mv using a 37-grain bullet. That's a muzzle energy of 173 foot-pounds, making this a pretty good varmint load for shooting within 100 yards or so, with a 75-yard maximum range preferred.

Other hyper-velocity loads have come along from various ammo crafters, all of them more powerful than standard 22 LR ammo. Bullets of the truncated-cone style have been used on some of these loads, such as Remington's Yellow Jacket brand, with a muzzle velocity averaging around 1475 fps with a 33-grain bullet.

22 Long Rifle Shot. The intention here was to create a shotgun effect with a 22-rimfire rifle. The shot used is referred to as dust, or snake shot; it measures only .04 inch in diameter, and there are 4,565 pellets to an ounce. The charge of shot is so light that this round is good only for shooting at very close range. Some smoothbore 22 rifles have been made for shot-shooting, and some marksmen enjoy shotgun games with these guns and loads.

22 WRF (Winchester Rim Fire). Although the 22 WRF is essentially obsolete, the modern shooter should nonetheless know some of its

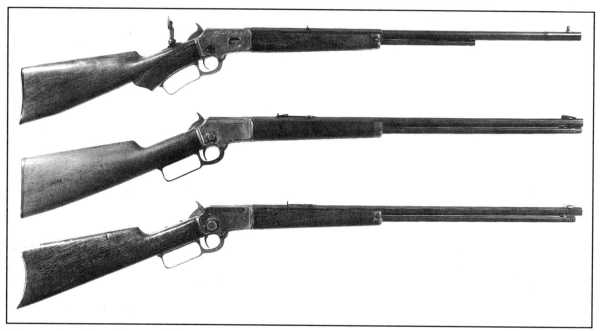

The most-used small-game rifle over the years has been the 22 rimfire, especially in Long and Long Rifle designs. These Marlins date back to the 19th century with (from top to bottom) Models 1891, 1892 and 1897.

background. Remember that there were hundreds of different rimfire rounds offered in the last century and during the early part of this one. The 22 WRF was an intelligent means of gaining more power than the 22 Long Rifle without going too far.

This cartridge handled a 45-grain bullet at about 1300 to 1400 fps mv (advertised at 1450 fps mv in the literature). A 22 Long Rifle with a 40-grain bullet at 1250 fps mv is worth 139 foot-pounds of muzzle energy. In contrast, the 22 WRF gained 169 foot-pounds of muzzle energy at 1300 fps mv and 196 foot-pounds of muzzle energy at 1400 fps mv. Some shooters found this increase in energy worthwhile for certain applications.

Winchester recently produced a modest run of 22 WRF ammo to "test the waters," in response to requests from customers desiring to shoot those fine old rifles originally chambered for the round. Other shooters claimed that they would use 22 WRF ammo in their rifles chambered for the 22 WMR (which is allowable, as

explained below). The idea was to provide a choice: the 22 WMR for full power, or the 22 WRF when full-blast 22 WMR punch was not needed. It all sounded great, but Winchester found 22 WRF sales less than sparkling, and the project was dropped. Fans of the 22 WMR weren't all that excited about dropping down in power after all, and apparently shooters excited about loading up those old 22 WRF rifles weren't interested in buying relatively expensive ammo to do so.

22 WMR (Winchester Magnum Rimfire). Although the 22 WRF was waning in popularity in the 1950s, it hung on. There was no factory cartridge on earth exactly like it. A shooter could handload his 22 centerfire to duplicate 22 WRF ballistics, but no rimfire round did the job. So Winchester decided to build a better 22 WRF.

The 22 WMR was brought out with a 40-grain bullet in full metal jacket (FMJ) and jacketed hollow-point versions. A longer case was designed so that older rifles chambered for the 22 WRF couldn't chamber the new 22-rimfire

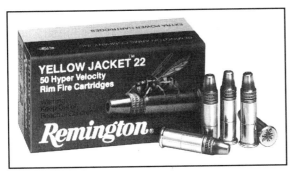

Offering more energy than the high-velocity 22 Long Rifle cartridge is the hyper-velocity 22 Long Rifle.

magnum cartridge. Right away, it was obvious that this was neither a jazzed-up 22 Long Rifle round nor a beefed-up 22 WRF, for the latter had a lead bullet just like other 22-rimfire rounds. The 22 WMR was different. Velocities of 2000 fps were advertised. From long barrels, these speeds were probably correct. Velocities of 1800 to 1850 fps were attained from barrels in the 22-inch domain. The FMJ bullet obviously was designed for fur hunters who didn't want to ruin pelts and for wild turkey hunters concerned about losing meat. As it turns out, the FMJ bullet, even where allowed, is not always right for the big bird. But it does work well on the trapline and for collecting fur-bearing varmints, such as foxes. It's also a fine small-game bullet.

Winchester had the exciting 22 WMR on paper in the 1950s. By 1959, the cartridge was a reality. "Announcing the all-new 22 Winchester Magnum Rimfire" read the first advertisement, which went on to state that "there's been a basic change in the entire concept of rimfire shooting—the first major breakthrough in two generations." It was all true. Winchester labeled its hot 22 rimfire a varmint and small-game round with "extra smashing power and a flatter trajectory." The company further stated that its 22-rimfire magnum was more powerful than the 38 S&W cartridge (not the 38 Special). From a test barrel, the 40-grain bullet was credited with 2000 fps at the muzzle, 1660 fps at 50 yards, 1390 fps at 100 yards, and 1180 fps at 150 yards. That made the 22 WMR about as powerful at 150

yards as the 22 Long Rifle was at the muzzle.

Muzzle energy was 355 foot-pounds. At 50 yards, 245 foot-pounds remained; at 100 yards, 170 foot-pounds remained; and at 150 yards, which Winchester saw as the outside range of the new 22 rimfire, 125 foot-pounds of energy was retained.

From the 6½-inch barrel of a revolver, the 22 magnum developed about 1550 fps mv with 210 foot-pounds of energy. At 100 yards, the 40-grain bullet traveled at more than 1100 fps, with an energy in the 115 foot-pound class. The 22 Long Rifle hollow-point, at an advertised muzzle velocity of 1365 fps, was worth about 150 foot-pounds at the muzzle, so there was no doubt that the new rimfire number was a whole division taller than the garden variety 22 LR, with far greater punch.

Shooters first saw the new round when it was unveiled at the 1959 NRA Annual Meeting in Washington, DC. The 22 magnum was thought to fit between the 22 LR and the 22 Hornet, which it did where both ballistics and cost were considered. A box sold for $2.60, for a bit over 5 cents a shot, in 1959. At the time, Hornet ammo cost about 12 cents apiece, and high-velocity 22 LR ammo went for about 1½ cents a pop. Compared to the 22 Long Rifle, the new round was expensive, but compared to the 22 Hornet, it was a bargain. And its FMJ bullet meant that, where allowed by law, the 22 WMR would make a fine small-game load.

There was an obvious parallel between the 22 WMR and the 22 WRF. The WRF was long

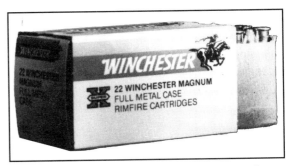

The excellent 22 WMR cartridge is offered in FMJ bullets, ideal for small game where they are safe to shoot and allowed by law.

advertised at 1450 fps mv with a 45-grain lead bullet for 210 foot-pounds of muzzle energy. Actual ballistics were closer to 1400 fps mv for the 22 WRF, which was born in blackpowder days with the Model 1890 Winchester pumpgun. (According to Major General Hatcher of the NRA staff, the WRF was called the 22-7-45 for a time: "22" for caliber, "7" for 7 grains of black powder, and "45" for bullet weight—true blackpowder nomenclature.) The 22 WRF was not entirely defunct when the 22 WMR appeared in the mid-20th century. In fact, both types were sold at gunshops for a while. The 22 WRF was not setting sales records in 1959 anyway, so it's not quite fair to say that the 22 WMR destroyed the old round, but the larger 22 magnum round certainly didn't help the smaller one.

1959, it used three firearms: a Savage Model 24 over/under, with 22 magnum barrel on top and .410 gauge below; a Smith & Wesson K-22 Masterpiece revolver; and a Ruger Single-Six. Winchester would chamber its popular Model 61 slide-action rifle for the 22 magnum in 1960. However, that rifle would be in the bone yard by 1963.

Many companies either hopped on the 22 magnum bandwagon early on in the round's history or intended to do so. Colt said yes with a forthcoming revolver. H&R was still thinking it over in 1959, as were Iver Johnson and High Standard. Mossberg planned a model immediately, with a longer action than those on its then-current 22 rifles. As noted, Savage, S&W, and Ruger had 22 WMRs on the market in '59.

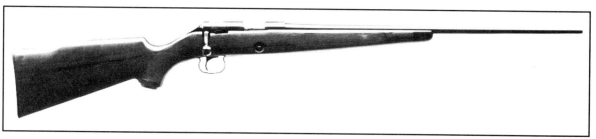

Classic 22-rimfire rifles have been replicated. This is Browning's version of the Winchester Model 52.

The two cartridges were so dimensionally close that the old 22 WRF would chamber and fire in 22 WMR rifles without a hitch. In fact, this was recommended: The owner of a new 22 WMR could use the less powerful 22 WRF when it suited him. Naturally, the reverse was not true. The 22 WMR was too long for the 22 WRF chamber. Conversions from 22 WRF to 22 WMR were never recommended, even though the 22 WMR was loaded to a mean pressure of about 24,000 psi maximum, the same as the high-velocity 22 LR, and bullets from the 22 WMR would stabilize in barrels of 1:16 rate of twist, the standard for the 22 LR.

Interestingly, Winchester was not the first arms company to accommodate the 22 magnum fan with a firearm. When the NRA ran its test in

Remington announced that it had no plans to produce a 22 WMR rifle; instead, it planned a unique—and, I might add, darned fine—20-caliber bottleneck rimfire very much like the bottleneck rimfires of blackpowder days. But the pretty little 5mm Remington was not born until a decade later, and it was 1970 before shooters could buy a rifle chambered for the round. Aside from Remington's bolt-action Model 592 rifle and a few T/C Contender barrels chambered for the 5mm Remington, gunmakers didn't pick up on the 20-caliber rimfire. Its 38-grain bullet at 2100 fps mv was possibly a shred ahead of the 22 WMR's 40-grain bullet at 2000 fps mv, due to the smaller bullet's slightly greater sectional density. But that advantage wasn't enough to save the 5mm.

Today, 5mm Remington ammo is harder to find than a shark in the Arizona desert. It's mostly a collector's commodity, quite high-priced. And no arms at all are chambered for the cartridge nowadays. Shooters can be as fickle as fashion lovers. They like and dislike, accept and denounce at will. The 5mm Remington rimfire was kicked out of the nest early on. The little 20-caliber rimfire with the bottleneck case was a fledgling that never had a chance to try its wings.

The 22 WMR, on the other hand, is as common as sand on the beach. Its 1.35-inch case (as compared to the 22 LR's 1.00-inch case) is treated to various bullet styles, and the original high-velocity ballistics have been maintained. The NRA test staff recorded 1990 fps mv from a 24-inch barrel with Winchester ammo in original tests. My chronographs show a slightly less scintillating bullet departure for current American-made 22 WMR ammo, but that's absolutely immaterial. All 22 magnum ammo tested for this work was supremely good.

WMR Ballistics. I ran chronograph tests with a 22-inch (not 24-inch) barrel; hence, the slightly lower-than-advertised mv. The first chronograph screen was 10 feet from the muzzle; mid-screens were at 12 feet. Four ammo brands were tested: Winchester, CCI, Federal and RWS. All were accurate from the test rifle, a bolt-action Marlin Model 25MN. One-inch center-to-center groups at 50 yards were common. Many 100-yard five-shot strings clustered around $1\frac{1}{2}$ inches center to center, shot "by hand" off the bench, usually with a mild wind blowing horizontally at the range. Although benchrest stability was excellent, wind did play a factor in grouping. Regardless, ammo accuracy proved sufficient for all small-game hunting, as well as varminting out to 150 yards. The 22 WMR's ballistics proved strong enough not only for small game and varmints, but also for javelina, the "wild pig" of the Southwest. Arizona allows the 22 WMR to be used on these animals, which run about 35 pounds dressed out.

22 WMR Ammo. Current 22-rimfire magnum ammo comes in several bullet styles. The 40-grain jacketed hollow-point is most popular for varmints. A 40-grain FMJ bullet is legal in some areas for wild turkey, small game and fur-bearers. RWS offers a 40-grain soft-point jacketed hollow-point load, as well as a 40-grain full patch. Incidentally, RWS ammo had the most energy. Its soft-point hollow-point bullet departed the muzzle at 2097 fps, and its 40-grain FMJ bullet left at 2025 fps mv.

Federal Cartridge Company's 50-grain jacketed hollow-point bullet has increased 22 magnum applications. The bullet earned a mv of 1550 fps from the 22-inch barrel, with sterling accuracy. Winchester's jacketed hollow-point

40- grain bullet was also superb.

With its various loadings and bullet styles, the 22 magnum is more flexible today than at any time since its inception. The 22 rimfire magnum fan just can't go wrong in ammo selection.

CENTERFIRE CALIBERS

25 WCF (Winchester Center Fire). Better known as the 25-20, the 25 WCF never died. It didn't even fade away. Ammo has been available since 1893. Moreover, new arms have been chambered for this round, including the Marlin Model 1894 CL lever-action repeater.

The 25-20 deserves mention as a cartridge for the small-game rifle because it's so versatile. It can be handloaded to duplicate the muzzle energies of the 22 WMR or can be boosted to full strength with an 87-grain bullet at around 1800 fps mv and a 60-grain bullet at 2300 fps mv. It's a specialty cartridge for small game, not a modern standard.

32 WCF. The 32 WCF, or 32-20, is pretty much the 25-20 necked up to shoot bullets of about 31 caliber. The 32 gets billing here because it too has survived over the years, having been introduced in 1892. Also a blackpowder round originally, the 32-20 found favor with small-game hunters who might have also wanted to bag a deer. Although the round is too small for deer, it was so used by some hunters of the past. It is also chambered afresh in the Marlin Model 1894 CL. The 32-20 is listed in Hornady's Fourth Edition handbook with an 85-grain bullet at 2300 fps mv and a 110-grain bullet at 2100 fps mv,

---

WIND DRIFT AND THE HIGH-VELOCITY BULLET

Drift, as already defined, is the departure of the bullet from its intended path due to rotational velocity. If the rifle carries a right-hand twist, then the bullet drifts right; a left-hand twist causes left movement of the bullet. Wind drift causes bullets to stray off course, too, sometimes greatly.

So target shooters were pleased when the 22 Long Rifle high-velocity round first came out. They knew that bullets at higher speeds drifted less than bullets at lower speeds, and so figured that the high-velocity 22 LR load would offer less wind drift. But it didn't work out that way.

The opposite proved true. Bullets from standard-velocity loads drifted less than bullets from high-velocity loads. Studies revealed that the cause of this effect was the "disturbed region," or region of disturbance. Much later, when high-speed photography became available, shadow graphs provided visual evidence of shock waves. It seems that bullets traveling slower than the speed of sound (roughly 1100 fps) are less affected by the atmosphere than are bullets traveling faster than the speed of sound. That 22 Long Rifle high-velocity bullet was, therefore, more susceptible to the ravages of wind than was the standard-velocity bullet, because the latter was more stable.

Bullets traveling much faster than the speed of sound are a different issue, however. These bullets are far more affected by the atmosphere than are subsonic projectiles, to be sure; but they still drift far less than slower missiles because of their much higher speed. The longer a bullet is subjected to the wind, the more time the wind has to push on it, in other words. So when bullets went from the speed-of-sound realm (as with the 45-70 Government in its original blackpowder load) all the way to 3000 fps and more (as with the 270 Winchester and its high-velocity sisters), the much faster bullets won the wind deflection battle. But for the 22 Long Rifle, a little gain in velocity (from the speed of sound to maybe 1200 to 1300 fps) was not sufficient to overcome the troubles caused by the region of disturbance. That's why the 22 Long Rifle high-velocity load drifts a little more in the wind than does the 22 LR standard-velocity load.

Cartridges larger than the 22 rimfire can be used for small-game hunting. The 32-20 Winchester is one of these, shown here (left) with a 30-30 round for comparison.

but squib loads (underloads) can be built to push either bullet at 22 LR velocities.

17 Remington. Tests with hard 23-grain bullets in this interesting little cartridge proved its value on small game. The bullet at 1800 fps mv performed perfectly on a cottontail rabbit hunt.

BIG-GAME CALIBERS

Squib loads, or underloads, can be prepared for big-game rifles to produce small-game ballistics. Various handbooks list loads to accomplish this, with both cast lead projectiles and jacketed bullets.

For test purposes, I handloaded a 308 Winchester cartridge using a Lyman cast bullet, No. 311465, 122-grain weight in alloy, plus 20.0 grains of Reloader 7 powder, for a muzzle velocity of 1625 fps. Obviously, this combination would make a nice small-game load.

Be sure to sight your rifle for the squib load—it may not be on target otherwise. The test rifle shot low and to the left with squib loads and had to be resighted to group at 25 yards.

THE RIFLE

The small-game rifle is built around the cartridge. It is the cartridge, or at least the load used in that round, that makes it a contender in the small-game field. Obviously, just about any rifle can serve; earlier I discussed a 308 Winchester big-game cartridge loaded to serve the small-game hunter. Thus, trying to define the small-game rifle is nearly impossible. A single-shot 22-rimfire rifle is entirely adequate for squirrel hunting and Western cottontails, for example. The only reason to move away from the single-shot is a desire to carry and use a different type of rifle on small game. It's not because the single-shot 22 rimfire is inadequate.

My most-used small-game rifle at the moment is a Kimber bolt-action clip-fed repeater chambered for the 22 LR cartridge (in which I also use the 22 Long CB Cap for short-range work). This rifle wears a Weatherby 1.5X–5X scope sight—the lower power for running or extremely close shots, the higher power for perfect bullet placement at longer distances. The Kimber provides target accuracy and has an excellent trigger. It's capable of head shots on rabbits and squirrels every time the shooter does his part.

Nonetheless, a careful hunter with an old Remington rolling-block single-shot from the last century can bag all the small game he wants if he hunts a good area. He can do the same with a big-game rifle loaded down with mild-mannered hand-rolled recipes. That's why the rifle itself receives low billing in a discussion on small-game shooting instruments.

Sights. The particular sight arrangement used on a small-game rifle is more important than the rifle itself. Sights must suit conditions. I was happy to have the Kimber with the excellent Weatherby scope while rabbit hunting on a ranch recently. I generally don't shoot running cottontails, because I'm afraid of losing meat if the bullet should rake through from back to front. I found cottontails in the sagebrush that had to be

taken from very close range; with the scope on low power, locating and shooting them was easy. Later on, I found cottontails along a drainage ditch. They were fairly wild, jumping out of the ditch and running, but most of them stopped within 50 to 75 yards. So I simply jacked up the scope to high power for more precise bullet placement.

On the other hand, I've hunted areas where iron sights were fine. What's important is that the sights of the small-game rifle match the conditions.

Sighting-In. Almost as important as the sight is how the rifle is sighted in. A cottontail rabbit offers a two-inch-wide target for a head shot (which, in deference to the good meat, should be the only shot taken). A rifle chambered for the 22 LR and sighted in at 100 yards can cause the shooter to miss closer shots, and most

The small-game rifle can also be a plinking/practice tool. A few tin cans and a safe backstop make a perfect setup for practice.

The muzzleloading rifleman can enjoy small-game hunting with a small-bore "squirrel rifle," especially in calibers 32 and 36 with patched round balls.

rabbits are taken well under 100 yards from the muzzle. It's better to sight in for 85 yards maximum range, thereby allowing the rifle to hit dead-on around 20 yards—the range at which most squirrels and Western cottontails are taken. So the 22 should be sighted in for about 20 yards, which will put the bullet back on again at around 85 yards for the 22 LR load.

The 22 WMR can also be sighted in for about 20 yards. This sighting will put the bullet back on target at more like 125 yards than 85 yards, but that's not a problem. For the 25-20, 32-20, 17 Remington and squib loads in big-game rifles, a sight-in of about 20 yards also works well.

Remember that the bullet path is always underneath the scope. At very close range, such as five to 10 yards, the crosswire should be held slightly above the target. Otherwise, the bullet may strike low and hit the edibles.

BLACK POWDER FOR SMALL GAME

There are now several million shooters in this country who are doing things the old way—the blackpowder way. Two bore sizes excel for small-game hunting: the 32 and the 36. Not that other calibers won't work—they will—but these two calibers stand out.

The 32 caliber, nearly ideal, shoots a 45-grain round ball, while the 36 caliber shoots a 65-grain round ball. Both can achieve around 2000 fps mv with FFFg black powder or Pyrodex P. Both can also achieve 22 Long Rifle muzzle velocity by appropriately reducing the powder charge. Small-diameter round balls drift significantly in the wind, but small-game hunting is usually a close-range proposition anyway. Here are some sample loadings of each caliber:

32 caliber Navy Arms Country Boy Rifle/ 26-inch barrel
    20 grains volume FFFg—1671 fps mv
    50 grains volume FFFg—2070 fps mv
36 caliber Mowrey Squirrel Rifle/ 32-inch barrel
    20 grains volume FFFg—1416 fps mv
    50 grains volume FFFg—1981 fps mv

Despite the Mowrey's longer barrel, the Country Boy achieved higher muzzle velocity for the same loads. But both rifles proved accurate, and both are entirely worthy for small-game hunting.

MOUNTAIN BIRDS

These aren't small game in a strict sense, but in parts of the West, certain mountain grouse and partridge may be hunted with a rifle, and certainly a small-game rifle is best for the job. These birds are usually taken at extremely close range, often measured in feet instead of yards. The warning sounded earlier goes double here—aim slightly higher than the target. A scope crosswire held on the bird's head and neck region may put the bullet right into the breast, the most edible portion of the carcass. A rifle especially for mountain grouse hunting should be a 22 rimfire, preferably shooting solid-point Long Rifle loads. I prefer match-grade ammo for its extra accuracy, which gives the best chance for a head shot. The head of even the largest blue grouse is tiny, and match-grade ammo makes the possibility of hitting the target just a little better.

THE CHOICE

If I were forced to hunt with only one small-game rifle for the rest of my life, it would be chambered for the 22 LR cartridge and capable of handling other members of the 22 rimfire family, such as the Short, Long and CB Long. It would be an accurate rifle, scope-sighted. There are dozens of fine telescopic sights on the market these days that fit 22s.

The 22 rimfire is best for small-game hunting because you never outgrow it. Ammo is inexpensive, so it's also a great choice for plinking. A shooter without a 22 rimfire in his gun collection is missing out on the most-used rifle on the North American continent.

THE WILD TURKEY/ JAVELINA RIFLE

10 It may seem strange classifying these two fine, but entirely different, game species in the same niche, but it turns out that a good wild turkey rifle is a good javelina rifle and vice versa. For instance, rifles chambered for the 22 WMR (Winchester Magnum Rimfire) are legal in many areas for javelina, and a good marksman has no trouble tagging the peccary with this round. Meanwhile, the same 22 WMR rifle is also legal for wild turkey hunting in numerous areas and is considered adequate for these big birds in the hands of the same good marksman. A small-bore blackpowder rifle is also ideal for both species. So are reduced loads and, under certain conditions, full-throttle loads in big-bore rifles.

A well-worn real estate cliché claims that the three most important points in selling a house are location, location and location. In selecting a wild turkey and javelina rifle, the three most important factors are cartridge, cartridge and cartridge. The lesson learned in the last chapter on the small-game rifle is repeated here: Just about any style of rifle will do, but the caliber has to be right, as does the load.

THE WILD TURKEY

The wild turkey has become such a popular "big- game" bird in North America that it's now recognized by its own national organization, the National Wild Turkey Federation, which was founded in 1973 and has more than 30,000 members. There are several varieties of wild turkey in America, and every state except Alaska is home to these birds. Numbers were down at one time, but not today. Nebraska, for example, started a wild turkey transplant program in 1958, with 28 birds released. Now it has an estimated 22,000 birds. Texas has 600,000. Colorado estimates 11,000 birds; Wyoming, 18,000; New Mexico, 30,000; and Montana, 40,000. Game departments estimate a total of two to three million birds in America.

The shotgun is commonly considered *the* firearm for wild turkey. But many hunters have found the rifle to be more suitable where they pursue the big bird. This is especially true for hunting flocks that inhabit mountainous regions, of which there are many, as well as birds that live in hilly country or even along streams that flow through good habitat.

There are two ways to rifle-hunt the wild turkey. One is to go forth with a rifle so accurate that a head/neck shot is viable. The other is to use a bullet constructed to stop the big bird, with minimal damage to the prized meat. Naturally, a combination of these two approaches is most desirable—good accuracy with a tough bullet,

Fadala took this wild turkey with an iron-sighted 22-rimfire magnum rifle by Anschutz.

with accuracy paramount. A head/neck shot with even the most explosive projectile obviously would ruin little, if any, edible meat. But this shot is not always available. In the Western mountains, for example, it's possible to get a good clean standing shot at long range—too far for the head/neck hit. How far? Careful hunters try to get as close as possible, but until a person has hunted wild turkey in the rimrocks he should refrain from criticizing another who feels that a 100-yard shot is entirely sportsmanlike.

THE JAVELINA

The javelina, or peccary, is also called a "wild pig," although it's more accurately termed a musk hog. Records prove that this big-game animal of the Southwestern United States and Mexico is actually pretty small. A dressed weight of 30 to 35 pounds is common; hogs dressing out at 40 to 45 pounds are considered prize animals. Javelina can be a problem to locate, but they aren't hard to stalk. Success rates in the 20 to 30 percent realm reflect the fact that these little musk hogs are small and the country they live in is large, not that they are wary and difficult to stalk. Because of their poor eyesight, javelina don't readily see hunters, but a keen sense of smell coupled with radar-like ears can uncover a hunter instantly. The careful outdoorsman stalks with the wind in his face and walks only where his boots won't crunch rocks and his pant legs won't scrape brush. Shots at 50 yards and under are achieved rather easily. Seldom will a hunter have to shoot beyond 100 yards, unless he's spooked the herd.

Because of the close-range factor on javelina and the comparatively small size of the wild turkey (Ben's bird is big, but he's no deer), these two species can be harvested with the same rifle. The javelina/wild turkey rifle isn't of any specific action or style, however. It can be a highly accurate target-type rifle with a variable scope capable of high magnification, or it can be an iron-sighted muzzleloader.

Rifle style discounted, what about the cartridge or blackpowder load for turkey and javelina?

THE 22 WMR

Two cautions should be observed when using the 22 WMR rifle for bagging wild turkey or javelina. The full-metal-jacket (FMJ) bullet is legal for wild turkey in some areas, but the hunter should avoid it unless he's a good caller and knows that his shot will be from close range. At 20 or 30 yards, it is entirely possible to place the little 40-grain "full patch" bullet precisely. That means a dead-center strike in the pinion area,

where wing and body meet. The bird will drop swiftly with such a strike. On the other hand, the FMJ bullet will zing right through a bird, doing very little internal damage unless it hits vital organs. (This is not always the case with the FMJ in 22-caliber centerfires, however; more on this later.) It's best, all in all, to avoid the FMJ bullet when using a 22 WMR for wild turkey. Save this bullet for small game (where its use is allowed by law) or for any circumstance where minimal pelt damage is desired.

The jacketed hollow-point bullet is a better choice for wild turkey. Even these bullets don't *always* produce dramatic wound channels in the big bird. I highly recommend the 22 WMR load

This javelina was tagged by the author with a custom Model 94 Winchester 30-30 rifle built by Dale Storey.

made by RWS. This load carries a 40-grain, soft-pointed hollow-point bullet—lead is exposed at the tip of the bullet, plus there is a hollow cavity. Not only is this bullet more disruptive of tissue, it also leaves the muzzle at a higher velocity than American-made ammo. This statement casts no aspersions on American-made 22 WMR ammo, which is highly accurate and ideal for most applications. But I have chronographed muzzle velocity figures of 2150 fps with the RWS 22 WMR ammo. (Not always easy to find, RWS ammo is available to dealers from The Old Western Scrounger, Inc., 12924 Highway A-12, Montague, CA 96064.) This isn't cheap ammo, just good ammo.

The ever-present dilemma exists, of course: A bullet that causes little damage saves meat, but the game might be lost. On the other hand, a bullet that drops game on the spot may ruin meat, but at least the game is down. Exact bullet placement saves the day with the more explosive projectile. Some meat will be lost even with correct bullet placement, but it's still the best compromise available. It's unethical to use ammo that's not designed to drop game quickly.

The 22 WMR works on javelina because, as stated earlier, these little pigs have Mr. Magoo eyesight. They can be stalked for a close shot, ensuring precise bullet placement. Federal Cartridge Company offers a heavier bullet that works well on javelina when hitting the chest—a 50-grain jacketed hollow point. Of course, velocity is not as high as with a 40-grain bullet, but energy and penetration are good. A javelina at 20 to 50 yards offers a perfect opportunity for the hunter to put one well-placed shot into the vitals, including the head shot. At 50 yards, the Federal 50-grain 22 WMR bullet will completely penetrate the javelina's skull, for an instantaneous and humane kill. The RWS 40-grain, soft-pointed hollow-point load is also deadly on the javelina when shot at the chest or head. The 22 WMR is not noted as the ideal cartridge for either wild turkey or javelina, but a good marksman can bag both species cleanly with the round. (*Note*: The 5mm Remington rimfire is also useful for wild turkey hunting, but this cartridge is no longer chambered in production rifles.)

John Fadala poses with a tom taken with a Marlin 22-rimfire magnum bolt-action—an ideal rifle for the job, especially when loaded with hollow-point ammunition.

22 CENTERFIRE REDUCED LOADS

Any 22 centerfire can be handloaded to duplicate the ballistics of the 22 WMR; therefore, it's only logical that subloads in any of the 22 centerfires must be considered at least on par with the 22 WMR for both wild turkey and javelina. Plus, a 22 centerfire can also be used in the full-power mode for these two game species.

The difference in using the hot 22 centerfire on javelina or wild turkey is one of meat loss. The wild turkey is far more susceptible to damage than is the larger and tougher javelina. So there is no reason to load down a 22 centerfire for javelina. A high-speed bullet through the chest cavity will bring it down quickly with no loss of edible meat. That same high-speed bullet is like a meat grinder when it passes through the breast of a wild turkey, however. Recommendation: Use subloads in the 22 centerfire for wild turkey, but retain full-throttle 22-centerfire loads for javelina. A few examples of 22-centerfire handloads for wild turkey, but *not* for javelina, follow.

22 Hornet Reduced Load. Many consider the 22 Hornet, in its full-power load, the best wild turkey cartridge. Others, however, think it's too explosive on the birds.

Light-jacketed varmint bullets at standard 22 Hornet velocities are quite destructive on wild turkey. A harder projectile at a more modest muzzle velocity is better—for example, a 55-grain bullet with 10.0 grains of IMR-4227 powder and a standard small rifle primer. Depending on barrel length and individual barrel/chamber factors, muzzle velocity runs around 2250 to 2300 fps with this load. It makes a fine turkey-taker, even for 125-yard shots.

A 55-grain Hornady FMJ bullet is available for the 22 Hornet. This accurate bullet works well on wild turkey, where allowed by law. But of course the solid bullet requires more careful placement, because it doesn't impart as much energy as an expanding missile. The subload shown here can also be used with the 218 Bee cartridge.

222 Remington Reduced Load. The accurate 222 Remington makes a good wild turkey round. It too can be loaded down to reduce meat loss. A 60- to 63-grain bullet generally is hard-jacketed enough to diminish the usual explosiveness of this varmint cartridge. The 60- to 63-grain bullet can be loaded with 15.0 grains of IMR-4198 powder for around 2250 fps mv, depending on barrel length and individual rifle traits. The 223 Remington also digests this same

wild turkey load, as does the 222 Remington Magnum. A 55-grain Hornady FMJ bullet can be substituted in this load.

22-250 Remington Reduced Load. This and its high-speed cousin, the 220 Swift, are not themselves ideal wild turkey rounds. The larger-capacity case is not quite as conducive to accurate underloads as are the 222 Remington and small rounds. Nevertheless, make no mistake about it—a centered hit with a full-power 22-250 varmint load will destroy much meat on a wild turkey. Therefore, underloading is necessary for this round and its counterparts.

A test rifle chambered for a 22-250 Remington proved quite accurate with a 60-grain bullet and 17.0 grains of IMR-4227 powder, with muzzle velocity running about 2200 fps. The Hornady 55-grain FMJ bullet also can be used in this cartridge with the same load, with a repeated

Interestingly, one cartridge loaded two ways can serve for both wild turkey and javelina. On the left is the 30-30 Winchester cartridge loaded with a cast-lead bullet. Such a bullet can be driven at only 22 LR velocities for a good close-range wild turkey round. On the right is the same 30-30 cartridge, but in its regular form, ideal for javelina.

A bolt-action rifle chambered for one of many different cartridges can be used for both wild turkey and javelina, especially by a handloader who can alter the loads for each species. This Kimber Model 84 Varminter is chambered for the 17 Remington, 221 Remington Fireball and 223 Remington, all good cartridges for turkey and javelina.

caution: Ensure that the hard bullet at modest velocity is well placed.

22 CENTERFIRES WITH HIGH-SPEED FMJ BULLETS

It would seem that an FMJ bullet at any speed would work well on wild turkey, because it would zoom through without much tissue disruption. This is not true, however. A high-speed FMJ bullet may well zip through a fairly large or tough target without much disruption. But the bullet produces a shock wave in front of it, which can destroy tissue. Also, the bullet may tumble in the target, causing a buzz-saw effect on the edibles.

Because of these factors, a high-velocity FMJ bullet is not right for wild turkey hunting and, in fact, may be *illegal* in a number of areas. The FMJ bullet is definitely illegal for javelina hunting in some regions.

OTHER WILD TURKEY/JAVELINA CARTRIDGES

The 22 Hornet. Many hunters consider the 22 Hornet in its full-charge mode to be ideal for wild turkey. Naturally, the 22 Hornet has plenty of power for wild turkey hunting; however, this medium-velocity round can destroy the bird's entire breast section. For this reason, the reduced load discussed earlier is recommended instead of a varmint load. The hunter who handloads should consider building a 22 Hornet reload that is just right for the specific conditions in question. For example, where the big birds are taken cross-canyon, as occurs in some mountainous

areas, a 55-grain bullet at 2400 fps mv may be necessary. This velocity is readily achieved with 10.5 grains of IMR-4227 powder. On javelina, the 22 Hornet should be used at full power, either in a factory load or a handload. A good javelina handload is the 55-grain expanding bullet and 11.5 grains of Winchester 680 powder, for 2500 fps mv.

The 218 Bee also can be loaded to this velocity with a 55-grain bullet. Reloading manuals that show the 218 Bee generally offer various loads that make good javelina medicine. The 218 Bee also should be loaded down for wild turkey hunting—except for long-range purposes, in which case a 55-grain bullet in the 2400 to 2500 fps mv realm is called for.

The 222 Family. The 222 family—222 Remington, 222 Remington Magnum and 223 Remington—all offer more punch than is needed for wild turkey hunting. Reduced loads are called for, as discussed above. On javelina, factory loads and high-velocity handloads are preferred for these rounds; for example, a 55-grain bullet at around 3100 fps mv, achieved with a number of different powders. Check a reloading manual for specific guidance.

The 22 PPC USA. Of special interest is this cartridge chambered in a bolt-action rifle, such as the Sako varmint model. The reason for this round's special notation is its benchrest-quality accuracy. On javelina, or where wild turkey can be hunted with a rifle, this accuracy brings fine results. It makes for specific bullet placement, which means an instant harvest. In the 22 PPC, full-power loads should be used for javelina, with subloads used for wild turkey. A good 22 PPC load for javelina is the factory offering from Sako. Also good is a 50- to 55-grain bullet at around 3100 fps mv, which can be easily gained with 25.0 grains of H-322 powder.

Larger 22 Centerfire Cartridges. All the rest of the 22 centerfires beyond 22 PPC USA size are more powerful than necessary for turkey hunting, but are ideal for javelina. This doesn't throw cold water on the theory that the javelina cartridge is also a wild turkey cartridge, because excellent reduced loads are available for the 219 Zipper, 225 Winchester, 224 Weatherby, 22-250 Remington and 220 Swift.

The 6 PPC USA. The 6 PPC USA cartridge fits the wild turkey/javelina rifle definition because of its high accuracy potential. On javelina, it should be used with the factory load (full power) or an upper-end handload with a 70- to 75-grain bullet at around 3000 fps mv, which is achieved with various loads, such as 26.0 grains of H-322 powder.

The 25-20 Winchester. This round came along in 1893 and never went away. Although no rifles were chambered for the 25-20 for a long time, ammo continued to flow from factories. Now the 25-20 is back, chambered for the Marlin Model 1894 CL rifle. Thousands of old, but serviceable, rifles were made in this caliber as well. The 25-20 is a mild-mannered plinker and small-game round, but it's also a fine wild turkey/javelina cartridge. The low-velocity factory load is just about ideal for wild turkey hunting. The 86-grain factory bullet at about 1450 fps mv isn't an explosive missile. This same load certainly will work for javelina. The reloader can pep up the 25-20 with a 60-grain bullet and 10.0 grains of IMR-4227, for about 2000 fps mv. An 86-grain bullet can be loaded in the 25-20 to produce around 1600 fps mv with 9.0 grains of IMR-4227 powder—an effective close-range javelina load.

Caution: Use only bullets with blunt noses in 25-20 rifles that have tubular magazines. Pointed bullets in tubular magazines may cause primer detonation during rifle recoil.

The 32-20 Winchester. Although the 32-20 shoots bullets of about 31-caliber size—a bit on the large size for wild turkey—this big sister of the 25-20 is another fine wild turkey/javelina round. Its low-velocity bullet doesn't ruin a lot

Nicole Fadala poses with her own wild turkey and a bird taken by her father. Nicole got hers with a 6mm-222 rifle loaded down.

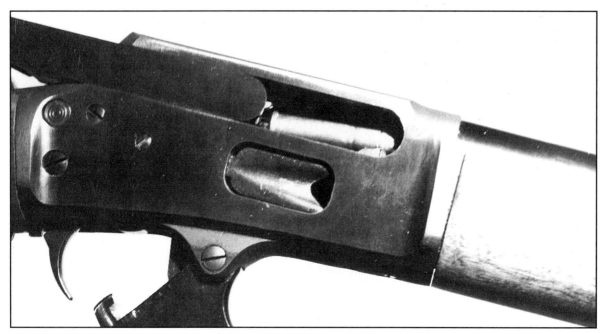

An excellent turkey cartridge is the old-time 32-20 Winchester, which is still factory loaded. Here it's being fed into a modern Model 1894 CL Marlin lever-action rifle.

of meat, yet sustains sufficient power for both of these game species.

The 32-20 came out in 1882, about a decade before the 25-20 Winchester was developed. This round wasn't chambered in rifles for a number of years, but now it's again offered in a modern rifle, the Marlin Model 1892 CL. The 32-20 is also chambered in the old, but shootable, Winchester Model 1892 rifle. In the past, many other rifles were chambered for this cartridge, including the Savage bolt-action.

The current factory load for the 32-20 Winchester shows a 100-grain bullet at 1210 fps mv. It's easy to see that this load isn't explosive, and yet it's plenty for wild turkey and javelina. As with the 25-20, the 32-20 also can be handloaded to make it more versatile. Hornady has an 85-grain, .312-inch-diameter bullet for the 32-20. This bullet is designed to expand and should be used on javelina with full-strength loads. In the new Marlin Model 1894 CL rifle, a load of 16.0 grains weight of IMR-4227 powder drives this 85-grain bullet at 2200 fps mv— plenty of power for javelina. This bullet can be loaded down to about 1700 fps mv with 12.0

grains of Winchester 680 powder. A good turkey load is the harder-jacketed 100-grain 32-20 bullet with 12.0 grains of IMR-4227 powder for about 1600 fps muzzle velocity.

The 17 Remington. This little hellbender may be considered an odd addition to our collection of wild turkey/javelina cartridges. But in fact, the 17 Remington makes a marvelous wild turkey cartridge with reduced handloads and is a deadly javelina round with factory loads or full-scale handloads.

First, how to make a 17 Remington into a fine wild turkey cartridge: Get the right bullet. This means a harder projectile than normally used; the Bullberry 24.5-grain 17-caliber bullet is ideal. (Check your local dealer for availability.) This bullet, combined with 17.0 grains of IMR-4198 powder, produces a muzzle velocity of about 3600 fps. This is high velocity, indeed, although well below the usual 4000 to 4100 fps mv potential of the 17 Remington. The tiny bullet in this harder-jacketed version, even at such a high starting velocity, has proven effective on wild turkey without undue meat damage when aimed at the bird's pinion area. For javelina, 24.0

grains of IMR-4320 can drive a custom 17-caliber, 25-grain bullet close to 4075 fps mv. Chest hits result in instant kills.

THE BIG-BORE RIFLE

No big-bore rifle, such as the 270 Winchester or 30-06 Springfield, can be considered ideal for either wild turkey or javelina. But these rounds must be included here because they are used on both species. In fact, more javelina are harvested with big-bore big-game cartridges than with lesser rounds more ideal for the animal. And in mountain states, it's common to see turkey hunters afield with the same big-game rifles. Some wild turkey hunters carry big-bore rifles because deer season and turkey season coincide in some areas. In such a locale, the only proper strategy is to carry a rifle suited for deer.

The choice has to run in favor of ruining some wild turkey meat rather than hitting a deer with a load that is too light. But there is a better way: the squib load for the big-game rifle, particularly with a cast-lead bullet. Bullet casting is a hobby in its own right. Thousands of shooters in this country fire tons of lead downrange annually. The *Lyman Cast Bullet Handbook* shows dozens of good bullets for popular big-bore cartridges and numerous loads. These loads vary from low to medium velocity, the former being great for wild turkey. A long list of loads for all the big bores would be unwieldy, but the following sample load will show how cast-lead bullets can turn a big-game round into a wild turkey taker.

The 308 Winchester is a good example, because it's a highly popular and accurate cartridge that uses cast as well as jacketed bullets. Numerous cast bullets and loads are available for the 308. A good light bullet for wild turkey hunting with the 308 is the 122-grain Lyman Mould No. 311465. This bullet in a harder form, at least No. 2 alloy, can be driven at around 1750 fps mv with 20.0 grains of Reloader 7 powder. Another good lead projectile is out of Lyman's Mould No. 311291. Although this is a 169-grain bullet in No. 2 alloy, its low velocity precludes violent expansion and it can be a fine turkey missile. A charge of 26.0 grains of IMR-3031 puts this bullet out of the muzzle at about 1700 fps.

One problem, of course, is slipping the turkey load into the chamber of the rifle once the birds are spotted. The hunter after both deer and gobblers will keep his rifle loaded for the bigger prize. But in a deer/wild turkey hunting situation, a hunter generally sees the birds while he's still-hunting, walking quietly through the terrain with the wind in his face. This gives him a chance to remove the deer round from his magazine and replace it with the cast bullet turkey load.

THE MUZZLELOADER

A 32- or 36-caliber muzzleloader shooting a round ball is superb for wild turkey hunting. Both caliber rifles can be loaded to produce plenty of muzzle velocity and thus sufficient energy for wild turkey, with a flat enough trajectory for 100-yard shots. Actually, shots are usually closer—more typically in the 50-yard realm—

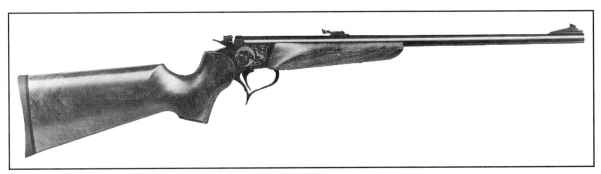

Fadala's current wild turkey rifle is the Thompson/Center single-shot Contender Carbine in 17 Remington chambering. He prefers the Bullberry 24-grain, 17-caliber bullet for turkey in this rifle.

especially when the birds are hunted along creekbottoms or wherever foliage or calling means a close encounter.

The beauty of the small-caliber round ball is its penchant for clean harvests on wild turkey without explosiveness. The pure lead 45-grain, 32-caliber round ball or 65-grain, 36-caliber round ball tends to punch a straight wound channel. Common sense dictates that the pinion area remains the target, of course. A good wild

charge for 1700 to 1800 fps mv, depending on barrel length. A Mowrey 36-caliber rifle with 28-inch barrel (all-steel version) got 1826 fps mv with a 65-grain round ball and 40 grains of FFFg black powder.

A 38- or 40-caliber muzzleloader is also worthy in the turkey field, but these two sizes are not very popular. Both also work fine for javelina. Actually, *any* blackpowder rifle is a good javelina rifle. If a small-bore rifle used for wild

The javelina is a small big-game animal, but it's a prize just the same.

turkey load for the 32-caliber muzzleloader is 40 grains of FFFg black powder or an equivalent volume load of Pyrodex P powder. (Pyrodex should be loaded by volume, not by weight.)

With this load, the Thompson/Center 32-caliber Cherokee with its 24-inch barrel earned a muzzle velocity of 1612 fps. The 36-caliber sootburner can be loaded with the same powder

turkeys is employed on javelina, the load should be upped to a safe optimum level. For example, the same short-barreled T/C 32-caliber Cherokee got 1733 fps mv with 50 grains of FFFg and a 45-grain round ball. A 36-caliber CVA Squirrel Rifle fired a 65-grain round ball at 1982 fps mv using 50 grains of FFFg black powder. These are good javelina loads in the small bore because, at 20 to 50 yards, it's really no trick to put the little 32- or 36-caliber ball right on the money for a perfect head shot.

Not to be left out for either wild turkey or javelina are other blackpowder rifles and calibers, as well as elongated projectiles. However, a wise hunter does not load up the heaviest charge possible with the largest bullet for wild turkey.

THE 32-RIMFIRE RIFLE

What? You've never even seen a 32-rimfire rifle? Few are around, to be sure. But Navy Arms Company recently offered 32- rimfire ammo, and this little rimfire is certainly part of the wild turkey/javelina family of rounds.

The 32 rimfire, with bullets in the 80- to 90-grain class at about the speed of sound, provides good close-range power for wild turkeys. The expert would have no problem putting a wild pig in the pot with the same rimfire load. After all, this round is more potent than the 22 WMR, which is legal for both wild turkey and javelina in some areas.

There is no plan for widespread reintroduction of the 32 rimfire, nor has a rifle been so-chambered for years. But the fact remains that a rimfire larger than 22 caliber would serve the wild turkey fan quite well in certain settings, especially for called-in birds, and the patient hunter also could count on the round to bag a javelina.

It's easy to see now why the wild turkey/javelina rifle was all but dispensed with earlier. There's no *specific* wild turkey/javelina rifle, because just about any properly loaded rifle will do. An accurate rifle that the shooter handles well, with the right load and, preferably, with a good trigger that promotes bullet placement, is a good turkey/javelina gun.

My favorite turkey/javelina rifle is a Thompson/Center Carbine with a 21-inch barrel, chambered in 17 Remington. The barrel is long enough to realize the potential of the 17 Remington cartridge, but the overall package remains short, light and handy enough to pack around the woods for wild turkey and the Southwest desert mountains for javelina. Accuracy is sufficient for hunting both species. For javelina, I load the little 17 for full power: a 25-grain bullet at over 4000 fps mv. For wild turkey, I download. On going reload tests include modest powder charges of IMR-4198 or H-4198 for muzzle velocities in the 3000 fps domain, with plenty of power for turkey within normal shooting distance. The aforementioned Bullberry bullet has proved reliable in harvesting without ruining a lot of meat.

THE WOODS AND BRUSH RIFLE

11 Like the small-game rifle and the turkey/javelina rifle, the woods/brush rifle depends upon a special cartridge to do its work. However, by its nature this rifle style is particularly suited to quick, close-range action. If the stay-put benchrest rifle is a stone, the woods/brush rifle is a bird. The benchrest piece is made to sit heavily in one spot, settled firmly for a shot. The woods/brush rifle is designed to fly into action.

Some readers may remember a favorite old rifle that weighed plenty, had a long barrel and came to shoulder as fluidly as a hippo doing the tango. Yet its owner did fine with that rifle in brush and woods. Granted. A smart rifleman learns to overcome. He manages to squeeze the most from any style rifle under a multitude of circumstances. But that's not the aim of the woods/brush rifle. The goal here is to define that specific rifle best-suited for the millions of hunters who go forth in heavy cover every year in pursuit of white-tailed deer, bears, wild boars, mule deer of the forests, elk, moose and other big-game animals that prefer tight places.

The scene is brush and timber, not necessarily in the mountains. Mountain shooting can be long-range, even in the timber, because a hunter can see from his side of the hill to the other, or from one canyon slope to the next. Our

timber rifle is for the multitude of locations that require close-range shooting, often at quick-moving targets. Everything said of the woods/brush rifle and its rounds pertain to this kind of country.

THE CARBINE

The carbine inevitably comes to mind for woods/brush work. While a carbine is considered a rifle, a rifle is not necessarily a carbine. A simple definition of carbine is "short rifle." This also means a short barrel. But how do short barrels affect recoil, noise, accuracy and velocity?

Any reduction in rifle weight increases recoil because the heavier the firearm, the less it "kicks." However, removal of an inch, two inches, even four or six inches of barrel does not take away all that much from a rifle's overall weight. Less weight up front may tend to increase the up-lifting of the barrel, however, which in turn may give an *impression* of greater recoil.

But in practical terms, the short barrel is not guilty of causing heavier recoil. So eliminate increased recoil for the truncated barrel. What about noise? No doubt about it—a short barrel sounds louder to the shooter. Arguably, if the powder charge were consumed within the confines of the bore, or nearly so, the shorter barrel

Mule deer as well as white-tailed deer can be found in brush or timber. A rifle suited for this setting is generally fast-handling and easy to aim quickly.

would bark no louder than a longer one. However, the shorter barrel generally does not consume the entire powder charge quite as effectively as the longer barrel for most big-game cartridges, so the shorter barrel makes more noise than the longer barrel. Chalk up one black mark against the stubbier tube: more noise, coupled with more muzzle blast.

Then there is accuracy. Is a long barrel inherently more accurate than a short one? Not really. Short barrels can be quite accurate. In fact, a short, stiff barrel can be more accurate than a long "whippy" barrel.

That leaves muzzle velocity, of which the shorter barrel can lose out. But it's not so simple, because muzzle-velocity loss per inch of barrel is not a constant. The general "rule of thumb" that declares 25 fps loss for every inch of barrel is a joke. There can be no single answer to barrel length/velocity loss because it all depends upon the cartridge, the load in question and the individual rifle. I tested a 270 Winchester by reducing its 24-inch barrel inch by inch and chronographing shots until the barrel was 20 inches long. Velocity did indeed fall as the barrel was lopped off, but not by 25 fps or any other standard figure. The first big surprise: slow-burning H-4831 powder continued to give the best muzzle velocity in this 270 rifle, even when the barrel was only 20 inches long.

The second surprise was a velocity loss of only 111 fps with a 130-grain Remington bullet from a 24-inch barrel to a 20-inch barrel (a drop from 3135 fps mv to 3024 fps mv). If that seems close to the oft-mentioned 25 fps mark, note that with a 150-grain bullet in the same rifle, velocity fell from 2975 fps mv to 2901 fps mv when going from a 24- to 20-inch barrel—only a 74 fps loss for this particular rifle with this particular H-4831 load.

One advantage of the single-shot style rifle for brush hunting is the generally shorter overall length. Here a bolt-action and single-shot with the same barrel lengths are compared.

Other rifles in other calibers showed different velocity losses per inch of barrel. A 30-06 Springfield suffered considerably, even with heavier bullets, when its barrel was whittled down from 24 inches to 18.5 inches. Heavier projectiles, one may assume, would cause better consumption of the powder charge, thereby showing less velocity loss as the barrel grows shorter. But in this test rifle, all bullet weights suffered more than a little as the barrel grew ever shorter. To condense the figures, consider a velocity of 3000 fps for a 150-grain bullet in the 24-inch barrel, this with 59.0 grains of IMR-4350 powder. Using the same bullet, same case, same primer, same 59.0 charge of IMR-4350 powder, but in the 18.5-inch 30-06 barrel, velocity fell from 3000 fps to 2690 fps—a loss of 310 fps for 5.5 inches, or around 56 fps per inch.

Let's look at one last cartridge: the 308 Winchester. I chronographed two different rifles in this session, one with a 22-inch barrel, the other with an 18.5-inch barrel. Velocity difference was minor between the two. For example, a Norma factory load with a 150-grain bullet earned 2758 fps mv from the 22-inch barrel, 2746 fps mv from the 18.5-inch barrel. Remember, of course, that this test used two different rifles, rather than one rifle with its barrel shortened, and that does make a difference. But the fact remains that the 308 Winchester cartridge did not suffer great velocity loss in the 18.5-inch barrel—at least not when compared to a 22-inch barrel.

Other tests on these 308 rifles included RWS Match ammo with a 168-grain bullet: 2523 fps mv for the 22-inch barrel, 2504 fps mv for the 18.5-inch barrel. A factory load with a 180-grain bullet also revealed little velocity loss: Winchester ammo with a 180-grain bullet achieved 2533 fps mv from the 22-inch barrel and 2529 fps mv from the 18.5-inch barrel.

What about handloads? The minor losses between barrels continued to hold up with a variety of reloads, from 150- to 190-grain bullets.

RIFLE WEIGHT

Nobody enjoys carrying an overly heavy rifle. However, stability is always important, even for close-range brush/timber hunting, and more vital than overall weight of the brush/timber rifle is *balance.* The butt-heavy or muzzle-heavy rifle will not snap to the shoulder with the precision of a well-balanced rifle. Before going out into the "thick stuff," the shooter should pre-test the rifle he intends to carry. This is easy enough to do: Pick up the rifle, making sure that it is unloaded. Hold the rifle as you would when stillhunting in the brush or woods. Now close your eyes. Snap the rifle to your shoulder, with eyes still shut, as if a white-tailed deer suddenly bounded out of a thicket in front of you.

Hold it. Don't move. Leave the rifle to shoulder exactly as it came up. Adjust nothing. Now open your eyes. Are you looking through the scope, or are the iron sights aligned? Has your

obviously. But it is not, fortunately, a matter of total individuality. There is leeway. A shooter can adjust to accommodate an LOP that is not absolutely correct for his body build or physical size. That's why it's not necessary for a hunter to run to his gunsmith for an LOP adjustment just because the LOP is not absolutely perfect for him. On the other hand, if LOP is fairly far off, a trip to the gunsmith is highly recommended. Fortunately, the problem has an easy remedy.

The gunsmith measures the shooter and matches shooter and rifle, establishing the correct LOP. He cuts the stock off appropriately, attaches the recoil pad, and the new LOP is just right for the individual shooter. If the stock is too short, spacers can be added, as well as a re-

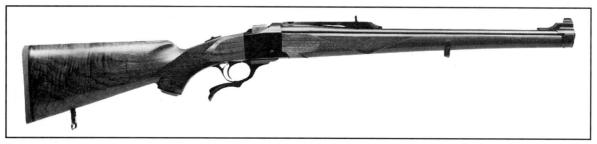

For very short overall length, look to this Ruger No. 1 International single-shot carbine, available in 30-06.

face made contact with the buttstock in such a manner that you would have to adjust your hold on the rifle in order to obtain a sight picture of that make-believe deer? A properly balanced, well-fitted rifle will come to your shoulder ready to go into action. Sure, a slight adjustment may be necessary, but not an entire reshifting in order to regain a sight picture.

STOCK FIT

Stock fit is also essential for fast action in close. The first consideration is LOP: length of pull. LOP is the distance from the trigger to the center of the buttplate. It's easy to see that if this measurement is too long, the buttstock will get hung up on the hunter's clothing or strike his armpit before it settles into his shoulder properly. If LOP is too short, the rifle tends to lever upward upon firing, often making it quite uncomfortable to shoot. LOP differs for different-sized people,

coil pad. If the stock is too short and already wears a recoil pad, a thicker pad may do the trick or spacers can be added to lengthen LOP.

Another important stock dimension is the comb—or top ridge of the stock—upon which the shooter rests his cheek. It may be too high or too low, in which case the shooter must adjust his head so that he can see the sights.

The professional gunsmith can correct several other stock dimensions to ensure a better fit, such as pitch, toe-out and toe-in. If the shooter tries the little closed-eyes test and finds he is not at all greeted by a sight picture when he opens his eyes, a trip to the gunsmith is in order.

STOCK MATERIAL

The quick-handling ability of the brush/woods rifle is not affected by the stock material. The ordinary wood stock has served for eons and still does. The newer composite and synthetic

One of the author's favorite brush rifles is a Mannlicher carbine made in 1921. It's chambered for the 9×56mm Mannlicher cartridge, which is comparable to a 358 Winchester in power.

An effective combination for Fadala is the 308 Winchester cartridge chambered in the Ruger Model 77 International carbine—good power from a short rifle.

John Fadala holds his father's Ruger Model 77 International in 308 Winchester. Note 2.5X-8X Bushnell variable scope. The low setting is ideal for fast action in brush and timber.

stocks are also excellent. But what about rough conditions? Won't the newer stock materials hold up better than wood for the rifle that has to accompany the hunter through tangles and tree limbs? Sure. On the other hand, the traditional wood stock has also worked well in tough terrain for a very long time and still does. The final decision regarding stock material for the brush/woods rifle is a personal one.

THE SAFETY

"I would have gotten a shot at that deer, but I couldn't get the safety off!" If you haven't said these words, you've probably heard them. There is no such thing as one ideal safety or one perfect safety location. If a hunter can swiftly slip off the safety on his rifle, he has the right safety. There are many ways to carry a rifle in the brush/timber setting, of course. One good way to carry a lever-action rifle with exposed hammer, for example,

is with the chamber empty. The hunter works the lever as the rifle is on its way to his shoulder. Anyone who does not think this is a fast way to get a clean shot off, as well as a good safety precaution, simply has not practiced the method. But how to carry a rifle in timber or brush country is not the point here—the safety is, and all the shooter need ask himself is this: "Can my rifle be carried in the safest manner possible, while still allowing me to get the rifle into action as speedily as possible?"

SIGHTS

Sights may be the most important element of the brush/timber rifle. Stock fit depends upon what sights are used. A rifle can be said to fit the shooter only when he can bring the firearm to shoulder without having to go through an overt contortion of his body in order to achieve a sight picture. The scope sight tends to rest higher

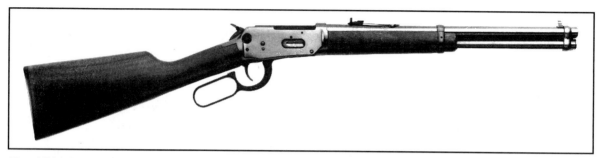

The 16-inch barrel Winchester 94 Trapper carbine is a good choice for tight quarters.

above the barrel than the iron sight, although an open iron sight on a ramp can indeed stand tall. Be certain that the sights fit the rifle. That's the bottom line. But which sights are best on a brush/timber rifle?

In Africa, I interviewed a number of professional hunters about sights for fast-action in thick country, especially on dangerous game. The majority of these hunters said the open iron sight was best. However, a minority felt otherwise, and that minority was vocal and convincing. Some professional hunters agreed that iron sights were best for close work—but not *open* iron sights. These men had tried the peep sight and found it extremely fast. After all, the correct way to use a peep sight is to look through, not at, the aperture, ignoring the "hole," in fact. The eye automatically centers at the greatest point of light anyway. Therefore, the hunter only has to look through the aperture, paste the front sight on target and pull the trigger, instead of having to align a rear sight and front sight.

One professional hunter disagreed with both iron sight camps. "The low-power scope is far and away the fastest sight in the bush I've ever used," he said. And his commentary made sense. His favorite scope was the 1.5X-5X variable. Obviously, the scope was carried at all times on its lowest setting to gain a very wide field of view, so wide that even the barrel could be seen in the sight picture. Scope power is advanced for shots that demand precise bullet placement.

It's difficult to argue against a scope sight in the brush, provided two things: field of view is wide and the hunter's face settles into the comb of the stock so that he automatically looks directly into the ocular lens of the scope, with no adjustment of his head on the buttstock.

It may seem a dodge to say that sight choice is also a matter of individual preference, but that's the bottom line. Some hunters can shoot superbly with open irons, others are great with peep sights and still others find the scope sight the fastest.

THE BRUSH CARTRIDGE

"Boy, she sure makes a great brush cartridge!" These words, usually said about a larger-caliber round that shoots a fairly heavy projectile, are just a bunch of bananas. No cartridge

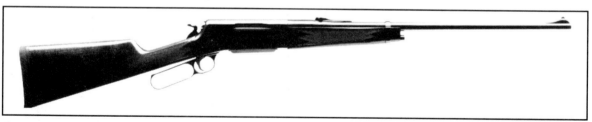

A superb brush/woods rifle is the sleek Browning lever-action Model 81 BLR, especially in caliber 358 Winchester. The value of the big bore here is not so much pushing brush aside, but rather a heavy bone-breaking bullet that can anchor a big-game animal on the spot.

smashes brush out of the way without the bullet taking a detour. This is not to say that a 35 Remington isn't better at getting through brush than a 222 Remington. But that's just about as far as the brush cartridge vehicle carries the story.

A simple test—shooting at a target set up behind a screen of brush— revealed the truth about bullets in the brush. In one test a 180-grain spitzer (pointed) bullet out of a 30-06 at a mv of 2700 fps, with a striking velocity of about 2500 fps, scored more bull's-eyes on the brush target than a 45-70 Government 405-grain bullet hitting the brush at around 1000 fps.

Momentum (mass times velocity) may indicate better brush performance. However, the best bet for a woods/brush hunter is to select a cartridge that matches the game being hunted, thereafter making all attempts to put the bullet

procure venison chops. On the other hand, if a fellow just happens to be terribly good with a bolt-action 375 Magnum in terms of fast-action shooting with precise bullet placement, nobody can tell him the big Model 70 is not a brush rifle. But without regard to that individual, the little 94 is better suited to fast and close shooting.

A look at any catalogue of rifles reveals a great many brush rifles made today (not to mention those offered in the past that are now out of production). Remington's Model 7400 semiauto rifle with 18.5-inch barrel in 30-06 chambering is a fine brush/woods rifle. Browning's Model 81 lever gun with 20-inch barrel in calibers 308 Winchester or 358 Winchester is another good brush/timber rifle, as is Marlin's Model 336 in 30-30 or 35 Remington.

Consider the 358 Winchester round for one

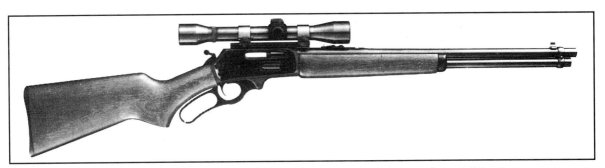

The lever-action rifle, such as this Marlin 30AS, is fast in the brush and timber. Whether to use a scope or not is a question best answered by the individual rifleman.

on target by sending it through holes in the brush, rather than counting on the bullet to thrust brush out of the way.

GOOD BRUSH RIFLES

"Handy" is an apt word to describe the brush/woods rifle. That may seem simple, but it works. Imagine before you two rifles. One is the Model 94 Winchester carbine—old Slab-Side, if you will. The other is the fine Winchester Model 70—the African model chambered for the 375 H&H cartridge. Which of these rifles is best for brush and timber? Don't fall into the trap. Of course the 94 will come to shoulder quicker than the bigger rifle. And if we're talking about deer in the thicket, a 375 H&H is hardly necessary to

moment: This 35-caliber cartridge, based on the 308 Winchester case, shoots a 200-grain bullet at around 2500 fps mv. That's a lot of mashed potatoes in the brush and timber, and a 250-grain bullet is available for those hunters who want even more power.

Remington's Model 7600 slide-action 30-06 with 18.5-inch barrel is another made-for-the-brush rifle. Of course the Model 94 is still with us, only better, with the Angle Eject action and a 356 Winchester cartridge as well as a 307 Winchester, 7-30 Waters, and the good old 30-30 round.

Remington's Model 7 bolt-action rifle is also brush/woods oriented with its 18.5-inch barrel and calibers like the 308 Winchester. Ruger's

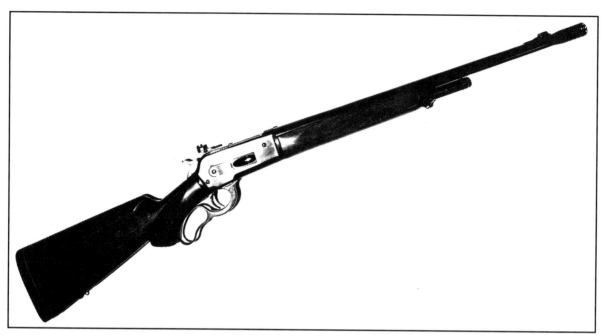

This customized Model 71 Winchester was built by Dale Storey for hunting big game in the brush, especially bears and moose in Alaska. It's chambered for the wildcat 450 Alaskan cartridge. Note muzzle brake to help control the effects of recoil.

The muzzleloader is no more or less a brush rifle than any other type of shoulder arm. The idea, however, that a heavy bullet from a large bore frontloader will cut through brush like a needle through paper is false. Even large bullets are deflected by brush and limbs.

The Marlin 1894S lever-action rifle is available in a number of handgun calibers, including the 41 Magnum, 44 Magnum and 45 Colt—all big-bullet shooters for close work in brush and woods.

Another good rifle for close-in work is Sako's full Mannlicher Carbine. It is available in 243 and 308 Winchester for deer-sized game, and in larger calibers for hunters who want more power in an 18½-inch-barrel arm.

Model 77 International is another fine brush/woods rifle with 18.5-inch barrel. My own 77 International in 308 sees action in thick cover every year. Sako offers a special rifle for close-in work: the Sako Carbine. It's just right in 308 Winchester for deer-sized game, but also available in calibers 338 Winchester and 375 H&H Magnum for hunters who want a lot of power in a short rifle with an 18.5-inch barrel.

The Steyr-Mannlicher has a full-stock carbine offered in a multitude of good American and European rounds, such as the 30-06 and 308, as well as a 9.3×62mm and 8×68S. Ruger's No. 1 International represents close-range action in a single-shot rifle chambered for good rounds such as the 7×57mm and 30-06. A snappy little rifle that can't be left out of the close-range picture is Thompson/Center's Contender Carbine with its 21-inch barrel. This fine single-shot is chambered for the 35 Remington cartridge, admired by brush-shooters for decades, as well as the 30-30 Winchester and 44 Remington Magnum. A 45-70 interchangeable barrel is also offered for the T/C Carbine.

This is a condensed list; many other suitable brush/woods rifles exist. There are even multiple-barrel rifles that qualify for brush/woods work on big game. The modern hunter who wants a firearm for heavy cover is blessed with choice, and a lot of it.

THE MOUNTAIN/ PLAINS RIFLE

12 The mountain rifle and the plains rifle can be considered as one because their requirements are often the same: accuracy, a flat-shooting cartridge, and a scope sight, preferably one capable of high magnification. A high-velocity bullet delivered over long range with precision and high remaining energy is required for long shots.

Before going on, some statements about long-range shooting are in order. First, it is unethical for a hunter to shoot far if his rifle is incapable of good grouping and high-energy delivery at long range. Second, it's unethical for a hunter to shoot at distant big game if he isn't proficient at long-range shooting. Third, it's wrong to take a long shot at big game when a prudent stalk will provide a much closer shot. When hunting large game, the best shot is always the closest one.

However, a close shot is not always possible in the West, or in many other areas where big game is normally sighted at long range and stalking possibilities are minimal. Just as it's wrong to shoot at long range if the rifle and the hunter aren't capable of accuracy at far distances, it's equally foolish to deny the careful and talented marksman a powerful, accurate rifle.

A proper plains/mountain rifle is more ac-curate at 300 yards than some other rifles are at 100 yards. And some shooters can place three shots at 300 yards into a smaller group than some shooters with less accurate rifles can manage at 100 yards. Moreover, some high-intensity cartridges deliver more energy at 300 yards than many other popular cartridges can deliver at the muzzle.

What, then, is the mountain/plains rifle? When the "mountain man" crossed the Mississippi River in search of Rocky Mountain beaver pelts in the 1800s, he learned something about his rifle. The Pennsylvania longrifle that served him so well in the East was not suitable for the West. That's why the stout, big-bore, half-stock plains rifle was born.

In this century, hunters learned the same thing—that Western or any open-country hunting calls for a rifle that meets long-range requirements. The 30-30 Winchester cartridge in the Model 94 Winchester rifle was once a hard-to-beat combination for the West. In 1895, when the 30-30 came along, it was a flat-shooting round compared to blackpowder numbers such as the 45-70, with its looping, low-velocity trajectory. The 30-30 is still a great round. It offers a special reward to the modern hunter who is willing, even in open country, to get relatively close. Furthermore, except when compared with

Using his Storey Modern Plains Rifle, Fadala harvested this buck from long distance. While the power of a 7mm Magnum is not necessary for antelope, at long range it is wise and prudent to have that extra margin of energy.

true long-range cartridges, the 30-30 shoots far.

Today, however, current hunting seasons are comparatively short, competition in the field is keen, and big-game animals seem better educated than their predecessors. The mule deer buck that used to stop for a look back before topping the rise now pops over without so much as a go-to-the-devil as he disappears. That's why contemporary open-country hunters have turned to long-range plains/mountain rifles.

The unique aspects of Western big-game hunting lie in the terrain and the species hunted. The land varies; there are riverbottoms and creekbottoms, black timber forests in big canyon country, high mountains, and wide open plains. Big-game animals range from the little Southwestern javelina to the ponderous bull moose. Therefore, the true nature of the mountain/plains rifle is versatility. A versatile tool is usually a jack-of-all-trades, master of none. This is true of the all-around Western big-game rifle. It's good for everything, but not perfect for anything. It's not the best brush rifle, but it may be called on for Western riverbottom white-tailed bucks. It's not ideal in the black timber, where the hunter must get on target swiftly, but it works there. It shines brightly in the high mountains—but although it's well-suited to that terrain, again it's not absolutely ideal. On the plains, it's also excellent, but again not perfect.

If the all-around Western big-game rifle isn't ideal, then why not choose one special rifle for one use and another for a different use? That would be fine, but most Western hunters carry one rifle for all big game—the plains/mountain rifle.

The most-used Western big-game rifle is a scope-sighted bolt-action model. Across the back window of almost every pickup truck heading for the hunting field in any region of the West rests one of these rifles. Most are 30-06s. While the 270 Winchester and 7mm Remington Magnum have made inroads, the famous '06 remains number one in ammo sales west of the Mississippi River. Following the 30-06 Springfield in popularity are, in order, the 270 Winchester, the 7mm Remington Magnum, and the 243 Winchester. The 25-06 Remington is also popular, and the 300 Winchester Magnum enjoys good sales as well. The 338 Winchester Magnum is

Fadala's plains rifle is built around the strong Model 700 Remington action. Note the powerful Bausch & Lomb variable scope sight.

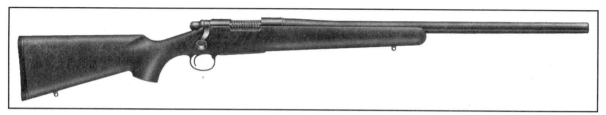

Rifles built around stiff actions and heavy barrels, such as this Remington Model 700 VS, are capable of long-range work due to inherent accuracy, but also because of good weight for field steadiness.

better represented than one might think. The accurate 308 Winchester sees action, as does the fine 7mm-08 Remington. But the archetype of all Western big-game rifles remains, without a doubt, a bolt-action, scope-sighted 30-06. There's more to the Western rifle story than statistics, however—there's also the game that it's used for.

These three plains rifles, all built by Dale Storey of DGS, Inc., (Casper, Wyo.) are: (left) caliber 6.5-06 and (middle and right) 7mm Remington Magnums. The author's rifle (right) weighs an intentional 11.5 pounds.

The action of this Storey Modern Plains Rifle is the Mauser 98. Scope is Bausch & Lomb 6X-24X.

Most Western sportsmen hunt mule deer. A great many hunt elk and pronghorn as well. Hunted less frequently but in surprisingly large numbers is the Western white-tailed deer. Blacktails are numerous in some areas on the West Coast, and on a more limited basis there are moose, sheep and Rocky Mountain goats. The Southwestern hunter has a chance to include javelina on the list, as well as the little Coues deer or Sonoran whitetail. These species differ in both size and habitat. Yet the Western hunting rifle works everywhere, on all these animals, because of its versatility.

Dissect the Western big-game rifle and many individual attributes unfold. For example, the stock—a scoped bolt action—is relatively straight in design, with little drop at the comb. The comb must be high enough for the shooter's eye to center the scope. The buttstock generally wears a recoil pad, although my favorite 7mm

Magnum carries a steel buttplate. The Western rifle also has a sling or carrying strap attached to the stock.

Once upon a time, most Western rifles wore a barrel of 24 inches; a few were 26 inches. Overall weight was about 9 to 9½ pounds with scope. Now, the Western rifle's barrel generally runs 22 to 24 inches in length, and gross weight is about 8½ pounds.

The "mountain rifle" concept had something to do with the Western rifle going on a diet. The idea of a sleek, trim, lightweight, high-country shooting instrument was extended to a general hunting rifle style. No hunter wants to pack more pounds than he has to. On the other hand, when the moment of truth presents itself, putting that bullet exactly on target is the goal. The shot is, after all, the bottom line. Some hunters can handle a superlight rifle under field conditions, but most of us cannot. Before hiking over a saddle or hill, a hunter should stop to catch his breath so he'll be as steady as possible should a buck or bull present itself. Hard hiking takes its toll on everyone, and when the heart is ticking like a clock up where the air is rarified, a firearm with sufficient mass settles down for a steady shot. I've found that a rifle of about 8½ pounds is stable.

A writer once noted that marksmanship in the hunting arena was overrated. In other words, a hunter need not be a good shot to harvest game. But think about it: Is there a trophy on your wall that didn't need to be hit before it could be tagged? Marksmanship is essential. The only way to cluster bullets on target or direct them to an exact point of aim on distant game is by good shooting with an accurate rifle. The Western hunt generally demands farther shooting, so the more accurate your rifle, the better.

Both the hunter and the rifle he's carrying must be capable of shooting tight groups at 100, 200, and even 300 yards. How tight? One test rifle, a custom pre-'64 Model 70 in 7mm Remington Magnum built by Frank Wells, has produced witnessed 1-inch groups at 200 yards. Those three-shot groups with handloads fall into

the realm of fantastic for a hunting rifle, and such amazing shooting isn't necessary for a hunting rifle. But imagine the confidence a hunter gains from such rifle accuracy!

SCOPES—HUNTING WITH ACCURACY

Integral to accuracy is the rifle's sight. You can shoot only as well as you can see the target, and you see the target best with a scope. Not all rifles should carry a scope, though. A muzzle-loader and open sights go together. Some brush rifles are fitted purposely with iron sights, as are certain dangerous-game rifles. And some rifles don't wear a scope well. A fine Mannlicher carbine I'm partial to does not have a scope mounted, because its design won't allow the bolt to clear the tube. But for most Western rifles, a scope sight—preferably a variable-power model—is ideal.

The variable-power scope enhances the Western rifle's versatility. Hunting whitetails in a creekbottom? Put the scope on low power for the jump shot. Antelope? Carry the scope on medium power, but be ready to switch to high magnification for the longer shot.

Common sense dictates that the scope be set

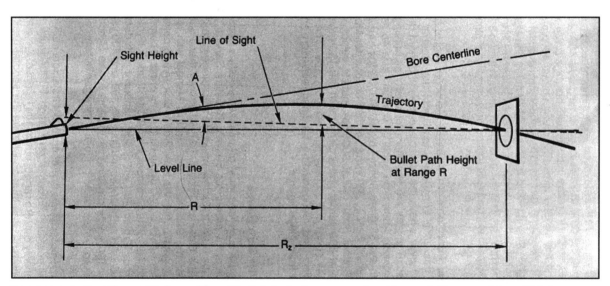

Long-range shooting calls for a rifle with flat trajectory, meaning the cartridge must be of high velocity. This drawing shows the path of the bullet from muzzle to target, along with line of sight and bore centerline.

This magnified view of antelope at long range illustrates what the shooter sees through his powerful telescopic riflesight.

on low power for a broad field of view, then turned up for the farther shot. "I don't use variables," some hunters say, "because I always set them on 4X anyway." Do these people drive their cars at exactly 38 miles per hour in or out of town? When a piece of machinery offers a range of applications, the wise person takes advantage of that feature.

The 2.5X-8X variable scope is an excellent choice. The lower power offers a wide field of view, while the higher magnification defines the target. I harvest most of my big game with the scope on its highest setting because of my particular Western hunting style—a lot of binocular work for game sighting in the distance, followed

by a stalk for the closest possible shot. High magnification improves bullet placement on the target, even for 100-yard shots. For example, no winner of a serious benchrest competition takes the prize with his scope set at 4X.

Prove the value of high magnification to yourself. Shoot at a target with the variable set at 2.5X. Then shoot again with it set at 8X. Decide which power provides the best chance of putting the bullet where you want it. A few seasons ago, I filled my additional deer tag with a deer that was standing about 100 paces away, with only its head and neck clearly visible. The scope—a 3.5X-10X—was screwed up to 10X. I took a rest over a fallen tree. The bullet centered where the head and neck join. The kill was instantaneous, with virtually no meat loss.

CARTRIDGES FOR WESTERN HUNTING

The mountain/plains rifle is very much a product of its cartridge. Of the four most popular rounds, the 243 Winchester (No. 4 on the list) is great for deer and antelope but isn't powerful enough for elk. A fantastic marksman can prove

RWS factory ammo and a 162-grain bullet.

Individual rifles vary in velocity, so not every Big 7 will turn up this velocity with a 160-grain bullet. But every 7 Mag tested put the 160- to 162-grain pill out at 3100+ fps with handloads. Nosler Loading Manual Number Three lists a 160-grain bullet at 3110 fps from a 7mm Remington Magnum loaded with H-870 powder. That's a lot of chili pepper. The power holds up

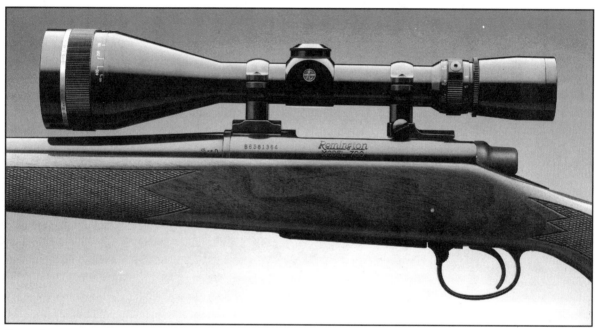

You can't hit it if you can't see it, and that is why modern scope makers offer choices such as this Leupold 3.5X-10X variable with adjustable objective.

that statement false by always putting the little 24-caliber bullet perfectly on target, but in general, the 243 is not an elk or a moose round.

Of the 30-06, 270, and 7mm Magnum, the last is the best all-around load because it includes and extends the ballistics of the first two. Anyone carrying an '06 or 270 is a smart Western hunter. But the 7mm Magnum, especially with handloads, gives the slam of the 30-06 with the trajectory of the 270. Using H-1000 or IMR-7828 powders, a test 7mm Remington Magnum rifle chronographed a mv of 3200 fps with a 160-grain bullet. If that sounds out of line, consider that the chronograph showed a mv of 3165 fps with

"out yonder" because a 7mm 160-grain bullet has a high sectional density and a good ballistic coefficient. The 7mm Weatherby Magnum is also an ace for long-range big-game hunting and is every bit as powerful as the 7mm Remington Magnum.

My feelings about a 7mm Magnum for Western big game are obvious, but a Big 7 is not necessary. Many hunters don't like that much push on the shoulder. The fine 7mm-08 Remington and the 308 Winchester "kick" less. Neither delivers the long-range authority of a bigger round, but a little extra stalking for perfect shot placement brings top results with these shorter car-

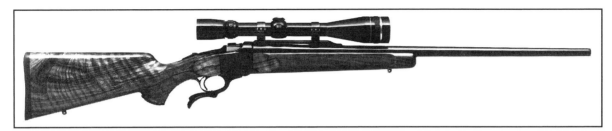

Another of Fadala's long-range favorites is his Ruger No. 1 rifle chambered for the 270 Weatherby Magnum cartridge. Fadala's personal handloads with IMR-7828 powder realize a muzzle velocity of 3400 fps with a 140-grain bullet from this cartridge.

tridges. The popular 25-06 is also excellent. Leave out elk, and a number of smaller cartridges fill the bill for the West as long as they have a flat-shooting trajectory that allows a practiced hunter to hit targets at a couple of hundred yards and beyond. Sighted 3 inches high at 100 yards, the 270 and 30-06 fall on target again at around 275 yards (with handloads). The 7 Mag is in the bull's-eye at about 300 yards. But is there enough power left out there to dispatch big game cleanly? Think of it this way: the 7mm 160-grain missile at 3100+ fps reaches 300 yards with more pasta

Fadala is a big fan of the 7mm Remington Magnum for long-range work. His Plains Rifle is so-chambered. Bullets in the 150-grain class have been chronographed at 3300 fps mv using IMR-7828 powder and H-1000 powder in handloads.

Weatherbys, noted for their fast-shooting magnum cartridges, make excellent long-range plains rifles. The Vanguard VGX (above), for example, is chambered for the long-range 270 Weatherby Magnum round.

than the fine old 300 Savage round has at the muzzle.

No one can dictate to the American hunter. He's a self-reliant outdoorsman with a lot of field knowledge and shooting ability. He knows what he wants and why. Admittedly, there are a few trailblazers who can get more done with a lever-action 30-30 than others can muster with a scoped '06. But the "average" Western hunter chooses a scoped, bolt-action, big-game rifle based on experience, study, and savvy, not on whim. He's tried plenty of rifles and cartridges. But his ballot is cast for a medium-weight, accurate, big-game rifle topped with a good glass sight to take advantage of the cartridge's inherent long-range power potential. With that one rifle, he can tag a javelina in the prickly pears, an antelope on the sagebrush plains, a whitetail in the thicket, or a bull elk breaking through the black timber.

THE 270 VERSUS THE 30-06

13 The 30-06 Springfield is clearly the most popular cartridge in the West and among the top few contenders for first rank in the East. Worldwide, the 30-06 is a household name among shooters. The 30-06 is so famous, so popular, and so well loved that it seems almost strange that it could be challenged by any cartridge. Yet it has been for years.

The 7mm Remington Magnum is considered a better all-around cartridge than the 30-06 by ballistics students, who can easily prove that the former shoots faster and flatter with more energy and only a little more recoil. But No. 2 is not the 7mm Magnum—it's the 270 Winchester. Is the 270 Winchester better than the 30-06?

The flames of this controversy have burned across the pages of gun magazines for decades, igniting cracker-barrel debates at gunshops and heated arguments among shooters from coast to coast. After a time, the hotbed cooled. Little if anything was resolved, and by all appearances the fire had gone out of the debate. But kick the thick layer of white ash lying over the 270-versus-'06 argument and red hot coals glow beneath, ready to be fanned into flame at the least provocation. The debate lives on because the argument actually constitutes one of the more practical "which-is-best?" cartridge clashes ever.

Based on sales, the 30-06 remains the No. 1 big-game cartridge west of the Mississippi River, with the 270 on its tail. Every time a hunter decides on a new big-game rifle for the West or any open country hunting, he at least considers a choice between No. 1 and No. 2. Which will it be? There's no argument concerning how most buyers decide. The '06 is king. Period. But the prince has been waiting to dethrone its parent cartridge since 1925, and many shooters wonder why its ascension to the throne has never occurred. The 270's challenge for dominance has almost closed the gap at times. But gunners who spend hard cash for rifles and ammo have continued to choose the '06 over the 270.

Born in 1903, the 30-06 began life as the 30-03 cartridge, produced by the U.S. Government as an Army round. In 1906 the 30-03 was shortened by .07 inch and given a new name: "Ball Cartridge, caliber 30, Model of 1906," firing full-metal-jacket military bullets (ball). Its title was shortened soon thereafter, and it is now referred to as the 30-06, 30-'06, or Springfield.

The 30-03 was initially loaded with a 220-grain bullet. The new 30-06 fired a 150-grain bullet at higher velocity with a flatter trajectory. The lighter bullet in the 30-06 also developed a little less recoil energy. The 30-03 was all but forgotten and the '06 went on to fame, not only

The 30-06 Springfield began life as a military cartridge chambered in this bolt-action rifle, the Springfield Model of 1903.

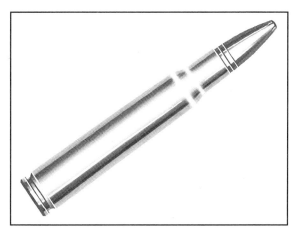

The 30-06 cartridge is one of the most successful rounds ever developed. This Remington factory load with 165-grain Core-Lokt soft-point bullet could be used successfully on game from javelina to elk.

with military men, but also in the hands of sportsmen.

Before you could say "Let's go hunting!" the 30-06 became a standard big-game round. American sportsmen—particularly those who had used the round in the military—had great faith in it. The 30-30 still outsold the 30-06, but there was no argument that the '06 was the more versatile of the two. Some shooters went overboard for the round. A few got downright carried away. One book written on the topic of American shooting listed the 30-06 as the best deer cartridge, best elk round, best varmint number, best target-shooting cartridge, ad nauseum. Wildcatters necked the case up, necked it down, shortened it, and "blew it out" with various new shoulder angles, including the Venturi design. The 30-06 fathered more wildcats than any other cartridge case.

THE BATTLE THAT WAS INEVITABLE

What some considered heresy was committed in 1925 when the beloved 30-06 was necked down to 7mm caliber—truly 7mm. Seven-millimeter cartridges, such as the 7mm Mauser, always fired .284-inch diameter bullets, making them about 7.2mm in size. The new 270 Winchester carried a .277-inch diameter bullet—a

true 7mm. The resulting case (2.540 inches) was insignificantly longer (.046 inch) than the '06. Shooters either fell in love with the 270 or despised it. Devotees of the 30-06 viewed the 270 as a demented stepchild that should be kept chained in the attic. Something about the 270 made some shooters break out in hives and go bug-eyed. It seemed to these sportsmen that necking the original round down to 27 caliber spoiled the perfect marriage of case size and caliber found in the '06.

But 270 fans held their ground. Some of the country's leading gun writers adopted the cartridge and wrote glowingly of it, not just ballistically, but almost religiously. Townsend Whelen, for example, called it "a very remarkable load," the round responsible for the most instantaneous one-shot deer harvests. F.C. Ness, well-known gunwriter of the 1930s, felt that the 270 with a 130-grain bullet was a better killer than the 30-06 with a 180-grain bullet. Phil Sharpe had seen the 270 round in 1923—two years before

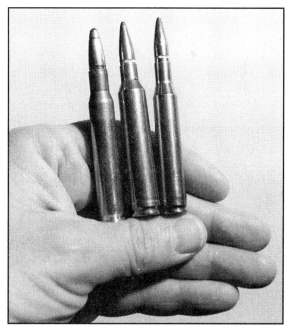

The three most popular big-game cartridges of the West are: (from left) the 30-06, 7mm Remington Magnum and the 270 Winchester. Of the three, the '06 is No. 1 in sales.

its public introduction—and liked its lighter kick. The 270 was ready to go then, but Winchester held it back from American riflemen for two years. So comparisons between the '06 and 270 actually began in 1923, before a rifle could be purchased in that caliber, and the two rounds have danced on the griddle ever since. Few shooters simply spoke of the 270 and what it could or could not do. Whenever the 270 was mentioned, it seemed imperative to talk about the '06 in the same breath.

As everyone knows, famous gunwriter Jack O'Connor was devoted to the 270. He collected big game with 270s in many parts of North America and other continents. He tirelessly defended the round in print against its detractors. It seemed that Jack once took a 270 to Africa mainly to prove a point. He had been reading about 270 bullets bouncing off of African fauna for so long he grew tired of it. He bopped a big waterbuck, a zebra stallion (a very tough animal), and many other species. "Relatively few paying customers have ever taken a .270 on sa-

The 30-06 shows its all-around "middle ground" nature when compared with cartridges such as the 220 Swift, a specialty round.

fari," O'Connor wrote acidly in the March 1967 *Outdoor Life*, "as most have been brainwashed in favor of heavy bullets."

John Moyer, staff member of the Chicago Natural History Museum, wrote in a 1950 issue of *American Rifleman* that sourdough Alaskan hunter Harold Looken had turned to the 270 for moose, finding it a better killer than his previous favorite, the 30-06 with 220-grain bullets. John Jobson, a long-time writer for *Sports Afield*, also declared the 270 Winchester his favorite cartridge. Necking the 30-06 down to 27 caliber, he said, "turned out to be one of the better things in life." It was his favorite deer, elk, and bear round. Jobson insisted that the 130-grain bullet was sufficient even for larger big game. A hunter named Tom Bolack dropped a new world-record polar bear with one shot from his 270, using a 130-grain Remington Bronze Point bullet. A full list of well-known riflemen who preferred the 270 would be long enough to fill this chapter.

At the same time, though, a list of '06 fans would be just as long. Interestingly, the 30-06 list would have to include some of the fellows who loved the 270. Such a roster could start with Jack O'Connor. O'Connor was one of the more practical gunwriters—just because he favored the 270 doesn't mean that he preached against the 30-06. He carried an old sporterized 30-06 Springfield from Mexico to the Yukon. Mrs. O'Connor also harvested much game in Africa with an '06. In a 1962 issue of *Outdoor Life*, O'Connor wrote that "for all kinds of jobs in the open and in timber, at long range and short, there isn't anything any more versatile than this perpetual best seller, the 56-year-old .30-06." He also mentioned he preferred the '06 over the 270 for certain timber hunting.

Visions of the '06 in the game field bring trophy hunter Grancel Fitz to mind. Fitz hunted just about everything with the round. He used it for Shiras moose in 1959. He used it for elk and also took many deer with it. By the time Fitz was a mature hunter, his Remington Griffin & Howe 30-06 with its Hensoldt 2¾X scope was weathered and trailworn, but he went about dropping everything with it anyway. He never saw a need for a different caliber or rifle, and preferred 180-

Greg Thompson, now an MD with the Mayo Clinic, took his first antelope with the cartridge many consider the finest all-around round ever designed, the 30-06 Springfield—good on the plains and in the mountains as well as any other habitat.

grain and 220-grain bullets for most of his hunting instead of the faster 150-grain bullet.

Elmer Keith bore no love for the 270 Winchester. He was no great fan of the 30-06 either; however, he greatly preferred the Springfield over the 270, mainly because the '06 could shoot heavier bullets. Keith was decidedly a big bullet man. This famous gunwriter accepted the '06 as tolerable for elk with its weightiest projectiles, but gave the round little credit with lighter missiles. He gave the 270 no credibility in the big-game field for anything larger than deer.

Another well-known advocate of the 30-06

was Stewart Edward White, who hunted broadly and wrote widely of his exploits. The novelist was a 30-06 fan from the start, owning one of the first sporterized Springfields built by gunmaker Bob Owen. Clyde Ormand, a fine big-game hunter and well-known writer, always said good things about the '06, too.

Yes, the list of 30-06 devotees is a long one. More time and money was spent on development of the '06 than on any other military round. As a hunting cartridge, the '06 no doubt has had more editorial ink spilled on it than any other cartridge in the 20th century.

DOWN TO HARD SCIENCE

Both the 30-06 and the 270 have long had a following of well-known riflemen. But what about the ballistic facts? When a modern-day hunter is faced with choosing No. 1 or No. 2, how does he go about it scientifically, with sentiment left out?

First, look at accuracy. The 270 is often described as the more accurate of the two. It's not. Never was. Never will be. Accuracy is determined largely by good bullets from good barrels, as Dr. Mann pointed out many decades ago. Fire precision bullets from precision barrels and accuracy is the rule. Cartridge case design is important to accuracy, as proved by the 6mm PPC USA round and the 308 Winchester, but the case design of the 270 and the '06 aren't that different. Accuracy differences between the two rounds are a matter of loads, barrels, actions, and other criteria that pertain to good bullet grouping. Neither round is inherently more accurate than the other.

Factory ammo is another point of comparison. Which cartridge is loaded more closely to its potential by ammo crafters? The 270 gets the nod. *Extended Ballistics*, a manual published by Pachmayr, Inc., of Los Angeles, lists 379 chronographed factory loads. Those with the 150-grain bullet in the 30-06 departed the muzzle at 2850 fps, 2910 fps, 2920 fps, 2970 fps, and similar velocities—roughly 130 to 190 fps below optimum handloaded potential, which is close to 3100 fps mv for the 150-grain bullet. My test '06 loads, with the 150-grain bullet in a 24-inch barreled rifle, averaged 3076 fps at 10 feet from the muzzle. In comparison, the 130-grain 270 bullet was listed at factory muzzle velocities of 3060 fps to 3140 fps.

The 270 has received some favorable press on velocities that are difficult to duplicate. Rifles chronographed for this work in 270 caliber with 24-inch barrels and top-end handloads produced muzzle velocities of about 3150 fps, although printed figures of 3200-plus fps have been listed. Nonetheless, the fact remains that 270 factory loads did come closer to handload potential than did 30-06 factory loads.

What about bullets? It's true that 270 bullets, being smaller in diameter, gain good sectional density with less bullet weight as compared to 30-06 missiles. For example, the 130-grain Hornady flat-base 270 bullet has a sectional density of .242 and a ballistic coefficient of .374. In contrast, a 180-grain 30-caliber bullet, also from Hornady and with the same ballistic shape, has a sectional density of .271 and a ballistic coefficient of .431. A 165-grain 30-caliber bullet of the same brand and ballistic shape has a sectional density of .248 and a ballistic coefficient of .400.

Ballistically speaking, the 130-grain 270 bullet and the 165-grain 30-06 bullet are quite close. There is only one difference: The 30-06 bullet weighs 35 grains more. So the weight difference between these two bullets is not much more than the weight of a 22 Short bullet. But consider the bullet comparison via percentages. The 165-grain bullet is roughly 20 percent heftier than the 130-grain bullet, a difference that is statistically and ballistically significant.

The 270 Winchester, center, flanked by the '06 on the left and 7mm Remington Magnum on the right, is the favorite round of thousands of big-game hunters and gunwriters.

What about projectile versatility? The range of good big-game bullets for the 270 runs from 130 grains to 180 grains. (The 180-grain 270 bullet is not well known, but such a missile is available from Barnes.) Big-game bullets for the 30-06 range from 150 to 250 grains, the heavyweight also offered by Barnes. Lighter bullets work well in both rifles; however, the heavier bullets are made for big-game hunting, with proper jacket/core design. The span in weight is 50 grains for the 270 and 100 grains for the 30-06, giving the 30-06 a wider latitude in big-game bullet selection.

Clearly, the 30-06 wins the battle in terms of energy delivered at any range. The 270's 130-grain bullet at 3150 fps mv earns a muzzle energy of 2865 foot-pounds. At 300 yards, according to ballistics tables, the bullet is still traveling at about 2400 fps, for a delivered energy of 1663 foot-pounds. The 165-grain '06 bullet taking off at a flat 3000 fps mv gains 3298 foot-pounds of muzzle energy; at 300 yards, it is still winging along at approximately 2300 fps, with 1939 foot-pounds of energy—not enough of a difference to do cartwheels over, but ballistically significant.

Surely, the 270, with its reputation as one of

Bullet selection remains a top reason for the continued success and popularity of the 30-06. Shown from left are 11 different 30-caliber projectiles: 100-grain Speer Plinker, Hornady 110-grain spire point, Sierra 125-grain hollow-point, Speer 130-grain, Speer 150-grain, Hornady 165-grain BT, Nosler 165-grain, Sierra 170-grain (for 30-30, but can be loaded to 30-30 ballistics in the '06), 180-grain Nosler, 200-grain Nosler and 220-grain Winchester Silvertip.

How about trajectory and delivered energy from *optimal* handloads? The 130-grain 270 bullet can be fired at 3150 fps mv, sometimes a shade faster, while the 165-grain 30-06 bullet generally achieves 2950 to 3000 fps mv. Looking at the best velocities generally realized from handloads for the 270 with H-4831 powder, 3150 fps is the maximum in most test rifles with 24-inch barrels. Using Winchester 760 powder in the 30-06 in a test rifle with a 24-inch barrel produced a velocity of 2989 fps at 10 feet from the muzzle, which can be honestly translated to 3000 fps at the muzzle.

the flattest-shooting big-game rounds in the world, requires a lot less "Arkansas elevation" at long range than the '06 demands. But in actual tests, does the 270 really shoot flatter? Sighted dead on at 200 yards with the 130-grain 270 bullet at 3150 fps mv, bullet drop is about 6.5 inches at 300 yards. In contrast, the 165-grain 30-06 bullet at 3000 fps mv, sighted at the same zero of 200 yards, drops about 7.0 inches at 300 yards. So the difference is about 7 percent in favor of the 270.

Looking further into the matter of trajectory and delivered bullet energy downrange, the 270

Nosler's 220-grain Partition bullet (above) makes the 30-06 an excellent rifle for elk/moose in the timber.

with the 140-grain boat-tail bullet beginning at 3000 fps mv has a muzzle energy just shy of 2800 foot-pounds and a 300-yard energy of about 1840 foot-pounds. It shoots a shade under 7 inches low at 300 yards when sighted dead on at 200 yards. When using a 165-grain boat-tail bullet

instead of a flat-base bullet in the 30-06, 300-yard figures improve, too. Now the '06 has just under 2100 foot-pounds of remaining energy at 300 yards, and it strikes the target just under 7 inches low at that distance—same as the 270.

These are ballistics facts with all of the romance strained out of the matter. A machine has done the testing, not a man. The subject is ballistics, not personal feelings. But a hunter chooses a cartridge for reasons other than ballistics. Recoil, for example, is a consideration. Many 270 lovers have stated that their round is much more pleasant to shoot than the '06. Is it?

There are two kinds of recoil: the actual recoil energy delivered by a load in a particular rifle weight and "felt recoil." Both are important. Given identical recoil energy in two rifles of the same weight, the rifle with the better-designed stock will seem to "kick" less than the rifle with an ill-designed stock.

Consider two rifles of identical stock proportions and identical weights—one a 270, the other a 30-06. With scope and sling, both tip the scale at 8½ pounds. The 270, firing a 130-grain

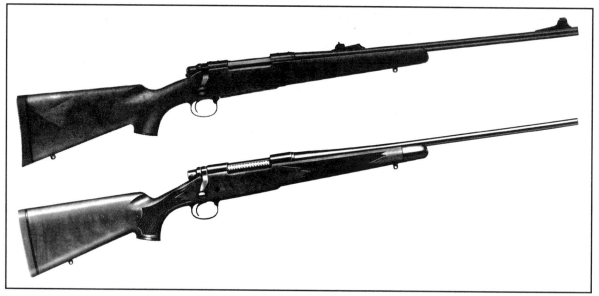

Rifles like these Remington Model 700s are contenders for all-around use in the West. The Model 700 AS (above) with synthetic stock is chambered for the 270 Winchester cartridge. The Model 700 Mountain Rifle (below) is light, but not overly so, and is offered in both 270 Winchester and 30-06 Springfield. This is the case with many rifles because the two rounds are close to the same length.

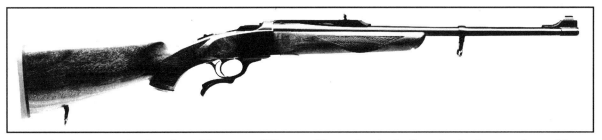

The 270 Winchester is chambered in many different rifle styles, including single-shots such as this Ruger No. 1.

The 30-06 wins the contest vis-à-vis the 270 because of bullets like these 150-grain Hornady BT, which can be driven at or close to 3100 fps mv from a 30-06 rifle.

bullet with 60.0 grains of H-4831 and a muzzle velocity of 3150 fps, has a recoil energy of 20 foot-pounds. In comparison, the 30-06 with a 165-grain bullet backed by 60.5 grains of Winchester 760 for a muzzle velocity of 3000 fps has a recoil energy of 25 foot-pounds. So the 30-06 has 20 percent more recoil here than the 270, so the recoil factor goes in favor of the 270.

The 270-versus-30-06 argument may never die for two reasons. First, while the two rounds are not identical, neither are they that far apart, making it difficult to downgrade either one. Second, they both fall into the same mystical pigeonhole called the "all-around" cartridge. If a

shooter were forced to choose either the 270 or 30-06 for Western big-game hunting, from antelope to elk, he could get by with either round quite nicely, as many hunters have over the years. Nonetheless, one truth stands out: The rounds are similar, but in terms of raw ballistics, the 270 is inferior to the 30-06. The 270 does not shoot flatter, in practical big-game terms, and does not deliver as much downrange energy as the '06. Its selection of hunting bullets is narrower, too. It isn't a shred easier to reload, nor is it one degree more accurate. However, it is powerful enough in the hands of a careful hunter to cleanly harvest all Western game, and it offers less recoil than the '06.

A shooter deciding on the basis of ballistics alone would have to take the '06. That's not sentiment—that's fact. But riflemen choose cartridges today as they always have—individually and personally. Both the 270 and 30-06 are selected on the basis of their do-it-all abilities. On that score, the 7mm Weatherby Magnum and 7mm Remington Magnum give both of these popular rounds more than a run for their money, as the next chapter on the all-around big-game cartridge reveals. But the fact that neither the 270 nor '06 are ballistically the world's best all-around cartridges will never prevent shooters from choosing them, because both work admirably in the big-game field. They develop sufficient power to get the job done, and many shooters feel that they don't need a magnum with the extra recoil that goes with it. They're happy with the '06 and 270, as sales records prove.

THE ALL-AROUND HUNTING RIFLE

14 Black timber stands denser than the hair on a grizzly bear's hide, plains flatter than a silver dollar, roller coaster hills, riverbottom thickets, catclaw jungles, cactus flats, oxygen-rare peaks above timberline—all of these and many other features describe the vast regions of big-game habitat. It seems impossible at first to come up with a single rifle-and-cartridge combination that would work in all of these areas.

The Rocky Mountains can serve as a test ground for the all-around rifle because of the tremendous variation in that range, which extends from Mexico to the Arctic, topped by Mount McKinley's 20,300-foot peak. A firearm/cartridge combination that works well in the Rockies will serve just about anywhere—if not perfectly, at least well enough. However, choosing a single rifle for big-game hunting in the Rockies is like finding a perfect hat for all seasons. It can be done, but it requires compromise.

In the past, the all-around rifle conflicted with the all-around cartridge. While the 30-06, for example, was considered the premium all-around cartridge for many decades, the Model 1895 Winchester lever-action was the only popular and easily obtainable non-bolt-action rifle for years. A lot of water passed beneath the bridge of time before the 30-06 found its way into a slide-action firearm. Although the 30-06 was chambered in a military semiautomatic rifle early on, it took Remington to bring out a sportsman's semiautomatic rifle for this caliber. Those hunters who felt that a bolt-action rifle wasn't to their liking didn't have a 30-06 option for a long time.

Today, that has changed. All-around cartridges have found their way into all action types, from single-shots to semiautos. Of course, the most popular big-game rifle for all-around hunting with a high-intensity cartridge remains the bolt-action design. This is the single most popular rifle. Usually, it's chambered for the 30-06, 270 or 7mm Remington Magnum, especially for the West, with plenty of 243s right behind that trio. The '06, 270 and 7mm Magnum are considered all-around calibers, referred to here as the "Big 3." They do it all, from bagging a creekbottom whitetail buck to dropping a bugling bull elk across a canyon.

THE KING OF ALL-AROUND CARTRIDGES

The 7mm Magnum (both the Remington and Weatherby versions) is considered the king of all-around cartridges. Weatherby had his 7mm

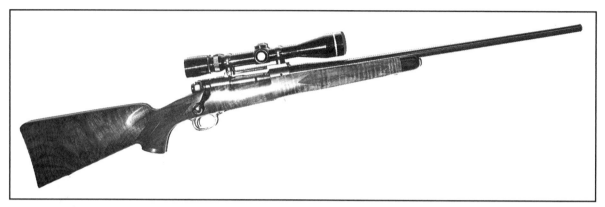

Fadala's most-used all-around rifle is his Frank Wells custom pre-64 Model 70 Winchester chambered for the 7mm Remington Magnum cartridge.

off the drawing board in 1944. Remington followed with its famous round in 1962. Both will drive a 139- or 140-grain bullet in the 3300 to 3400 fps mv realm for long-range antelope or deer hunting, and also push a 160-grain missile at 3000 to 3100 fps mv for elk or cross-canyon deer. The elk and moose hunter can depend on a long 175-grain bullet at 2900 to 3050 fps mv for the big stuff. The 7mm 195-grain Barnes bullet loaded with H-870 powder will develop a muzzle velocity of nearly 2800 fps. Such versatility certainly puts the 7mm at the top of the all-around cartridge class.

The all-around rifle has been sought after for years, *and found*, although it has varied over time. A hundred years ago, it was a lever-action repeater in any of the good blackpowder calibers, such as 45-70. The practiced rifleman learned to get extra range from these slow-motion "punkin throwers" through familiarity with their looping trajectory. The heavy bullet made a long wound channel and broke bones, so hunters of the past did well with this blackpowder cartridge on all sorts of big game. The nimrods of old had plenty of time to hunt, often taking long treks into the outback. More time in the field translated into increased opportunities for the good shot. In an interview concerning one of his early hunts, Elmer Keith said the adventure was planned as a three-month Rocky Mountain campout for big game. Three *months*! Today's hunter is lucky to have more than a weekend. And competition for

game in the field is much keener now than it was in the past.

That's why the long-range precision rifle is preferred these days for hunting in the West. And the same all-around rifle is one that also serves, as noted, in both open and dense terrain, making it a versatile firearm for both the East and the West—and for most of the world as well.

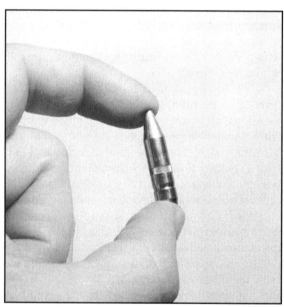

The all-around cartridge widens its range of usefulness through bullet selection. This is the Cone Point RWS 162-grain 7mm bullet, which offers good expansion without jacket loss.

THE ALL-AROUND CARTRIDGE COMES IN MANY SIZES

Many hunters prefer to specialize, though. Hunting the little javelina of the Southwest, for example, is usually a close-range proposition. After finding the herd with binoculars and stalking quietly with the wind in his face, the hunter commonly collects the nearsighted little porkers within 50 yards. A 270, 30-06 or 7mm Magnum

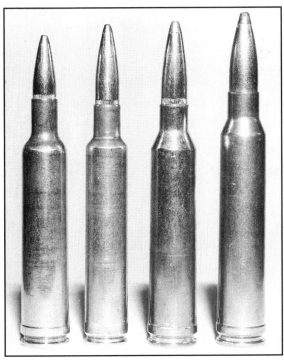

All-around cartridges come in many sizes. These four rounds are: (from left) the 257 Weatherby Magnum, 6.5-06 Improved wildcat, 7mm Remington Magnum and 300 Winchester Magnum.

is not necessary for a 50-pound pig 50 yards from the rifle muzzle. Chapter 10 discussed the specialty javelina/wild turkey rifle, but the all-around rifle, remember, is still the most-used for these species.

If javelina offer close-in shooting, then pronghorn antelope represent the other end of the spectrum. The pronghorn is often taken at 200 yards—even 300 yards and farther by prac-

ticed riflemen. Any one of the Big 3 will do the job splendidly. But you don't need this much cartridge for a prairie goat that weighs about 100 pounds dressed out. The popularity of the 243 Winchester and 6mm Remington was founded on antelope and deer hunting, and either will cleanly drop such quarry out to 300 yards or so. The hunter won't observe any demonstrable difference between a chest-hit buck taken with a

Things change. Today, the 30-06 (left) has taken over as the all-around cartridge, a role once fulfilled by the 44-40 Winchester cartridge (right).

243 and one taken with a 270. (But he will, of course, see a difference if the little bullet doesn't land in the vitals.) The fine 240 Weatherby Magnum is a hotter 24 caliber that does the same job as the smaller 6mms with flatter trajectory and more fanfare, making it an excellent long-range round.

The 25-caliber family consists of terrific Rocky Mountain rounds for deer and antelope harvesting. The 250 Savage and 257 Roberts are ballistically similar when both are handloaded with 100-grain bullets. A popular wildcat is the 257 Roberts Improved, which adds about 200

Hunter Gene Thompson took this pronghorn with the only big-game rifle he uses in the West for all of his hunting: a Model 700 Remington chambered for the 30-06 cartridge.

Although the all-around rifle/cartridge is no longer considered to be a lever-action 30-30, this combination still harvested more big game under various conditions than any other. Nancy Fadala poses with mule deer she tagged with a Storey custom 30-30 rifle.

vorite cartridge. He considered it a fine all-around number ideal for big game when the rifleman placed his bullet correctly. A good handload for this hot 25-caliber magnum round, by the way, was listed in the May 1984 *American Rifleman*, in which Colonel Charles Askins achieved over 3400 fps mv with IMR-4831 powder and a 120-grain bullet. Two test rifles chambered for the 257 Weatherby chronographed in excess of 3400 fps mv with this load. At 300 yards, the 120-grain bullet starting at 3400 fps mv delivers close to 1800 foot-pounds of retained energy. And it shows. The rocket-like crack of the bullet terminates in a strike like an express train.

The 257 Weatherby is a fine all-around cartridge in a bolt-action rifle, capable of instant kills on medium-sized game. But another round is also a long-range wonder for the Rockies, even though it's not nearly as popular as other all-around cartridges. This is the 264 Winchester, a 1959 creation that many thought would send the standard 270 Winchester to the showers. It never happened. The 264 kicks out a 100-grain bullet at 3600 fps mv, but its long 140-grain bullet at 3200 fps mv is the better choice for big-

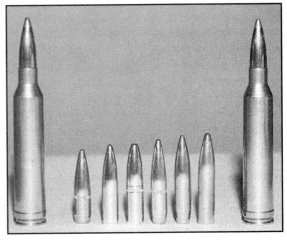

The 7mm Remington Magnums stand as sentinels on either side of the variety of bullets they take: (from left) 139-grain Hornady BT, 160-grain Nosler Partition, 160-grain Speer Grand Slam, 162-grain Hornady BT, 175-grain Sierra BT, and the long 195-grain Barnes bullet.

fps mv over the standard round when shooting the 100-grain bullet.

A ballistic notch up from the 25s, the 25-06 is a well-thought-of round in the West, and deservedly so. Handloaded properly, a 25-06 with a 120-grain bullet departs the muzzle at 3000 to 3200 fps. At the latter speed, the bullet arrives at 300 yards still doing about 2400 fps, with over 1500 foot-pounds of energy remaining.

The epitome of 25-caliber power is the fabulous 257 Weatherby Magnum. Although this round was born when many of us were still in short pants, not nearly enough hunters took notice of this powerful 25-caliber magnum on belted brass until their hairlines were receding. The 257 Weatherby was Roy Weatherby's fa-

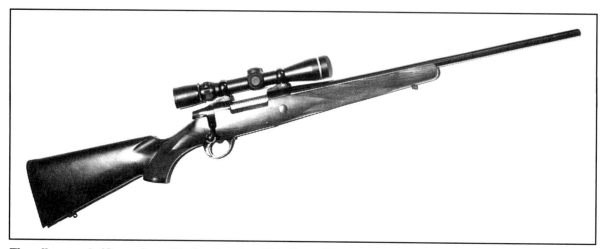

The all-around rifle varies with the shooter. This 7mm-08 Sako is just right for its owner, Nancy Fadala, who enjoys the light recoil, but excellent results offered by this combination. Nancy has taken antelope, deer, elk and other game with this rifle.

game hunting. Sighted 3 inches high at 100 yards from the muzzle, this bullet is about 3.75 inches high at 200 yards, on the money at 300 yards, and about 8.75 inches low at 400 yards. This, fellow shooters, is known as flat trajectory. In the hands of a careful hunter, the 264 Winchester round chambered in an accurate rifle will take all North American big game and a great many big-game animals elsewhere. I used the 264 Winchester in Africa for a succession of one-shot, big-game kills.

The fine 270 Winchester is still a wonderful Rocky Mountain round and all-arounder. As noted earlier, Jack O'Connor carried a 270 Winchester in Africa. Although it falls into a love/ hate category mentioned in the previous chapter, thousands of hunters continue to use the 270 on everything from wild turkeys to elk. The 270 is a flat-shooting round that, in the hands of an able rifleman, can handle just about any game we have in this country. But those who suggest that the 270 and the Big 7s (7mm Weatherby Magnum and 7mm Remington Magnum) are ballistic twins aren't looking closely enough at the facts. Good factory ammo for the 7mm magnums, Weatherby or Remington rounds, and correct handloads for these same numbers, gain from these cartridges what their birthright commands—a 160-grain bullet at 3100 to 3200 fps

Four excellent all-around cartridges are: (from left) the famous 270 Winchester, the 7mm Remington Magnum, 30-06 Springfield and 300 Winchester Magnum. Each is capable of taking any species of North American big game when the marksman does his part.

Fadala made one of the longest shots of his hunting career on this Southwestern Coues deer. He used his favorite all-around caliber: the 7mm Remington Magnum. Too much for the small Coues deer? Perhaps, but not for long-range shooting.

mv and a long 175-grain bullet at 2900 to 3000-plus fps mv. No 270 Winchester load can match these figures.

What about the 7mm family in general? All of these cartridges are good. The 7×57 Mauser has been recognized as one of the world's great all-around cartridges, with extensive use in Africa. The newer 7mm-08 Remington, based on a necked-down 308 Winchester case, is one of the finest mid-sized cartridges, capable of better ballistics than its case size might suggest.

Of course, the 30s also are an excellent family of rounds for all-around hunting. The 30-caliber cartridge is highly American, and it's really

no surprise that the well-loved 30-06, with modern loads, is still one of the best all-around cartridges. The 30-06 will do it all in the Rockies, which means that it will handle hunting situations in many other parts of the globe as well. A test rifle in 30-06 chambering once drove a 150-grain bullet just a cat's whisker under 3100 fps at the muzzle, and a 165-grain bullet only a shade below 3000 fps. The former sights in 3 inches high at 100 yards, and the bullet hits about 4 inches high at 200 yards from the muzzle, roughly 1 inch low at 300 yards, and about 10.5 inches low at 400 yards. The range of bullets available for the 30s is wider than the Mississippi, too, with

These Winchester Model 70s are fine all-around rifles, both chambered for the 7mm Remington Magnum cartridge.

everything from little plinkers of 90 and 100 grains (and even lighter) to brutes of 220 to 250 grains.

Some 30s larger than the '06 also make good all-arounders. The 300 Winchester Magnum, for example, is a terrific cartridge capable of driving a 180-grain bullet at about 3100 fps mv with H-1000 powder in a handload. The much older 300 Holland & Holland Magnum remains a fine cartridge, too, with similar ballistics. And, of course, many hunters travel the world with the great 300 Weatherby Magnum as their main game-taker. The Mark V Weatherby rifle is not only strong, it is also highly accurate right out of the box. Factory ammunition for it is always up to par as well.

Although cartridges of the 30-06 clan and the larger 30-caliber magnums are notable all-

arounders for big game all over the world, the smaller 308 Winchester cannot be left out of the picture. American hunters in Africa are usually surprised to learn that the 308 is one of the most-used rounds on the continent. Ammo availability is the reason, but the 308 can be an effective all-around cartridge nonetheless. Tests with the 308 revealed handload ballistics of 2500 fps mv with a 190-grain bullet—sufficient indeed for most big game anywhere.

WHY CHOOSE HIGH-POWER ROUNDS?

Flat trajectory is a major reason for the success of high-intensity cartridges in the Rocky Mountains. Flat shooting is not always necessary, but it comes in handy abroad as well as in North America. As noted earlier, those big-bullet, blackpowder busters of the past put plenty of

The all-around rifle adapts to terrain. Nancy Fadala got this mule deer in a forested area with her Sako 7mm-08 rifle shooting Remington factory ammo with a 140-grain bullet.

game down, but compared to today's hot rounds, those hunters had to get pretty close to the target.

Most all-around high-velocity cartridges can be sighted in to print groups 3 inches high at 100 yards. This handy sight-in rule takes advantage of the trajectory potential of most high-velocity rounds. For example, my 257 Weatherby Magnum so sighted delivers a 120-grain bullet 3.5 inches high at 200 yards and right on at 300 yards. Although anything past 300 yards is getting into the *extra-long-range* category, this load puts the 120-grain bullet only 7.5 inches low at 400 yards from the muzzle. The 7mm magnums produce similar trajectories. Neither the 30-06 clan nor the 308 Winchester is quite so flat-shooting, but even they produce a trajectory that would have startled both the 19th-century black-powder shooter and the early 20th-century marksman.

The great 7mm magnums, firing 160-grain bullets at 3100 to 3200 fps mv and sighted to strike 3 inches high at 100 yards, put their projectiles about 3.5 to 4 inches high at 200 yards, on target to about 1 inch low at 300 yards, and only 8 to 9 inches low at 400 yards. The big 175-grain bullet at about 3000 to 3100 fps mv is not far off of this line of trajectory. It's quite an elk-taker in the Rocky Mountains and has a great reputation for big game the world over. The 7mm magnums are, as recognized earlier, the tops of all-around cartridges, because their bullets have great sectional densities and ballistic coefficients. They "carry up" well, retaining much of their original energy—and they penetrate deeply on big game.

The variety of all-around cartridges is tremendous. This category includes the 243 Winchester, 6mm Remington, 240 Weatherby, 250 Savage, 257 Roberts, 257 Roberts Improved, 25-06 Remington, 257 Weatherby, 264 Winchester (the one with the 140-grain bullet at 3200 fps mv), 270 Winchester, 270 Weatherby, 7mm-08, 7×57 Mauser, 284 Winchester, 280 Remington, 7mm Remington Magnum, 7mm Weatherby, all the 30s, the big 300 Weatherby Mag-

num, and a host of wildcat rounds and foreign cartridges. The usual rifle is a bolt-action model, but as stated earlier, today's hunter can have an all-around cartridge in a single-shot, pump, semiauto—even in a multiple-barrel rifle. With only a few exceptions, however, it's safe to say that today's all-around rifle will wear a glass sight. My vote is, as always, for the variable.

Today's variable scope is generally compact and lightweight, with a bright image and a great range of magnification. A 2.5X–8X scope, for example, provides a wide field of view at lower power for those quick close shots that present themselves in just about any type of terrain, while a twist of the power ring provides target-like magnification for longer shots. The variable-power scope is a versatile sight, which is why it fits so perfectly on the all-around rifle. The hunter should use it to full potential, carrying the rifle with the scope on its lower setting for the possible up-close shot and remembering to increase the power for the long shot.

The right rifle for the Rocky Mountains and most of the world is in the high-power class, chambered in one of many different models and calibers. The selection of caliber and rifle depends on the individual hunter and his perceived needs in the big-game field. My choice for an all-around rifle/cartridge combination for North America (and just about anyplace else) is a bolt-action repeater chambered for either a Weatherby or Remington 7mm Magnum. This rifle would weigh 8 1/2 to 9 1/2 pounds, have a sling or carrying strap, and wear a variable-power telescopic sight.

BIG BORES & MIDDLE MAGNUMS

15

This chapter deals with an important branch of hunting cartridges, divided into two parts. Part I covers the true big-bore cartridges—elephant rounds, if you will; and Part II discusses an entirely different cartridge—the "middle magnum."

North American shooters have always had a great fascination for elephant rounds, even though they do not truly fit into the domestic hunting picture, except for possibly the coastal grizzly, the huge Kodiak or brown bear. Then it's always wise to carry a rifle that can put the stop to a charge. More than one Alaskan guide has turned to the 458 Winchester or a similar powerhouse to safeguard the life of a client, as well as his own, when a big bruin decided to make a two-legged snack for himself. While the true big-bore cartridge finds a use here, the great majority of big-bore rifles in this country are owned by persons who enjoy shooting and studying these brutes strictly for their own personal interest.

The "middle magnums" aren't ordinarily known as elephant rounds, although the 416 is indeed strong enough for pachyderms. Rather, they are the 41-caliber-or-under cartridges meant primarily for African game and hardly what a hunter would carry in the whitetail thicket.

THE BIG ONES

The two cartridges discussed here are the huge 460 Weatherby Magnum and the powerhouse 458 Winchester. Many other 45-caliber magnum cartridges are available to the American shooter, such as the 458 Lott, 450 Ackley Magnum, and other 45s built on magnum brass. Also, dozens of 45-caliber wildcat magnums can be custom-ordered, as well as a host of foreign big bores. But these rounds aren't nearly as attainable as the 460 Weatherby Magnum and 458 Winchester Magnum.

These big 45-caliber cartridges aren't needed for general North American hunting—not for moose, elk or, for that matter, bears. Even the largest quadruped on this continent, the mighty bison, does not require the blow delivered by this class of cartridge. Truly, they are dangerous-game rounds, developed for use on ponderous beasts with thick hides or, at the very least, the power and speed of an African lion, with fang and claw for weapons.

The 458 Winchester Magnum. First available in 1956, the 458 Winchester Magnum was America's answer to the British big-bore elephant round. Winchester introduced the cartridge in its special Model 70 African rifle, a heavy, well-constructed firearm suited to the recoil of the 45-caliber magnum. The cartridge proved far

Bill Fadala shoots his father's custom 458 Winchester. This rifle is equipped with a muzzle brake. Note the B&L variable scope with 1.5X option for ultra-close-range work.

The unloaded 30-06 cartridge case measures 2.494 inches long from head to mouth. The 458 Winchester cartridge case is 2.500 inches long, only .006 inch longer than the '06. A belted, fairly straight-walled, 2 1/2-inch case is sufficiently large to hold over 80 grains weight of ball powder, plenty to achieve 2100 to 2150 fps mv with a 45-caliber, 500-grain bullet and 1900 to 2000 fps mv with a 600-grain bullet. Handloads with 350- and 405-grain bullets at 2400 to 2500 fps mv could stop any charging bear. (The latter bullet, intended for the 45-70 Government, is explosive in the 458.) But the 500-grain FMJ and soft-point have remained favorites in this round, both achieving a muzzle energy of over 5000 foot-pounds. A 500-grain bullet from the 458 behind 80 grains of W-748 powder chronographed at exactly 2150 fps from a 24-inch barrel test rifle, for a muzzle energy of 5133 foot-pounds.

The 460 Weatherby Magnum. Weatherby's entire reputation for cartridges lies in bigger

The 7mm Remington Magnum round (left) is excellent for game larger than deer, such as elk and moose, but not as large as elephants. The other three rounds (from left), the 458 Winchester, 460 Weatherby Magnum and 500 Van Horn Express, could handle pachyderms.

more accurate than anyone expected, with minute-of-angle clusters not at all rare on the range. Bullets of 300 to 600 grains were hand-loaded in the 458, with 500-grain soft-points and full-metal-jacket (FMJ) "solids" the rule from ammo companies.

The 458 was built with 470 Nitro Express ballistics in mind. The famous 470 was always considered enough cartridge for elephants by the British hunters who carried rifles so-chambered. Typical of many English big bores, the 470 appears even more powerful than it is. Its ballistic claim to fame was a 500-grain bullet loaded to achieve a muzzle velocity of 2000 to 2200 fps. Winchester engineers knew they could produce a cartridge capable of pushing a 500-grain bullet at the same muzzle velocity from a modest-sized case; one no longer than a 30-06 round, but of course much "wider."

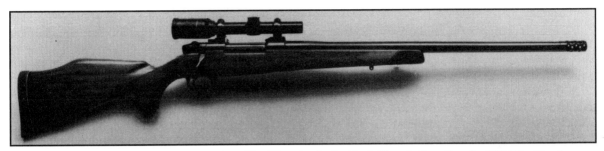

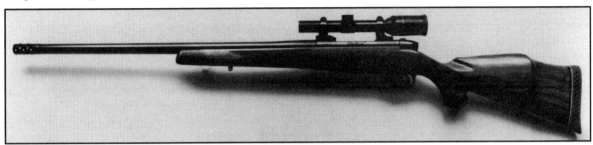

The world's most powerful commercial rifle: Weatherby's Mark V, a bolt-action in 460 Weatherby Magnum. This model, shown right view (above) and left view (below), is equipped with Accubrake, scope and sling swivels.

and better. This fine company has designed some stout fodder in its time, and thus far the 460 is the biggest of the Weatherby line.

The 460 came along in 1958, two years after the 458 Winchester was on the street. The 460 is built on 378 Weatherby Magnum brass opened up to accept bullets of .458-inch diameter. It was intended for a shooter who either felt a need for the biggest or had an interest in such a blaster. To date, it remains the world's single most powerful commercial cartridge. Other more powerful rounds aren't readily encountered by the American sportsman.

With handloads, the 460 Weatherby Magnum can push a 350-grain bullet at a muzzle velocity of 2950 fps and develops 6765 foot-pounds of muzzle energy. (Compare that to the 30-06 with a 180-grain bullet at 2800 fps mv for 3134 foot-pounds of muzzle energy.) The 460 can drive a 500-grain bullet at 2600 fps mv for an energy rating of 7507 foot-pounds.

Warning: It is unwise to underload cartridges of this size. Doing so can bring on a hangfire, whereby the powder charge is not instantly ignited; injury could result.

THE MIDDLE MAGNUMS

These cartridges are American standards. They range from over 30 caliber to under 417—an entirely arbitrary category, but viable for the sake of discussion, because these rounds are useful in American hunting (albeit only on the largest game). No wildcats are included in this roundup—there are too many to consider. Foreign rounds unlikely to be found in an American gunshop were also omitted. The 375 H&H Magnum and 358 Norma Magnum qualify because they can be readily purchased in the U.S.

These middle magnums wouldn't have to be belted to qualify as magnums, but all members of this clan do have belted cases. In other words, if the 35 Newton weren't pushing up posies in the graveyard of obsolescence, it would definitely qualify as an American middle magnum, even though it is beltless.

These rounds are magnums because they burn a lot of powder. An exact limit of qualification is difficult to establish, but the middle magnums generally consume 70 to 100+ grains of fuel—larger in capacity than the 30-06. Therefore, the 35 Whelen, granted factory rank

Over the years, the semiautomatic has been chambered for the 30-06 Springfield cartridge, a round considered adequate for large game. Today, semiauto options have increased with rifles such as this Browning BAR chambered for the powerful 338 Winchester round.

not long ago, would not qualify as an American middle magnum according to these criteria.

The survey includes only current cartridges. The powerful A-Square rounds are mentioned but not detailed simply because these excellent heavy punchers are not usually available at the gunshop. The A-Square numbers are definitely in the middle magnum bag, and then some, with plenty of energy to qualify as jumbo-stoppers.

The list includes the 8mm Remington Magnum, followed by the 338 Winchester Magnum, 340 Weatherby Magnum, 358 Norma Magnum, 375 H&H Magnum, 378 Weatherby Magnum, 416 Remington and 416 Weatherby Magnum. The 416 Rigby is loaded in the U.S. but is not yet an all-American, although it may be soon. The superior Ruger Magnum Rifle is chambered

to back their clients on coastal grizzlies). Furthermore, mid-range calibers are versatile because they push medium-heavy bullets at medium to high velocities, generally shooting flatter than blunt-bulleted pachyderm rounds.

Mid-calibers pack a wallop. Remember that "power" generally goes up with caliber, all other things being equal. This point was brought out in Chapter 3 for the series of cartridges all based on the 30-06 case from calibers 6mm through 375. As the caliber went up, so did ballistic impetus. However, recall that the 338-06 provided better downrange figures than the 35 Whelen in tests because, weight for weight, 1/3-inch bullets have better ballistic properties than 35-caliber bullets.

The middle magnums shoot excellent bullets

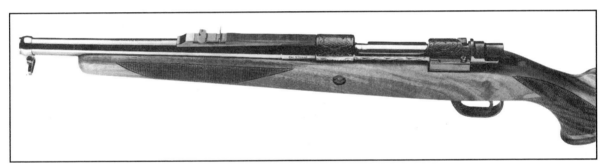

Another fine rifle chambered for some of the world's most powerful cartridges is the Parker-Hale Model 81 African.

for the 416 Rigby, for example, and at least two professional custom gunmakers tell me that they've received significant orders for the English-born 416 Rigby. But for now, the eight rounds listed above, plus the two A-Square powerhouses, comprise the class of American middle magnums.

A shooter may wonder why middle magnums were invented. If middle magnum power is desirable, then why not go all the way to big-bore magnum punch? It's a matter of horsepower. If a vehicle is required to pull a camp trailer, a stout engine is necessary, but a power plant big enough to tug a semi-truck up Pike's Peak is not. It also doesn't make sense to pit elephant cartridges against moose, or for that matter big bears (although as mentioned, some Alaskan guides do like a 450 Alaskan or 458 Winchester

of high sectional density and, depending on projectile profile, good ballistic coefficient. The following sections present some history of each round, a glance at promised factory ballistics, a few select handloads as garnered from the literature (many of which were personally chronographed to verify stated figures) and, finally, a sample of sight-in and trajectory figures with one bullet selected for the purpose of longer-range shooting. The "rule of three"—to sight in three inches high at 100 yards with flat-shooting rounds—was applied where possible. Such a sight-in generally provides hold-on capability all the way out to 300 yards and a bit farther, depending of course on the size of the target (a deep-chested quarry allows greater latitude for bullet drop).

8mm Remington Magnum. Although this

THE MIDDLE MAGNUMS

The three charts that follow list factory loads, handloads and their trajectories, the first as found in print, the second from test results slightly rounded off to make comparisons neasier (for example, 75.7 grains would be rounded off to 75.5 grains). The trajectory sight-in data was prepared both mathematically and at the shooting range using my own drop tests. Downrange ballistics were chronographed with Oehler Skyscreens.

Cartridge	FACTORY LOADS			SAMPLE HANDLOADS		
	Bullet Size (in grains)	Muzzle Velocity (fps)	Muzzle Energy (foot-pounds)	Bullet Size (in grains)	Powder Load	Muzzle Velocity (fps)
8mm Rem. Magnum	185 220	3080 2830	3896 3912	175 220	85.5 gr. H-4831 80.0 gr. H-4831	3200 2900
338 Winchester Magnum	225 250	2780 2660	3860 3927	250 300	70.0 gr. IMR-4350 69.0 gr. H-4831	2700 2450
340 Weatherby Magnum	210 250	3250 3000	4924 4995	250 300	80.0 gr. IMR-4831 88.0 gr. H-870	2800 2500
358 Norma Magnum	250	2800	4350	225 250	75.0 gr. IMR-4350 74.0 gr. IMR-4350	2900 2750
375 H&H Magnum	270 300	2690 2530	4337 4263	270 300	72.0 gr. IMR-4320 78.5 gr. IMR-4350	2700 2600
378 Weatherby Magnum	270 300	3180 2929	6062 5698	270 300	115.0 gr. H-4831 112.0 gr. H-4831	3100 2900
416 Remington Magnum	400	2380	5031	300 400	90.0 gr. Reloader 15 82.0 gr. Reloader 15	2850 2450
416 Weatherby Magnum	400	2700	6476	400	117 gr. Reloader 22	2700

round, the first member of the middle magnum clan, hasn't entirely caught on with American shooters, those who've studied the round and shot game with it have high respect for it.

Gunmaker Dean Zollinger of Idaho worked up a series of loads for the 8mm Remington Magnum in his own custom rifles. Dean was happy, and surprised, with the long-range effectiveness of the 8mm Rem. Mag. on cross-canyon mule deer and elk. Colonel Charles Askins, who

has vast safari experience, also likes the Big 8. Askins's many encounters with African fauna have made him a walking encyclopedia of loads and field results. He has concluded that the 8mm Remington Magnum is a long-range round of high merit.

The 8mm Remington Magnum came along in 1977. Remington wanted to offer the hunter a powerhouse cartridge with true long-range big-game potential. The 8mm Rem. Mag. can be

MIDDLE MAGNUMS VELOCITY/ENERGY FIGURES

Cartridge	Bullet	Velocity/ Energy	Muzzle	100 Yards	200 Yards	300 Yards
8mm Remington Magnum	175-grain spitzer flat-base bullet	V	3200 fps	2936	2687	2454
		E	3987 f-p	3348	2805	2339
	220-grain spitzer boat-tail bullet	V	2900	2728	2563	2409
		E	4108	3635	3207	2834
338 Winchester Magnum	250-grain spitzer boat-tail bullet	V	2700	2548	2401	2261
		E	4064	3603	3199	2837
	300-grain round-nose bullet	V	2450	2160	2010	1600
		E	4000	3109	2692	1706
340 Weatherby Magnum	250-grain spitzer boat-tail bullet	V	2800	2645	2494	2349
		E	4350	3882	3453	3063
	300-grain round-nose bullet	V	2500	2206	2050	1740
		E	4164	3243	2800	2017
358 Norma Magnum	225-grain spitzer boat-tail bullet	V	2900	2690	2466	2265
		E	4203	3616	3039	2564
	250-grain spitzer flat-base bullet	V	2750	2365	2035	1733
		E	4199	3106	2299	1668
375 H & H Magnum	270-grain spitzer flat-base bullet	V	2700	2511	2331	2160
		E	4372	3780	3258	2798
	300-grain spitzer boat-tail bullet	V	2600	2414	2244	2061
		E	4502	3882	3354	2886
378 Weatherby Magnum	270-grain spitzer flat-base bullet	V	3100	2895	2698	2508
		E	5763	5026	4364	3773
	300-grain spitzer boat-tail bullet	V	2900	2701	2512	2333
		E	5601	4861	4201	3624
416 Remington Magnum	400-grain spitzer bullet	V	2380	2145	1923	1718
		E	5031	4087	3285	2620
416 Weatherby Magnum	400-grain soft-point bullet	V	2700	2460	2215	1970
		E	6477	5376	4359	3448

viewed as a 300 H&H Magnum case blown out and necked up to accept .323-inch diameter (8mm) bullets, or as a 375 H&H Magnum with straighter walls necked down to hold .323-inch bullets. Either way, the result is a large-capacity case capable of burning 80+ grains of powder. As the table shows, the 8mm Remington Magnum meets all obligations of middle-magnum performance, with muzzle energies in the 4000 foot-pound arena.

338 Winchester Magnum. Born in 1958, the 338 Winchester Magnum didn't catch fire immediately. Before long, though, this belted magnum had an impressive list of fans. For one thing, 1/3-inch bullets offer high sectional density in mid-weights. For another, the 338 Win. Mag. wasn't built on a full-length 300 H&H case, but rather on a shortened, blown-out case, so it held a hefty powder supply but still worked through standard length bolt actions.

MIDDLE MAGNUMS TRAJECTORY/SIGHT-IN*				
Cartridge	Bullet	100 Yards	200 Yards	300 Yards
8mm Remington Magnum	220-grain spitzer boat-tail bullet at 2900 fps mv	+3	+4.5	−1
338 Winchester Magnum	250-grain spitzer boat-tail bullet at 2700 fps mv	+2	0	−8
340 Weatherby Magnum	250-grain spitzer boat-tail bullet at 2800 fps mv	+2	+1	−7
358 Norma Magnum	225-grain spitzer boat-tail bullet at 2900 fps mv	+2	+1	−7
375 H & H Magnum	300-grain spitzer boat-tail bullet at 2600 fps mv	+2.5	+1	−8
378 Weatherby Magnum	300-grain spitzer boat-tail bullet at 3100 fps mv	+2.5	+1	−5
416 Remington Magnum	400-grain spitzer flat-base bullet at 2380 fps mv	+2.5	−1	−14
416 Weatherby Magnum	400-grain spitzer flat-base bullet at 2700 fps mv	+2.5	0	−6

* With bullet of high ballistic coefficient only

Comparisons between the 338 Winchester Magnum and the 375 H&H Magnum began almost immediately after the 338's inception. Long for its caliber, the .338-inch, 300-grain bullet "carried up" better than the 300-grain, .375-inch bullet, so the 338 seemed to be a 375 in downrange power. But the notion that the 338 and 375 were ballistic twins has eluded close scrutiny. Not a 375 H&H (and never intended to be), the 338 Win. Mag. is something else: a super-reliable big-game round capable of thumping any animal in North America plus many big bullies in Africa and Asia.

Two professional guides of my acquaintance took up with the 338 Winchester early on. Charles J. Keim, the Alaskan outdoorsman and master guide, found the 338 Winchester just about perfect for everything in the Great Land, from deer to what we then called the "brown bear" or Kodiak (now classified as a regular grizzly). Alaskan master guide Harold "Zeke" Schetzle also fell in love with the 338 Winchester Magnum. Harold collected bears on Kodiak Island with his 338, but he also found this middle magnum the best all-around cartridge for other Alaskan game. "I like the 338 when I'm hunting Sitka blacktails," says Zeke, "because Sitka blacktails live where grizzlies roam." Although the 338 remains his favorite, Zeke reports that he uses the 375 H&H Magnum "for the extra insurance" to back his clients in big-bear country. One bear required two well-placed 375 bullets to stop its charge.

The 338 A-Square cartridge richly deserves a place in the family of middle magnums. In factory form, this missile-launcher jets a 250-grain bullet out of the muzzle at a velocity of 3120 fps, for 5403 foot-pounds of muzzle energy.

340 Weatherby Magnum. Another "bigger 338" is the 340 Weatherby Magnum, which has been around since 1962. This is a typical Weatherby creation, intended as a more powerful 338 Winchester Magnum. Although the 338 Win. Mag. didn't send the world of shooting on a dizzy roller coaster ride of joy, it certainly didn't crawl under a bush and die either. It was as natural as snow in Siberia that Weatherby would build a hotshot 33-caliber round to increase 338 Winchester ballistics. The Weatherby cartridge shoots the same 33-caliber bullets that the 338 uses, of course, only it does so faster, from a larger cartridge case. Ten grains more powder increased velocity by about 100 to 150 fps.

Some shooters felt it was too much to pay for too little reward. The 340 made more noise and produced more recoil, but didn't deliver that much more bullet speed. Were these detractors correct? It depends on where significant velocity improvement starts. In some instances, 100 to 150 fps is considered fairly good ballistic improvement for a bullet. Certain 308 Winchester and 30-06 loads differ by only 150 fps, for example, yet the 30-06 is considered a notch above the 308 in power.

The 340 Weatherby factory load can drive a 200-grain bullet at 3200 fps. My test rifle didn't quite realize this speed, but it did achieve 2800 fps with a 250-grain bullet and 2500 fps with a

Even a small bull moose is big. Fadala took this giant in Wyoming with one shot from his 7mm Remington Magnum, using a 160-grain Barnes X-Bullet handload.

300-grain bullet. As the chart shows, the 340 Weatherby is anything but short of power and so is more than deserving of a solid place in the list of American medium magnums.

358 Norma Magnum. The 358 Norma is also a solid member of the family. If this round has a problem, it's in the matchup of the cartridge case and the bullet size. The round came out in 1959, right on the heels of the 338 Winchester Magnum. Its overall case length was set down as 2.508 inches; in comparison, the 338 Winchester Magnum runs 2.500 inches, the same length as the 458 Winchester Magnum.

Ballistically speaking, the 358 Norma Magnum is a 338 Winchester necked up to handle .358-inch bullets. Whether this is good or bad is beside the point; only testing will reveal its qualities. The 358 Norma Magnum shoots bullets in the same weight category as the 338 Winchester Magnum with similar powder charges—but the scale tips a bit in favor of the 338 because, weight for weight, its bullets have higher sectional density. This is exactly the same situation already noted for the wildcat 338-06 compared with the 35 Whelen. Not to say that the 358 Norma is anything other than a powerful middle magnum suitable for any game that walks our continent. But the cartridge is not as popular as the 338 Winchester among American sportsmen.

375 H&H Magnum. This cartridge has been around for so long, we tend to forget that it's a transplant. It was first offered to British shooters in 1912, then quickly found its way into hunting camps all over the world. The 375 H&H is known as *the* all-around cartridge—not just for North America or Africa, but for the entire globe. Our chapter on the all-around cartridge/rifle did not draw the same conclusion, because the 375 H&H is not right for the American Rockies or for many other American hunting areas. Shooting across a canyon for mule deer is much better accomplished with a 7mm Magnum, for instance. Nevertheless, with a 375 H&H a hunter can go anywhere for anything, up to elephants, if he places the bullets properly.

Custom gunmaker Dale Storey worked up a series of special handloads for his hand-made

375s. An Oehler 35P chronograph ticked out some impressive numbers for Dale's handloads on its handy adding-machine tape, one being a 270-grain bullet at more than 2800 fps. Incidentally, I used a 375 H&H widely in Africa and I wasn't impressed when the 375 H&H and a Cape buffalo met. Buffs are tough as truck-tire rubber wrapped around steel, and that means multiple hits are necessary when using the 375 H&H. But reports from several experienced professional hunters have convinced me that the 458 Winchester is more effective on buffs.

378 Weatherby Magnum. Since there is a standard 375, one might expect a 375 from the boys at Weatherby, and of course there is. The modern version of Weatherby's 375, the 378

The 375 H&H Magnum has long been considered one of the best all-around cartridges for large game. Even elephants have been tackled with this round.

Weatherby Magnum, was introduced in 1953. Unlike the 375 Weatherby—a blown-out version of the 375 H&H—the 378 was all new, with a 2.908-inch-long case and a 100+-grain case capacity. This dinosaur-slayer can drive a 300-grain bullet at 2900 fps, a 270-grain bullet at 3100 fps, and a 350-grain bullet at more than 2700 fps.

As the chart shows, the 378 Weatherby Magnum's energy rating is phenomenal. Note how much punch is left at 300 yards with a Sierra 300-grain boat-tail bullet starting at 2900 fps. (Incidentally, the 375 A-Square round offers about the same ballistic numbers as the 378 Weatherby Magnum.)

The 416s. Caliber 416 caught the fancy of American shooters in the late 1980s, and its priests consider it the greatest thing since painless dentistry. The 416 offers a superb bullet diameter. But shooters who insist that the 416 Rigby or 416 Remington eats 458 Winchesters for breakfast should study the situation a bit more closely.

The story—to make the comparison look good for the 416—goes that for all these years the 458 Winchester has never really gained its advertised bullet velocity, and that 1900 fps with a 500-grain slug is about maximum. Dale Storey and I proceeded to the range with our 458s to test this hypothesis. We set up chronographs and

ton Magnum case, it fills a gap between the 375 H&H Magnum and the 458 Winchester Magnum. With its 2.85-inch overall case length, it works in long-action rifles, such as Remington's special Model 700 with long bolt.

The 416 Remington and 416 Rigby rounds are ballistic peas in a pod for all practical purposes. A 400-grain bullet at 2450 fps represents their ballistic promise. Devotees of the 416 who insist that its streamlined bullets have it all over the 458's whale-nosed bullets forget Barnes's 500-grain, .458-inch spitzers and Swift's .458-inch, 500-grain A-Frame spitzers. The Swift 45-

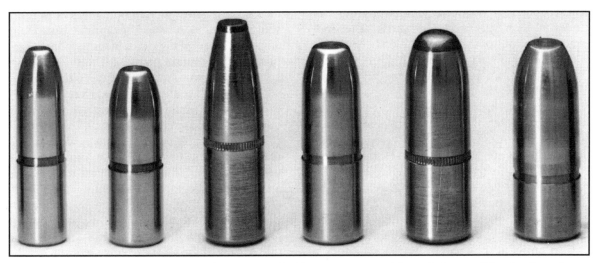

Rifles for truly big game require bullets to match. Here are some of Speer's best, all in the Grand Slam style (left to right): 338 caliber, 275-grain solid; 375 caliber, 300-grain solid; 416 caliber, 400-grain soft point; the same in solid form; 45 caliber, 500-grain soft point; and the same in solid form.

commenced to document ballistics. The two test rifles—Dale's with a 22-inch barrel, mine with a 24-inch barrel, and W-748 fuel in both—earned 2150 fps with 500-grain bullets. So it boils down to a 41-caliber, 400-grain bullet versus a 45-caliber, 500-grain bullet.

Both Remington's and Weatherby's 416s are supremely fine rounds capable of killing ponderous beasts with one well-placed shot. They are not 458s, nor would we want them to be. In America, these 416s are more useful than 458s.

The 416 Remington is a fine cartridge. Developed in 1989 and based on the 8mm Reming-

caliber spitzer is just as "pointy" as the 416's 400-grain missiles. Nonetheless, the 416 Remington remains more useful than the 458 for American game. The 416 wouldn't be entirely out of place for elk in timber, and a hunter after moose or big bears in Canada and Alaska would do well with a 416 (although the 30-30 has dropped more moose and bears than the 416 will ever collect). The 416 Remington is a well-balanced, accurate middle magnum.

The 416 Weatherby is, predictably, more of a good thing. It's built on the 460 Weatherby case necked down to shoot 416-caliber projec-

Rifles for powerhouse cartridges must be designed to withstand the abuse delivered by the recoil of these rounds. Chambered for the 8mm Rem. Mag., 375 H&H Magnum, 416 Rem. Mag. and 458 Win. Mag. is Remington's Model 700 Safari with synthetic stock.

tiles. The 416 doesn't whip the 460 Weatherby Magnum for power. It is accurate, as proved with a test rifle that produced three-shot groups of under-an-inch spread at 100 yards. The 400-grain bullet out of the big 416 Weatherby Magnum case achieved a muzzle velocity of 2600 fps. The resulting foot-pounds of energy puts the 416 Weatherby in the realm of superpower cartridges, but this round remains a middle magnum because it shoots a bullet from the middle magnum category.

The 416s are excellent rounds and will do fine in Africa. Dangerous game isn't dangerous when it's 100 yards away from the hunter, so these cartridges many never replace larger-bullet numbers with their greater missile weight. But they'll do the job all the same—not only on the Dark Continent, but also in Alaska, where they make great grizzly stoppers.

The middle magnums are some of the most powerful cartridges offered across-the-counter to North American sportsmen. For most applications, they're too large and too specialized. The "average" North American hunter gets by quite well without a middle magnum. But many sportsmen prefer the extra insurance that these powerhouse rounds provide. The middle mags aren't timber/woods rounds alone, although they serve well in forest and thicket. They also make excellent long-range harvesting machines for the hunter who practices with them and sights in his rifles correctly. A cool marksman with a solid rest could drop an elk cleanly with a middle magnum round at long range. These rounds have a fairly flat trajectory, which eliminates considerable bullet drop guesswork, and provide terrific impact at all ranges. All of the middle magnums have a place, with the 375s capturing the title of best all-around cartridge worldwide, the 33s possessing as fine a ballistic missile as could be asked for, and the 416s having the power to stop deadly beasts at close proximity.

THE SUCCESSFUL VARMINT RIFLE

16 The varmint rifle considered here is the "real thing." It's not a behind-the-barn-door firearm that gets dragged out now and then when the chicken coop is raided by a coyote. This varmint rifle is a professional.

Without three major attributes—varmint-cartridge chambering, super accuracy and a high-magnification scope sight—the varmint rifle is just another longarm. The medium-weight varmint rifle is not a benchrest rifle. It can be carried in the field without undue strain, although it's no flyweight. Flyweights don't have the field stability necessary to produce the results that varmint hunters demand from a rifle.

The most popular action for the varmint rifle is the bolt. But there are (and have been for a very long time) single-shot varmint rifles of excellent quality. The pump-action, semiauto and lever-action gun can all be used with success on varmints.

But these are not varmint rifles by the definition we set down here. The cowhand who slips his lever-action 30-30 out of the scabbard to take a poke at a sheep-eating coyote is varmint hunting, but that doesn't make his carbine a varmint rifle any more than a cocker spaniel is a bear hound just because he barks at one. Multiple-barrel rifles and all other action types fall into the same category. All can be used on varmints, but they aren't true varmint rifles. Accuracy factors keep most rifles out of the varmint class. But even the most accurate big-game rifle isn't a varmint piece, because it doesn't qualify under caliber restrictions.

The 22 Long Rifle rimfire cartridge has dropped more varmints than all the varmint cartridges in the world, but this round doesn't make the list for the purpose of this chapter. The 22 WMR is a fine varmint cartridge for 150-yard—even 200-yard—shooting, and it borders the list of varmint rounds. It is highly recommended for varminters.

For our purposes, varmint cartridges of "professional" status are centerfires—every one of them. They are confined by caliber to include 17s through 24s. Caliber 14 and 20 centerfires are too rare to worry about here, and although only one factory 17 is available, it's too good to omit. On the other end of the list is the 24-caliber bullet, or 6mm size. Some fine cartridges shoot this bullet size with great accuracy, and the 24s deserve high honors in the varmint field.

The 25-caliber cartridge is also used on varmints with fine results. But there has to be a cutoff. If the 25 is admitted, then why not the 6.5mm (26 caliber)? And if 26s are OK, why not the 270 as well? Therefore, this list of varmint rounds concludes with caliber 24, a good stopping point on the upper end of the scale.

Recoil, after all, does play a role in varminting. Some varmint hunters take only a few shots per day. But in many areas, varmint-class wildlife abounds, and a marksman may get off numerous shots in a day. In a true varmint cartridge, recoil should be minimal to allow pleasant firing of multiple rounds when the demand calls for it. Keep in mind that a varmint rifle is also a target machine. And a target rifle should be manageable, with only modest recoil.

These days, it's a good bet that the varmint rifle will see more action on the target range than in the field. Where woodchucks once excavated farm fields, few of these marmots exist. Populations of this and other varmints have been reduced in favor of growing crops. Even in the West, large prairie dog colonies aren't always easily found. So the specialized tackdriver, a rifle chambered for a mild round, gets most of its workouts at the range. The plan is to punch neat groups in paper. This is not benchresting, as such, because the varmint rifle is not a benchrest rifle. It's a matter of building fine handloads and/or tuning a rifle to produce superior groups at 100, 200, 300 yards and farther. So it is that today's varmint rifle is also a paper-puncher. As such, it must be chambered for a cartridge that doesn't buffet the shooter each time he touches off a shot.

VARMINT BULLETS

The varmint bullet is unique. The need for accuracy demands that varmint bullets carry all traits of precision. These bullets are concentric, not lopsided. Their jackets are uniform. Their bases, whether flat or boat-tail, are symmetrical. They are of uniform weight, with only very slight variation.

Although all factors of bullet integrity must be observed, the varmint bullet must be something else, too—explosive. The varmint rifle was created for instant dispatch of varmint-class species, which means quick bullet expansion for instant delivery of energy. Jackets for varmint bullets are on the thin side. Designs include hollow-point and soft-point configurations. The whole idea is bullet frangibility.

Such a design also reduces the chance of ricochet, as the bullet will self-destruct on contact with the ground. This is an important factor. On a farm, ranch, or any area where livestock may occupy the same grounds inhabited by varmints, it's comforting to know that a fired bullet will self-destruct on the ground or on the varmint, not bounce off the ground and continue its journey. The 22 Long Rifle bullet doesn't travel fast enough to blow up on contact with varmint or ground, and it tends to ricochet. The 22 WMR is also known for bouncing off the ground. The varmint hunter should make it a point to tell the farmer or rancher that the rifle being used may have a loud report, but that it is safer than a rimfire. The landowner may not realize that the quiet little 22 may actually be less safe over in the "back 40" than the louder varmint cartridge with its self-destructing bullet.

VARMINT CARTRIDGES

Here, all of the following cartridges are surveyed on the basis of the following criteria: ac-

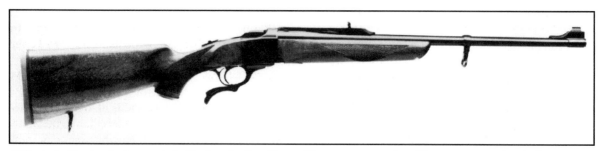

Although the typical varmint rifle is a bolt-action with scope, varmint rifles can come in all forms and sizes. This Ruger No. 1 is offered in various chamberings that serve admirably for varmint hunting.

The coyote is a large non-game species and is often hunted with powerful rifles.

curacy, trajectory, bullet blow-up, noise, recoil, wind drift and power.

17 Remington. Tiny, with virtually no felt recoil, the 17 Remington is one of the most interesting varmint cartridges ever developed.

Accuracy: The accuracy level of the 17 is acceptable. Although the 17-caliber rifles tested for this work did not exhibit benchrest accuracy, minute-of-angle groups were common. IMR-4320, IMR-4198 and H-4895 powders all gave good accuracy in test rifles.

Trajectory: Sighted in only 2.5 inches high at 100 yards, the little 25-grain bullet was back on zero at a full 300 yards from the muzzle. That is flat shooting!

Bullet blow-up: Bullets from the 17 Reming-

ton self-destruct readily. No ricochet was encountered in testing. Bullets from the 17-caliber centerfire turn into confetti.

Noise: Modest. Compared with larger varmint cartridges, the 17 is quiet—not as quiet as the 22 Hornet or 218 Bee, but nearly so.

Recoil: There is simply no felt recoil with the 17. The nudge on the shoulder is difficult to detect at all.

Wind drift: The 17 Remington has the asset of high velocity and the detriments of low bullet mass and ballistic coefficient. Time of flight is quick. The bullet covers ground fast, giving the wind less of a chance to push on the projectile. So the end result is better wind drift properties for the little 17 than may be imagined. In a 20-

m.p.h. crosswind, the little bullet drifts between 8 and 10 inches off course at 200 yards with a muzzle velocity of 4075 fps.

Power: The 17 Remington is a strange cartridge in its effect on game. Smaller targets, such as prairie dogs, all but disappear when struck. Larger targets, such as marmots (woodchucks and rockchucks), seem to go into stop-motion when hit. Coyotes within a range of a couple hundred yards also stop in their tracks on bullet contact. Retained energy is around 460 to 480 foot-pounds at 200 yards with a muzzle velocity in the 4000- to 4100-fps domain.

The big strike against the 17 is that because of its tiny bore, it fouls in the field rather quickly. Because bore surface is minimal, there's less bore to hold fouling. Even with the cleanest-burning powder and good ignition, the 17-caliber cartridge tends to dirty the bore quickly. In addition to powder residue, the bore also fouls from bullet jacket metal. In fact, metal fouling is probably more serious than powder fouling. The shooter can overcome this problem by carrying a breakdown rod, a bristle brush attachment and solvent into the field. Good solvents include Shooter's Choice, J-B Cleaning Compound and Flitz. These agents should be removed from the bore after they do their job. A bullet should never be fired through a bore that has cleaning agent residue in it. Other than the fouling problem, the 17 centerfire is a fine round.

22 Hornet and 218 Bee. Ballistically, these two rounds are close enough to share the same berth. Both push a 50-grain, .224-inch bullet at a muzzle velocity of around 2800 fps.

Accuracy: Neither round is a benchrester, yet both shoot with sufficiently close bullet clustering for varmints at 200 to possibly 250 yards. An accuracy test with a Winchester Model 70 chambered for the 22 Hornet netted groups of just under 1-inch size for five shots at 100 yards.

Trajectory: The 22 Hornet and 218 Bee shoot flat enough for their power limits. Sighted 2.5 inches high at 100 yards, the 50-grain bullet is back on target at 200 yards and about 4 inches low at 250 yards. Since 250 yards is about the limit for these rounds, trajectory is sufficiently flat.

Varminting is specialized shooting and hunting. Here, John Fadala uses a Marlin 22 WMR on the plains. His method is to spot prairie dogs and then approach to within 150 yards before shooting.

Bullet blow-up: Light-jacketed bullets in these cartridges explode well. For example, the Hornady 50-grain SX bullet did not ricochet, even at remaining 200-yard velocities. Harder-jacketed bullets do not self-destruct as readily.

Noise: These rounds are quiet as varmint cartridges go. They make far less noise than the 220 Swift, for example.

Recoil: There is no recoil problem here, since both cartridges are exceedingly mild.

Wind drift: Modest ballistic coefficient and modest velocity team up negatively with the Hornet and Bee. The 50-grain bullet starting at 2800 fps drifts about a foot off target at 200 yards in a 20 m.p.h. crosswind.

The heavy barrel of a varmint rifle, as shown here on this Savage Model 112-FV, is excellent not only for field stability, but also for distribution of barrel heat. A heavy barrel is slower to heat up than a thinner-walled barrel.

Power: Both cartridges have ample power for smaller varmints to 250 yards and larger varmints (fox, coyote) to 200 yards. Remaining energy at 200 yards for a 50-grain bullet starting at 2800 fps mv is about 450 foot-pounds.

The 222 Family. For practical purposes, the 222 Remington, 223 Remington and 222 Remington Magnum are in the same class, despite devoted shooters of each cartridge who claim that their specific round is vastly superior to the other two. An increase of 100 fps mv over the standard 222 Remington is about it for the 223 and 222 Magnum.

Accuracy: The 222 Remington and 222 Remington Magnum have both competed favorably in benchrest competition. The 223 also is certainly a highly accurate round, in the right rifle. These cartridges can produce 1/2-inch groups with five shots at 100 yards.

Trajectory: All three of these rounds are solid contenders for 300-yard varminting, with the 50-grain bullet departing the muzzle at 3300 fps (as high as 3400 fps for the 222 Remington Magnum and 223 Remington). Sighted 2 inches high at 100 yards, bullets drop back into zero at about 225 yards and fall about 6 inches low at 300 yards. A sight-in of 2.5 inches at 100 yards puts the group back on line at about 250 yards and only 4 inches low at 300 yards.

Bullet blow-up: Bullet upset is excellent with this trio of rounds. The lighter-jacketed missile will withstand 222 family velocity.

Noise: The 222 family falls in between the Hornet/Bee and the big 220 Swift for noise level.

Recoil: All three rounds are exceedingly light in recoil. This factor makes rifles chambered for the 222 family easy to shoot consistently at the target range or in the varmint field for numerous shots.

Wind drift: The 50-grain bullet starting at 3300 to 3400 fps mv drifts off course about 8.5 inches at 200 yards in a 20-m.p.h. crosswind.

Power: At 200 yards, the 222 family delivers around 685 foot-pounds of remaining energy when the 50-grain bullet begins at 3300 to 3400 fps mv.

22 PPC USA. This benchrest cartridge is pure dynamite in the varmint field. It delivers sufficient power for varmints to at least 300 yards, but its strongest point is accuracy.

Accuracy: The 22 PPC USA is a cartridge of benchrest accuracy, with five-shot groups in the 1/3-inch and smaller category. Because of this accuracy, the 22 PPC USA often accounts for hits

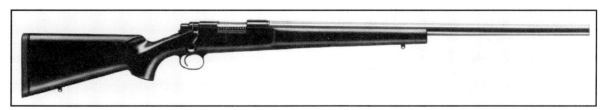

Another fine varmint rifle is this bolt-action Remington 40-XB "Varmint Special" with Kevlar stock.

at very long range.

Trajectory: Although 3400 fps mv is often given as a maximum velocity for the 22 PPC USA, speeds up to 3600 fps mv have been achieved with N-201 powder and the 50-grain, .224-inch bullet. At this velocity, the 22 PPC can be sighted 3 inches high at 100 yards for a zero of 300 yards. But for hunting smaller varmints, it's best to sight 2.5 inches high, which will put the bullet 3 inches high at 200 yards.

Bullet blow-up: The 22 PPC shoots 50-grain bullets just fast enough to cause self-destruction on contact with the ground and on varmints.

Noise: The 22 PPC makes no more *perceptible* noise than the 222 family of rounds. It does

One of the best varmint cartridges ever offered the shooter is the 22 PPC USA (left), shown here with the short 7.92×33mm Kurz cartridge to illustrate its compactness.

burn a little more powder than the 222 group and no doubt makes a bit greater muzzle blast, but a shooter would be hard-pressed to tell the difference in the field or at the range.

Recoil: Once again, recoil is simply no problem. The little 50-grain bullet and modest powder charges preclude heavy recoil.

Wind drift: A 50-grain bullet, beginning at 3600 fps mv with N-201 powder, drifts off course about 7.5 to 8.0 inches at 200 yards in a 20-m.p.h. crosswind.

Power: About 800 foot-pounds at 200 yards is realized for a 50-grain bullet at 3600 fps mv.

219 Zipper. The 219 Zipper is capable of yielding ballistics identical to the 22 PPC USA. However, in its factory form this cartridge isn't noted for the accuracy level achieved by the 22 PPC USA or the 222 family. Nonetheless, it is a useful round for varminting.

225 Winchester. In muzzle velocity, the 225 Winchester surpasses the 219 Zipper by about 200 fps. Consequently, the 225 has a slightly flatter trajectory for the 50-grain, .224-inch bullet, along with slightly less wind drift and mildly increased 200-yard energy. This round has not achieved great popularity, although it came out in 1964 and is still loaded by Winchester.

The 225 Winchester is a powerful varmint round, delivering almost 900 foot-pounds of remaining energy at 200 yards with the 50-grain bullet at 3800 fps mv. Sighted in 2.5 inches high at 100 yards, it's back on target at a full 300 yards from the muzzle. The 50-grain bullet at 3800 fps mv drifts about 7.5 inches off course at 200 yards in a 20-m.p.h. crosswind.

224 Weatherby Magnum, 22-250 Remington and 220 Swift. These three rounds are lumped together because they all deliver a 50-grain bullet at 3800 to 3900 fps. They are wicked long-range varmint cartridges, but they also make more noise than the smaller cartridges of the varmint class.

Accuracy: Out of proper barrels, all three cartridges are capable of delivering accuracy in the .50- to .75-inch range at 100 yards from the bench. (As always, these general statements are subject to individual rifle variation.)

Trajectory: These are the flatliners of the

varmint clan. A 50-grain bullet departing the muzzle at 3800 to 3900 fps can be sighted to strike dead on at 300 yards, hitting 2.5 inches high at 100 yards.

Bullet blow-up: Obviously, a 50-grain bullet screaming away at these velocities blows up readily on contact with either varmint or earth.

Noise: None of these three is as quiet as the varmint rounds that burn less powder. In fact, they can be fairly noisy, and anyone hunting with them on farm or ranchlands should explain to the landowner that these speedsters' bullets blow to bits on contact with the ground.

Recoil: Recoil is no problem with these cartridges, but some shooters may find that these hot 22s *seem* to "kick" because of their noise. In fact, recoil is mild when compared to that of big-game cartridges.

Wind drift: A 50-grain bullet beginning its journey near 3900 fps mv drifts a little over 7 inches at 200 yards in a 20-m.p.h. crosswind.

Power: Patient, skilled hunters have compiled good harvest records on deer-sized game with these big 22-caliber centerfires. But these cartridges are illegal in many areas, because of their small caliber and light bullet. This trio of

The 22-caliber Ballistic Tip bullet in 55-grain form is made for explosiveness. It's built for all 22 centerfires capable of achieving more than 3200 fps muzzle velocity.

Varmint rifles require the correct projectile. This is Nosler's 70-grain 6mm Ballistic Tip bullet, ideal when handloaded in the 6 PPC USA and other 6mm cartridges.

rounds is entirely capable of dropping varmints out to 400 yards, though. Remaining energy at 200 yards with the 50-grain bullet at 3900 fps mv is more than 900 foot-pounds.

6 PPC USA. This is the current accuracy king of the benchrest clan. It makes an extremely fine varmint cartridge with medium-weight (70-grain) bullets at 3200 to 3300 fps mv.

Accuracy: Groups in the .25-inch zone are not uncommon with this cartridge in the right rifle. Groups of .30- to .35-inch size at 100 yards from the bench are readily achieved.

Trajectory: With the 70-grain bullet at 3200 fps mv, the 6 PPC USA can be sighted in 2.5 inches high at 100 yards, which puts the group back on target at 250 to 265 yards and only a couple inches low at 300 yards.

Bullet blow-up: Using special varmint bullets with lighter jackets, the 6 PPC USA offers plenty of bullet upset on varmint or ground.

Noise: The 6 PPC USA does not seem to make much more noise than the 22 PPC USA. To some observers, it has a less "sharp" report than the high-speed 22s. Of course, it makes more noise than the 22 Hornet or 218 Bee.

Recoil: Rifles chambering the 6 PPC are generally fairly heavy. The test rifle used for this work was a Sako Varminter in the 9-pound class. Felt recoil was absolutely minimal.

Wind drift: A 70-grain bullet starting at

One of the hottest varmint cartridges of all time is the once-wildcat 22-250, which is now a factory standard. Two rounds are shown here flanking the 30-06.

act makeup of the load.

Recoil: In varmint-type rifles, the 243 Winchester and 6mm Remington are not kickers using varmint loads and 70-grain bullets. In extremely light rifles with hunting loads and heavier bullets, there is some felt recoil. All in all, though, these aren't bad rounds in the recoil department.

Wind drift: A 70-grain bullet taking off at 3400 fps mv drifts a little more than 8 inches off course at 200 yards in a 20-m.p.h. crosswind.

Power: Obviously, these rounds are capable of taking deer. Even with a 70-grain varmint bullet starting out at 3400 fps mv, energy at 200 yards is well over half a ton.

The varmint rifle is one of the best buys in the modern world of shooting. It's mild-mannered, fun to shoot, accurate and amply powerful for smaller species. Arms companies

around 3200 fps mv drifts off course about 9 inches at 200 yards in a 20-m.p.h. crosswind.

Power: This 6mm cartridge is sufficiently powerful for varmints, even of the coyote class, to more than 400 yards. Retained energy at 200 yards for the 70-grain bullet at 3200 fps mv is around 950 foot-pounds. Energy for the same bullet at the same starting speed is almost 550 foot-pounds all the way out to 400 yards.

The 243 Winchester and 6mm Remington. For all practical purposes, these two rounds are ballistic twins. They can be loaded with a 70-grain varmint bullet at 3400 to 3500 fps mv.

Accuracy: Both of these rounds are inherently accurate, shooting minute of angle with no problem. Groups in the .50- to .75-inch realm are possible with certain rifles.

Trajectory: A sight-in of 3 inches high at 100 yards puts the 70-grain bullet dead on target at 300 yards.

Bullet blow-up: At 3400 to 3500 fps mv, the 70-grain bullet of varmint construction blows to bits on contact with the ground.

Noise: These rounds are on par with the 220 Swift for noise, depending, of course, on the ex-

Jackrabbits are classified as varmints in most areas and are fair game all year long. This hare was taken with a 25-grain Remington bullet from a Sako 17 Remington rifle.

One of the author's favorite varmint rifles is the bolt-action Sako chambered for the 17 Remington cartridge. This little round shoots a 25-grain bullet at over 4100 fps muzzle velocity, which worked perfectly on this rockchuck.

know this, and are now offering the shooter the greatest array ever of special varmint rifles—those that bear good weight for stability, are chambered for great varmint cartridges, can achieve high levels of accuracy and are suited for mounting the finest state-of-the-art scope sights.

TODAY'S IMPROVED FACTORY AMMO

17 Factory ammunition is better than it has ever been in the history of cartridges. That's not an author's generosity—it's simple and provable fact. Today's factory fodder is more accurate than ever, more powerful in many loads, and entirely reliable. Ammo from abroad as well as our homeland graces sporting goods shelves, making the selection of cartridges extremely wide.

About five billion rounds of ammunition are produced in this country annually. By far the majority of this ammunition is 22 rimfire in nature, but plenty of centerfire ammo is manufactured. This chapter discusses many of the companies that supply us with this plethora of good shooting material.

CCI

CCI produces some of the world's best 22-rimfire ammunition in a vast variety of loads, from the meek 22 CB Long to the powerful 22 WMR, including shotshells in 22 Long Rifle and 22 WMR. The company's Green Tag ammunition is for the target-minded. Those who enjoy putting small game on the table with the 22 rimfire will appreciate CCI's SGB (small-game bullet). In keeping with the CCI concept—a load for everything—the SGB offers a blunt-nosed bullet that delivers a good blow to squirrels, rabbits or other small animals, while at the same time avoiding the explosiveness of a hollow-point projectile.

CCI also produces a broad selection of handgun ammo, mentioned here because several rifles today use handgun ammunition, including the 9mm Parabellum, the particular caliber of Marlin's semiautomatic Model 9 Camp Gun rifle. Rifles in 45 ACP, 44 Magnum and other calibers can shoot high-quality reloadable CCI ammo, as well as economy-priced, but excellent non-reloadable rounds with aluminum cases.

FEDERAL CARTRIDGE COMPANY

This trusted ammo company has been in business many years, to the benefit of any shooter who has tried their products. In the past, it would have been a simple matter to list Federal's offerings. Today, the list is virtually endless. Federal has some of the finest 22-rimfire ammo made anywhere, including a 50-grain bullet for the 22 WMR. There is also a 22 CB Long and a number of 22 Long Rifle loads.

Federal's centerfire ammunition begins with the 222 Remington and encompasses the 22-250, 6mm Remington, 257 Roberts, 7×57 Mauser, 280 Remington, 7-30 Waters, 7.62×39mm So-

FEDERAL PREMIUM LINE BALLISTICS

PREMIUM SAFARI RIFLE

USAGE	FEDERAL LOAD NO.	CALIBER	BULLET WGT. IN GRAINS	GRAMS	BULLET STYLE	FACTORY PRIMER NO.	VELOCITY IN FEET PER SECOND (TO NEAREST 10 FEET) MUZZLE	100 YDS.	200 YDS.	300 YDS.	400 YDS.	500 YDS.	ENERGY IN FOOT/POUNDS (TO NEAREST 5 FOOT/POUNDS) MUZZLE	100 YDS.	200 YDS.	300 YDS.	400 YDS.	500 YDS.
3	P300HA	300 H&H Magnum	180	11.66	Nosler Partition	215	2880	2680	2480	2290	2110	1940	3315	2860	2455	2100	1780	1500
3	P300WD2	300 Win. Magnum	180	11.66	Nosler Partition	215	2960	2750	2540	2340	2160	1980	3500	3010	2580	2195	1860	1565
3	P338A2	338 Win. Magnum	210	13.60	Nosler Partition	215	2830	2590	2370	2150	1940	1750	3735	3130	2610	2155	1760	1435
3	P338B2	338 Win. Magnum	250	16.20	Nosler Partition	215	2660	2400	2150	1910	1690	1500	3925	3185	2555	2055	1590	1245
3	P375C	375 H&H Magnum	250	16.20	Boat-tail SP	215	2670	2450	2240	2040	1850	1680	3955	3335	2790	2315	1905	1565
4	P375D	375 H&H Magnum	300	19.44	Solid	215	2530	2170	1840	1550	1310	1140	4265	3140	2260	1605	1140	860
4	P375F	375 H&H Magnum	300	19.44	Nosler Partition	215	2530	2320	2120	1930	1750	1590	4265	3585	2995	2475	2040	1675
3	P458A	458 Win. Magnum	350	22.68	Soft Point	215	2470	1990	1570	1250	1060	950	4740	3065	1915	1205	870	705
4	P458B	458 Win. Magnum	510	33.04	Soft Point	215	2090	1820	1570	1360	1190	1080	4945	3730	2790	2080	1605	1320
4	P458C	458 Win. Magnum	500	32.40	Solid	215	2090	1870	1670	1480	1320	1190	4850	3880	3085	2440	1945	1585
4	P416A	416 Rigby	410	26.57	Soft Point	215	2370	2110	1870	1640	1440	1280	5115	4050	3165	2455	1895	1485
4	P416B	416 Rigby	410	26.57	Solid	215	2370	2110	1870	1640	1440	1280	5115	4050	3165	2455	1895	1485
4	P470A	470 Nitro Express	500	32.40	Soft Point	215	2150	1890	1650	1440	1270	1140	5130	3965	3040	2310	1790	1435
4	P470B	470 Nitro Express	500	32.40	Solid	215	2150	1890	1650	1440	1270	1140	5130	3965	3040	2310	1790	1435

Usage Key: 1 = Varmints, predators, small game   2 = Medium game   3 = Large, heavy game   4 = Dangerous game

PREMIUM RIFLE SIERRA BOAT-TAIL

USAGE	FEDERAL LOAD NO.	CALIBER	BULLET WGT. IN GRAINS	GRAMS	BULLET STYLE	FACTORY PRIMER NO.	VELOCITY IN FEET PER SECOND (TO NEAREST 10 FEET) MUZZLE	100 YDS.	200 YDS.	300 YDS.	400 YDS.	500 YDS.	ENERGY IN FOOT/POUNDS (TO NEAREST 5 FOOT/POUNDS) MUZZLE	100 YDS.	200 YDS.	300 YDS.	400 YDS.	500 YDS.
1	P223E	223 Rem. (5.56x45mm)	55	3.56	Boat-tail H.P.	205	3240	2770	2340	1950	1610	1330	1280	935	670	465	315	215
1	P22250B	22-250 Rem.	55	3.56	Boat-tail H.P.	210	3680	3280	2920	2590	2280	1990	1655	1315	1040	815	630	480
2	P243C	243 Win. (6.16x51mm)	100	6.48	Boat-tail S.P.	210	2960	2760	2570	2380	2210	2040	1950	1690	1460	1260	1080	925
1	P243D	243 Win. (6.16x51mm)	85	5.50	Boat-tail H.P.	210	3320	3070	2830	2600	2380	2180	2080	1770	1510	1280	1070	890
2	P2506C	25-06 Rem.	117	7.58	Boat-tail S.P.	210	2990	2770	2570	2370	2190	2000	2320	2000	1715	1465	1240	1045
2	P270C	270 Win.	150	9.72	Boat-tail S.P.	210	2850	2660	2480	2300	2130	1970	2705	2355	2040	1760	1510	1290
2	P270D	270 Win.	130	8.42	Boat-tail S.P.	210	3060	2830	2620	2410	2220	2030	2700	2320	1980	1680	1420	1190
2	P7RD	7mm Rem. Magnum	150	9.72	Boat-tail S.P.	215	3110	2920	2750	2580	2410	2250	3220	2850	2510	2210	1930	1690
3	P7RE	7mm Rem. Magnum	165	10.69	Boat-tail S.P.	215	2950	2800	2650	2510	2370	2230	3190	2865	2570	2300	2050	1825
2	P3006D	30-06 Spring. (7.62x63mm)	165	10.69	Boat-tail S.P.	210	2800	2610	2420	2240	2070	1910	2870	2490	2150	1840	1580	1340
2	P3006G	30-06 Spring. (7.62x63mm)	150	9.72	Boat-tail S.P.	210	2910	2690	2480	2270	2070	1880	2820	2420	2040	1710	1430	1180
3	P3006L	30-06 Spring. (7.62x63mm)	180	11.66	Boat-tail S.P.	210	2700	2540	2380	2220	2080	1930	2915	2570	2260	1975	1720	1495
2	P308C	308 Win. (7.62x51mm)	165	10.69	Boat-tail S.P.	210	2700	2520	2330	2160	1990	1830	2670	2310	1990	1700	1450	1230
3	P300WC	300 Win. Magnum	200	12.96	Boat-tail S.P.	215	2830	2680	2530	2380	2240	2110	3560	3180	2830	2520	2230	1970

+P ammunition is loaded to a higher pressure. Use only in firearms so recommended by the gun manufacturer.

PREMIUM RIFLE NOSLER PARTITION

USAGE	FEDERAL LOAD NO.	CALIBER	BULLET WGT. IN GRAINS	GRAMS	BULLET STYLE	FACTORY PRIMER NO.	VELOCITY IN FEET PER SECOND (TO NEAREST 10 FEET) MUZZLE	100 YDS.	200 YDS.	300 YDS.	400 YDS.	500 YDS.	ENERGY IN FOOT/POUNDS (TO NEAREST 5 FOOT/POUNDS) MUZZLE	100 YDS.	200 YDS.	300 YDS.	400 YDS.	500 YDS.
2	P6C	6mm Rem.	100	6.48	Nosler Partition	210	3100	2830	2570	2330	2100	1890	2135	1775	1470	1205	985	790
2	P243E	243 Win.	100	6.48	Nosler Partition	210	2960	2730	2510	2300	2100	1910	1945	1650	1395	1170	975	805
2	P257B	257 Roberts (Hi-Vel.+P)	120	7.77	Nosler Partition	210	2780	2560	2360	2160	1970	1790	2060	1750	1480	1240	1030	855
2	P270E	270 Win.	150	9.72	Nosler Partition	210	2850	2590	2340	2100	1880	1670	2705	2225	1815	1470	1175	930
2	P7C	7mm Mauser (7x57mm Mauser)	140	9.07	Nosler Partition	210	2660	2450	2260	2070	1890	1730	2200	1865	1585	1330	1110	930
2	P280A	280 Rem.	150	9.72	Nosler Partition	210	2890	2620	2370	2140	1910	1710	2780	2295	1875	1520	1215	970
3	P7RF	7mm Rem. Magnum	160	10.37	Nosler Partition	215	2950	2730	2520	2320	2120	1940	3090	2650	2250	1910	1600	1340
2	P7RG	7mm Rem. Magnum	140	9.07	Nosler Partition	215	3150	2920	2700	2500	2300	2110	3085	2650	2270	1940	1640	1380
2	P3030D	30-30 Win.	170	11.01	Nosler Partition	210	2200	1900	1620	1380	1190	1060	1830	1355	990	720	535	425
3	P3006F	30-06 Spring. (7.62x63mm)	180	11.66	Nosler Partition	210	2700	2470	2250	2040	1850	1660	2910	2440	2020	1670	1360	1110
3	P308E	308 Win. (7.62x51mm)	180	11.66	Nosler Partition	210	2620	2430	2240	2060	1890	1730	2745	2355	2005	1700	1430	1200

viet, 300 Savage, 308, 300 Winchester Magnum and some not-as-popular cartridges as the 303 British, 8mm Mauser and 32 Winchester Special. A 44 Remington Magnum load for rifles is listed with a 240-grain bullet at 1760 fps mv, as well as a 45-70 load with a 300-grain bullet at 1880 feet per second muzzle velocity.

Federal has long offered the hunter a good bullet in its Hi-Shok brand, but the company also makes a Premium line of ammo with Sierra and Nosler Partition bullets. The Premium Safari line lists the 375 H&H Magnum, the 416 Rigby (once

FEDERAL PREMIUM LINE BALLISTICS

WIND DRIFT IN INCHES 10 MPH CROSSWIND					HEIGHT OF BULLET TRAJECTORY — AVERAGE RANGE				LONG RANGE						TEST BARREL LENGTH INCHES	FEDERAL LOAD NO.
100	200	300	400	500	50	100	200	300	50	100	200	300	400	500		
0.7	2.9	6.7	12.4	20.1	-0.2	⊕	-3.4	-12.4	+0.7	+1.7	⊕	-7.4	-21.3	-43.2	24	P300HA
0.7	2.8	6.6	12.3	20.0	-0.2	⊕	-3.1	-11.7	+0.6	+1.6	⊕	-7.0	-20.3	-41.1	24	P300WD2
0.8	3.5	8.3	15.4	25.4	-0.2	⊕	-3.7	-13.6	+0.8	+1.8	⊕	-8.1	-23.7	-48.6	24	P338A2
1.1	4.5	10.8	20.3	33.6	-0.1	⊕	-4.6	-16.7	+1.1	+2.3	⊕	-9.8	-29.1	-60.2	24	P338B2
0.9	3.6	8.5	15.9	26.1	+0.4	⊕	-5.3	-17.6	+1.7	+2.7	⊕	-9.6	-27.6	-55.6	24	P375C
1.7	7.2	17.6	33.9	56.5		-1.1	-9.1	-27.5	+0.5	⊕	-7.0	-24.2	-55.8	-106.5	24	P375D
0.9	3.9	9.1	17.0	27.8	0	⊕	-5.0	-17.7	+1.2	+2.5	⊕	-10.3	-29.9	-60.8	24	P375F
2.5	11.0	27.6	52.6	83.9	⊕	-1.5	-11.0	-34.9	+0.1	⊕	-7.5	-29.1	-71.1	-138.0	24	P458A
1.9	7.9	18.9	35.3	56.8	⊕	-1.8	-13.7	-39.7	+0.4	⊕	-9.1	-32.3	-73.9	-138.0	24	P458B
1.5	6.1	14.5	26.9	43.7	⊕	-1.7	-12.9	-36.7	+0.4	⊕	-8.5	-29.5	-66.2	-122.0	24	P458C
1.3	5.7	13.6	25.6	42.3	⊕	-1.2	-9.8	-28.5	+0.6	⊕	-7.4	-24.8	-55.0	-101.6	24	P416A
1.3	5.7	13.6	25.6	42.3	⊕	-1.2	-9.8	-28.5	+0.6	⊕	-7.4	-24.8	-55.0	-101.6	24	P416B
1.6	7.0	16.6	31.1	50.6	⊕	-1.6	-12.6	-36.2	+0.8	⊕	-9.3	-31.3	-69.7	-128.6	24	P470A
1.6	7.0	16.6	31.1	50.6	⊕	-1.6	-12.6	-36.2	+0.8	⊕	-9.3	-31.3	-69.7	-128.6	24	P470B

WIND DRIFT IN INCHES 10 MPH CROSSWIND					HEIGHT OF BULLET TRAJECTORY — AVERAGE RANGE				LONG RANGE						TEST BARREL LENGTH INCHES	FEDERAL LOAD NO.
100	200	300	400	500	50	100	200	300	50	100	200	300	400	500		
1.3	5.8	14.2	27.7	47.6	-0.3	⊕	-2.7	-10.8	+0.4	+1.4	⊕	-6.7	-20.5	-43.4	24	P223E
0.8	3.6	8.4	15.8	26.3	-0.4	⊕	-1.7	-7.6	0	+0.9	⊕	-5.0	-15.1	-32.0	24	P22250B
0.6	2.6	6.1	11.3	18.4	-0.2	⊕	-3.1	-11.4	+0.6	+1.5	⊕	-6.8	-19.8	-39.9	24	P243C
0.7	2.7	6.3	11.6	18.8	-0.3	⊕	-2.2	-8.8	+0.2	+1.1	⊕	-5.5	-16.1	-32.8	24	P243D
0.7	2.8	6.5	12.0	19.6	-0.2	⊕	-3.0	-11.4	+0.5	+1.5	⊕	-6.8	-19.9	-40.4	24	P2506C
0.7	2.7	6.3	11.6	18.9	-0.2	⊕	-3.4	-12.5	+0.7	+1.7	⊕	-7.4	-21.4	-43.0	24	P270C
0.7	2.8	6.6	12.1	19.7	-0.2	⊕	-2.8	-10.7	+0.5	+1.4	⊕	-6.5	-19.0	-38.5	24	P270D
0.5	2.2	5.1	9.3	15.0	-0.3	⊕	-2.6	-9.8	+0.4	+1.3	⊕	-5.9	-17.0	-34.2	24	P7RD
0.5	2.0	4.6	8.4	13.5	-0.2	⊕	-3.0	-10.9	+0.5	+1.5	⊕	-6.4	-18.4	-36.6	24	P7RE
0.7	2.8	6.6	12.3	19.9	-0.2	⊕	-3.6	-13.2	+0.8	+1.8	⊕	-7.8	-22.4	-45.2	24	P3006D
0.7	3.0	7.1	13.4	22.0	-0.2	⊕	-3.3	-12.4	+0.6	+1.7	⊕	-7.4	-21.5	-43.7	24	P3006G
0.6	2.6	6.0	11.0	17.8	-0.1	⊕	-3.9	-13.9	+0.9	+1.9	⊕	-8.1	-23.1	-46.1	24	P3006L
0.7	3.0	7.0	13.0	21.1	-0.1	⊕	-4.0	-14.4	+0.9	+2.0	⊕	-8.4	-24.3	-49.0	24	P308C
0.5	2.2	5.0	9.2	14.9	-0.2	⊕	-3.4	-12.2	+0.7	+1.7	⊕	-7.1	-20.4	-40.5	24	P300WC

These trajectory tables were calculated by computer using the best available data for each load. Trajectories are representative of the nominal behavior of each load at standard conditions (59°F temperature; barometric pressure of 29.53 inches; altitude at sea level). Shooters are cautioned that actual trajectories may differ due to variations in altitude, atmospheric conditions, guns, sights, and ammunition.

⊕ "Nosler" and "Partition" are registered trademarks of Nosler Bullets, Inc.

WIND DRIFT IN INCHES 10 MPH CROSSWIND					HEIGHT OF BULLET TRAJECTORY — AVERAGE RANGE				LONG RANGE						TEST BARREL LENGTH INCHES	FEDERAL LOAD NO.
100	200	300	400	500	50	100	200	300	50	100	200	300	400	500		
0.8	3.3	7.9	14.7	24.1	-0.3	⊕	-2.9	-11.0	+0.5	+1.4	⊕	-6.7	-19.8	-29.0	24	P6C
0.7	3.1	7.3	13.5	22.1	-0.2	⊕	-3.2	-11.9	+0.6	+1.6	⊕	-7.1	-20.9	-42.5	24	P243E
0.8	3.3	7.7	14.3	23.5	-0.1	⊕	-3.8	-14.0	+0.8	+1.9	⊕	-8.2	-24.0	-48.9	24	P257B
0.9	3.9	9.2	17.3	28.5	-0.2	⊕	-3.7	-13.8	+0.8	+1.9	⊕	-8.3	-24.4	-50.5	24	P270E
1.3	3.2	8.2	15.4	23.4	-0.1	⊕	-4.3	-15.4	+1.0	+2.1	⊕	-9.0	-26.1	-52.9	24	P7C
0.9	3.8	9.0	16.8	27.8	-0.2	⊕	-3.6	-13.4	+0.7	+1.8	⊕	-8.0	-23.8	-49.2	24	P280A
0.8	3.3	7.7	14.1	23.4	-0.2	⊕	-3.2	-11.9	+0.6	+1.6	⊕	-7.1	-20.7	-42.0	24	P7RF
0.6	2.7	6.2	11.5	18.7	-0.3	⊕	-2.6	-9.9	+0.4	+1.3	⊕	-6.1	-17.7	-36.0	24	P7RG
0.9	8.0	19.4	36.7	59.8	-0.3	⊕	-8.3	-29.8	+2.4	+4.1	⊕	-17.4	-52.4	-109.4	24	P3030D
0.9	3.7	8.8	16.5	27.1	-0.1	⊕	-4.2	-15.3	+1.0	+2.1	⊕	-9.0	-26.4	-54.0	24	P3006F
0.8	3.3	7.7	14.3	23.3	-0.1	⊕	-4.4	-15.8	+1.0	+2.2	⊕	-9.2	-26.5	-53.6	24	P308E

impossible to find in an American factory load), the 458 Winchester Magnum and the 470 Nitro Express, an English cartridge of renown. The Safari Premium line, built for show as well as go, provides beautiful cartridges, handsomely boxed.

Incidentally, Federal's shotgun slugs with sabots are super accurate in rifled-bore shotguns; in 12 gauge, a 50-caliber bullet is encased in a sabot. Finally, Federal's match ammo includes a 30-06 load with a 168-grain Sierra match bullet at 2700 fps muzzle velocity.

FIOCCHI OF AMERICA

This Italian-made ammunition is high-grade all the way, as my personal tests revealed. My interest was the company's line of 22-rimfire ammo, including match grades. A 22 Short standard velocity starts the list, followed by a 22 Long Rifle standard velocity load. Then there is a high-velocity load called the 22 Long Rifle Ultra-Sonic, along with a hollow-point version of the same. Of particular interest, however, is a hyper-velocity 22 LR load dubbed the Wasp. Using a 37-grain hollow-point, this load proved especially effective on smaller varmints of prairie dog to jackrabbit size.

Silhouette loads, Biathlon and Exacta match ammo are included in the Fiocchi rimfire list, along with a 22 Short Golden Match and a 22 Long Rifle Subsonic. Also tested in a rifle was this company's 44 Magnum ammo with a 200-grain jacketed hollow-point bullet. In test media, this load created a large channel of disruption, indicating good transfer of bullet energy to target.

GARRETT CARTRIDGE COMPANY

This unique ammo-making concern deals in what must be called "super loads" in 44 Remington Magnum and 45-70 Government calibers. Rifles loaded with heavy-duty Garrett 44 Remington Magnum ammo have more than ample deer-taking authority for brush and woods. Loaded with bullets up to 330 grains weight, these 44 Magnum rounds deserve the title "magnum."

Several fine 45-70 Garrett loads turn the old-time round into a firebreather, including one with a 400-grain Barnes X-Bullet (solid copper). Out of a strong-action rifle, this spitzer bullet (not

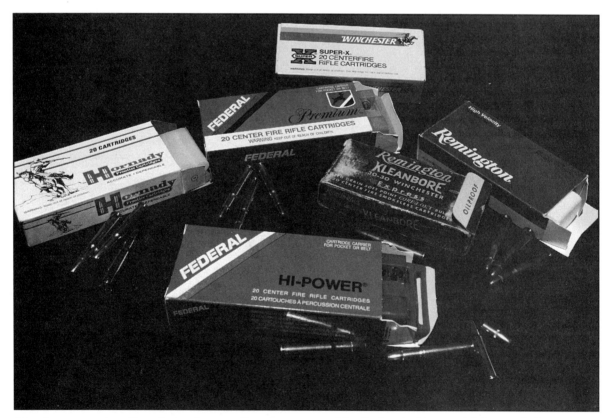

American ammo crafters have always offered an array of loads for a given popular round. Among these boxes of 30-30 Winchester ammo is an old box of Remington Kleanbore.

approved for older rifles or designs) shoots far flatter than standard 45-70 ammunition, delivering considerable power at longer ranges.

HANSEN CARTRIDGE COMPANY

This interesting ammo company decided to provide shooters with something special. Excellent 22-rimfire ammunition at good prices remains an important part of the Hansen lineup, but there is much more. For example, the popular 7.62×39mm Russian cartridge is offered with a 123-grain full-metal-jacket bullet as well as a 123-grain soft-point bullet, both with a muzzle velocity of 2373 fps.

Top-grade 308 Winchester ammo is another Hansen offering, with both FMJ and soft-point bullets. The Hansen 30-06 has an especially appealing price tag. There are even 6.5mm Japanese rounds available with 139-grain FMJ bullets as well as practice 308 ammo with 11-grain plastic bullets. American and Canadian shooters who own British 303 rifles can buy ammo from Hansen with a 190-grain FMJBT (full-metal-jacket/boat-tail) bullet at 2335 fps mv. Among an ever-growing list of rounds is the 50-caliber Browning M33, or 12.7×99mm. This huge car-

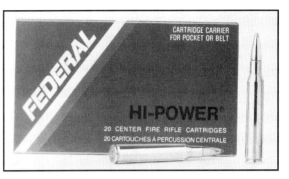

Factory loads with more power are in vogue, an example of which is Federal's Hi-Power brand 280 Remington load with 150-grain bullets.

tridge carries a 694-grain bullet at 2927 fps mv, with a muzzle energy of 13,000 foot-pounds.

HORNADY MANUFACTURING COMPANY

Known for its bullets, this company also has a factory ammo line. Naturally, the finished ammo uses the same Hornady bullet available to handloaders for so many years. The lineup begins with the 222 Remington cartridge with a 50-grain SX (Super Explosive) bullet at 3140 fps mv and ends with the 300 Winchester Magnum and a 190-grain Hornady soft-point boat-tail bullet. The usual popular cartridges fill the space between 222 and 300 Magnum, including the 220 Swift, 257 Roberts, 7×57 Mauser and 30 M1 Carbine rounds.

REMINGTON

Remington has gone to great lengths to supply shooters with interesting, unique, powerful ammunition for a huge range of applications, from the tiny 17 Remington through the heavy-bullet 416 Remington.

The 22-250 Remington is produced with a 55-grain pointed soft-point bullet and a 55-grain hollow-point bullet. There is also the 6mm BR (benchrest) Remington, with a 100-grain bullet at 2550 fps mv. Remington also offers the 25-20 Winchester, 32-20 and 32 Winchester Special in the lineup. The 7mm BR Remington is a unique benchrest round, with a 140-grain bullet at 2215 fps mv. Remington's 7mm-08, an accurate cartridge loaded with 120- or 140-grain bullets, is

Some factory ammunition is made with bullets from reloading companies, such as Federal's Premium with Nosler bullets. Shown here is the 257 Roberts w/120-gr. Nosler Partition bullet.

REMINGTON CENTERFIRE RIFLE BALLISTICS

CALIBER	REMINGTON Order No.	Wt.-Grs.	Style	Primer No.	Muzzle	100 Yds.	200 Yds.	300 Yds.	400 Yds.	500 Yds.
17 REM.	R17REM	25*	Hollow Point Power-Lokt®	7½	4040	3284	2644	2086	1606	1235
22 HORNET	R22HN1	45*	Pointed Soft Point	6½	2690	2042	1502	1128	948	840
	R22HN2	45	Hollow Point	6½	2690	2042	1502	1128	948	840
220 SWIFT	R220S1★	50*	Pointed Soft Point	9½	3780	3158	2617	2135	1710	1357
222 REM.	R222R1	50	Pointed Soft Point	7½	3140	2602	2123	1700	1350	1107
	R222R3	50*	Hollow Point Power-Lokt®	7½	3140	2635	2182	1777	1432	1172
222 REM. MAG.	R222M1	55*	Pointed Soft Point	7½	3240	2748	2305	1906	1556	1272
223 REM.	R223R1	55	Pointed Soft Point	7½	3240	2747	2304	1905	1554	1270
	R223R2	55*	Hollow Point Power-Lokt®	7½	3240	2773	2352	1969	1627	1341
	R223R3	55	Metal Case	7½	3240	2759	2326	1933	1587	1301
	R223R4	60	Hollow Point Match	7½	3100	2712	2355	2026	1726	1463
22-250 REM.	R22501	55*	Pointed Soft Point	9½	3680	3137	2656	2222	1832	1493
	R22502	55	Hollow Point Power-Lokt®	9½	3680	3209	2785	2400	2046	1725
243 WIN.	R243W1	80	Pointed Soft Point	9½	3350	2955	2593	2259	1951	1670
	R243W2	80*	Hollow Point Power-Lokt®	9½	3350	2955	2593	2259	1951	1670
	R243W3	100	Pointed Soft Point Core-Lokt®	9½	2960	2697	2449	2215	1993	1786
	ER243WA★	105	Extended Range	9½	2920	2689	2470	2261	2062	1874
6MM REM.	R6MM1	80‡	Pointed Soft Point	9½	3470	3064	2694	2352	2036	1747
	R6MM2§	80‡	Hollow Point Power-Lokt®	9½	3470	3064	2694	2352	2036	1747
	R6MM4	100*	Pointed Soft Point Core-Lokt®	9½	3100	2829	2573	2332	2104	1889
	ER6MMRA★	105	Extended Range	9½	3060	2822	2596	2381	2177	1982
6MM BR REM.	R6MMBR	100	Pointed Soft Point	7½	2550	2310	2083	1870	1671	1491
25-20 WIN.	R25202	86*	Soft Point	6½	1460	1194	1030	931	858	797
250 SAV.	R250SV	100*	Pointed Soft Point	9½	2820	2504	2210	1936	1684	1461
257 ROBERTS	R257	117	Soft Point Core-Lokt®	9½	2650	2291	1961	1663	1404	1199
	ER257A★	122	Extended Range	9½	2600	2331	2078	1842	1625	1431
25-06 REM.	R25062	100*	Pointed Soft Point Core-Lokt®	9½	3230	2893	2580	2287	2014	1762
	R25063	120	Pointed Soft Point Core-Lokt®	9½	2990	2730	2484	2252	2032	1825
	ER2506A★	122	Extended Range	9½	2930	2706	2492	2289	2095	1911
264 WIN. MAG.	R264W2	140*	Pointed Soft Point Core-Lokt®	9½M	3030	2782	2548	2326	2114	1914
270 WIN.	R270W1	100	Pointed Soft Point	9½	3320	2924	2561	2225	1916	1636
	R270W2	130*	Pointed Soft Point Core-Lokt®	9½	3060	2776	2510	2259	2022	1801
	R270W3	130	Bronze Point™	9½	3060	2802	2559	2329	2110	1904
	R270W4	150	Soft Point Core-Lokt®	9½	2850	2504	2183	1886	1618	1385
	ER270WA	140	Extended Range Boat Tail	9½	2960	2749	2548	2355	2171	1995
7MM BR REM.	R7MMBR	140*	Pointed Soft Point	7½	2215	2012	1821	1643	1481	1336
7MM MAUSER (7x57)	R7MSR1	140*	Pointed Soft Point	9½	2660	2435	2221	2018	1827	1648
7MM-08 REM.	R7M081	140	Pointed Soft Point	9½	2860	2625	2402	2189	1988	1798
	R7M083	120*	Hollow Point	9½	3000	2725	2467	2223	1992	1778
	ER7M08A★	154	Extended Range	9½	2715	2510	2315	2128	1950	1781
280 REM.†	R280R3	140	Pointed Soft Point	9½	3000	2758	2528	2309	2102	1905
	R280R1	150	Pointed Soft Point Core-Lokt®	9½	2890	2624	2373	2135	1912	1705
	R280R2	165	Soft Point Core-Lokt®	9½	2820	2510	2220	1950	1701	1479
	R280R4§	120*	Hollow Point	9½	3150	2866	2599	2348	2110	1887
	ER280RA	165	Extended Range	9½	2820	2623	2434	2253	2080	1915
7MM REM. MAG.	R7MM2	150	Pointed Soft Point Core-Lokt®	9½M	3110	2830	2568	2320	2085	1866
	R7MM3	175	Pointed Soft Point Core-Lokt®	9½M	2860	2645	2440	2244	2057	1879
	R7MM4	140*	Pointed Soft Point	9½M	3175	2923	2684	2458	2243	2039
	ER7MMA	165	Extended Range	9½M	2900	2699	2507	2324	2147	1979
7MM WBY. MAG.	R7MWB1	140	Pointed Soft Point	9½M	3225	2970	2729	2501	2283	2077
	R7MWB2	175	Pointed Soft Point Core-Lokt®	9½M	2910	2693	2486	2288	2098	1918
	ER7MWB4★	165	Extended Range	9½M	2950	2747	2553	2367	2189	2019
30 CARBINE	R30CAR	110*	Soft Point	6½	1990	1567	1236	1035	923	842
30 REM.	R30REM	170*	Soft Point Core-Lokt®	9½	2120	1822	1555	1328	1153	1036
30-30 WIN. ACCELERATOR®	R3030A	55*	Soft Point	9½	3400	2693	2085	1570	1187	986
30-30 WIN.	R30301	150*	Soft Point Core-Lokt®	9½	2390	1973	1605	1303	1095	974
	R30302	170	Soft Point Core-Lokt®	9½	2200	1895	1619	1381	1191	1061
	R30303	170	Hollow Point Core-Lokt®	9½	2200	1895	1619	1381	1191	1061
300 SAVAGE	R30SV3	180*	Soft Point Core-Lokt®	9½	2350	2025	1728	1467	1252	1098
	R30SV2	150	Pointed Soft Point Core-Lokt®	9½	2630	2354	2095	1853	1631	1432

★**New.** *Specifications are nominal. Ballistics figures established in test barrels. Individual rifles may vary from test-barrel specifications.* †*280 Rem. and 7mm Express™ Rem. are interchangeable.* ‡*Interchangeable in 244 Rem.* §*Subject to stock on hand.*

	ENERGY FOOT-POUNDS						SHORT RANGE Bullet does not rise more than one inch above line of sight from muzzle to sighting-in range.						LONG RANGE Bullet does not rise more than three inches above line of sight from muzzle to sighting-in range.							BARREL LENGTH
Muzzle	100 Yds.	200 Yds.	300 Yds.	400 Yds.	500 Yds.	50 Yds.	100 Yds.	150 Yds.	200 Yds.	250 Yds.	300 Yds.	100 Yds	150 Yds.	200 Yds.	250 Yds.	300 Yds.	400 Yds.	500 Yds.	
906	599	388	242	143	85	0.1	0.5	0.0	-1.5	-4.2	-8.5	2.1	2.5	1.9	0.0	-3.4	-17.0	-44.3	24"
723	417	225	127	90	70	0.3	0.0	-2.4	-7.7	-16.9	-31.3	1.6	0.0	-4.5	-12.8	-26.4	-75.6	-163.4	24"
723	417	225	127	90	70	0.3	0.0	-2.4	-7.7	-16.9	-31.3	1.6	0.0	-4.5	-12.8	-26.4	-75.6	-163.4	24"
1586	1107	760	506	325	204	0.2	0.5	0.0	-1.6	-4.4	-8.8	1.3	1.2	0.0	-2.5	-6.5	-20.7	-47.0	24"
1094	752	500	321	202	136	0.5	0.9	0.0	-2.5	-6.9	-13.7	2.2	1.9	0.0	-3.8	-10.0	-32.3	-73.8	24"
1094	771	529	351	228	152	0.5	0.9	0.0	-2.4	-6.6	-13.1	2.1	1.8	0.0	-3.6	-9.5	-30.2	-68.1	24"
1282	922	649	444	296	198	0.4	0.8	0.0	-2.2	-6.0	-11.8	1.9	1.6	0.0	-3.3	-8.5	-26.7	-59.5	24"
1282	921	648	443	295	197	0.4	0.8	0.0	-2.2	-6.0	-11.8	1.9	1.6	0.0	-3.3	-8.5	-26.7	-59.6	
1282	939	675	473	323	220	0.4	0.8	0.0	-2.1	-5.8	-11.4	1.8	1.6	0.0	-3.2	-8.2	-25.5	-56.0	24"
1282	929	660	456	307	207	0.4	0.8	0.0	-2.1	-5.9	-11.6	1.9	1.6	0.0	-3.2	-8.4	-26.2	-57.9	
1280	979	739	547	397	285	0.5	0.8	0.0	-2.2	-6.0	-11.5	1.9	1.6	0.0	-3.2	-8.3	-25.1	-53.6	
1654	1201	861	603	410	272	0.2	0.5	0.0	-1.6	-4.4	-8.7	2.3	2.6	1.9	0.0	-3.4	-15.9	-38.9	
1654	1257	947	703	511	363	0.2	0.5	0.0	-1.5	-4.1	-8.0	2.1	2.5	1.8	0.0	-3.1	-14.1	-33.4	24"
1993	1551	1194	906	676	495	0.3	0.7	0.0	-1.8	-4.9	-9.4	2.6	2.9	2.1	0.0	-3.6	-16.2	-37.9	
1993	1551	1194	906	676	495	0.3	0.7	0.0	-1.8	-4.9	-9.4	2.6	2.9	2.1	0.0	-3.6	-16.2	-37.9	24"
1945	1615	1332	1089	882	708	0.5	0.9	0.0	-2.2	-5.8	-11.0	1.9	1.6	0.0	-3.1	-7.8	-22.6	-46.3	
1988	1686	1422	1192	992	819	0.5	0.9	0.0	-2.2	-5.8	-11.0	2.0	1.6	0.0	-3.1	-7.7	-22.2	-44.8	
2139	1667	1289	982	736	542	0.3	0.6	0.0	-1.6	-4.5	-8.7	2.4	2.7	1.9	0.0	-3.3	-14.9	-35.0	
2139	1667	1289	982	736	542	0.3	0.6	0.0	-1.6	-4.5	-8.7	2.4	2.7	1.9	0.0	-3.3	-14.9	-35.0	24"
2133	1777	1470	1207	983	792	0.4	0.8	0.0	-1.9	-5.2	-9.9	1.7	1.5	0.0	-2.8	-7.0	-20.4	-41.7	
2183	1856	1571	1322	1105	916	0.4	0.8	0.0	-2.0	-5.2	-9.8	1.7	1.5	0.0	-2.7	-6.9	-20.0	-40.4	
1444	1185	963	776	620	494	0.3	0.0	-1.9	-5.6	-11.4	-19.3	2.8	2.3	0.0	-4.3	-10.9	-31.7	-65.1	15"
407	272	203	165	141	121	0.0	-4.1	-14.4	-31.8	-57.3	-92.0	0.0	-8.2	-23.5	-47.0	-79.6	-175.9	-319.4	24"
1765	1392	1084	832	630	474	0.2	0.0	-1.6	-4.7	-9.6	-16.5	2.3	2.0	0.0	-3.7	-9.5	-28.3	-59.5	24"
1824	1363	999	718	512	373	0.3	0.0	-1.9	-5.8	-11.9	-20.7	2.9	2.4	0.0	-4.7	-12.0	-36.7	-79.2	
1831	1472	1170	919	715	555	0.3	0.0	-1.9	-5.5	-11.2	-19.1	2.8	2.3	0.0	-4.3	-10.9	-32.0	-66.4	24"
2316	1858	1478	1161	901	689	0.4	0.7	0.0	-1.9	-5.0	-9.7	1.6	1.4	0.0	-2.7	-6.9	-20.5	-42.7	
2382	1985	1644	1351	1100	887	0.5	0.8	0.0	-2.1	-5.6	-10.7	1.9	1.6	0.0	-3.0	-7.5	-22.0	-44.8	24"
2325	1983	1683	1419	1189	989	0.5	0.9	0.0	-2.2	-5.7	-10.8	1.9	1.6	0.0	-3.0	-7.5	-21.7	-43.9	
2854	2406	2018	1682	1389	1139	0.5	0.8	0.0	-2.0	-5.4	-10.2	1.8	1.5	0.0	-2.9	-7.2	-20.8	-42.2	24"
2448	1898	1456	1099	815	594	0.3	0.7	0.0	-1.8	-5.0	-9.7	2.7	3.0	2.2	0.0	-3.7	-16.6	-39.1	
2702	2225	1818	1472	1180	936	0.5	0.8	0.0	-2.0	-5.5	-10.4	1.8	1.5	0.0	-2.9	-7.4	-21.6	-44.3	
2702	2267	1890	1565	1285	1046	0.4	0.8	0.0	-2.0	-5.3	-10.1	1.8	1.5	0.0	-2.8	-7.1	-20.6	-42.0	24"
2705	2087	1587	1185	872	639	0.7	1.0	0.0	-2.6	-7.1	-13.6	2.3	2.0	0.0	-3.8	-9.7	-29.2	-62.2	
2723	2349	2018	1724	1465	1237	0.5	0.8	0.0	-2.1	-5.5	-10.3	1.9	1.5	0.0	-2.9	-7.2	-20.7	-41.6	
1525	1259	1031	839	681	555	0.5	0.0	-2.7	-7.7	-15.4	-25.9	1.8	0.0	-4.1	-10.9	-20.6	-50.0	-95.2	15"
2199	1843	1533	1266	1037	844	0.2	0.0	-1.7	-5.0	-10.0	-17.0	2.5	2.0	0.0	-3.8	-9.6	-27.7	-56.3	24"
2542	2142	1793	1490	1228	1005	0.6	0.9	0.0	-2.3	-6.1	-11.6	2.1	1.7	0.0	-3.2	-8.1	-23.5	-47.7	
2398	1979	1621	1316	1058	842	0.5	0.8	0.0	-2.1	-5.7	-10.8	1.9	1.6	0.0	-3.0	-7.6	-22.3	-45.8	24"
2520	2155	1832	1548	1300	1085	0.7	1.0	0.0	-2.5	-6.7	-12.6	2.3	1.9	0.0	-3.5	-8.8	-25.3	-51.0	
2797	2363	1986	1657	1373	1128	0.5	0.8	0.0	-2.1	-5.5	-10.4	1.8	1.5	0.0	-2.9	-7.3	-21.1	-42.9	
2781	2293	1875	1518	1217	968	0.6	0.9	0.0	-2.3	-6.2	-11.8	2.1	1.7	0.0	-3.3	-8.3	-24.2	-49.7	
2913	2308	1805	1393	1060	801	0.2	0.0	-1.5	-4.6	-9.5	-16.4	2.3	1.9	0.0	-3.7	-9.4	-28.1	-58.8	24"
2643	2188	1800	1468	1186	949	0.4	0.7	0.0	-1.9	-5.1	-9.7	2.8	3.0	2.2	0.0	-3.6	-15.7	-35.6	
2913	2520	2171	1860	1585	1343	0.6	0.9	0.0	-2.3	-6.1	-11.4	2.1	1.7	0.0	-3.2	-8.0	-22.8	-45.6	
3221	2667	2196	1792	1448	1160	0.4	0.8	0.0	-1.9	-5.2	-9.9	1.7	1.5	0.0	-2.8	-7.0	-20.5	-42.1	
3178	2718	2313	1956	1644	1372	0.6	0.9	0.0	-2.3	-6.0	-11.3	2.0	1.7	0.0	-3.2	-7.9	-22.7	-45.8	24"
3133	2655	2240	1878	1564	1292	0.4	0.7	0.0	-1.8	-4.8	-9.1	2.6	2.9	2.0	0.0	-3.4	-14.5	-32.6	
3081	2669	2303	1978	1689	1434	0.5	0.9	0.0	-2.1	-5.7	-10.7	1.9	1.6	0.0	-3.0	-7.5	-21.4	-42.9	
3233	2741	2315	1943	1621	1341	0.3	0.7	0.0	-1.7	-4.6	-8.8	2.5	2.8	2.0	0.0	-3.2	-14.0	-31.5	
3293	2818	2401	2033	1711	1430	0.5	0.9	0.0	-2.2	-5.7	-10.8	1.9	1.6	0.0	-3.0	-7.6	-21.8	-44.0	24"
3188	2765	2388	2053	1756	1493	0.5	0.8	0.0	-2.1	-5.5	-10.3	1.9	1.6	0.0	-2.9	-7.2	-20.6	-41.3	
967	600	373	262	208	173	0.9	0.0	-4.5	-13.5	-28.3	-49.9	0.0	-4.5	-13.5	-28.3	-49.9	-118.6	-228.2	20"
1696	1253	913	666	502	405	0.7	0.0	-3.3	-9.7	-19.6	-33.8	2.2	0.0	-5.3	-14.1	-27.2	-69.0	-136.9	24"
1412	886	521	301	172	119	0.4	0.8	0.0	-2.4	-6.7	-13.8	2.0	1.8	0.0	-3.8	-10.2	-35.0	-84.4	24"
1902	1296	858	565	399	316	0.5	0.0	-2.7	-8.2	-17.0	-30.0	1.8	0.0	-4.6	-12.5	-24.6	-65.3	-134.9	
1827	1355	989	720	535	425	0.6	0.0	-3.0	-8.9	-18.0	-31.1	2.0	0.0	-4.8	-13.0	-25.1	-63.6	-126.7	24"
1827	1355	989	720	535	425	0.6	0.0	-3.0	-8.9	-18.0	-31.1	2.0	0.0	-4.8	-13.0	-25.1	-63.6	-126.7	
2207	1639	1193	860	626	482	0.5	0.0	-2.6	-7.7	-15.6	-27.1	1.7	0.0	-4.2	-11.3	-21.9	-55.8	-112.0	24"
2303	1845	1462	1143	806	685	0.3	0.0	-1.8	-5.4	11.0	18.8	2.7	2.2	0.0	-4.2	-10.7	-31.5	-65.6	

*Inches above or below line of sight. Hold low for positive numbers, high for negative numbers.

one of the finest new cartridges to come along in recent times. Remington also offers the Accelerator cartridge in 30-30, 308 and 30-06, all three shooting a 55-grain 22-caliber bullet contained in a plastic sabot. The 30-06 Accelerator achieves over 4000 fps mv.

The powerful one-of-a-kind 8mm Remington Magnum gives the shooter a 32-caliber high-power round that shoots a 185-grain bullet at close to 3100 fps mv. The one-time wildcat 35 Whelen is now a Remington standard, loaded with 200- and 250-grain bullets. The 416 Remington fires a 400-grain bullet at 2400 fps mv. The Remington load for the 444 Marlin has a 240-grain bullet at 2350 fps mv. Furthermore, Remington now loads two Weatherby cartridges, the 7mm WM and 300 WM. The age-old 44-40 Winchester remains on line, as well as the 45-70 Government, with a 405-grain soft-point bullet.

Remington has developed a new Extended Range line of ammo, with a flat-base bullet design that has a sharp profile and a boat-tail bullet of spitzer form. This ammo is intended to do what its name implies—pick up yardage for a number of cartridges. As this is written, the following cartridges are treated to this special Extended Range loading:

In an effort to give the shooter better ammo than ever, Remington has produced its Extended Range line. Here are two Extended Range factory loads: the 280 Remington (left) and 7mm Remington Magnum, both with 165-grain bullets.

- 270 Winchester with a 140-grain boat-tail bullet
- 7mm-08 with a special 154-grain bullet
- 280 Remington with a 165-grain bullet
- 7mm Remington Magnum with a 165-grain bullet
- 30-06 with 152-grain flat-base, 165-grain boat-tail and 178-grain flat-base bullets
- 308 with 165-grain boat-tail and 178-grain flat-base bullets
- 300 Winchester Magnum with 178-grain flat-base and 190-grain boat-tail bullets
- 300 Weatherby Magnum with 178-grain flat-base and 190-grain boat-tail bullets

RWS

This famous German company offers a full lineup, with some of the most unique, accurate and powerful ammunition loaded anywhere. A long line of 22-rimfire ammo, from BB Cap to 22 WMR, starts the list. RWS has a 22 WMR load with a 40-grain hollow-point soft-point bullet that was chronographed at over 2100 fps

Innovation is a big part of factory ammo. Here is Remington's unique Accelerator load with a 55-grain, 22-caliber bullet encased in a plastic sabot so that it can be fired from a 30-30 rifle.

muzzle velocity. RWS 7mm Remington Magnum ammo with a 162-grain bullet was chronographed at 3165 fps mv. Across the board, printed data matched personally chronographed data with the sampling of RWS ammunition that was tested.

The *Ballistic Data* manual offered by RWS contains a long lineup of both American and European cartridges, along with trajectory data and sight-in suggestions. The booklet begins with the 22 Hornet soft-point bullet and FMJ bullet, going next to the 222 Remington and 5.6×50mm Magnum. The old 22 Savage is loaded here as the 5.6×52R (R for rimmed). Their extensive collection of interesting cartridges includes such numbers as the 5.6×57mm (essentially a 22 caliber based on the 7×57 Mauser case in both rimless and rimmed styles), 243 Winchester, 6.5×57mm, 6.5×54mm Mannlicher round, 6.5×68mm (much like our 264 Winchester Magnum), 270, 7×57mm Mauser, 7×64mm

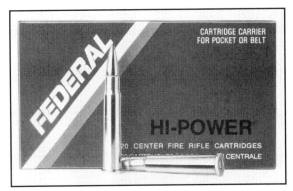

Foreign ammunition is offered by American companies, as illustrated by Federal's 150-grain load for the 303 British cartridge.

(like a 7mm-06), 7mm Remington Magnum, 308, 30-06 and 300 Winchester Magnum. The progression continues with various 8mm rounds, including full-power loads for the 8mm Mauser, as well as 9.3s, the 375 H&H, a 10.75×68mm

Ammo companies do not have exclusive right of manufacture, which is why one company can load a cartridge brought out by another firm. This Winchester 280 Remington ammunition (with 140-grain Power Point bullets) is a prime example.

with a 347-grain bullet and, finally, a 404 Rimless with a 401-grain bullet. Accuracy tests with RWS 308 Match ammo resulted in half-inch 100-yard five-shot groups.

SAKO

Sako exports only two of its excellent lines of ammunition to America: the 22 PPC USA and the 6mm PPC USA. In both instances, ammunition is highly accurate, a trademark of this company's products. My own chronographing of these two factory loads proved a muzzle velocity of 3459 fps for the 22 PPC USA and 3078 fps for the 6mm PPC USA, both figures recorded 12 feet from muzzle to first screen. Standard deviations were 8 fps for the 22 PPC and 12 fps for the 6mm PPC—good low numbers. Incidentally, Norma also offers these two cartridges today.

WEATHERBY

As one would expect, Weatherby concentrates on ammunition of its own design. The company known for high velocity doesn't spare the get-up-and-go on its own ammunition. Starting with the 224 Weatherby Magnum (a 55-grain bullet at 3650 fps mv), the list jumps to the 240 WM with three loads: an 87-grain bullet at 3500 fps mv and two 100-grain bullets, including a Nosler Partition, at 3395 fps mv. The great 257 WM comes next, with several loads, including an 87-grain pill at 3825 fps mv and a 120-grain Partition at 3290 fps mv. This is followed by the 270 WM (which doesn't seem to attract all that much attention in the press, but in fact ranks only behind the 300 WM in Weatherby sales), the famous 300 WM with its 180-grain bullet at 3300 fps mv, the 340 WM, 378 WM and 416 WM. At the end of the list is the huge 460 WM, with its 500-grain bullet, listed at 2700 fps mv for over 8000 foot-pounds of energy.

Tests with Weatherby 257 and 270 ammo showed chronograph figures on par with advertised velocities. Accuracy with Weatherby am-

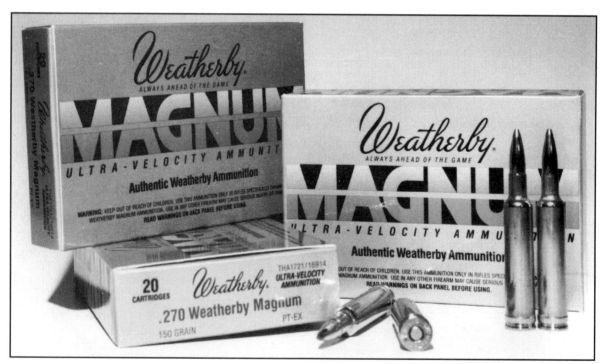

Weatherby is noted for ammo loaded to high velocity. The author chronographed this 270 Weatherby Magnum ammunition in 130- and 150-grain loads. Advertised and chronographed velocities were quite close.

WEATHERBY BALLISTICS

Cartridge	Weight In Grains	Type	VELOCITY in Feet per Second						ENERGY in Foot Pounds						BULLET DROP in Inches From Bore Line			PATH OF BULLET (Above or below Line-of-sight) For riflescopes mounted 1.5" above bore		
			Muzzle	100 Yds.	200 Yds.	300 Yds.	400 Yds.	500 Yds.	Muzzle	100 Yds.	200 Yds.	300 Yds.	400 Yds.	500 Yds.	100 Yds.	200 Yds.	300 Yds.	100 Yds.	200 Yds.	300 Yds.
.224 WBY MAG	55	Pt-Ex	3650	3192	2780	2403	2057	1742	1627	1244	943	705	516	370	-1.4	-6.3	-15.6	2.8	3.6	0
.240 WBY MAG	87	Pt-Ex	3500	3202	2924	2663	2416	2183	2366	1980	1651	1370	1127	920	-1.5	-6.4	-15.4	2.6	3.4	0
	100	Pt-Ex	3395	3106	2835	2581	2339	2112	2559	2142	1785	1478	1215	990	-1.6	-6.8	-16.4	2.9	3.6	0
	100	Partition	3395	3069	2766	2483	2216	1966	2559	2091	1698	1368	1091	859	-1.6	-6.9	-16.8	3.0	3.8	0
.257 WBY MAG	87	Pt-Ex	3825	3456	3118	2805	2513	2239	2826	2308	1878	1520	1220	969	-1.3	-5.5	-13.2	2.1	2.9	0
	100	Pt-Ex	3555	3237	2941	2665	2404	2159	2806	2326	1920	1576	1283	1035	-1.5	-6.2	-15.1	2.6	3.3	0
	100	Partition	3555	3292	3044	2810	2589	2377	2806	2406	2058	1754	1488	1254	-1.4	-6.1	-14.5	2.4	3.1	0
	117	Semi Pt-Ex	3300	2882	2502	2152	1830	1547	2829	2158	1626	1203	870	621	-1.7	-7.7	-19.3	3.7	4.6	0
	117	Partition	3300	2998	2717	2452	2202	1967	2829	2335	1917	1561	1260	1005	-1.7	-7.3	-17.6	3.2	3.9	0
	120	Partition	3290	3074	2869	2673	2486	2306	2884	2518	2193	1904	1646	1416	-1.7	-7.0	-16.7	2.9	3.6	0
.270 WBY MAG	100	Pt-Ex	3760	3380	3033	2712	2412	2133	3139	2537	2042	1633	1292	1010	-1.3	-5.7	-13.9	2.3	3.0	0
	130	Pt-Ex	3375	3100	2842	2598	2366	2148	3287	2773	2330	1948	1616	1331	-1.6	-6.9	-16.4	2.9	3.6	0
	130	Partition	3375	3119	2878	2649	2432	2225	3287	2808	2390	2026	1707	1429	-1.6	-6.8	-16.2	2.8	3.5	0
	150	Pt-Ex	3245	3019	2803	2598	2402	2215	3507	3034	2617	2248	1922	1634	-1.7	-7.3	-17.3	3.0	3.8	0
	150	Partition	3245	3036	2837	2647	2465	2290	3507	3070	2681	2334	2023	1746	-1.7	-7.2	-17.1	3.0	3.7	0
7mm WBY MAG	139	Pt-Ex	3400	3138	2892	2659	2437	2226	3567	3039	2580	2181	1832	1529	-1.6	-6.7	-16.0	2.7	3.5	0
	140	Partition	3400	3163	2939	2726	2522	2328	3593	3110	2684	2309	1978	1684	-1.6	-6.6	-15.7	2.7	3.4	0
	150	Pt-Ex	3260	3023	2799	2586	2382	2188	3539	3044	2609	2227	1890	1595	-1.7	-7.2	-17.2	3.0	3.8	0
	154	Pt-Ex	3260	3023	2800	2586	2383	2189	3633	3125	2681	2287	1941	1638	-1.7	-7.3	-17.2	3.0	3.7	0
	160	Partition	3200	3004	2816	2637	2464	2297	3637	3205	2817	2469	2156	1875	-1.8	-7.4	-17.4	3.0	3.7	0
	175	Pt-Ex	3070	2879	2696	2520	2351	2189	3662	3220	2824	2467	2147	1861	-1.9	-8.0	-19.0	3.4	4.1	0
.300 WBY MAG	110	Pt-Ex	3900	3441	3028	2652	2305	1985	3714	2891	2239	1717	1297	962	-1.2	-5.4	-13.5	2.2	3.0	0
	150	Pt-Ex	3600	3297	3015	2751	2502	2266	4316	3621	3028	2520	2084	1709	-1.4	-6.0	-14.5	2.4	3.1	0
	150	Partition	3600	3307	3033	2776	2533	2303	4316	3642	3064	2566	2137	1766	-1.4	-6.0	-14.4	2.4	3.1	0
	165	Boat Tail	3450	3220	3003	2797	2599	2409	4360	3799	3303	2865	2475	2126	-1.5	-6.4	-15.2	2.5	3.2	0
	180	Pt-Ex	3300	3064	2841	2629	2426	2233	4352	3753	3226	2762	2352	1992	-1.7	-7.1	-16.8	2.9	3.6	0
	180	Partition	3300	3077	2865	2663	2470	2285	4352	3784	3280	2834	2438	2086	-1.7	-7.0	-16.6	2.9	3.6	0
	220	Semi Pt-Ex	2905	2498	2126	1787	1490	1250	4122	3047	2207	1560	1085	763	-2.3	-10.2	-25.8	5.3	6.5	0
.340 WBY MAG	200	Pt-Ex	3260	3011	2775	2552	2339	2137	4719	4025	3420	2892	2429	2027	-1.7	-7.3	-17.4	3.1	3.8	0
	210	Partition	3250	2991	2746	2515	2295	2086	4924	4170	3516	2948	2455	2029	-1.7	-7.4	-17.6	3.1	3.9	0
	250	Semi Pt-Ex	3000	2670	2363	2078	1812	1574	4995	3958	3100	2396	1823	1375	-2.1	-9.1	-22.4	4.4	5.3	0
	250	Partition	3000	2806	2621	2443	2272	2108	4995	4371	3812	3311	2864	2465	-2.0	-8.5	-19.9	3.6	4.3	0
.378 WBY MAG	270	Pt-Ex	3180	2976	2781	2594	2415	2243	6062	5308	4635	4034	3495	3015	-1.8	-7.5	-17.8	3.1	3.8	0
	300	RN	2925	2576	2252	1952	1680	1439	5698	4419	3379	2538	1881	1379	-2.2	-9.7	-24.0	4.8	5.8	0
.416 WBY MAG	400	Swift A-Frame	2600	2365	2141	1930	1733	1552	6003	4965	4071	3309	2668	2140	-2.7	-11.7	-28.3	5.7	6.7	0
	400	RNSP	2700	2391	2101	1834	1592	1379	6476	5077	3921	2986	2249	1688	-2.6	-11.3	-27.9	5.7	6.8	0
	400	Mono Solid®	2700	2398	2115	1852	1613	1402	6476	5108	3971	3047	2310	1746	-2.6	-11.2	-27.7	5.7	6.7	0
.460 WBY MAG	500	RN	2700	2404	2128	1869	1635	1425	8092	6416	5026	3878	2969	2254	-2.6	-11.2	-27.4	5.6	6.6	0
	500	FMJ	2700	2425	2166	1923	1700	1497	8092	6526	5210	4105	3209	2488	-2.4	-11.1	-26.9	5.4	6.3	0

LEGEND: Pt-Ex=Pointed-expanding. Semi Pt-Ex=Semi pointed-expanding. RN=Round nose. FMJ=Full metal jacket.
NOTE: These tables were calculated by computer using a standard modern scientific technique to predict trajectories from the best available data for each cartridge. The figures shown are expected to be reasonably accurate of ammunition behavior under standard conditions. However, the shooter is cautioned that performance will vary because of variations in rifle, ammunition and atmospheric conditions. BALLISTIC COEFFICIENTS used for these tables are as published by Hornady and Nosler ballistic data compiled using 26" barrels.

A big plus in today's factory ammo is choice. Winchester 308 ammo, for example, is offered in 150-grain Silvertip or Power Point for deer-sized game, and 180-grain Silvertip or Power Point for elk and similar animals.

munition in Weatherby rifles was high-grade all the way, including the 416 and 460, both producing slightly under 1-inch center-to-center groups at 100 yards with three shots. The 257 WM with factory ammo created groups of .60 inch at 100 yards with five shots.

WINCHESTER

One of the oldest ammunition companies in America, Winchester continues to offer the

shooter an extensive choice of excellent products. The company has experimented with a number of different bullet styles and loads over the past few years, culminating in a new and exciting Supreme Line.

In a Dale Storey custom rifle, Winchester's Supreme in 22-250 Remington produced five-shot groups as small as .375 inch center to center. The Supreme Line was also tested with both 150- and 180-grain Silvertip Boattail bullets in 308

WINCHESTER SUPREME CENTERFIRE RIFLE AMMUNITION BALLISTICS

Cartridge	Symbol	Game Selector Guide	CXP Guide Number	Bullet Wt. (grs.)	Bullet Type	Barrel Length (In.)	Velocity In Feet Per Second (fps) Muzzle	100	200	300	400	500
22-250 Remington	S22250R52	V	1	52	HPBT	24	3750	3268	2835	2442	2082	1755
243 Winchester	S243W100	D,O/P	2	100	SPBT	24	2960	2712	2477	2254	2042	1843
270 Winchester	S270W140	D,O/P	2	140	STBT	24	2960	2753	2554	2365	2183	2009
7 MM Remington Mag.	S7MMRM160	D,O/P,M,L	3	160	STBT	24	2950	2745	2550	2363	2184	2012
30-30 Winchester	S3030W150	D	2	150	ST	24	2390	2018	1684	1398	1177	1036
30-06 Springfield	S3006S165	D,O/P,M	2	165	STBT	24	2800	2597	2402	2216	2038	1869
30-06 Springfield	S3006S180	D,O/P,M,L	3	180	STBT	24	2700	2503	2314	2133	1960	1797
308 Winchester	S308W150	D,O/P	2	150	STBT	24	2820	2559	2312	2080	1861	1659
308 Winchester	S308W180	D,O/P,M	3	180	STBT	24	2610	2424	2245	2074	1911	1756
300 Winchester Mag.	S300WM190	O/P,M,L	3D	190	STBT	24	2885	2698	2519	2347	2181	2023

Game Selector Guide: V-Varmint; D-Deer; O/P-Open or Plains; M-Medium Game; L-Large Game; XL-Extra Large Game. **CXP Class Examples:** 1-prairie dog, coyote,

Winchester for groups that hovered around .60 inch with five shots at 100 yards.

The Supreme Line has been expanded to include 22-250, 243 Winchester, 270 Winchester, 30-30 Winchester, 308, 30-06 and 300 Winchester Magnum loads, the last with a 190-grain boat-tail bullet. But the Supreme Line is hardly the only news from Winchester. The company continues to supply riflemen with ammunition in a great variety of calibers.

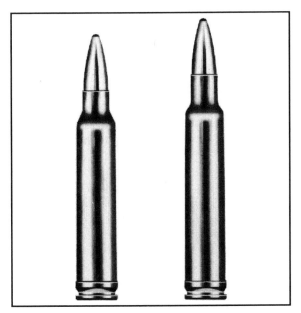

Ammo factories continually add to their inventory. Remington has long offered the excellent 300 Winchester Magnum load (left), and in recent times has added the 300 Weatherby Magnum to its list. Both Extended Range loads use 178-grain bullets.

The following are only those cartridges from the "old days." (Of course, Winchester also supplies a full line of currently popular rounds as well.) The 218 Bee is still on line with Winchester. So are the 25-20 Winchester and the 25-35 Winchester, the latter co-appearing in 1895 (along with the 30-30) in the Model 1894 Winchester rifle as America's first smokeless sporting rounds. The 303 Savage remains intact in the Winchester list as well, shooting a 190-grain Silvertip bullet. The 32 Winchester Special, for which many thousands of rifles were made, is available with a 170-grain bullet. The 32-20 Winchester is also on line. This cartridge dates back to the 19th century, but it has regained some of its former fame by being chambered once again in modern arms, including the T/C pistol and Marlin's Model 1894 rifle. The still-viable 35 Remington continues, as does the one-of-a-kind 348 Winchester, both with 200-grain bullets. Winchester supplies ammo for the 38-40 Winchester with 180-grain bullets, the 44-40 Winchester with 200-grain bullets and the 45-70 Government with 300-grain jacketed hollow-point bullets—three more rounds from former days that modern shooters have not forgotten.

A WORD ABOUT WILDCATS

The wildcat is simply a non-factory cartridge. If a wildcat cartridge "goes factory," as many do, that round is never again called a wildcat. Wildcats have had a strong influence on ammunition companies, which, in turn, has brought about some of the greatest factory rounds of all times. It would be no exaggeration to say that the majority of our most recent factory creations were at the very least prompted by a wildcat, if

Energy In Foot-Pounds (ft-lbs)						Trajectory, Short Range Yards						Trajectory, Long Range Yards						
Muzzle	100	200	300	400	500	50	100	150	200	250	300	100	150	200	250	300	400	500
1624	1233	928	689	501	356	-.1	0	-.7	-2.4	-5.1	-9.1	1.2	1.1	0	-2.1	-5.5	-16.9	-36.3
1946	1633	1363	1128	926	754	.1	0	-1.3	-3.8	-7.8	-13.3	1.9	1.6	0	-3.0	-7.6	-22.0	-44.8
2724	2356	2029	1739	1482	1256	.1	0	-1.2	-3.7	-7.5	-12.7	1.8	1.5	0	-2.9	-7.2	-20.6	-41.3
3093	2679	2311	1984	1694	1439	.1	0	-1.2	-3.7	-7.5	-12.8	1.9	1.5	0	-2.9	-7.2	-20.6	-41.4
1902	1356	944	651	461	357	.5	0	-2.6	-7.7	-16.0	-27.9	3.9	3.2	0	-6.2	-16.1	-49.4	-105.2
2873	2421	2114	1799	1522	1280	.1	0	-1.4	-4.3	-8.6	-14.6	2.1	1.8	0	-3.3	-8.2	-23.4	-47.0
2914	2504	2140	1819	1536	1290	.2	0	-1.6	-4.7	-9.4	-15.8	2.3	1.9	0	-3.5	-8.8	-25.3	-50.8
2649	2182	1782	1441	1154	917	.2	0	-1.5	-4.4	-9.0	-15.4	2.2	1.8	0	-3.5	-8.7	-25.5	-52.3
2723	2348	2015	1719	1459	1232	.2	0	-1.7	-5.0	-10.1	-17.0	2.5	2.1	0	-3.8	-9.4	-26.9	-54.0
3512	3073	2679	2325	2009	1728	.1	0	-1.3	-3.9	-7.8	-13.2	1.9	1.6	0	-3.0	-7.4	-21.1	-42.2

woodchuck; 2-antelope, deer, black bear; 3-elk, moose; 3D-all game in category 3, plus large dangerous game, i.e., Kodiak bear; 4-Cape buffalo, elephant.

not taken directly from the same drawing board.

The 7-30 Waters, designed by well-known gunwriter Ken Waters, is one example. Ken took the 30-30 case and necked it down to shoot 7mm (.284-inch diameter) bullets. He reasoned the new cartridge would have less recoil than the 30-30, while retaining sufficient power for deer-sized game. The cartridge became a factory round in 1984 when the Federal Cartridge company built its own version of the 7-30 Waters and United States Repeating Arms Company chambered the new cartridge in a Model 94 Winchester rifle. Handloads with a Hornady 139-grain flat-nose bullet designed to work through a tubular magazine create 2600 fps mv with several different powders.

Remington has been strong in taming wildcats to factory loads. Its 7mm-08 is the 308 Winchester case necked down to shoot 7mm bullets—an excellent and accurate round. One handload with the 7mm-08 showed a 175-grain bullet moving out at over 2650 fps mv. Other former wildcats include: the 22-250, the 250 Savage necked down to shoot 22-caliber bullets; the 6mm BR (Benchrest), a shortened 308 necked to 6mm and built to hold small rifle primers instead of large rifle primers; the 25-06 Remington, which is the 30-06 necked down to shoot 25-caliber bullets; the 280 Remington, a redesigned 7mm-06 round with longer case; the 7mm Remingtom Magnum, built on the style of numerous rounds that were wildcatted on shortened and blown-out 300 H&H brass necked to 7mm; the 35 Whelen, a 30-06 necked up to shoot 35-caliber bullets; and on the small end of the spectrum, the 17 Remington with a 25-grain bullet at over 4000 fps mv, which was originally a 17-caliber round based on the 223 Remington case. All of these fine cartridges were born as wildcats.

Wildcat cartridges are made essentially by reforming the brass case. The original case can be shortened, for example, and then forced through a series of reloading dies to give it a new shape. Or the case can simply be necked-up or necked-down, thereby changing its caliber.

A wildcat may also be fireformed. This is a simple, very effective operation. First, a chamber with a specific set of dimensions is cut in the rifle. A cartridge is fired in the new chamber and the brass swells out to match the configuration of the chamber. A new cartridge is born with one shot. An example is the 30-30 Improved based on the 30-30 Winchester case. The 30-30 Improved chamber is cut into the rifle barrel and, in this instance, factory ammo can be used to fireform new brass. When the original 30-30 cartridge is fired in the 30-30 Improved chamber, the case expands to meet the new dimensions of the chamber, giving it straight walls and a sharper shoulder. Obviously, the new case holds more powder than the older one, and, in addition, the new case also burns powder a bit more efficiently than the older slope-shouldered case; case life is therefore improved.

It seems that only moments after a new cartridge is on the market, it is seized upon by wildcatters and altered. Ammo factories would have a hard time beating wildcatters to the punch, and that is why the majority of our wildcat-gone-factory rounds were built in someone's personal reloading laboratory first. The following cartridges either started wild and ended up tamed by the factory, or began as wildcats and still are. Although they were selected on the basis of personal interest, they do stand up under the scrutiny of any applied tests of ballistics, trajectory and uniqueness.

17 Remington. Previously mentioned, this is the only 17-caliber commercial cartridge of the moment. A 25-grain bullet at 4000 to 4100 fps mv is this round's claim to fame.

22 PPC USA. This round has won many benchrest matches. It was brought from the world of wildcats to the land of factory rounds by Sako, and achieves amazing groups in a Sako varmint rifle. Furthermore, the 22 PPC can be loaded with a 50-grain bullet at 3600 fps mv, making it a deadly varmint cartridge combining flat-shooting trajectory, good energy and super accuracy.

226 Barnes. This interesting round never saw production and probably never will. It was noted as the 226 Barnes QT, the letters representing "quick twist." A rifle so-chambered required a barrel with a fast twist to stabilize a 22-

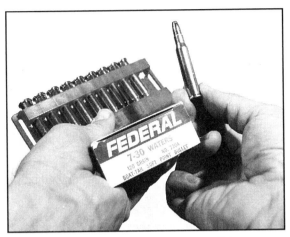

The now-factory 7-30 Waters began life as a wildcat, as did so many fine factory cartridges.

caliber (.226-inch) bullet that weighed 125 grains. This unique wildcat has been witnessed shooting through a moose!

6mm/222 Remington. The little 222 Remington necked up to hold 6mm bullets provides a wildcat that is capable of producing 250 Savage factory ballistics out to 200 yards. It is great for anyone who wishes to avoid recoil. Its effective range on deer-sized game with proper bullets and bullet placement is about 200 yards.

6mm PPC USA. Also useful for deer and antelope, this actually delivers more power than the 6mm/222 wildcat. It is known as the world's most accurate cartridge. Formerly a wildcat, it is now a factory round loaded by Sako.

257 Roberts Improved. This is simply the 257 Roberts with a 28-degree shoulder blown out to form straighter case walls. It gains about 200 fps mv over the standard 257 Roberts with a 100-grain bullet, with good case life. It's easy to work with, requiring only the fireforming of factory ammo in the improved chamber.

270 Savage. Another wildcat that never saw life as a factory round is the 300 Savage necked down to shoot .277-inch bullets. Now that we have the fine 7mm-08, this round is no longer as inviting as it once might have been. However, it would have made a wise wildcat in the Model 99 Savage, offering a mild-mannered round with plenty of ballistics for deer-sized game.

30-30 Improved. The blown-out 30-30 cartridge does not escalate velocities greatly, but it does offer the shooter somewhat better ballistics from a long-lasting cartridge case and it's no trouble to prepare, requiring only fireforming of factory ammo.

338-06. As explained in Chapter 3, 338 bullets in a blown-out 30-06 case produce excellent ballistics. The 35 Whelen was turned into a factory cartridge, but the 338-06 shows no signs of following suit.

450 Alaskan. A 45-caliber powerhouse built on the strong Model 71 lever-action Winchester rifle is almost ideal for close encounters of the grizzly kind in the Alaskan and Canadian bush. A 400-grain bullet at 2100 to 2200 fps mv is a lot of life insurance in such situations, especially from a fast-action rifle, but the 450 Alaskan remains a wildcat.

500 Van Horn Express. The 500 VH Express (which should be the 510 VH Express due to its 51-caliber bullet) is a significant wildcat with terrific ballistics for dangerous game of African proportion. This wildcat shoots a 500-grain bullet 2500 fps mv for a muzzle energy of almost 7000 foot-pounds, or a 600-grain bullet at 2175 fps mv for a muzzle energy of over 6300 foot-pounds. The amazing aspect of this powerhouse is the fact that the round works through a standard length bolt action.

The ammunition makers of the world have

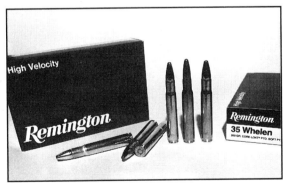

Another example of a factory cartridge that was a wildcat for decades is the 35 Whelen. Note the 30-06 cartridge (center) for comparison.

always tried to build what shooters want. This is far more than good business on their parts—it's a tradition that started in the last century. Those who design ammunition for the public are shooters themselves. They are curious. They are demanding. They want the best possible ammunition for their rifles, and that quest manifests itself in factory ammo that benefits all shooters.

HANDLOADING FOR RIFLES

18 In effect, handloading predates the cartridge. Every load fired from a muzzleloader was put together "by hand." The tradition never died.

The practice of handloading cartridges is only slightly older than the cartridge itself. Rifle companies such as Winchester sold handloading tools to match their rifles, so that a sportsman could reload the expensive brass case. Reloading components—bullets, powder, empty brass cases, primers—were available from the start for the rifleman who wanted to put together his own ammo.

In blackpowder days, reloading was a simpler matter because of the nature of the propellant. The handloader didn't need a scale. He simply poured powder into the resized case with a dipper, leaving enough room to seat the bullet. Smokeless powder changed all that. Carefully weighing the smokeless charge became essential due to increased pressure created by the new powder.

WHY RELOAD?

The previous chapter revealed that today's factory ammunition is better than at any time in shooting history. Factory ammo is powerful, accurate, reliable and available. Then why reload? There are at least seven good reasons.

The first (although not the most important) reason is economy. Reloading enables a rifleman to enjoy his sport at a considerable savings.

The second reason is cartridge versatility. A wide range of factory ammunition is available, but not nearly as wide as home-rolled fodder. For example, factory loads for the 30-06 Springfield cartridge offer bullet weights from 110 to 220 grains—a wide selection. However, the handloader can prepare 30-06 ammo with lighter or heavier bullets. Moreover, he can create 30-06 loads with greater-than-factory power or far lower power. He can cast his own projectiles, loading them, if he wants, to mere 22 Long Rifle muzzle velocity for plinking, practice, or even small-game hunting.

A third reason for handloading is the making of custom ammunition—pet loads, if you will. The handloader can experiment (using a loading manual only) until he finds the specific combination of bullet, powder type, charge weight, case and primer that his particular rifle shoots best.

The handloader can also prepare rounds for rifles that would otherwise serve only as wall-hangers. This is reason number four to reload: the ability to make ammo that is either obsolete or otherwise difficult to buy in factory form. A good example is the 32-40 Winchester cartridge. Ammunition is not entirely obsolete for this old-

It all begins with a loading manual, such as this two-volume set by Hornady. All information in the manual must be strictly adhered to for safety as well as for the best results.

timer, but it is difficult to locate. Not long ago, a fine Model 94 Winchester rifle was lying fallow until handloads of mine brought it back to usefulness. A set of RCBS dies; Hornady and Speer 32-caliber, 170-grain bullets; IMR-4064 powder; and standard rifle primers provided the right equipment, fuel and spark for ignition.

But what about 32-40 cartridge cases? No cases were for sale in my area. So I formed some from 30-30 brass by running them one time through a resizing die. Now the 32-40 rides again—in style.

A fifth reason for reloading is power. Some factory ammunition is loaded to full potential, but much of it is not. This is not a black mark against ammo companies; they do so because they have no control over the guns in which their products are used. The 30-06, for example, is loaded with a 180-grain bullet to about 2700 fps mv by most factories. A careful handloader who owns a strong bolt-action rifle in perfect condition can boost the punch of the '06 with a 180-grain bullet to over 2800 fps mv.

Sometimes the difference in power between factory ammo and handloads is even more pronounced. For example, some factory 300 H&H Magnum ammunition gains only a little bullet speed over the 30-06, while the handloader can turn the 300 H&H into a true magnum.

A sixth reason for reloading is accuracy. Although factory ammunition is now available in super-accurate loads, it is impossible for the factory to provide "personal" ammo for a given rifle. A pet load allows the shooter to build ammo that works well in his particular rifle. In some instances, increased accuracy for reloads is substantial.

A seventh reason for handloading is simply that it's enjoyable. It's a hobby in its own right. Thousands of reloading fans in this and other countries would continue to make their own ammunition even if it was more expensive than buying factory loads. Handloading is rewarding because it's relaxing, and it's also a science unto itself. Consider the fact that without handloading, there would be no wildcat ammunition. The research invested in that field has brought about some of the finest factory rounds we enjoy today.

These are some of the reasons that handloading is so popular. Is it safe? Handloading is as safe as the shooter's routine, his knowledge and his desire to make only the best product, while closely following the information in a reloading manual.

TOOLING UP

Reloading Manual. The reloading manual is vital to the reloading process. Manuals contain all pertinent details to the load. Perfect agreement between loading manuals is impossible because of variations in the exact firearm or testing device

Every detail in the manual should be followed. These two powders, for example, bear the same number, 4831, but not the same name. They do *not* produce the same results in handloads.

used to gather velocity information. It is wise to own several manuals and study them for loads that may work especially well in a particular rifle.

The Reloading Bench. One of the first considerations when reloading is finding a place to work and a surface on which to work. A reloading bench is ideal. Those who would reload thousands of rounds a year should consider a first-class, heavy-duty, permanent bench. The casual reloader can get by with a less rigid surface.

The Press. A reloading press is the basic tool of reloading. It supplies the mechanical force to resize cases and seat bullets. Compact loading tools are an exception, in that no press is required. However, extended reloading, case forming and other operations demanding considerable application of force call for a press. There are many different kinds of presses; check the catalogs available at sporting goods stores.

Shell Holder. A shell holder that matches the cartridge head size is necessary to stabilize the cartridge case in the press.

Priming Tool. Cases can generally be re-primed on the reloading press. Some hand-held priming tools also do an excellent job.

Dies. A set of dies is necessary to reform the case to near-original dimensions so it will once again fit the chamber of the rifle and allow the bullet to seat at the correct depth. Some die sets offer the ability to crimp the mouth of the case into a bullet cannelure.

Scale. With some basic reloads that use certain powders, it is possible to reload by volume using a dipper. But the serious reloader should have a scale, a precision instrument designed to weigh powder to $1/10$ grain or so (there are 7000 grains in 1 pound). Some scales are electronic, such as the RCBS Model 90, which offers a display window and readout of the powder charge weight.

Powder Measure. A precision powder measure is a time-saving device and can produce remarkably accurate loads. Benchrest loads are usually built with the use of a powder measure. Of course a scale is necessary to set the measure, so the powder measure doesn't preclude the need for an accurate scale.

Funnel. Simple as it is, the funnel is vital for introducing the weighed powder charge into the cartridge case. Of course, the powder measure will have a built-in funnel, while loads from a scale are put into the case with a separate funnel.

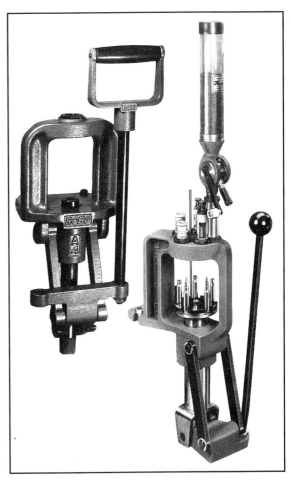

Uncomplicated and extremely powerful, the RCBS press (left) will form cases and handle many reloading operations. A modern sophisticated unit like the Hornady Pro-7 Progressive Press (right) performs several loading operations automatically.

Case Block. A case block is simply a device used to hold cartridge cases during the reloading process. It prevents powder spillage.

Trimmer. The trimmer is used to reduce the neck length of a cartridge case. Cases that stretch

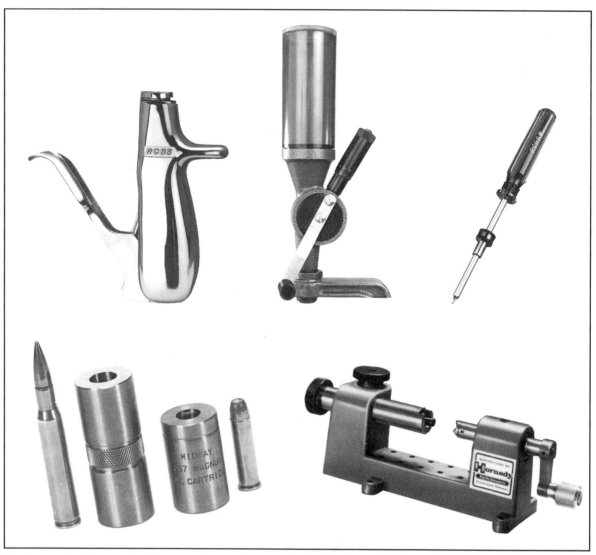

Modern reloading tools offer speed as well as precision in handloading. Clockwise from top left are: a popular RCBS hand-held unit for repriming cases; an RCBS powder measure; a deburring tool for cleaning the flash hole of the cartridge case; a Hornady case trimmer; and case-length gauges made by the Midway Company.

beyond the acceptable limit can produce high pressures, because the mouth of the case can pinch the bullet in the leade or throat of the chamber, thus retarding the bullet's normal escape from the case. Too much friction at this particular juncture can cause trouble. Trimming maintains cases at a safe length.

Trim Die. Rather than use a trimmer to tailor

cases, a special trim die can be inserted in the reloading press and the case run up into that die. Any portion of the case mouth that protrudes beyond the top of the die is removed with a file, then the mouth of the case is deburred and chamfered to make it uniform.

Deburring Tool. This small tool is used to chamfer the mouth of the cartridge case to ease bullet entry and to make the brass in this area of the case uniform in thickness.

Primer Pocket Cleaner. As the name suggests, this tool cleans powder residue from the primer pocket.

Bullet Puller. A bullet puller of some kind is necessary to withdraw a bullet from a loaded round. The puller is useful when the handloader wishes to break down a round for any reason.

Tumbler. The tumbler is used to clean cartridge cases, mostly for cosmetic reasons but also to remove powder fouling from within the case.

Case Lube. Vital to resizing the fired brass case is a special lube that prevents galling, or sticking of the case in the die. Some dies of carbide material do not require case lube.

Stuck Case Remover. Should a cartridge case become stuck in the die, this device serves to withdraw the stuck case.

THE HANDLOADING PROCESS

Case Inspection. The first step in reloading the spent cartridge case is inspecting for cracks. Checking for a loose primer pocket will come later, but at this point it's imperative to inspect the case visually for a split neck or any other form of brass fatigue. Worn cases are discarded.

Case Cleaning. The case can be cleaned in a tumbler with cleaning medium at this point. Excessive buildup caused by media inside of the case can reduce case capacity, so cases do not—and probably should not—be tumbled every time the reload is fired. Brass cleaner, generally in cream form, can also be used to clean the cartridge case.

Lubrication. A pad treated with case lube may be used to distribute the lubricant on the case. Some prefer to use their hands: A dab of lube is placed in one palm, and both hands are rubbed together to put a film of lube on both palms. Two to several cases at a time, depending on the size of the cartridge, can be lubed by rubbing the cases in between the palms. A tiny dab of lube inside of the case mouth is useful to lube

For case cleaning, dry media such as Formula 2 Corn Cob is placed in a cartridge-cleaning apparatus. These two different models from Midway do the job.

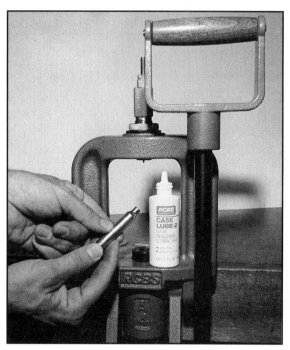

The empty case is first lubed to prevent galling in the resizing die.

The case is resized by running it up all the way into the resize die.

that area, but only one out of every three or four cases should be so treated. If every case mouth is lubed, the buildup of lube within the die becomes excessive.

Decapping/Resizing. The resize die is screwed into the press. It should be set to make contact with the shell holder for full-length resizing. A lubed case is placed in the shell holder, and the arm of the press is activated to drive the case fully into the resize die. This performs two functions: The case is returned to near-original dimensions (never perfect), and at the same time the spent primer is expelled by a decapping pin.

Full-length resizing is highly recommended for everything except benchrest competition shooting. Anyone who thinks the average hunting rifle will show marked accuracy improvement from neck-sizing the case only should experiment for himself. He will find that if there are accuracy differences at all (which is doubtful), they will be insignificant. On the other hand, a neck-sized-only case will stick in the chamber of the rifle far sooner than a full-length resized case.

Trimming. My personal preference leans toward the trim die rather than a trimming tool. At this point, the resized (and still lubed) case is installed in the trim die. Any portion of the case resting above the top of the trim die is filed away.

Deburring. The deburring tool is now put to work, even if the case did not require trimming. This step guarantees a beveled case mouth, which makes bullet seating easier, and provides a more uniform neck area for the case.

Cleaning the Primer Pocket. The primer pocket is quickly cleared of fouling with the primer pocket cleaning tool. The primer pocket need not be cleaned every time. If the cartridge case is to be reprimed as part of the resize/decap step, the case may be left in the shell holder throughout the resize/deprime/prime step.

Repriming the Case. Of course, a new primer must be installed in the resized case. If this has not been done in the press as a part of the resize/decap step, it can be done now with a separate priming tool.

After depriming, the brass case is fitted with a new primer. On this press, the operation is accomplished at the top of the unit.

After the correct powder charge has been weighed and introduced to the case, the bullet is seated. The finished product is a professionally reloaded cartridge.

Charging the Case. A correct powder charge is introduced into the resized/primed case at this point. Details are discussed later in "Choosing the Load."

Bullet Seating. The seater die is installed in the press in place of the resize die. It should not be fully inserted; rather, a gap should be left between the base of the resize die and the shell holder. A bullet is carefully inserted, base down of course, into the neck of the cartridge case. As the ram is worked, pushing the case up into the seater die, the bullet is guided into the opening of the die. Then the cartridge is released and the ram is worked fully, but slowly and without slamming, until the bullet is seated in place.

Setting the Bullet Seater Die. There are several ways to determine overall cartridge length. Ideally, the nose of the bullet should end up slightly off of the rifling in the leade, and not wedged into the rifling. This advice comes from winners of world benchrest matches. On the other hand, the bullet must be seated deeply enough so that the cartridge will fit the magazine of the rifle. One gauge that can be used is a factory round. The factory round is carefully run up into the seater die with the stem of the seater die screwed out. Then the stem of the seater die is screwed downward until it makes contact with the nose of the bullet. This ensures that the length of the reload matches the length of that particular factory load.

Choosing The Load. The loading manual is the last word—always. Never exceed a maximum load listed in the manual. A little velocity gain— or probably none at all—is not worth extra pressure. Furthermore, there is a possibility that pressure will be increased with so little velocity appreciation that using more powder would be a total waste of fuel.

There are several ways to choose a load. One is to study the detailed information provided in the manual. Sometimes, but not always, there will be a notation telling the reader which powder

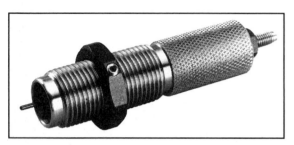

The reloading die set provides case resizing, case forming, decapping and bullet seating operations. A close look at an RCBS Decap Die reveals superb workmanship with extremely precise tolerances.

and powder charge is best. The manual's researchers have found the particular powders and/or powder charges to give the best results, especially in terms of accuracy.

Another method of selecting a powder is to choose one that most closely offers 100 percent load density. This means simply that a safe and prudent charge of a specific powder fills the air space in the case. In theory, a full case of powder is best for accuracy. Start from below and work up. If a maximum charge is 50.0 grains of a given powder, the shooter may wish to try 45.0 or 46.0 grains first, working up in half-grain increments toward the maximum charge, but testing each load at the range. It could turn out that one of the trial loads (below maximum charge) is most accurate.

WARNING: Do not reduce powder charges below the minimum recommended levels for large-capacity cartridges using slow-burning powder. Reduced charges of slow-burning powder in large-capacity cases can cause a pressure excursion. Even medium-sized cases, such as the 270 Winchester, using slow-burning powder should not be loaded below the level shown in the manual. Half-charges could cause a terrific rise in pressures. A 270 Winchester cartridge loaded with about half of its normal recommended charge of H-4831 powder, for example, caused a dangerous pressure problem, locking the bolt of the rifle and in fact damaging the rifle.

Tenth-of-a-Grain Loads. Working up in half-grain increments is recommended for the

vast majority of cartridges. Loads of 50.5 grains and 50.6 grains can seldom be differentiated, because as efficient as smokeless powder is, it isn't efficient enough to merit such small powder differences. Therefore, half-grain increments generally serve the shooter well.

An exception is the 17-caliber cartridge. Due to the tiny bore size and consequent minor bore volume of the 17, extremely close loading is necessary. In some instances, a $1/10$-grain difference, as with charges of 18.5 grains versus 18.6 grains, can affect the results. Serious benchrest competition is another possible exception. However, considering that most benchrest shooters use a powder measure instead of a powder scale, the $1/10$-grain increment must not be that important, even to seekers of the one-hole group.

Selecting Primers. Some shooters seem to think that following the loading manual means selecting a given bullet and powder charge without regard for the primer used to build the load. Primers do make a difference, though, as a recent test of 308 Winchester accuracy loads proved. In this test, one batch of ammo was made up with standard primers, and another batch was built with CCI BR-2 Large Rifle Bench Rest Primers. The latter proved more accurate in this particular test. Furthermore, a test of reduced loads for grouse hunting, also in a 308 Winchester, revealed that benchrest primers provided better accuracy with reduced loads of fast-burning powder.

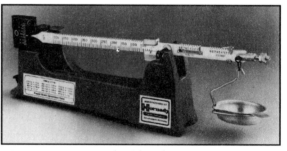

A reloader's bullet/powder scale is essential to creating accurate loads. This is a standard scale with high reliability in the $1/10$-grain domain. Electronic scales are also available to today's handloaders.

One way to get started in handloading is with a complete outfit like this RCBS Rock Chucker Master Reloading Kit.

On the other hand, magnum primers have been shown to improve hunting load velocities. The most startling example that comes to mind is the 257 Weatherby Magnum cartridge, which gained a full 200 fps mv by switching from standard primers to Federal No. 215 magnum primers.

Accounting for Cartridge Case Variation. It is essential to use the cartridge case noted in the loading manual, because case capacity varies. For example, two 30-06 cases of different brands varied 2.0 grains in capacity. Military brass is generally thicker walled than commercial brass, which means that if these cases (such as 308 or 30-06) are used, powder charges meant for commercial cases should be cut.

Ideally, it is wisest to use the exact brand of cartridge case recommended in the loading manual chart. However, it is also acceptable to cut powder charges when using brass known to have less powder capacity.

Spotting Signs of Pressure. Loading-manual researchers have the advantage of pressure guns to relate specific pressures for their loads in test barrels. Shooters don't normally own pressure guns. The best way to stay within the parameters of safety is to remain at or below the maximum powder charge listed in the loading manual. However, it is also important to recognize when pressure problems exist. Here are a few visual signs:

1. Significant cratering of the primer, in

which there is a raised ridge all around the indentation made by the firing pin.

2. Difficulty extracting the fired cartridge case, especially if the brass is new and not fatigued. (Sometimes fatigued brass will also cause sticky case extraction.)

3. The bolt opening with difficulty or not at all.

4. A loose primer pocket. If after a couple reloads, the primer pocket won't hold a new primer snugly, chances are pressures are fairly stiff.

5. Blown primers. Obviously, a hole all the way through the primer indicates very high pressures.

6. Case-head expansion. The head of the case, or the belt on a belted magnum case, can be measured after the first firing of the round. Use a micrometer to get an exact reading. If the next shot shows a head or belt expansion over .001 inch, this indicates brass flow caused by high pressures.

7. Headstamp engraving. If the headstamp area of the cartridge reveals overt and obvious impressions made by the bolt face of the rifle, this illustrates a condition of high pressure. Minor engraving is normal, with the imperfections of the bolt face marked on the headstamp. Also look for engraving caused by the extractor. A shiny mark on the headstamp made by the extractor, if overt and obvious, can indicate a condition of high pressure.

8. Damaged cartridge case. The most obvious sign of high pressure is the separated head, in which the back end of the cartridge breaks away from the rest of the case. Sometimes the fore-part of the case remains stuck in the chamber of the rifle and must be removed with a cleaning rod or, in severe cases, by a gunsmith.

Accounting for Rifle Variation. Individuality among rifles is especially important in handloading. A rifle of tight chamber and/or bore dimensions may demand lighter loads than will a rifle with more generous dimensions. This is why starting below the maximum recommended load is so important when reloading. If the rifle is sensitive to pressures, the shooter will find out by working his loads up in half-grain increments.

The first signs of pressure tell the shooter to stop and back up a load.

TESTING YOUR HANDLOADS

Chronographing Loads. The dedicated handloader often has access to a chronograph. Chronographs have improved greatly over the years. The Oehler 35P Proof chronograph used in connection with this work provides two read-

Before and after. The loading tray (above) is essential to prevent powder spillage from the charged case. When the job is done, reloaded ammo can be stored in boxes (below), such as these offered by the Midway Company.

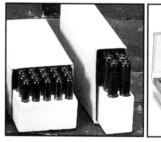

outs for each shot fired through its Sky-screens. Furthermore, results are printed on a tape. The machine automatically provides five important pieces of information:
- lowest velocity in the string
- highest velocity in the string
- spread between high and low velocities
- average velocity
- standard deviation

It is currently popular for some gunwriters to devalue the last factor. However, standard deviation is a function of variance, and a low standard deviation in a handload tells the reader that his ammunition is reliable. It is not proof of accuracy, because accuracy depends on many factors, from bullet concentricity and precision to bore condition, rifling, the shooting situation and many other elements. However, a low standard deviation does suggest that the ammunition in question is reliable.

Furthermore, the only real way to know what a given load does in a specific rifle is to chronograph that load in that rifle. Some remarkable variations have been noted. Speer, the famous bulletmaking company, found differences as high as 200 fps mv in two 270 rifles using identical handloads.

As mentioned so many times, variation is the rule, not the exception. It would be rare for two rifles to give identical velocities right down the line—although large differences are also rare. For all practical purposes, the velocities given by the loading manuals are close enough. But the only way a shooter can know *exactly* what his rifle yields with a given load is to chronograph that rifle with that load.

The Dry Run. Cartridges should be checked to ensure that they fit the rifle perfectly. First, load the round into the magazine. Second, with the muzzle of the rifle pointed in a totally safe direction, feed the round into the chamber of the rifle, to see if it feeds properly through the magazine and also to make sure that it fits the chamber. A reload may look perfect, but the case—even if full-length resized—may not have been returned to specifications that allow it to chamber in the rifle. This may mean a stuck case in the field, and at the worst possible moment.

THE HANDLOADER'S DIARY

Trusting results to memory is foolish and can be dangerous. Every handloader should keep a diary of his range work. Every nuance of reload behavior must be recorded, including accuracy and how the load functioned in the rifle. Then the shooter can go back to his records to find out what loads worked best in a specific rifle. That's how pet loads are born. A recipe box is useful as a shooting diary, each card representing a particular date with weather conditions and elevation of the test range.

Handloading is and always has been an important aspect of rifle shooting. Custom loads expand the range of usefulness of any centerfire rifle, while also providing a savings that translates into more shooting for the money. Several top companies provide a long list of high-grade reloading equipment, and the components for handmaking ammunition are better than ever, with more useful powders than ever before, precision bullets in hundreds of variations, the finest in brass cartridge cases, more primer types than existed in the past and a huge body of reloading data. There has never been a better time to be interested in handloading.

BUYING A CUSTOM RIFLE

19 The tradition of custom gunmaking in this country began long before the appearance of telephones, automobiles, knickers or nickel beer. The Kentucky/Pennsylvania longrifle that sent the Redcoats running and supplied meat for the leather-stockinged explorers of our Eastern seaboard was primarily a hand-made affair; it was put together by a single artisan, often working in a one-room building that was his entire shop. By today's standards, the gunmaker's tools were crude. Many were hand-powered. Some were water-driven implements often built by the tradesman himself. If the old-time gunmaker had any help at all, that aid came in the form of an indentured servant, who was generally a young man assigned to the master for a period of time. The object of this apprenticeship was obviously the learning of a trade. The "servant-student" went on to become a gunmaker in his own right. The system was a European holdover and, like it or not, it worked.

The art of hand-making firearms never died. Early on, there began a guild-like operation, where locksmiths made locks and barrelmakers made barrels. Finally, Henry Ford's assembly-line process of manufacture took over in the gun industry. Factory-made arms proved an ideal way to build good products for the "average" buyer, but custom gunmakers have never been lacking in this country. No matter how many fine factory arms came along, there was always room for the custom gunmaker.

Today, custom-crafting rifles is as vital as ever. Every year, new custom armsmakers set up shop, most of them on a part-time basis, some full-time. Gunsmithing schools continue to train these men (women have not taken to the trade in numbers as yet), and the old apprenticeship program is also far from defunct. Busy gunsmiths all over the country hire young men to help in the shop and to learn the trade as they work.

There is a sufficient number of wood and metal experts in the U.S. to meet a constant demand for fine custom rifles. Sometimes the demand exceeds the work force. That is why a buyer of a custom firearm must often wait a year or longer for his rifle. Modern shooters appreciate the art of the hand-made rifle; many of us want at least one custom arm in our collection.

But money is a barrier between shooters and custom rifles. Hand-made items command a higher dollar outlay than factory-made products. That's why the first custom rifle ordered by a shooter is often the last one. It's also why the rifle should be just what the shooter ordered—in design, caliber and other appointments.

Who needs a custom rifle? Nobody. Who

wants one? The shooter who appreciates something special. The marksman who considers the rifle a tool and nothing but a tool won't be happy shelling out greenbacks for a custom rifle. The factory rifle of the hour is supremely good in all respects, from accuracy to function. A shooter buys a custom rifle because he views the longarm as art as well as a tool. He wants something personal, something special. He may also buy a custom rifle to obtain what he cannot buy over the counter, although that situation is less true today because factories are producing just about anything a shooter could want.

Factory rifles are available in high grades. For example, Remington not only offers higher grades of factory rifles for sale, but also has a custom shop from which special rifles are crafted. These are best called semi-custom rifles, in that they're not entirely unique from one model to the next but are highly refined over the standard factory model. Sako is another manufacturer of show rifles that exceeds the usual over-the-counter firearm. For example, Sako's Deluxe and Super Deluxe rifles are built on high-figure French walnut stocks, with hand-cut checkering, a special high-gloss stock finish topped off with rosewood forend tip and grip cap, plus a handsome deep blued metal finish. So beauty alone is not a reason to buy a custom arm. The best reason to buy one is to have a rifle that is unique and is at least in part what the individual rifleman desires—*his* rifle.

True custom rifles are built one at a time. That does not mean that a gunmaker must necessarily take a plank of wood and create a stock from it, or that he cannot work on chambering a number of barrels simultaneously or in some other way streamline the task. But custom-building a rifle is a hands-on endeavor.

A custom rifle is usually built for a particular customer; that is, it is rarely built on speculation—although a few custom arms are also put together with the idea of finding a customer after the fact. Uniqueness plays a role in the custom arm. This is not to say that a builder won't have a trademark; most builders do. The makers of some custom arms are rather easily identified by a certain recognizable style.

There is nothing quite so unique in the world of rifles as a custom model. This is the author's custom Model 94 built by Dale Storey.

However, a custom rifle is not the same as a *customized* rifle, which is simply an alteration of a regular rifle. The military rifle with a new sporting stock, a bolt bent to miss the scope tube

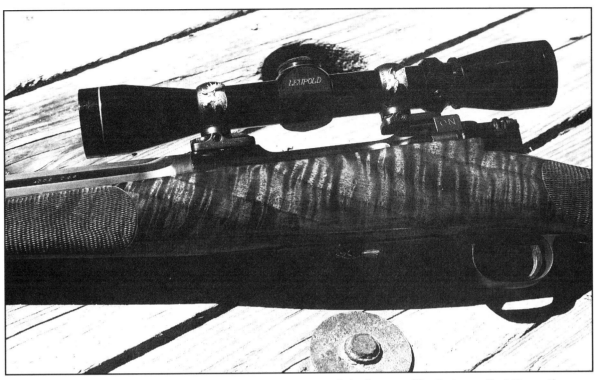

This custom-made Springfield rifle is a far cry from the original army rifle that supplied the action.

and even a new trigger and trigger guard remains a customized rifle, not a custom rifle. Most of the time, a custom rifle is contracted for. A shooter decides that he wants something unique, or he sees workmanship that he admires. He seeks out the gunmaker, and the two of them get together on a plan that results in a one-of-a-kind rifle.

CHOOSING THE GUNMAKER

The first step in obtaining a custom rifle is choosing the right gunmaker. Reputation is one good calling card. Fine 'smiths have built sterling reputations for themselves. But there are some new boys on the block who are very good, too. So, if possible, you should study samples of a gunmaker's work to see if his style is what you, the prospective buyer, wants. Gunmakers generally work in one "school" or another. Some 'smiths can build various styles, but most find a style that suits them and stay with it. For example, certain craftsmen make muzzleloaders of the Lancaster school, a specific type of Pennsyl-

vania longrifle, while other blackpowder rifle-makers build plains rifles.

Most of today's artisans work with the bolt-action rifle, especially of the "American classic" design. This particular bolt-action style is associated with Bob Owen, who became famous in the early 1900s for building rifles with clean, "classic" lines.

But if a rifleman does not feel qualified to judge custom workmanship, he should have someone else evaluate the workmanship for him. Just because a rifle is home-made doesn't make it worthy of being called a custom firearm.

When a prospective buyer finds a gunmaker whose work suits his taste, an agreement is drawn up. The 'smith agrees to build a rifle of certain specifications, and the client agrees to pay a certain price. Generally, the client pays the 'smith half of the total amount before the work starts. This keeps the 'smith from having to work out of his own pocket, so to speak, buying parts with his own money. It also commits the buyer, who now has an investment in progress. He must

John Fadala poses with a 7mm Remington Magnum rifle, custom built on a pre-64 Model 70 action by Dean Zollinger of Rexburg, Idaho.

pay the second half of the bill on delivery of the rifle or he may lose part or all of his investment.

A realistic delivery date should be agreed on. If the 'smith gives references, it won't hurt to ask a previous customer how long he had to wait for his rifle. Fine art takes time, but there are limits. Michelangelo could have done two Sistine Chapels in the time it takes for some gunsmiths to hew out one stock. Some slack is necessary, but a year to 18 months is a reasonable waiting time for a gunmaker to finish his creation.

TAILORING RIFLE TO BUYER

Customer Input. "It's going to be my rifle. I'm paying for it, and I'll have exactly what I want." That's how some buyers feel—but they are entirely wrong. Yes, the customer will be the owner of the firearm and, yes, he is paying for it—but customer input goes only so far. A perfect example of this is a rifle I contracted for many years ago, a custom-made muzzleloader. I wanted a rugged, somewhat bulky half-stock rifle of the "Hawken" type. The gunmaker felt that this particular breed of rifle was too clubby, unnecessarily hefty, and not all that handsome. He found an original rifle in a museum that was ruggedly built. It had once been a long-barreled Pennsylvania rifle, but its owner had the barrel freshed out (rebored) to a larger caliber and the flintlock ignition converted to a percussion system. The barrel had obviously been shortened to 34 inches. The gunmaker got his way, and I ended up with a beautiful, serviceable and historically oriented rifle that has since proven itself ideal in the field.

The point is this: The customer is not always right, especially when it comes to hand-made firearms. It's not only the gunmaker's right to guide the buyer to a rifle that's correctly designed and executed—it's his responsibility.

Design. A custom rifle is designed with a purpose in mind. Beauty is important, but so is function. The workings of a rifle should never be forsaken for beauty. It's a piece of art, yes, but the custom rifle is still a shooting instrument. Building a custom rifle with only looks in mind is a great mistake, unless that rifle's true reason for existence is to hang on a wall. An example of a custom rifle built for show is a seven-pound 458 Winchester with a petite and graceful sliver stock. But nobody would shoot that rifle more than once. It kicks like two mules in tandem. It's a pretty rifle but is ill-designed for its intended purpose, containment of one of our more powerful cartridges.

Watch out for gimmicks. They're cute when first encountered, but after a while the wild stuff makes our eyes grow weary. Consider a brilliant green bathroom appointed with gold fixtures. It might be sharp-looking at first glance, even unique, but after a time the homeowner will wish for more restful colors. The customer should get what he wants, to a point, but when in doubt about any specific aspect of the custom rifle, leaning to the conservative side is usually a wise move. Always remember that your first custom rifle may be your last.

Ensuring Rifle Fit. A custom rifle should fit its owner perfectly. The gunmaker should take note of his customer's physique and shooting stance so he'll know proper drop at comb, length of pull, pitch, cast-off or cast-on, and other stock dimensions.

Selecting the Wood. Many beautiful woods are available, even in today's dwindling supply of exotics and scarcity of highly figured woods of even the most common species, such as American black walnut. Good gunstock wood is strong, yet on the lightweight side. For example, ironwood is strong, but gunstocks of this material would weigh a great deal—fine for the bench, but hefty for field use and extremely difficult for the stockmaker to work with. Good stock wood should be "pretty," at least in comparison with plain white figureless pine for crate-building.

French walnut, which is the same genus and species as English walnut, is high on the list of good gunstock woods. Some French walnut, which can possess fancy grain patterns, is beautiful. French walnut "works" well, taking checkering cleanly and sharply. Claro walnut is a high figure wood. It may warp slightly sooner than French, but all in all, a stock of Claro walnut is just fine. Bastogne is another good stock wood. Mesquite can be pretty. It's strong and stable, but also heavy—just right for some magnum calibers, but perhaps a bit too dense for other rifles.

Stockmakers generally have planks of wood on hand for the customer to study. The plank or semi-inletted stock is wetted a little to display its grain structure.

The higher grades of wood can destroy your wallet. It's not uncommon these days for a piece of top-grade French walnut to run $1000 or more. For a lifetime investment, the cash outlay is worth it—but your budget has to be ready for the price tag.

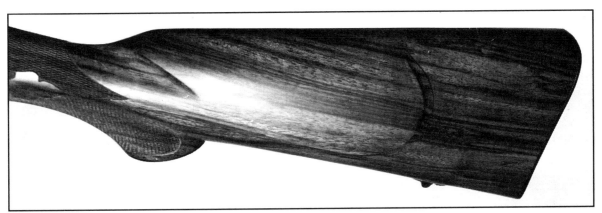

Slim lines mark the work of many modern gunmakers. This buttstock is the design of Dean Zollinger.

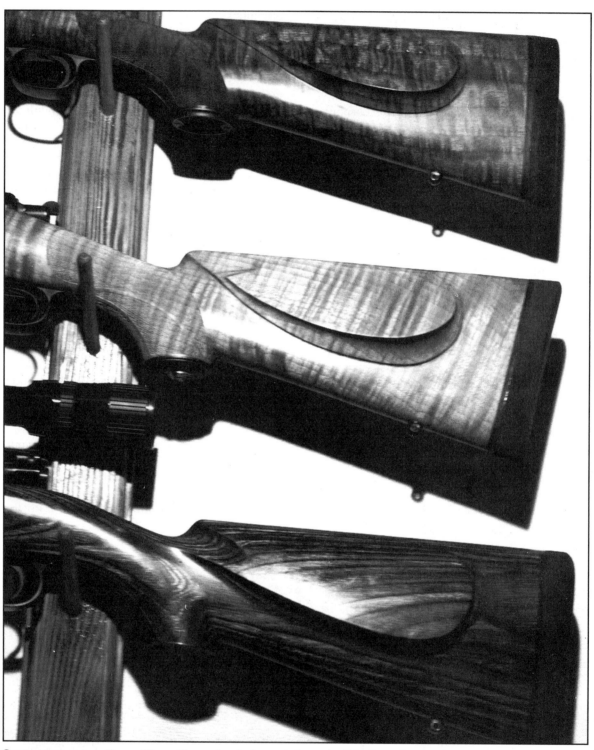

Custom means options. These three cheekpiece styles are all built by gunmaker Dale Storey. Note the variations in the wood grain as well as the checkering and pistol-grip caps.

Power tools are as indispensable as hand tools to custom work. Here, a stock outline is cut from a plank using a power band saw.

The best buy is the best plank the customer can afford, because such wood increases in value, provided that the stock made from it is executed properly. Most importantly, the wood should match the finished product. A rifle is a balanced piece of art. For example, tigertail maple is ideal for a muzzleloader, and it fits beautifully with some modern rifle designs, too. However, most modern bolt-action rifle designs do not necessarily lend themselves to tigertail maple. This fiddleback wood somehow seems out of place with the deep-blue metalwork of the modern rifle. It would be wiser to go with a less-figured piece of American walnut in this case.

Economizing on wood is not economy at all. The wood will be shaped, inletted and checkered, and these steps cost at least as much as the plank, generally more. There is no point in spending a lot of money for the extras if the basic piece of wood is poor.

The Right Cartridge. The cartridge must be chosen with great wisdom. All aspects must be assessed: What will this custom rifle be used for? Deer only, deer and antelope or deer and elk? What terrain will be hunted—timber, brush or the high mountains?

The previous chapters on cartridges and rifle styles can help here. The "all-around" caliber, from the 270 Winchester all the way up to 300 Magnum, is usually a safe bet if the rifle is headed for the Rocky Mountains or similar areas. There are so many excellent rounds that choosing a bad one is more difficult than picking a good one. Anybody with a 30-06, for example, has plenty of hunting latitude. The 270 is flexible, too. And the 7mm Magnum, Weatherby or Remington version, is a king among all-around cartridges.

The bigger calibers bark more and buck more, so if game smaller than elk is the rifleman's aim, he should forget the larger magnums and go with the more pleasant numbers. The 7mm Remington Magnum and 7mm Weatherby Magnum mark the upper power scale.

Wildcat or factory standard? Interviews with custom riflemakers indicate that a great many custom rifles are built in wildcat calibers. The reasoning is this: The customer has ordered a special rifle; he should have a unique cartridge rather than an everyday cartridge to match that rifle. But this reasoning may be faulty. A custom rifle chambered for a special round is interesting, but usually of no real practical improvement.

On the other hand, there is no doubt that a wildcat cartridge embodies a uniqueness not found in a standard number from the ammo factory. A number of wildcat rounds are being chambered in customs these days, including the 280 Remington Improved, a blown-out version of the regular round. Here the intent is to approach the ballistics of the 7mm Remington Magnum with a beltless case, and it does. My opinion, though, is that the shooter who wants 7mm Magnum power should buy a 7mm Magnum.

The Metalwork. Many modern gunmakers do much of their own metalsmithing, although there is also a guild approach to metalwork, whereby specific metal parts may be purchased. For example, the three-position safety is a feature many riflemen prefer. A custom wing safety of

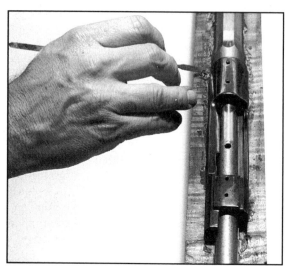

Here, a barreled action is being glass-bedded into a stock.

this type can be installed on rifles that were not originally designed for one. For example, a custom rifle may be built on the Remington Model 700 action, upon which a wing safety can be installed. A custom safety of this type may run $200 by the time it's installed. Scope bases can also be customized. So can sights and sight ramps, as well as many other metal features. A 'smith may contour his own barrels and modify an action in his own unique manner. Again, it's a matter of matching and mating so that metal and wood become a unit. Metal finishing may be done in-house or by a separate shop. A popular metal finish these days is the matte style, which is a sort of "Parkerized" approach, bead-blasted to give a rich but not shiny surface. All of these metalwork touches add to the custom rifle's uniqueness and appeal.

Finishing the Work. The stock must be inletted and shaped. The action must fit snugly into its mortise to ensure accuracy and security against recoil splitting the stock. The barrel must be inletted perfectly into its channel. Cheekpiece, wrist, forearm—all lines must match so that the finished product has a graceful and flowing appeal. This sort of woodworking requires talent.

If the custom rifle stock is to be checkered, the pattern is generally devised by the gunmaker, with approval by the customer. Checkering is

for show. It has a bit of function, but how many of us have had a non-checkered rifle fall out of our hands due to lack of friction? So checkering may help a rifleman hang onto his piece—a little—but in the main, cutting nice lines into wood is for appearance.

Checkering is measured in lines per inch, and the range is wide. Some of the very finest checkering, in the 28- to 32-line-per-inch range, is beautiful, but such checkering is not always necessary and of course costs more because it requires more time. Sufficient checkering about the wrist and forearm of a rifle, using patterns that wrap around while staying with somewhat conservative panels, is often the best way to go. Checkering that goes beyond tasteful to gaudy may tend to reduce a custom stock's overall visual appeal.

Then there is stock finishing. Wood finishes have almost become trademarks for many gunmakers. Custom stockmakers have spent countless hours experimenting with wood blocks to achieve that perfect finish—a finish that's *in* the wood, not on it, and that protects the wood without looking thick. There are almost as many different wood-finishing methods as there are custom gunmakers.

Fine parts result in high-quality custom rifles. These pistol-grip caps offer three variations.

In a checkering cradle, this composite stock awaits checkering. Today's gunmakers have a multitude of optional stock materials with which to work.

As for engraving, some custom 'smiths do a bit of their own, but, generally speaking, engraving of fine rifles is the work of a specialist in this art. When contracting for a rifle, engraving and embellishments of any kind, such as inlays, should be clearly decided on well ahead of time. Samples of the engraver's work should be studied by someone who knows good work when he sees it. Professional-quality engraving enhances a rifle markedly. Poor engraving does nothing to elevate a custom rifle's value.

The Dollar Value. What does a buyer get for his money? Consider what a gunmaker must do to construct a true custom rifle. It may not be entirely unique in all aspects, but the hand-made rifle can be distinguished from a factory rifle at about a city block's distance. The custom also is not a semi-custom rifle—a standard model with some special features. Remember that the custom rifle is a unique, individual firearm.

But Does It Shoot? A custom rifle must function with perfect reliability: rounds feeding up from the magazine flawlessly, action smooth as greased marbles, safety sharp and precise, with a trigger as crisp as a fresh cracker.

The rifle should be accurate. A well-tuned factory rifle shoots so well that it's unfair for a customer to ask that a hand-made rifle do much better. However, a number of riflemakers build for super accuracy. For example, Dale Storey is known for his light (not flyweight, but lightweight) rifles that shoot with high-grade accu-

The custom craftsman at work. Here, Dale Storey labors over the stock of a new creation.

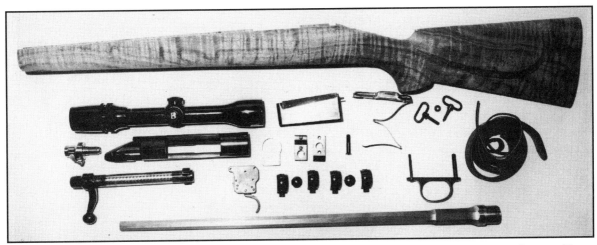

These are nothing but parts now, but when the custom gunmaker works his craft, a handsome rifle will be the result.

racy. Storey often uses an octagon barrel on his custom rifles, which may help to account for stiffness. His rifles, of round or octagon barrel, are often capable of half-inch five-shot groups at 100 yards from the bench.

Such accuracy is not uncommon for custom rifles. A 7mm Magnum built by Frank Wells is another example of a custom rifle that hovers around the half-inch range. A Storey Conversion (a Model 94 Winchester custom) breaks into the one-inch-group domain when the light is right for a clear picture with its iron sights.

While a great deal of the joy in owning a custom rifle is the simple pleasure derived from handling and looking at it, if it doesn't shoot well, it's just a pretty plaything. That's all right if it's what the shooter wants—but most custom rifles are for using, not displaying. Therefore, accuracy is important. The gunmaker should be asked what he expects for group size from a particular rifle. Once again, there's nothing wrong with a prospective buyer contacting the gunmaker's former customers to learn how his rifles shoot. Of course, such information is not always reliable. Many rifles are capable of shooting far tighter groups than their owners can manage.

THE MODERN CUSTOM RIFLE

The "modern" custom rifle is becoming more prevalent. Such a rifle isn't for show. It doesn't even have a stock of high-grade wood. This is the custom rifle built specifically for the field. It may have a synthetic or laminated stock.

A good example of this genre is a particular custom rifle built by Dale Storey, who calls it his "Modern Plains Rifle." It's a heavy-barreled rifle with a synthetic or laminated stock for strength and accuracy. It's chambered for a flat-shooting round, such as the 7mm Remington Magnum. The rifle is not light. All tolerances are held to a high degree of precision. Topped with a high-magnification scope, the powerful plains rifle is generally capable of dealing out one-inch groups at 200 yards. My own Storey Modern Plains Rifle has accounted for a number of fine trophy pronghorn antelope, taken at distances that I never would have attempted with a less accurate or less powerful rifle.

The art of custom rifle-building may be old indeed, yet there is something new in this field every year. New stock designs. New finishes. New safeties. New barrels. New materials. But the old tradition lives on. The custom rifle is always a combination of function with beauty. Wood-to-metal fit is flawless. Checkering stands up to the scrutiny of a magnifying glass. All lines flow together so that the eye is treated to a visual symphony. The custom arm is a good investment, too, when it is well-designed and properly constructed. All in all, robbing the piggy bank to

The gunmaker shapes the wrist of the stock with a file.

buy a custom longarm is worth it. Just make sure that you know up front what you're paying for and when you're going to see the finished product.

THE POPULAR AIR RIFLE

20 Thousands of riflemen first began shooting with a rifle that works not by powder, but by air. This does not make the "pellet gun" a toy. The air rifle has long been considered a serious shooting instrument. Missiles propelled by air were used in European wars centuries ago, and our own Lewis and Clark carried a large-bore air rifle on their 19th-century expedition into the West. It is recorded that the Indian peoples along the way were more impressed by the air rifle than by the powder-burning muzzleloaders carried by the Lewis and Clark party. Today, some of the most accurate shooting instruments in the world are air-powered. A recent test of an RWS Model 75 match-grade air rifle produced one-hole groups of only .20 inch at 10 meters (33 feet).

Most of all, air rifles maintain their popularity among American shooters as hunting tools. Small game and pests are the major considerations of air rifle shooters. As a beginning outdoorsman, I hunted with a Louisiana man who'd moved to my home town, then Yuma, Arizona. Mr. Mullens taught me the right reasons to bag game, including the most important one: food. That's why he admired the only rifle I owned at that time, a 17-caliber Diana made in Germany that my uncle brought back from Berlin in 1945.

Mr. Mullens appreciated the rifle's accuracy. "If you get close, Sam, you can do well with that air rifle," he said. He was right. If I got close enough to direct the tiny lead pellet where it belonged—head shots only—cottontail rabbits, springtime jackrabbits, bullfrogs and small varmints were mine.

The unknowing may think, "That was then, but this is now. Those hunting air rifles of the World War II era are gone for good. Nowadays they're probably not so well made." Wrong. Today's top-of-the-line hunting air rifles are better than ever; they're more accurate and more powerful than their predecessors. If the older air rifle was acceptable on small game, the current precision air rifle is ideal at close range. Selecting a modern air rifle for small-game hunting, along with pest control and plinking, is not entirely easy, but that's because all high-grade models have merit. About the only way to decide on one specific model as a small-game air rifle is to examine the problem with a specific set of criteria in mind.

Before considering an air rifle for hunting, the rifleman must examine the game laws of his state or region. Air rifles for small game are legal in a number of states, but laws do vary. In some areas the air rifle is legal for rabbits, squirrels and other small game, as well as for mountain birds, such as blue grouse. But each rifleman must check his local laws.

Cost is also a factor. A good air rifle is worth the money. But as with all well-made items that last a long time and are entirely dependable, prices for good air guns are not low. The air rifle is a long-time investment, though, and should be purchased with that fact in mind. It is also a precision instrument. Therefore, the top models bear price tags that reflect their quality. A good air rifle often costs more than a medium-grade 22-rimfire rifle.

TYPES OF AIR RIFLES

Choice of mechanism is extremely important. Three basic types of air rifles are sold widely today: pneumatic (pump), CO_2 (gas operated) and spring piston.

The Pneumatic Rifle. The pneumatic rifle offers variable power, like having several air rifles

The modern precision air rifle is well balanced, has a fine trigger and exhibits top accuracy. When scoped, as shown here with an adjustable objective-type sight, an air rifle can put pellets right on target out to 20 or 25 yards.

all in one. Three or four pumps are sufficient for close-range shooting, especially plinking. If more power is desired for increased pellet velocity, the pneumatic is pumped more, which gives the pellet flatter trajectory as well as increased energy. Pneumatics are smooth operating, quiet and economical. There is no uncoiling spring to make noise, as in the spring-piston model, and no CO_2 cartridges are required.

The CO_2 Rifle. CO_2 rifles are more convenient than pneumatics. They require no pumping. Compared to the spring-piston model, CO_2s are quiet—perhaps a little louder than the average pneumatic rifle, but quiet enough. The CO_2 is more expensive to shoot than the pneumatic or spring-piston, but it still offers a reasonable cost-per-shot value.

The Spring-Piston Rifle. The spring-piston air rifle has gained great popularity in the past few decades. It has many attributes. (This does not reflect negatively on either the pump or CO_2 air rifle, both of which are excellent choices for plinking and small-game hunting.) The spring-piston air rifle gains full power with one stroke. It is known for its high velocity. Spring-piston rifles offer a choice of break-open or lever cocking. Most popular spring-piston air rifles are a little heavier and slightly bulkier than pneumatic and CO_2 rifles. But for most small-game hunting, which usually involves quiet walking over a relatively small area, the extra mass is not detrimental.

I chose an RWS Model 48 Diana as a test model for this chapter. (Perhaps nostalgia had a bearing on this choice.) The Diana's uncoiling spring caused no noise problems. Its side-lever cocking mechanism proved easy to operate. Variable pellet velocity was out of the question with this spring-piston design, but this factor wasn't considered as important as the Diana's ability to reach full power with a single cocking of the side lever.

The Model 48 exhibited the simplicity of the spring-piston air rifle style: cock, insert a pellet, aim and shoot. Accuracy of this non-target air rifle was amazing, with groups of near one-hole size at 10 meters, not far behind the previously tested match air rifle.

The spring-piston air gun dates back to the 1500s. One manipulation of the break-barrel design generates full power.

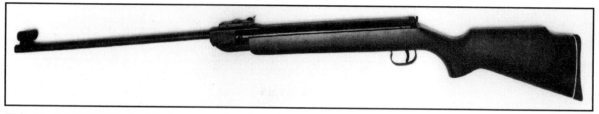

This Model 36 RWS air rifle is representative of the spring-piston style. It's also an example of the precision that's built into the best "pellet guns."

AIR RIFLE BALLISTICS

Ballistics are always an important consideration in the choice of a hunting implement. There must be no delusion about gaining 22-rimfire power with an air rifle. If a rifleman wants or needs that much authority for a given shooting application, he should carry a 22-rimfire rifle. The air rifle is not a long-range tool. Hunting small game within 20 yards or so with perfectly adequate harvesting power is a reality; but farther than about 25 yards—depending on the specific air rifle, its pellets and the shooter—the little missile loses much of its authority. The Model 48 registered about 1000 fps mv with a 17-caliber, 7.8-grain pellet. That's only 17 foot-pounds of energy. Compared with the "lowly" 22 Short, with its 29-grain bullet at 1250 fps mv and 85 foot-pounds of energy, that's not much punch. But experience in air-gun hunting will prove that this range of power is enough for the 20- to 25-yard shot at small-game animals, with head shots the rule.

I know that the air rifle is ideal for quiet, safe, close-range small-game hunting, because a rancher friend of mine has a problem. Rabbits invade his ranch-yard every winter, doing hundreds of dollars in damage to lawn and shrubs, shredding every piece of vegetation they get their teeth into and doing their fair share of eating up grain and other foods put out for domestic animals. But the rancher doesn't hunt, and he doesn't want people with 22 rifles plinking at rabbits in what amounts to his front yard. This front yard isn't one of the postage stamp-sized hunks of grass surrounding the average tract home in Suburbia, USA; it's more like a couple of football fields stuck together. Nonetheless, rabbits are near buildings. The hunting plan is simple: Walk along the walls of the buildings, carefully, shooting only away from the structures and out toward the open fields, which in winter are devoid of livestock. Before I began my air-gun excursions, the rancher was thinking of requesting special permission from the game department to trap rabbits. He's not worried now. The problem is under control.

The comparatively quiet, inoffensive, short-range modern air rifle is perfect for careful application in similar settings. Hunting small game with air power has long been a reality for young marksmen. Today's air rifle makes the situation equally ideal for adults who wish to hunt areas where even a 22 rimfire is not quite right due to population density.

The big difference between using an air rifle and a 22 rimfire is, as already recognized, range. At 50 yards, even 75 yards or more, a scoped 22-rimfire rifle is highly effective. Air-rifle hunting takes more patience than does 22-rimfire hunting. But it is effective because Western small game is usually abundant and can be approached to within 10-yard shots.

The quiet Model 48 high-precision high-power air rifle is just right for this type of hunting. It has accuracy to burn, grouping from .20 inch to about .33 inch at 10 yards, depending on the type of rest used. Groups open up only when shooting conditions deteriorate. The width of a cottontail rabbit's head, at least that of the Western "brush rabbit," is around two inches. The precision hunting air rifle is capable of keeping all of its pellets inside that diameter at 20 to 25 yards, about the farthest a hunter should try for rabbits with an air rifle. Accuracy is vital, because pellet placement is essential to the one-shot harvest on small game.

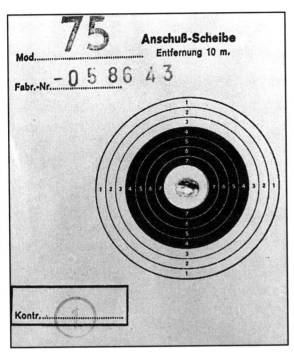

75 Anschuß-Scheibe
Mod........................... Entfernung 10 m.
Fabr.-Nr............... **- 0 5 86 43**

Kontr................................1

This is the kind of accuracy that can be expected from a target air rifle: a one-hole group at 10 meters for 10 shots.

The test air rifle wore good iron sights; however, a scope would promote even better accuracy. Scopes designed for low-recoiling 22-rimfire rifles don't always fare well on spring-piston air rifles, sometimes getting scrambled up inside from the slam-bang effect of the uncoiling spring and driving piston. A special air-gun scope is in order, one built to take the type of recoil punishment dealt out by the spring-piston air rifle. RWS makes such scopes to match its rifles. Bushnell also offers air-rifle scopes in various magnifications.

The adjustable objective lens can be a highly important feature on an air-rifle scope, because it allows focusing on near targets as well as on more distant targets. An RWS Model 300 scope I tested focused clearly from a few feet from the muzzle to infinity. A rabbit sitting under a bush—brown on brown—can be difficult to see clearly for perfect pellet placement. But the scope could be focused quickly under these circumstances for a perfect sight picture. The adjustable

objective lens also works beautifully in an indoor shooting range, for focusing at short distances.

PELLET CHOICES

The 17-caliber pellet is a wise choice because of its good velocity, adequate penetration on small game and reasonable trajectory. Many styles of 17-caliber pellets are available from various companies: economical plinking pellets, small-game pellets and high-precision match-grade pellets intended for competition shooting as well as steeple-shaped lead pellets and diabolo-shaped pellets with flat noses.

The hunting pellets available today are better than ever. The old-style diabolo is still good, but the modified diabolo, such as the Super-H-Point by RWS, penetrates better. Another highly regarded pellet is Beeman's Silver Bear. Pointed pellets, such as Beeman's Silver Sting and Silver Jet and the RWS Superpoint, are also ahead of the standard diabolo for hunting, offering better penetration than the older-style pellet.

The round-nose pellet is an excellent design and may be the best for penetration. The RWS Superdome, a round-nose pellet, is excellent on rabbits at 10 to 20 yards, with one-shot performance the rule. The Superdome penetrates fully on the head shot and also on the occasional chest shot, which is sometimes the only opportunity offered the rifleman and is an ethical aimpoint

The game of silhouette shooting is also played with the air rifle. This is Crosman's Airgun Silhouette Target System.

John Fadala shoots a Model 45 RWS air rifle with scope sight. The inherent accuracy of the high-tech air rifle suggests a glass sight. On the other hand, close-range shooting can be accomplished with the excellent iron sights provided on these air rifles.

with today's powerful air rifle. There is also a hollow-point, or nose-cavity point, pellet that offers greater expansion than the round-nosed pellet. It seems to work better than the round-nose design on chest-hit cottontails. Individual preference is no doubt accountable for pellet selection, because there are numerous pellet styles today that offer fine accuracy along with game-taking ability.

High velocity for a 17-caliber air rifle is in the 1000 fps mv realm. This is not high velocity as we regard bullet speed, so why not go with larger-caliber pellets to gain more authority? There are excellent 20-, 22- and 25-caliber pellets on the market. Beeman's 25-caliber Ram Point

pellet is an example of a "big-bore" air-powered missile. However, careful hunters who use an air rifle properly don't seem to have any trouble collecting game with the 17-caliber pellet, which explains the continued popularity of this small-caliber "bullet." The idea is not to put the pellet entirely through a small-game animal, but rather to penetrate deeply enough to reach a vital zone while at the same time transferring the pellet's energy, be it ever so scant, to the target. Good pellets penetrate the target to the vitals but not necessarily beyond, which means they expend most of their energy in the game, rather than beyond it. In short, the 17-caliber pellet continues to rule with a popularity that began a very long time ago.

While seldom used for anything other than plinking, target work and small game, the pellet rifle can be ideal on mountain grouse and partridges where allowed by law. I tried the air rifle on blue and ruffed grouse as a test for this chapter, finding once again that the 17-caliber high-speed pellet at close range was effective. Both birds fell instantly to head/neck shots, as would be expected. These unsophisticated mountain birds are seldom hunted. Most live a year or two, just long enough to procreate, and then they're gone to rain, snow, cold or predators. Because these birds are hunted infrequently by man, close shots—often measured in feet, not yards—are the rule. Blue grouse sometimes burst from un-

A closer look at air-gun pellets (from left to right): the standard diabolo, the plinking or "hobby"-type pellet, and the hunting pellet, this one RWS's Super-H-Point.

derfoot, only to crash-land on a branch 40 yards away. Then the air-rifle hunter slowly closes the gap, takes a rest, aims and squeezes off. Usually, the result is a bird for the pot.

The modern air rifle not only is an important shooting tool for the beginner, but also is equally important for the veteran marksman who likes to keep in tune by using a shooting range in the basement or plinking at a tin can in front of a backstop. Pellets are still cheap to purchase, making this practice an inexpensive pastime. Meanwhile, the "pellet gun" is also a serious match rifle, as well as a small-game arm for use in areas that aren't ideal for rimfire rifles or shotguns. Western hunters may even take mountain

A rifle is no better than its ammunition. Pellets are uniform and precise, even in the "plinking" or "hobby" style, and more so in target form. From top to bottom are: target pellets, plinking pellets and hunting pellets.

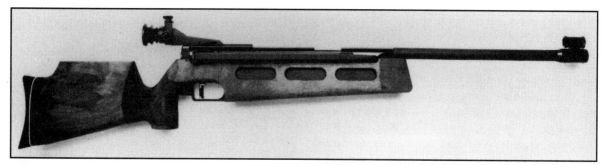

This RWS Model 75 Match rifle has double pistons, designed to negate recoil.

birds with the air rifle, especially out of a big-game camp, where noise should be kept to a minimum. Over the years, the air rifle has become more sophisticated, more accurate and more useful than ever, with ammunition to match.

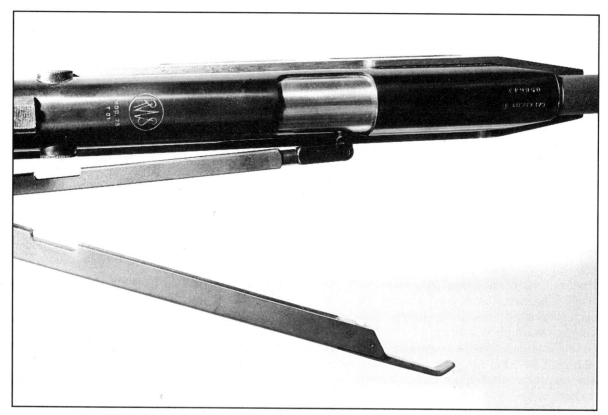

The Model 75 target air rifle is of the side-lever type, but still a spring-piston system. The shooter cocks the rifle by pulling the lever back toward his body.

THE MUZZLELOADER'S SPECIAL APPEAL

21 Most shooters believe that the blackpowder rifle is basic and simple, whereas the modern rifle is complex and involved. If anything, the reverse is true, for the modern cartridge makes it so. Although handloading is popular these days, shooting the modern cartridge rifle need be no more involved than buying a box of rounds and loading one or more into the firearm.

Not so with black powder. Every shot is put down by hand. The shooter is involved not only with making his muzzleloader work, but also with maintaining it. No single chapter in a book can deal with all of the fine points of black powder as a propellant or muzzleloader shooting as an activity. However, it is possible to lay a foundation for the enjoyment of one of the most rewarding shooting games of our time: firing the old-style longarms of the past. At least five million modern shooters do it. There must be a reason.

WHY SHOOT A MUZZLELOADER TODAY?

The muzzleloader brings a new understanding of firearms to today's shooters. It teaches a rifleman about the way things used to be and provides a sense of arms history. The game of muzzleloading is challenging, and meeting that challenge provides a special brand of reward. All of these factors and many more bring today's shooter back in time to guns that were outdated before the invention of the computer, yet never became extinct.

A look at *American Rifleman* magazine proves this last statement. Blackpowder shooting has always been represented in the magazine, from its inception to this day. Muzzleloading never died out. Custom frontloaders have been made in this country from our earliest history to this hour. Perhaps some of the finest hand-made longarms the world has ever seen are being built right now. But there remains a reason for taking up the frontloader that has nothing to do with gun history, pageant, spectacle, nostalgia, firearms interest, challenge or reward. It's a simple matter of getting something extra, and it cannot be denied.

One of the major reasons the blackpowder rifle remains high in popularity is the special muzzleloader-only hunting season. States from coast to coast have scheduled these seasons. Owning and shooting a blackpowder rifle means that a hunter can take advantage of seasons not open to those who don't shoot an old-style firearm. Special hunts are held in areas that are off limits to modern long-range rifles. For example, a farm area in Idaho is closed to hunting with a

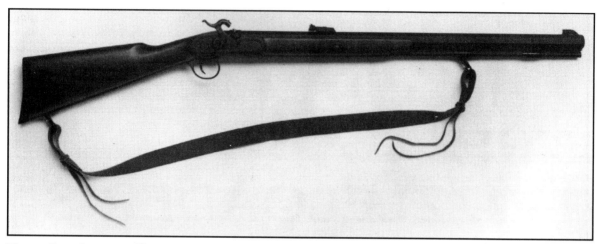

The well-made non-replica muzzleloader remains the most popular style of blackpowder rifle shot today. This Thompson/Center Big Boar Rifle is a non-replica muzzleloader in 58 caliber.

modern rifle, but the blackpowder fan is allowed to take whitetails in that locale. Some blackpowder seasons predate regular hunting times. Colorado's special blackpowder hunt for deer and elk opens before the regular season, for instance. There are also special late seasons, ideal in areas where migration brings game down from the high country. So, from a practical point of view, knowing how to handle the old-time smokepole provides something extra for big-game hunters.

BLACKPOWDER PROPELLANTS

The frontloader represents what might be called an "open" system. The rifle does not possess a locked breech. Rather, there is an exit at the breech, which serves as an entrance for ignition. Because of the Venturi principle, gas doesn't tend to jet back out of the channel to the breech. Crudely speaking, it's a matter of how gas reacts when contained in a device that has two orifices, one larger than the other. The gas tends to exit the larger orifice far more readily than it escapes through the smaller one—not perfectly, but well enough to allow muzzleloaders to function. Even the flintlock, which has a visible "hole" in one of its barrel flats for flame to dart through on its way to the main charge in the breech, does not shoot that much fire from its touchhole. *Some* escapes, yes, with a puff of smoke as well, but most of the gas goes out the

front as it pushes a projectile on its way.

The point is, the frontloader is strictly a blackpowder machine. Smokeless powder generates too much pressure to work safely in this so-called open system. Furthermore, smokeless powder and black powder have different burning profiles. Two propellants work in muzzleloaders: black powder, represented in this country by GOEX; and Pyrodex, a replica black powder from Hodgdon's. The properties of these fuels rest in complicated formulas. In fact, the U.S. Navy ran a survey of black powder in the 19th century that cannot be understood by anyone lacking a high understanding of physics, mathematics and ballistics. So these are the only

The percussion cap provides the ignition spark for the caplock-style rifle.

Only black powder or Pyrodex is allowable in the muzzleloader. Simply because a powder is black does not make it safe! On the left is a can of modern smokeless powder. It looks black, but using it in a muzzleloader could easily cause the firearm to burst, possibly injuring the shooter.

powders that the muzzleloader rifleman will deal with. They are safe in frontloaders, although they don't burn the same. Going into their unique properties would require an entire chapter of its own.

FLINTLOCK OR CAPLOCK?

Also known as a percussion system, the caplock is far more popular today than the flintlock (although the latter functions far better than modern writers like to pretend). A good flintlock has a faster lock time than one may think, and when properly managed, it "goes off" far more regularly than some would have us believe. If flinters were as primitive and haphazard in function as detractors say, the early American settlers would never have tasted venison steaks or roast turkey. Nonetheless, a newcomer to the sport must be advised that the percussion system is easier to work with, simpler to master and, therefore, recommended.

MUZZLELOADER STYLES

The Original. Surprisingly, original muzzleloaders are not quite as rare as we might think, and some of them are quite affordable. On a trip to New Jersey, I viewed a collection of muzzleloaders that included more than 25 models in fine condition, most of them for sale at under $500. Originals are seldom seen at the gun range, because so many are collectors' items. The inclusion of originals here is not a recommendation at all; it's simply a reminder to the reader that original muzzleloaders are still available. Shooting them is another matter, of course. No original should be fired until it is fully inspected by a professional blackpowder gunsmith.

The Replica. Replicas were designed to offer the modern shooter a copy of an old-time rifle. With a replica, a shooter can fire a historically designed muzzleloader without going to an original. The concept of replication was and remains a fine idea. A blackpowder fan wishing to emulate the past should consider this form of frontloader.

The Non-Replica. A huge market exists for a rifle that functions in every way like an original, but without duplicating anything from the past. The most popular muzzleloader of the day remains the non-replica rifle, often called a Haw-

Today's shooters enjoy the muzzleloader for many reasons. This replica offers historical value as well as shooting enjoyment.

The modern muzzleloader has gained a large following. Here, the author shoots a Knight MK-85, an in-line ignition frontloader with modern appointments.

ken, although it in no way resembles an original plains rifle. These are accurate, well-made firearms that get the job done. They are ruggedly constructed, for the most part, and shooters find them a good buy.

The Rifled Musket. The name seems to be a contradiction. A musket was essentially a smoothbore longarm popular in military service. However, when this style of longarm was rifled, it became known as a rifled musket. Oddly, the rifled musket is not as popular as one might expect. This type of muzzleloading rifle is usually a replica of a past model, so it has historical significance and value. But more than that, the rifled musket is powerful, accurate and a true frontloader, so it meets game department requirements for special blackpowder hunts. Naturally, individual exceptions may pertain, but all in all the rifled musket is simply a strongly made and accurate frontloader. It shoots elongated projec-

tiles, which look very much like modern cast-lead projectiles that are loaded in a cartridge.

An example of a rifled musket is Navy Arms Company's Volunteer rifle. This rifle is "only" caliber 45, not an overly large bore for a frontloader. But because it shoots conical bullets, the Volunteer carries authority. It's capable of shooting 500-grain lead bullets at around 1500 fps mv, enough oomph to take the largest game in North America in the hands of an expert hunter. In its day, the rifled musket was often used for target competition, including 1000-yard matches. It's easy to see that this particular blackpowder rifle style has a lot going for it, but it has never gained the popularity of the non-replica Hawken-like charcoal burner.

The Modern Muzzleloader. The modern muzzleloader is just that—it normally, but not always, has in-line ignition. This means that the flame from the percussion cap goes directly to the powder charge in the breech, rather than following a circuitous route. Stocks are contemporary in design, and the safety is usually a modern type as well. Modern muzzleloaders are often scope-ready, so that a glass sight can be mounted.

Rate of twist is rapid, so the modern muzzleloader shoots conicals better than round balls. It uses not only the Minie and Maxi types of projectiles, but also modern jacketed pistol bullets. A sabot (sah-bow) makes this possible. The sabot is a plastic cup into which the jacketed bullet fits. The bullet/cup unit is run downbore on the powder charge. When the unit exits the muzzle, the light cup falls away and the jacketed bullet speeds to the target rotating on its axis, the spin translated to the bullet via the cup, which is engraved by the rifling in the bore. Sabots are not a new concept. The idea goes back to French blackpowder days, the term originally meaning "shoe."

Traditionalists don't like the modern muzzleloader, which is easy to understand. However, thousands of blackpowder shooters feel differently about these rifles. Not only do they shoot well, but they also are easy to maintain. In most cases, the breech system comes out and cleaning can be done from the breech end instead of the

Hand-made frontloaders have been built for centuries and are still crafted by hand today. Here gunmaker Dale Storey puts the finish on a custom muzzleloader stock.

Muzzleloaders have a high potential for good accuracy. This Dale Storey custom rifle was treated to a B&L target scope. Using round balls, one-inch groups at 100 yards were obtained. Note this rifle's sidehammer style, with the percussion cap nipple located on the barrel flat.

muzzle end of the rifle, making the job faster and easier.

The well-made modern muzzleloader is here to stay. Some game departments have taken exception to this concept, however, and in certain regions the 20th-century version of the thunderstick is outlawed for special blackpowder-only hunts. The way game departments usually exclude the modern muzzleloader is to insist that the rifle's nipple be external. In-line ignition frontloaders have nipples that aren't always externally mounted. The modern muzzleloader remains an accurate and well-made rifle, and it *is* a muzzleloader, because powder and projectile are introduced downbore.

The Sidelock. The sidelock, or mule ear, frontloader is yet another type offered the modern shooter. The hammer is mounted on the side of the lock, offering in-line ignition, in effect. The nipple seat is an integral part of the breech, so fire from the cap darts directly into the powder charge in the chamber. Under-hammer rifles offer the same sort of ignition system. While the sidelock is not all that popular, it does represent another viable blackpowder rifle choice.

Custom Muzzleloaders. Hand-made frontloaders are still offered to the rifleman by a rather large number of professional builders. These rifles, when crafted by true experts, are beautiful as well as functional. The custom muzzleloader represents the cream of the trade; but of course it's also tagged with a price that reflects its value.

These are some of the choices facing the modern rifleman who wants to add blackpowder shooting to his sport. It's impossible to position one rifle type over another, because when properly built, each works well. Each individual shooter must make his choice based on his desires and taste, and also on the firearm's intended uses. If he chooses to emulate the 19th-century Western mountain man, a replica is necessary because it fits the historical picture. But if his goal is hunting during a special season, then the choice must reflect his personal preferences as well as the law. A frontloader that's not allowed in the game field won't do a hunter much good.

BLACKPOWDER CALIBERS AND BALLS

Cartridge caliber is given its own important chapter in this book. Muzzleloader caliber is equally important, if not more so. As the caliber goes, so goes the frontloading rifle. High velocity as we know it is impossible with black powder. Therefore, caliber is all to the round ball, and it's also quite important to the conical. Since high speed is out, the only way to gain power with black powder is with missile mass. On the other hand, a big bore is all wrong in the small-game/plinking field.

32 Caliber. This fantastic bore size should be even more popular than it already is. A 32-caliber round ball is a terrific small-game missile, weighing 45 grains in .310-inch diameter. Naturally, the ball diameter is smaller than the stated caliber, because the round ball wears a patch around it in the bore. A 45-grain, 32-caliber ball at 1900 to 2000 fps—an entirely possible muzzle velocity—is a fine wild turkey load. The same ball at 1200 to 1400 fps mv is great for small game and plinking. (The beauty of the muzzleloader is its versatility in the field. All a shooter needs to do to change the muzzleloader's character is alter the powder charge.) The 32 has another high point—if a shooter makes his own cast-lead round ball, he can enjoy a 32-caliber muzzleloader for less shooting cost than even the 22 rimfire.

36 Caliber. This is another excellent small-game/plinker caliber. With a 65-grain round ball of .350-inch diameter, the 36 is ideal for wild turkeys with top loads of powder, but it can also be tamed down by loading less fuel downbore.

38 Caliber. A good round ball size, the 38 caliber is not at all popular in the blackpowder rifle at this time.

40 Caliber. The 40-caliber round-ball rifle was once quite popular, but over the years this size has steadily decreased in popularity.

45 Caliber. There's nothing wrong with a 45-caliber round ball in terms of usefulness, ex-

cept that it's on the light side for big game, yet on the heavy side for small game. A 45-caliber ball of 133 grains weight is common—a good target size. Even at 2000 fps mv, that's not much potency, especially considering the fact that a round ball loses speed/power rapidly in the first place and ever more rapidly as caliber decreases. On the other hand, a 45-caliber conical missile is plenty heavy.

50 Caliber. At this bore size, the .490-inch round ball weighs 177 grains, offering enough mass to be a good deer-taker, and is suitable for larger game if projectile placement is perfect. Naturally, a 50-caliber conical has plenty of weight behind it. Conicals in 50 caliber come in all sorts of styles and weight. Buffalo Bullet Company offers modern-style 50-caliber conicals in a number of weights and designs, including hollow-point and hollow-base models.

54 Caliber. When shooting round balls, the 54 offers a unique situation. The 54-caliber ball weighs enough to gain considerable authority at usual blackpowder hunting distances, and yet

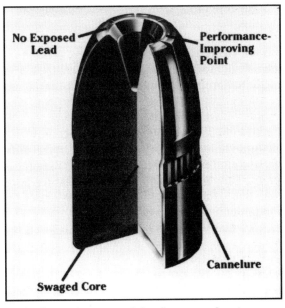

Today's modern muzzleloaders can shoot a jacketed bullet such as this Hornady XTP Pistol Bullet, which is designed to expand at muzzleloader velocities. The jacketed bullet is encased in a sabot of bore dimension.

The sabot is an old idea that still works. Here are jacketed pistol bullets encased in plastic sabots.

Over 58 Caliber. Round-ball sizes over 58 require even larger powder charges to gain reasonable muzzle velocities and trajectories. These big doses of powder produce a lot of recoil. All in all, calibers over 58 are neither practical nor popular.

Round Versus Conical Balls. One of the oldest arguments in all of shooting is the round-ball-versus-conical debate. It is fashionable at the moment for gunwriters to downgrade the round ball. They claim that, on paper, it's terrible. But for some reason, it does a perfectly excellent job in the field, displaying accuracy and power.

There are only two caveats regarding hunting with the round ball. The first is that its size must provide sufficient mass for big game—preferably

it's not so heavy that it fails to achieve good muzzle velocity with reasonable powder charges. The .535-inch round ball weighs 230 grains and can reach muzzle velocities in the 1900 to 2000 fps range with FFg black powder or Pyrodex RS propellants. Meanwhile, a 54-caliber conical can be quite hefty. A favorite 54 conical is the 460-grain round-nose offered by Buffalo Bullet Company. This big bullet starts out at a larger bore size than some bullets achieve after impact on the target.

58 Caliber. The 58-caliber round ball requires a large charge of powder to gain good muzzle velocity and, in one sense, isn't as efficient as the 54-caliber round ball. On the other hand, a 58 is capable of terrific power. The Thompson/Center Big Boar Rifle in 58 caliber is an example of a conical-shooting rifle of high power. Heavy conicals, including 600-grain bullets, can be given muzzle velocities in the 1500 fps range, turning the 58 into a powerhouse.

The muzzleloader requires hands-on attention. Even this modern Cabela muzzleloader is fed from "up front."

a 50 caliber for deer-sized animals and a 54 caliber for larger game. The second caveat is range. When hunting deer-sized game, even with a 50-caliber ball, 125 yards should be considered maximum for most situations. On game larger than deer, such as elk, 75 yards is far enough. The round ball loses speed fast; therefore, it loses energy fast. But the hunter who gets close and puts a large-caliber round ball where it belongs will tag his game. The smaller-caliber round ball is of course good for target shooting, plinking, turkey hunting and small-game hunting. The conical offers a lot more mass per caliber than the round ball. For example, a 45-caliber, 133-grain round ball isn't much, but a 45-caliber, 500-grain conical is "big medicine."

Twist. The major consideration in selecting a blackpowder projectile is rifling twist. This is an involved subject; all that will be said here is that slow twist is for round balls and faster twist is for conicals. In blackpowder terms, slow is very slow and fast is not very fast. A 50-caliber ball-shooting rifle does great with a 1:66 rate of twist—one turn in 66 inches of ball travel. (See Chapter 5 for more information on bullet stabilization.) A 50-caliber conical shooter, such as a modern muzzleloader intended for elongated missiles, might have a 1:28 twist.

SIGHT-IN AND TRAJECTORY

Although it is not correct for every situation, a sight-in of 100 yards will serve the average big-bore muzzleloader quite well. This goes for conical as well as round-ball rifles. It may seem otherwise, but the truth is that both bullet types project about the same trajectory over normal blackpowder hunting distances. The round ball, with top loads, starts out at about 1900 to 2000 fps mv, while most conicals take off at about 1500 fps mv. Since the round ball loses speed more rapidly than the conical, both end up with similar trajectories. About 125 yards is far enough for certain bullet placement with either rifle. This statement, remember, pertains to round balls and to the usual Minie and Maxi conicals, not to the higher-sectional-density bullets used in the rifled musket or to some of the newer bullets used in the modern muzzleloader.

SURPRISING ACCURACY

Most of the time, blackpowder shooters are satisfied with less accuracy than their rifle is truly capable of. A blackpowder rifle that will group into four or even six inches at 100 yards will indeed harvest a lot of game, but groups of half that size are hardly impossible. Remember that every rifle is unique. A frontloader should be tested for accuracy with various missiles and loads until a "pet load" is found. When a scope sight is placed on a muzzleloader to more clearly discern the target, groups shrink, sometimes amazingly. A Dale Storey custom rifle fitted with a Bausch & Lomb target scope regularly made one-inch center-to-center groups from the bench, using only the patched round ball for ammunition.

EASIER CLEANING

If there's one major reason why more shooters don't try muzzleloading, it's the fact that black powder and Pyrodex necessitate a thorough rifle cleanup after shooting. Two recent developments have eased this task: lubes that keep blackpowder fouling soft and manageable, and new solvents formulated to break down black-

Through the technology of chemistry, the frontloader rifleman has a far easier maintenance job today than in the past. A few items from CVA that work well are patch solvent/bore cleaner, lube, prelubed shooting patches and treated cleaning cloth.

powder fouling quickly and thoroughly. The old-time water-cleaning method remains in force to this day, but cleaning mainly with solvents is becoming more popular as solvents become increasingly sophisticated and potent.

The blackpowder rifle is interesting and useful. It completes a shooter's knowledge of the sport, and it also opens the door to special blackpowder-only seasons. However, gaining the most from the muzzleloader requires study, and learning about a new type of shooting is part of the final reward.

USEFUL GEAR FOR THE RIFLEMAN

22 The popular image of the frontiersman riding through uncharted wilderness, with all his possessions strapped onto a packhorse trailing behind him, makes the modern shooter wonder how such men got by with so little. The dedicated rifleman couldn't carry his entire outfit on the back of a pack elephant, let alone a mule or horse. But that's not necessarily bad. It just shows how far we've come in a couple hundred years of shooting.

The following list is by no means complete, but it includes some handy, useful items for the contemporary shooter. The items are presented in no particular order.

SPOTTING SCOPE

The spotting scope saves a great deal of time on the range. Walking from bench to target is fine, but a spotting scope allows for quick location of bullet placement on the target without having to call a cease fire on the range while others are shooting.

SCOPE COVERS

Protection for expensive scope lenses is provided by covers. See-through plastic covers should be removed before shooting because they can distort the sight picture.

A spotting scope like this one—Bushnell's Sentry® Spotting Scope with Tripod—saves time and footwork at the rifle range and is an essential item for the shooter who uses the range frequently.

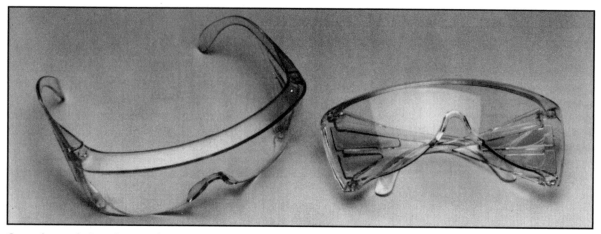

One piece of shooting equipment every marksman needs is safety eyeglasses. Savage Arms company supplies these shooting glasses with certain Savage rifles.

SHOOTING GLASSES

It is imperative that every shooter use protective lenses in front of his eyes. The obvious reason is to shield your eyes from gas or debris. This recommendation goes double for muzzle-loading shooters.

TOOLS

Many tools work well on the range or in the hunting camp to put a rifle back on track. The most obvious is the screwdriver. However, there are also a few compact multi-tool kits worth considering.

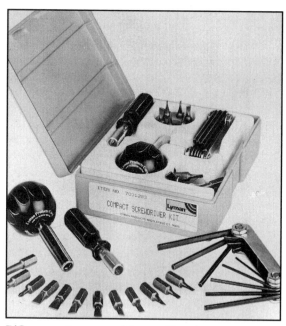

Rifles require screwdrivers. Here is a compact screwdriver kit from Lyman that provides a number of bits plus an allen wrench set.

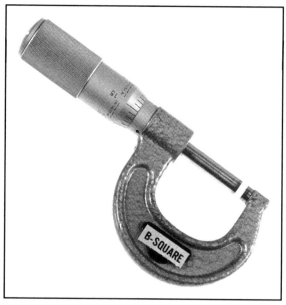

The advanced shooter can always use a micrometer to measure bullet diameters, or to check measurements of case heads or belts for expansion.

SHOOTING BAG

This is an essential kit for all shooters. The bag holds everything from screwdrivers and other tools for rifle/scope adjustment and maintenance, to cleaning rods and targets.

PORTABLE BENCHREST

A portable benchrest can be one of the best investments a shooter will ever make. While there is nothing like a solid bench at the rifle range, sometimes it is necessary to do some testing or sighting-in away from the range, and the portable benchrest is far and away superior to a lesser rifle-steadying device. Cabela's makes a good portable benchrest.

CARTRIDGE CARRIERS

Belt cartridge carriers these days are small and neat, comfortable to wear, and entirely workable. They keep ammo clean and accessible to the shooter.

A shooting bag can be any container that holds the essentials of the sport. This Uncle Mike's Sidekick Gear Bag can be used as an entire "range kit," holding not only shooting tools, but folded targets as well as cleaning equipment.

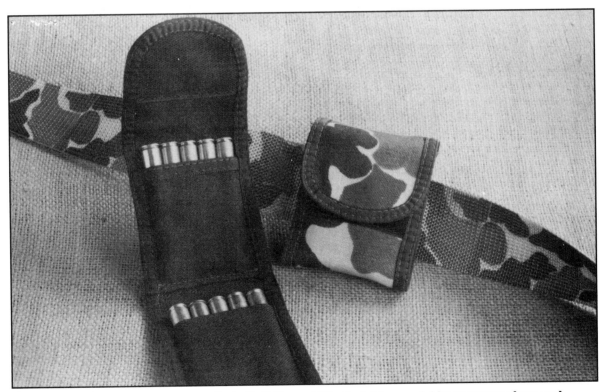

Cartridge carriers like this Uncle Mike's Fold-Down Rifle Cartridge model keep ammo clean and easily accessible.

HEARING PROTECTION

Muffs are excellent. Muffs combined with soft plugs that are inserted into the ear offer even more hearing protection.

These RCBS muffs offer the shooter hearing protection, which is imperative when shooting at the range.

The beauty of modern ear muffs, like these Browning Hearing Protectors, is that they fold for easy carrying.

BULLET TRAP

A pellet or bullet trap can be used to allow safe shooting under circumstances where a butt or other bullet-catching backstop is not available.

GEAR BAG

Not the same as the shooting bag, the gear bag is ideal for carrying extra clothing and other important items to the range. Available in an array of sizes and styles, many are constructed of nylon, which makes them lightweight to carry.

CLEANING KIT

The cleaning kit is simply a handy way to carry the basic tools needed for adequate rifle maintenance.

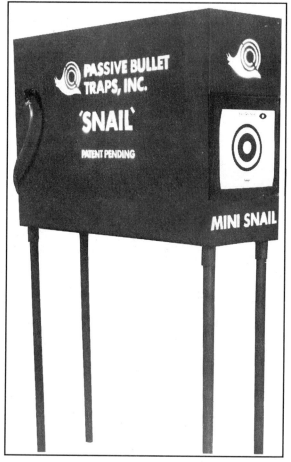

This Passive Bullet Trap does what its name implies—it traps and contains fired bullets.

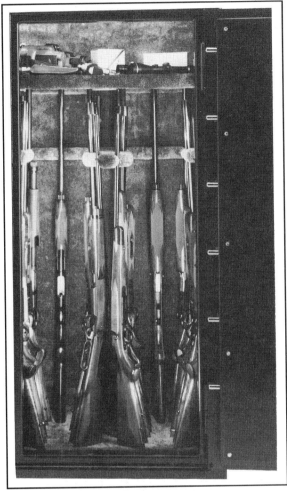

Gun safes, such as these "Gun Sportsman" models from Browning, are not only ideal for thwarting rifle loss, but are also considered childproof safety devices.

VAULT

A home vault for rifles is an expense worth considering for anyone who owns more than a few rifles. Even though the rifles may have little or no collector value, the vault thwarts handling of unsupervised guns.

CLEANING RODS

A breakdown cleaning rod is a requirement for the shooting bag. But a good idea is also to have a stout one-piece rod on the shooting range—not only for that once-in-a-lifetime stuck case, but also for defouling a rifle so that a

Uncle Mike's nylon rifle scabbard is at home on an "iron pony" as well as on the hayburning four-footed steed. A scabbard of this type protects the rifle from rough rides and scratches.

shooter can determine if an accuracy problem is due to bore fouling.

CLEANING SUPPLIES

Modern chemicals for rifle maintenance have come a long way. Shooters are encouraged to check the marketplace for the many good chemicals that promote a rifle's useful life.

SCABBARD

Those who sometimes go by horse need a rifle scabbard. The nylon scabbard of the hour is inexpensive and workable.

HARD GUN CASE

A hard gun case prevents rifle damage, especially in shipping or transporting firearms.

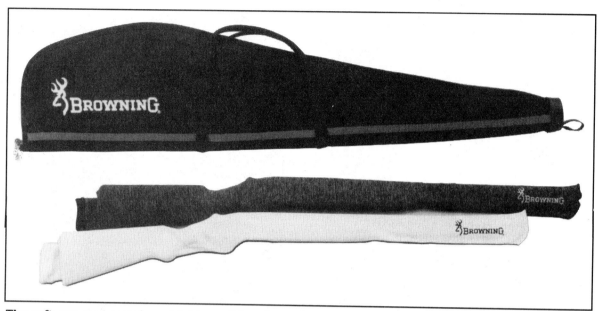

The soft gun case remains a highly useful and practical means of protecting the rifle from scratches. Shown are Browning's Signature Gun Case (top) and CamoGun Socks (bottom).

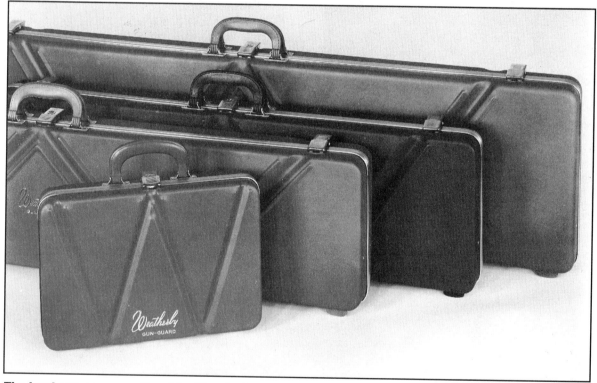

The hard gun case, as offered by Weatherby in a choice of sizes, affords the kind of protection necessary for air travel or any situation where rough handling is a possibility.

SOFT GUN CASE

In many situations, the soft gun case is more useful than a hard one. It takes up less space, and if the rifle is being transported on the back seat of a vehicle or in another manner that ensures a good ride, the soft gun case is sufficient to prevent scratches.

RIFLE RACK

The home version of the rifle rack is not necessarily ideal. It displays guns, sending out blatant signals to anyone who might have an interest in taking them. And it invites curious hands, even if the case is locked. However, in a vehicle the rifle rack is handy, keeping guns up and out of the way, yet easily accessible at the range.

TARGETS

Target design has improved in the past decade or two. Many aid the shooter in selecting a specific point of aim. If the shooter is still using the simple black bull's-eye, he should at least give other targets a try, especially some of the special sight-in targets available today.

BLACKPOWDER BOX

This is an addition to the standard shooting bag. A muzzleloader fan must have a multitude of tools, from nipple wrenches to short starters. The shooting bag alone is never large enough to carry all of the items needed when shooting a blackpowder rifle.

Scope covers protect the precious lenses of the expensive glass riflesight. These QD (Quick Detachable) Uncle Mike's scope covers snap out of the way for instant scope use.

EFFECTIVE RIFLE HANDLING

23 A modern marksman can know a great deal about ballistics and shooting technology, but if he can't shoot well in the field, his know-how has only academic application. The following rifle-handling techniques are practical, on-the-spot tips that should lead the rifleman to success in the field.

CARRYING THE RIFLE

When the shooter is afield, the crook of his arm is a fine place to carry a rifle; but in woods and brush, "at the ready"—gripping the rifle at its wrist and forearm—makes more sense. This way, the shooter need only lift the firearm to his shoulder and take aim, switching the safety to battery position as he mounts the rifle or nestles the buttstock into his shoulder.

In open terrain, or at any time when fast-action is unlikely, the sling comes into play. I believe a rifle without a sling is like a handgun without a holster: very inconvenient to carry. With a little practice, the slung rifle can be put into play in a couple heartbeats. Those who use packframes will want to mount a special hook on the vertical strut of the frame. This hook is used to receive the sling of the rifle.

SHOOTING THE RIFLE

Proper Foot Placement. Humans walk toes-forward, not crab-like in a sideways stance. When game is sighted, the feet are therefore out of position. Toes-forward is fine for shotgunning, but a rifleman should have his feet pointed roughly 45 degrees to the right of the target (for a right-handed shooter). It takes only a little practice for the rifleman to learn to rotate his body as the rifle comes to shoulder so that the shooting stance is correct and at the proper angle. The feet should be spread apart by about shoulder-width. All of this gives stability to the shot.

Breathing. As part of field-handling a rifle, the shooter should learn to take a full breath as part of the procedure in getting a rifle into action. This is a natural reaction to sighting game anyway, but the trick is letting out about *half* of that breath, then holding it as you settle the rifle for a shot.

Positioning the Face. The shooter's face should rest firmly on the comb of the stock for a steady shot. A shooter who lifts his face off of the stock will probably miss his target.

Relaxed Knees and Elbows. Knees and elbows should be kept free-moving and unlocked, because locked knees/elbows prevent body relaxation and the natural turning of the torso for

The sling is important in field-handling, not only for carrying the rifle, but also for aiding the steady shot. Here the rifle is carried on the packframe strut via the rifle sling.

a moving shot. Unlocked elbows and knees aid in the follow-through, which is the natural flow of the body's motion after the shooter pulls the trigger.

A Bird in the Hand. Master swordsmen advise that a sword be held like a bird—not too tightly or the bird will be injured, and not too loosely or it will fly away. The same can be said of the rifle. A white- knuckled grip on the forearm prevents full rifle control. The shooter should hold the rifle firmly, but only with big-bore, high-recoil rifles should he pull hard into the shoulder.

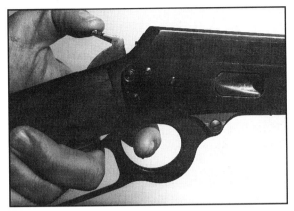

Field-handling means knowing your rifle. This Marlin rifle has an exposed hammer, but it also has a push-bolt safety. The rifleman must become proficient with both if he expects to maintain good field-handling.

Squeeze—Don't Yank—the Trigger. Never jerk the trigger. The idea is to maintain the sight picture at all times, not only before the firearm goes off, but even a short time after the bullet has departed the muzzle. This is proper follow-through. Jerking the trigger throws off the aim.

Winking. Ideally, the shooter should learn to shoot with both eyes open. The dominant eye takes over and aligns the sights. Shooters who cannot work with both eyes open should not worry about it, but they should test to see which eye is the dominant one, because an inability to shoot with both eyes open may indicate a left-eyed shooter trying to operate right-handedly.

To test for the dominant eye, extend an arm, holding the forefinger out. With both eyes open, align that finger visually on a distant object, as

This shooter uses the side of a tree as a rest. Note that the rifle stock does not touch the tree—only the shooter's left hand makes contact.

The sitting shot is very steady and can be quickly assumed. Here Dale Storey shoots with one of his custom Modern Plains Rifles using the sitting position.

if the finger were the front sight of a rifle. Now blink the left eye shut. If you're right-handed, the finger should remain lined up on the object. Open both eyes again, maintaining the forefinger on the object, and blink the right eye shut. The finger should appear to jump over to the right.

The Moving Target. The offhand stance is best for shooting at a moving target, with feet about shoulder-width apart and pointed about 45 degrees to the right of the target (for a right-handed shooter). With elbows and knees unlocked, swing the rifle, keeping the sights ahead of the moving target. The most important aspect of hitting the target now is proper lead, which varies with the speed and angle of the target. It also ensures that the rifle goes off when it is in motion. Stopping the motion of the rifle to pull the trigger generally results in a miss. The trigger should be tripped with the rifle in motion.

The Sitting Shot. Every rifleman should be able to hit a target of reasonable size at a reasonable distance "off his hind legs." But the sitting shot is better, especially with a hiking stick wedged under the rifleman's right ankle and held by his left hand in conjunction with the forearm of the rifle (for a right-handed shooter). Shooting from the seat of the pants is a field-handling must and riflemen should take this stance whenever it is possible to do so. Naturally, its value lies in increased steadiness. The following shooting position is even steadier, although more difficult to assume in the big-game arena.

The Prone Position. Lying on the ground with elbows planted firmly, legs spread apart and toes pointed outward is a field-handling posture that is hard to beat for putting a bullet on target. The sight picture is rock-steady from the prone position. The left elbow (for a right-handed

The running shot demands excellent rifle-handling techniques.

Although not the steadiest shooting position, the kneeling shot is still steadier than the offhand posture.

shooter) should be directly beneath the forearm of the stock, not cocked off at an angle, because the forearm controls the rifle. The buttplate of the rifle is firmly planted in the shooter's shoulder, but the elbow continues to support the rifle.

The Kneeling Shot. Better than the off-hand for steadiness, but not nearly as good as the sit-ting or prone shot, this field-handling stance is good when better positions cannot be assumed. This is sometimes the case due to brush or other obstructions that prevent the shooter from seeing when he takes a sitting or prone position. The problem with the kneeling shot is the right elbow (for a right-handed shooter), for it just sits out there in the breeze with no more support than it would have from the offhand posture.

IMPROVING GROUPS IN THE FIELD

A field group is the center-to-center cluster that a hunter normally achieves from a given rifle in a hunting situation, not off the bench. The object is better control of the rifle in the field, especially on long shots. The following three rules, if followed, will improve the shooter's field groups, a worthy goal for any rifleman.

1. Practice with a carefully sighted, accurate rifle. It is a waste of time to shoot a lesser rifle when trying to improve field-shooting skills.

2. Gain field-shooting experience. Varmint hunting—especially the mobile jackrabbit—is excellent practice.

3. Assume a rest, or at the very least an enhanced shooting posture when possible. This rule is obviously hinged to rifle control.

Begin improving field groups by first knowing the capability of your particular big-game rifle. Benchrest groups are the best practical means of ascertaining that level of rifle accuracy. Many human variables prevail at the bench, but by using a good rifle rest (such as the Hoppe's professional unit), human variables are minimized. Use proper benchrest practices: feet flat, right elbow planted firmly, padded to prevent a skid bruise from a heavy-recoiling rifle, variable scope set at highest power, eyepiece focused. Fire several groups. The five-shot group is statistically more reliable than the three-shot group, although the latter is totally acceptable for testing a hunting rifle. Naturally, group sizes vary widely in accord with inherent rifle accuracy as well as load quality and load/rifle compatibility.

The next step is to shoot groups from several field positions. In my tests for this chapter, I shot standing, sitting, kneeling and prone; plus I used a walking staff, packframe, boulder, tree trunk and fencepost, but no sling. Range was 200 yards. Although I did not take advantage of the Harris rifle bipod, it is an excellent implement, as is a unipod like the Underwood Rest with its special "T" leg arrangement for steadiness. In point of fact, all groups shrunk when rests were used, such as a packframe, padded rest from a boulder and so forth.

When hunting in timber, offhand shooting is often the rule, as it is when "jump-shooting" riverbottom whitetails. Offhand shots are often necessary in any terrain where the game "spooks out" in front of the rifleman. But offhand marks-

Here rocks serve as a platform for the shooter. Note that the shooter rests the full length of his forearm on the surface of the boulder for steadiness.

Fadala uses his walking staff to steady the rifle for a shot. The stick is ideal as a hiking aid, but can also serve to brace a shot in the field.

manship, even with an accurate rifle, is considered good for the average shooter if groups fall with a one-foot circle at 200 yards. A practiced *silueta* (metallic silhouette) rifleman betters this group considerably. Although the "hasty-sling" method of simply wrapping up in the carrying strap is often said to be of little practical value, my offhand field groups tightened when I lashed

the strap around my left arm with a quick twist.

Kneeling groups were smaller than offhand results, with "offhand fliers" greatly reduced. The sitting position improved the cluster again, to around 4+ inches at 200 yards with some fliers. There were fewer fliers outside the 6-inch Targ-Dot that was used for an aim point from the firm sitting stance as compared with the

Fadala uses his packframe as a solid rest in this sitting shot. The shooter can test accuracy for himself at the range by shooting with and without rest aids.

kneeling posture. Prone groups dwindled to about 3.0 to 3.5 inches center to center. Consistency was clearly improved over the sitting stance.

Using Field Rests. The most gratifying field groups came from using field rests. The packframe rest, employing the v-bar of the upper packframe strut, using the daypack's straps for padding, gave 200-yard groups that missed benchrest accuracy by only an inch at times. Groups of 2.0 to 3.0 inches with this field rest were common.

There are dozens of in-the-field steadying stances that a hunter can apply. The longest shot I ever made in the field was on a Coues deer in Arizona. I was hunting with a good friend who is now a guide in Colorado. John and I were on a high ridge looking across to another ridge of about the same altitude. My binoculars enabled me to spot a buck in an ocotillo jungle. But the buck was far. Stalk cross-canyon? I'd hunted Coues too long to trust that tactic. The buck wouldn't be there by the time we made it down into the bottom of that big hole, back up the other side, and then into range. So I settled my walking staff across two low rocks, assumed the prone position with the rifle's forearm resting across my hasty "benchrest," and I held a foot off-target for the wind and maintained considerable daylight over the deer's back. I fired. The buck fell.

The use of a bipod, tripod or other rest device, especially from the prone position as shown here, offers one of the steadiest field positions of all.

No rest—no buck. I'm convinced of it.

The walking staff. There's nothing new about this tool—travelers of Bible days carried a staff. It's a good walking/hiking aid. Good sticks are made of dead agave cactus stalks. Live ones must never be cut down. Doing so is illegal and, besides, the stick would be green. The dead stalk is dry and tough. Agave stalks grow mainly in the Southwest, are light as balsa wood and strong as oak. The staff is approximately hunter-tall. A 6-foot hunter would carry a walking stick of 5 1/2

to 6 feet in length. The upper third is covered with tanned buckskin for a grip, the top padded for a binocular rest.

A walking stick can assist offhand, kneeling, sitting and prone shots. The stick is used upright as a rest from the offhand or kneeling positions; or jammed under an ankle, while pinching rifle forearm and staff together; or from the sitting stance; or across a couple rocks or tree limbs. The rifle's forestock can be rested directly against the staff. The bullet will not be guided

Another makeshift field rest is a downed tree trunk. Once again, notice that the shooter does not rest any part of the rifle directly against the hard surface. In this instance, a hat is used as a cushion for the forearm of the rifle.

Using the side of an old fence post, this marksman steadies his Marlin Camp Gun for a good shot. Note that the rifle actually rests upon the shooter's left thumb and not against the wood.

off-target by this action, because the stick, unlike a fencepost or tree limb, *gives.* It is not rigid.

To get a solid rest, the squirrel hunter can also "hug a tree." The tree-hug steadies the rifle remarkably. The shooter wraps an arm around a tree, the hand of that arm holding the forestock of the rifle. Naturally, the tree must be small enough in diameter to allow this.

An ordinary fencepost can become a pretty good rest, too. The hand cushions the forearm of the rifle. The stock is not allowed to make contact with the post. Such contact can persuade the bullet to depart from its usual path. A boulder

can offer a fine rest. Again, the forestock of the rifle should be padded.

The hunter who fails to take advantage of the steadier field postures handicaps himself greatly. No matter how superior the benchrest accuracy of his big-game rifle, that accuracy potential cannot be realized in the field from the offhand stance. Under many circumstances, the offhand shot is the only shot. But a shooter who groups his rifle offhand at 200 yards, then tries a few groups from the sitting or prone position for comparison, will soon learn the advantage of proper field-handling of the rifle.

MODERN RIFLE MAINTENANCE

24 Shooters should maintain their rifles for several important reasons: among them, continued perfect function, pride of ownership and resale value. A fourth reason—equally as important—is accuracy.

The advent of smokeless powder precluded the necessity of virtually washing a bore out every time a rifle went to the range or on a hunt. The rifle could be maintained with much less effort. Primers remained corrosive, however, so wise shooters continued a stringent program of cleaning their longarms soon after use. Then the non-corrosive primer arrived. Many marksmen concluded that smokeless powder coupled with non-corrosive primers meant that a rifle never had to be cleaned. Even though modern ammunition is better than ever in terms of corrosion and residue, there is no such thing as perfectly clean-burning ammo. Powder residue is left behind after a round goes off, and such residue can bind the workings of any rifle action. Moreover, metal fouling occurs, too. A bore that is badly fouled with copper wash will not perform to its highest level.

MAINTENANCE EQUIPMENT

Listed below are a sampling of maintenance tools and devices available to shooters today that will promote the longevity and preserve the accuracy of their firearms.

The Cleaning Kit. This idea still remains vital today. It's simply a way for the shooter to obtain, in one package, the basic items necessary for rifle maintenance. Two kits that I have found excellent are the Hoppe's Wooden Presentation Kit and the Outers Universal Gun Kit. No cleaning kit contains every maintenance product, but the basic tools are all there.

The Cleaning Rod. Vital to bore maintenance is the cleaning rod, which is made in two basic styles: the takedown and the one-piece. From there, dozens of variations exist. The takedown rod offers portability; the one-piece rod is less subject to breakage. Many of us own both kinds, keeping the one-piece rod in the workshop, while the takedown fits into the shooting bag. Hunters who go far into the field should put a compact takedown cleaning rod in their daypacks. A stuck case may seem unlikely, but it is not impossible. The handy compact cleaning rod will knock a stuck case out right away. Furthermore, should debris or any foreign matter invade the bore, the cleaning rod will make short work of getting that material out.

Bore Brush. Essential to bore maintenance, bore brushes are available in various constructions. Metal bore brushes are especially good for

The cleaning kit contains all of the basic tools necessary for rifle maintenance. Naturally, the dedicated rifleman adds several other tools to his kit.

reaching down into the groove of the rifling to remove fouling. Incidentally, a neat holder for various calibers of bore brushes can be made with a hardwood block by simply drilling holes into the block to match the various stem sizes of the individual brushes.

The Muzzle Protector (Muzzle Guard). Built into some rods, these devices are designed to maintain the cleaning rod dead center in the bore, discouraging the rod from lapping the rifling, especially at the muzzle. Built-in muzzle protectors slide on the cleaning rod. Individual protectors, such as Outers Brass Muzzle Guards, can be purchased for the same purpose also. If a rifle must be cleaned from the muzzle, as in certain semiautomatic, slide-action and lever-action rifles, a muzzle protector is highly recommended.

Bore Guide. A bore guide is essentially the reverse of the muzzle guard. It is a device used to center the rod at the breech end of the rifle instead of at the muzzle. The guide is inserted into the breech and the cleaning rod goes through it. The guide ensures that the cleaning rod remains centered in the bore rather than dragging along the walls of the chamber.

Soft Cloth. A washed flannel cloth is useful in maintaining the exterior finish of the rifle. It is good for a simple wipe-down, and also useful in applying maintenance products to both stock and metalworks. Soft flannel cloth can also be cut into cleaning patches when necessary.

Cleaning Patches. Proper cleaning patches are available not only in the caliber of the rifle, but also made of materials that will not damage the bore. Using old rags for cleaning patches is unwise at best, since they may introduce abrasive particles to the bore.

Cotton Swabs. A few cotton swabs in the kit serve to clean or apply lubricant to hard-to-reach spots of the action. A swab soaked with solvent works well in removing fouling from parts of the action.

Pipe Cleaners. A few pipe cleaners should be kept in any cleaning kit. Pipe cleaners do about the same work as cotton swabs, but the two are not identical in function. The swab is a little better in careful application of chemicals, while the pipe cleaner is more useful in scrubbing out an orifice or getting into a crevice.

Toothbrush. A toothbrush makes a good scrubbing tool. Better for larger jobs is the bronze brush, offered by Outers.

The Jag. The jag is a screw-in device that adorns the top of the cleaning rod. It does not have a slot. The advantage of using a jag is that it will drop off of a soiled cleaning patch at the muzzle when cleaning from the breech of the rifle. Since the jag has no slot, the patch is therefore not dragged back through the bore.

The Slotted Cleaning Tip. Although the slotted cleaning tip does pull the patch back through the bore, it is a useful, workable, outstanding device for holding the cleaning patch. Every kit should have slotted cleaning tips that match the bore dimensions of the rifle.

Lubrication Oil. Hoppe's 9 Bench Rest is an example of a lubrication oil that "penetrates, lubricates, drives out moisture." Jonad Corporation has long offered the shooter exceedingly good preservatives, especially in the form of Accragard, which is a chemical designed to promote the long life of a barrel.

REMOVING METAL FOULING

Much useful knowledge about firearms has been derived from benchrest shooting. One of the best discoveries was how metal fouling affects bore condition. A jacketed bullet at high velocity leaves a memory of itself in the bore of the rifle. This trace of metal that rests on the rifling is most often copper wash, because most jackets are cupro-nickel. The all-lead or lead alloy bullet can also leave a trace of itself in the bore of the rifle,

cut to size to match various jobs.

Solvents of many types and brands also aid in lead removal. Hoppe's No. 9 is an example of a long-lived product engineered to reduce lead deposits in the bore, especially when used in conjunction with a bore brush. Other solvents that work on lead are as easy to locate as the nearest gunshop.

Copper Removal. Chemicals for cutting copper fouling also abound nowadays, whereas they once existed only in the wishes of shooters who had to scrub the bore with bristle brushes, and even then were not always successful in producing a metal-free rifling condition. Shooter's

A bore guide is used here to protect the breech of the rifle by maintaining the cleaning rod dead center in the bore.

a condition called leading. Chemical research of course has come to the rescue, and the marketplace is now full of good products designed to reduce metal fouling. This was not true even a decade ago.

Lead Removal. Birchwood Casey's Lead Remover Cloth is designed to do what its name promises—remove leading from the rifling. (This cloth also aids in the reduction of copper fouling, as well as attacking plastic residue from the use of plastic sabots.) The 9×12-inch cloth can be

Choice is a liquid solvent designed to attack all kinds of bore fouling, including lead, copper and powder. J-B Cleaning Compound is a cream that also promises to cut metal fouling. Flitz metal polish, used by some benchrest shooters, cuts metal fouling as well.

Since these chemicals are strong, always carefully follow the directions that appear on the packaging. A bottle of liquid Shooter's Choice, for example, lists six important steps for bore cleaning. They're worth outlining here because following a precise cleaning routine will produce the best results from a product.

1. The first step listed on the Shooter's Choice bottle is to wet two patches, pushing these individually through the bore to cut overt fouling. *2.* Take a tight-fitting bronze brush, soaked in the solvent, and pass it through the bore several times. *3.* Next, using three solvent patches, pass these individually through the bore. *4.* Now dry the bore with clean patches. The bore is ready to go, provided patches come out fairly white toward the end of the drying process. *5.* Protect the bore with rust inhibitor before storing the rifle. *6.* Finally, the shooter should prepare the rifle before shooting by using a single solvent-dampened patch followed by dry patches to remove oils from the bore.

LUBRICATING METAL PARTS

Cleaning is one thing. Lubricating is another. Lubrication is basically a deterrent to friction. A

Today's chemicals make rifle maintenance easier than ever. Hoppe's 9 Benchrest is an example of a chemical designed to attack metal fouling in the bore.

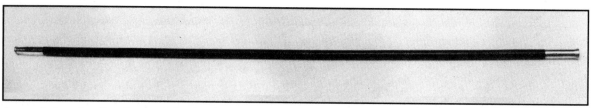

A good cleaning/loading rod, in this instance a CVA Lexan (just about unbreakable) ramrod, helps maintain the rifle in good condition.

dab of lube applied to the working parts of a rifle action promotes ease of use. Lubrication is also necessary for reducing wear, because friction actually ruins parts. The rifle action, similar to an engine, has a number of working parts that require lubrication.

Many good lubes are on the market today, and the good news is that over the years rifle lubes have continued to improve. We now have lubes that function in cold and hot weather like no products before them. Sometimes preservatives and lubes are one and the same, as in Outers Gunslick, which is a superior lube and a good rust preventative. Outers Tri-Lube, on the other hand, is one of our modern miracle chemicals. It offers superior lubrication, excellent rust pro-

tection, great powder fouling removal, good degreasing qualities and super water displacement—all in one product. But no single chemical does it all, from bore cleaning to perfect protection.

ACCURACY AND THE OILY BORE

Rifle variation disallows an across-the-board statement concerning the oily bore and accuracy, but it is safe to conclude that a bullet fired from an oily bore will most likely fly off course. This is an important consideration, especially for the rifleman who carefully sights in his firearm before hunting season, and then proceeds to oil the bore heavily before putting the rifle away. The hunter grabs the rifle from his gun safe and heads

BASIC RIFLE CLEANING PROCEDURES

There are any number of ways to approach rifle maintenance. Here is one method, which offers a good starting point for the rifleman.

1. Be absolutely positive that the rifle is unloaded. The cliché about a rifle going off during the cleaning process isn't fantasy; it happens. Make certain that the magazine and chamber are empty.

2. Run solvent-soaked patches through the bore several times. There is no prescribed number of patches or passes; it depends upon the condition of the bore.

3. Clear the bore of excess solvent with a few passes of dry patches.

4. If the bore is fouled with metal, now is the time to remove the copper wash. One method is to use a cream, such as J-B Compound or Flitz, applied to a patch. If metal fouling is severe, the same products can be applied to a bore brush. The combination of bore brush and compound does a good job of loosening metal fouling.

5. If one of the above compounds is used, removing all of it from the bore is imperative, because leaving traces of compound in the bore could cause damage when a bullet is fired. Cleaning patches on a jag or slotted tip, soaked in solvent, will do this job. Follow with dry patches.

6. Check for metal fouling by placing a bit of white cloth downbore a short distance. A piece of clean cotton will also do the trick. Push the cotton or cloth down a quarter-inch past the muzzle. Using a flashlight, or better yet, a bore light, shine the beam into the muzzle. The white cloth or cotton reflects light into the bore and the lands of the rifling will have a golden hue if metal fouling is present. If copper fouling is absent, the lands will appear dark in color.

7. Treat the cleaned bore with a light application of rust inhibitor or other metal preservative.

8. Clean the action with a toothbrush, commercial cleaning brush, cotton swabs, pipe cleaners and cloth, along with solvent to lift powder residue and old lube from metal surfaces. After all working parts are cleaned, rub each surface-to-surface contact lightly with lubricant. Naturally, the action of the rifle must be disassembled sufficiently to allow cleaning. The bolt-action rifle generally requires no more than bolt removal, for example, whereas other actions may call for more detailed takedown to reach working parts.

9. Wipe all exterior surfaces with a clean cloth and apply a trace of metal protector to them. Treat the stock similarly, using, of course, an appropriate product for the wood if the stock is made of wood. The stock may also be waxed, as with Birchwood Casey Gun Stock Wax in liquid or aerosol-spray form.

10. Store the rifle properly. This is essential not only to prevent the firearm from falling into the wrong hands, but also to protect it. The gun safe provides good storage for both reasons.

---

for the hills. The only problem is that his first shot out of the bore will probably be off the mark. A problem? It could be. If the game is close, and missing by a few inches is no miss at all, fine. But if precision is demanded, a couple of inches could make the difference between and hit and a miss. Then it's a problem.

A rifle I tested expressly for determining the effect of an oily bore shot the first group two inches to the right and three inches high every time at 100 yards from the bench. The next four shots centered in the bull's-eye. This discrepancy would be much more pronounced at longer ranges.

Another rifle reacted differently to the oily bore condition. Its first shot was six inches off the mark at 100 yards. The first bullet printed at the upper left-hand corner of the target. A third rifle, a muzzleloader (to test for that kind of firearm), also put its first patched round ball well

Maintenance means saving the rifle from harm in the first place. This Pachmayr canvas-covered aluminum case is a perfect example of protecting the firearm from harm.

ern miracle chemicals is ideal in promoting the long life of bores.

The story goes that most 22-rimfire rifles are worn out by cleaning rods, not by firing ammunition in them, and that is probably true. After all, the 22 rimfire is a mild cartridge that burns only a small powder charge. Typical 22 rifles, especially those with simple action designs and few working parts, require modest attention, whereas some shooters virtually attack their little 22s for the sake of good maintenance. All rifles need attention, and that certainly includes the 22 rimfire, but common sense should prevail.

SPECIAL CONSIDERATIONS

Certain firearms demand special handling when it come to maintenance schedules and methods.

The Air Rifle. Air rifles require infrequent piston lubrication. Do not use standard oils on air rifles, only the products designed for them. Dri-Slide, for example, is a molybdenum disulfate base product made for air rifles. It leaves a dry film on metal parts and does not cause buildup. Also, be certain that the bore of the air rifle is cleaned with a rod that fits exactly.

off the mark from an oily bore. In the latter case, the first hole in the target printed far to the left of the bull's-eye, with the next five shots centering straight-on.

While a rifle bore should be treated to conditioning before storage, it should be swabbed out before the rifle is fired. One clean patch will do, or if the shooter wishes to play it extra safe, he can push a solvent-soaked patch down first, followed by drying patches. Furthermore, overuse of chemicals is unnecessary and can be detrimental, rather than helpful. When a rifle is put into storage, a metal protector should be applied to the bore, but lightly, not heavily.

DAMAGE FROM CLEANING

All rifles require sensible, prudent and correct cleaning. A semiautomatic 22, for example, may all but cease to function if left uncleaned. The bore protector is ideal in preventing damage to the crown of the muzzle. And the use of mod-

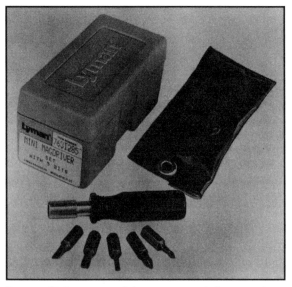

Proper-fitting screwdrivers prevent damage to screw heads; these are essential to good rifle maintenance.

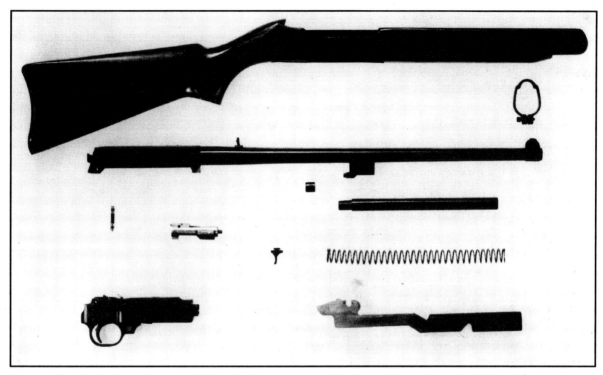

Some rifles lend themselves to field stripping more readily than others. Ruger's 44 Carbine is an example of a rifle that can be broken down into its component parts for occasional super-cleaning.

The Muzzleloader. Blackpowder arms demand special attention above and beyond the modern firearm. This is due to the fact that the powder is hygroscopic, i.e., water- or moisture-attracting. Fouling left behind by black powder or Pyrodex tends to collect moisture, which in turn can damage the steel of the firearm. So it is essential that the shooter remove powder residue from the bore and the "action". Many new products on the market do this and are far more sophisticated chemicals than those offered in the past. Moreover, modern paste and liquid lubes designed to thwart blackpowder fouling during the actual shooting process also help greatly in muzzleloader maintenance.

ADDITIONAL TIPS FOR RIFLE CARE

Here are a few additional tips that help to promote rifle longevity.

1. Dry-firing of bolt-action rifles is not quite so bad as dry-firing rifles that have exposed hammers, such as many lever-actions have. But,

all in all, the practice of clicking the rifle trigger without benefit of a dummy or live round in the chamber is not in the best interest of the rifle. Also, the simple safety rule of never pointing a rifle or any gun at an object you do not wish to shoot pertains to dry-firing.

2. Bringing a rifle from a cold to warm environment can make the steel "sweat." This in turn can cause rust. It's wise to watch a rifle that must be brought into shelter from the cold, wiping it frequently to ensure that moisture does not build up and remain on the metal. Naturally, going from cold to hot, or even the reverse, can cause scope sights to fog, although this condition occurs less frequently because of better sealing characteristics on modern scope sights.

3. An obvious but sometimes ignored rifle-care rule is keeping a rifle safeguarded in a rack or case when in transit. It takes only a modest bump to throw a scope out of whack, and not much of a blow at all to scratch a stock or bend an iron sight.

Many modern muzzleloaders allow cleaning from the breech through the removal of percussion system. This is the CVA Apollo modern muzzleloader.

4. All bolts and screws should be kept firmly in place. Loose screws can allow a stock, for example, to exhibit play between wood and metal. During recoil, this condition could cause a break or split in the stock.

5. Rapid-fire of a rifle, especially with a cartridge that burns a large powder supply, heats the barrel quickly, and a hot barrel is susceptible to extra-fast wear. Unless necessary, it is wise to avoid rapid-fire shooting.

Keeping a rifle "like new" requires routine care and maintenance. It also requires proper use of the right products. Today's rifleman is fortunate. Rifle-care tools and chemicals are in huge supply and improving all the time.

Preventive maintenance is desirable for all tools. The CVA cap cover and nipple protector set act not only as safety devices to prevent accidental rifle discharge, but the unit also keeps moisture out of the system.

INDEX